THE ULTIMATE SHOPPER'S CATALOGUE

Also by the author

The International Catalogue of Catalogues
The American Catalogue of Catalogues
The Catalogue of Catalogues
The New Catalogue of Catalogues

THE ULTIMATE SHOPPER'S CATALOGUE

WHERE TO GET HIGH QUALITY AND LOW PRICES BY MAIL AND PHONE

MARIA ELENA DE LA IGLESIA

PERENNIAL LIBRARY

HARPER & ROW, PUBLISHERS, New York
Cambridge, Philadelphia, San Francisco, Washington
London, Mexico City, São Paulo, Singapore, Sydney

NEXT EDITION

If you have any suggestions, recommendations, criticism or information for the next edition of this book, I would be very grateful if you would send them to me: Maria Elena de La Iglesia, ℅ Harper & Row, 10 E. 53rd St., New York, N.Y. 10022.

 For information address Harper & Row, Publishers, Inc., 10 East 53rd Street, New York, N.Y. 10022. Published simultaneously in Canada by Fitzhenry & Whiteside Limited, Toronto.

Copyeditor: Diane Conley
Designer: Abigail Sturges
Indexer: Natalia Schiffrin
Cover photo (Irish castle): Deirdre Stanforth

Library of Congress Cataloging-in-Publication Data

De La Iglesia, Maria Elena.
The ultimate shopper's catalogue.

"Perennial Library."
Includes index.
1. Mail-order business. 2. Catalogs, Commercial.
3. Shopping. I. Title.
HF5466.D455 1987 381'.1 86-45089
ISBN 0-06-055017-1 87 88 89 90 91 RRD 10 9 8 7 6 5 4 3 2 1
ISBN 0-06-096088-4 (pbk.) 87 88 89 90 91 RRD 10 9 8 7 6 5 4 3 2 1

CONTENTS

Acknowledgments vii
Preface ix
Introduction 1

Appliances and Electronics 9
Audio Equipment 21
Cars 33
Cigars 45
Clothes and Shoes 47
Computers 67
Fabrics and Fibers 79
Food 89
Gardening 101
General: Large Stores Overseas 115
General: Department Stores, Mail-order Houses and Telephone Buying Services in the United States 121
Haircuts 129
Health 133
Dental Work 133
Drugs 134
Hobby and Professional Equipment 137
House 143
China and Glass 143
Furniture 151
Heating 158
Kitchen Equipment 160
Linen 161
Paint 165
Wallpaper 167
Silver and Flatware 168

Insurance 173
Investment 181
Leather and Luggage 189
Musical Instruments 191
Office Equipment and Stationery 203
Perfume and Cosmetics 209
Pets 215
Photography 223
Publications 233
Records and Cassettes 241
Sports 247
Backpacking and Climbing 247
Bicycling 251
Boating 254
Fishing 260
Golf 264
Skiing 267
Tennis 269
Telephone Service 273
Toys 279
Travel 285
Watches 311
Appendixes
Manufacturers' Addresses 315
Parallel or Direct Imports (A.K.A. "Gray" Market) 324
Paying 325
Credit Cards 327
Shipping from Abroad 329
Avoiding and Dealing with Problems 331
Clothing Size Charts 335
Metric Conversions 336
Customs Charges 337

Index 343

ACKNOWLEDGMENTS

Warmest thanks to all the people whose names are scattered throughout the book, who, with great generosity, have given information and suggestions.

And many thanks to these contributors and advisers:

Art materials: Richard Osterwell, painter.

Audio equipment: Clement Meadmore, author of *All Sound and No Frills.*

Backpacking and camping: Jack Stephenson, sporting equipment manufacturer; John Fischer, Palisade School of Mountaineering.

Bicycles: Charles Flynn.

Boats: Practical Sailor.

Cars: Ed Henson.

Cigars: Allen Pasternack.

Clothes: Adele H. Russell, Merchandise Manager, Roots Clothiers.

Computers: John Jainschigg of Family Computer; Russ Walter, author and publisher of *The Secret Guide to Computers.*

Fabrics: Shirley Salerno, couturier.

Fishing: Angus Cameron; Jerry Hoffnagle.

Gardening: section written by Peter Schneider, amateur gardener.

Insurance: James Hunt, National Insurance Consumer Organization.

Investments: introduction written by J. Michael Reid, publisher of *Insider Indicator.*

Musical instruments: Brian Coogan, musician; Steve McGhee, violin maker; Nick Savene of Nick's Place store.

Pets: Margaret English, author of *Basic Guide to Dog Training and Obedience;* Beverley Miller, sheltie breeder; Dr. Jane Bicks, veterinarian.

Photographic equipment: introduction written by Harvey V. Fondiller, photographer, teacher, editor of photographic publications.

Skiing: Jack Stephenson, equipment manufacturer.

Telephones: New York Public Service Commission.

Travel: Ceci Smilie, Vice President, Inverness Travel; Clifton Cook, publisher of *JAX FAX.*

PREFACE

This book is for people who hate spending time searching for the best prices. Shopping is changing, and there are now many ways of paying less for whatever you want—buying at a lower price is increasingly popular across the country. But taking advantage of the changes isn't easy. Discount stores tend to be in out-of-the-way low rent districts, and buying from an untried and faraway discount mail-order firm takes guts. Besides, there is always the problem of whether seasonal sales are worth waiting for.

I hope that the most reluctant bargain hunter will find it easy to buy just about anything at a better price with this book in hand. I have asked professional and amateur experts when and where to buy, searched out the stores, compared their prices and done some testing myself. If you want to know what really happens when you have discounted furniture trucked from the South or order made-to-measure clothes from Hong Kong—read on.

M.E.L.

September 1986

THE ULTIMATE SHOPPER'S CATALOGUE

INTRODUCTION

A PENNY SAVED: ULTIMATE SHOPPER SOURCES AND STRATEGIES

A penny saved is *more* than a penny earned—it's up to a penny and a twenty-seventh, depending on your income tax bracket. I have gathered information on all the different ways that you can spend less and get more (or better). The major sources of good buys and strategies you can use are described here.

Mail and Telephone Sources

I have listed several kinds of mail and telephone sources, most of which are actually walk-in stores as well. One is the low-price city store. Stores of this kind tend to have small premises in out-of-the-way neighborhoods and are popular with people who don't mind shabbier surroundings and less service so long as they can get famous national brands and designer name goods at lower prices. These stores provide no-frills service, don't publish catalogues and don't give out much information. They just give price quotes. When you buy from them, you must know exactly what you want, and often you must provide a model number. You can get a model number from the manufacturer (see the list of manufacturers at the end of this book), *Consumer Reports* (the magazine that tests and rates consumer products) or another store.

Another kind of mail-order source is the specialist firm that sells such things as computers, gardening supplies, musical instruments, records, supplies for pets, tools and sports equipment. Such stores, many of which have national and international reputations, not only have lower prices but also usually have a far bigger and better inventory than any local store. Some of them actually provide better service than neighborhood stores, with specialists on staff willing to advise customers.

Then there are the overseas stores, which are not in any sense discount stores. Nevertheless, if you buy brand name goods in the country where they are made instead of in the United States, you save a great deal of money—usually a third to half of the price, even after paying postage and duty.

Sales

Selfridges, the London department store, claims that its founder, Gordon Selfridge, invented reduced-price sales when he was working at Marshall Field, Chicago, at the turn of the century. Since then sales have increased to such an extent that, in competitive urban areas, it sometimes seems as if there are no regular prices. Sales are no longer simply a way of getting rid of unwanted merchandise. They are now used as bait to lure us into the shops and away from competitors and discount stores. There are preseason sales, holiday sales at "high traffic" times, "promotional" sales created by manufacturers and, of course, postseason sales (which tend to have the best prices). On the whole, I have not found local sales worth waiting for, at least for price reasons alone, because most things are available at sale price or lower all year round at discount stores. Obviously, that doesn't apply if there is something you can't get by mail or if you have other reasons for buying locally. In those cases it is often well worth waiting for sales. In my discussions of various products throughout the book, I have noted when major seasonal sales tend to occur.

It is always worth trying the mail-order sources listed at sale time, at the end of summer and after Christmas, when many of them reduce their already low prices even further.

Do It Yourself

When doing it yourself seems worthwhile, either because it is so easy or because savings are tempting, I have given information and sources. However, the savings I mention certainly don't take into account the value of your time. I am assuming that if you weren't doing it yourself, you'd be watching television, reading a novel or indulging in some other financially unrewarding activity.

Buying Secondhand

Where appropriate I have included advice from experts as to what is worth buying secondhand. Some used goods are easier to judge than others, but the message is usually the same—great buys for people who really know what they are doing, but possible problems for people who don't.

OTHER WAYS

There are two other ways of buying at lower prices that are not dealt with in this book:

Haggling

If you live in a larger city, you may well be able to find a store locally that charges only about 10 or 15% above what the New York discounters are charging. If not, you can often get a discount by quoting a lower price you have found somewhere else (from a firm in this book, for instance). This is especially true with more expensive things such as cars, computers, electronics and sporting goods. Don't be tentative, be *firm*. Show the salespeople a magazine advertisement, or give them the name and number of the store so that they can verify your claim. A local firm probably won't actually meet a discount price, but you might get within 10%.

Off-price Stores and Factory Outlets

There are stores around the country that sell brand name goods, mostly clothes, at big discounts. At off-price stores brand name clothes can cost as much as 50% or even more off list price. Goods at these stores include overstock, out-of-season merchandise and sometimes irregular and "distressed" items that the off-price stores get from manufacturers, middlemen or full-price stores. Unlike discount stores, which keep a steady stock of certain lines of the first quality, these stores tend to vary stock according to what is available. Many of them sell seconds at really extraordinary prices.

One book that lists factory outlet and retail clearance stores around the country and is often updated is ***SOS: Save on Shopping Directory*** by Iris Ellis. Sold in bookstores or by mail from SOS Directory, 9109 San Jose Boulevard, Jacksonville, FL 32217.

HOW TO BUY BY MAIL OR TELEPHONE

Comparing Prices

Although the stores in this book sell at lower prices than most walk-in stores, to get the very lowest price on a particular item you should compare prices at the stores listed.

When you compare prices, make sure the products are exactly the same. Check to see, for instance, whether there are any variables or detachable parts that may or may not be included.

My neighbor Alice Eckstein tells me that she makes a chart that includes shipping costs when she compares. Don't forget that you don't pay sales tax when buying out of state, and that is a significant saving that often offsets shipping costs.

When There Is a Catalogue

Catalogues are seasonal, and many go out of print when the next one is being prepared. If you ask for a catalogue at that time, you may have to wait a couple of months before receiving an up-to-date one. With general catalogues, this is especially likely to happen from July to September, just before Christmas catalogues are published.

When There Is No Catalogue

When dealing with stores that have no catalogue, you must know exactly what you want. You have to get details regarding brand, size and color (and model number if applicable) before ordering. Advertisements, other stores, friends and *Consumer Reports* are obvious starting points for getting that information. Manufacturers are a very good source; most of them will send color brochures illustrating and describing their complete lines. Through them you can get a better idea of what's available than in neighborhoods stores, most of which have a limited selection.

Many firms without catalogues use toll-free numbers to give prices and information and in fact prefer to use the telephone rather than answer mail; this is especially true of computer stores, furniture stores, tire stores and wallpaper stores.

When asking for prices and when buying, make absolutely sure from the first quote what is included in the price, and also whether everything you need is included. It is infuriating to suddenly realize after calling several stores that something you need may or may not have been included in the price quotes you have collected. (This happened to me with the case for a camera I was buying.) This is most important with electronics and photographic equipment, which have accessories and removable parts, but also comes up with things like musical instruments with cases and removable mouthpieces.

You can consult *Consumer Reports* in the library or buy it from the address below.

***Consumer Reports*, Consumer Reports Subscription Department, Box 2480, Boulder, CO 80322. Telephone 800-525-0643.**
11 monthly issues and December Buying Guide, $16. Buying Guide only, $5.95 plus $2.15 postage *($4 in Canada and other countries),* from Consumer Reports Books, 540 Barnum Avenue, Bridgeport, CT 06608.

The *Buying Guide* is a paperback book of condensed listings from the magazines.

Buying by Telephone

A great new advance for the bargain hunter is the proliferation of toll-free 800 numbers. Some stores reserve the 800 numbers for orders only, but many give prices and information toll-free. They prefer you to telephone, rather than write, for price quotes. In fact, these numbers are multiplying so quickly that it is worth calling toll-free information (800-555-1212) to find out whether a store or manufacturer you want to communicate with has acquired an 800 number recently.

You direct dial overseas stores, but first dial operator to get the country code. I have given the area code for each shop along with its telephone number.

If you buy by telephone, always write a complete record of the order and the date so that you can refer to it later.

Paying with a Credit Card

Another great advance in mail and telephone shopping is the increased use of credit cards. It is much easier to use a card than go to the post office or bank for a money order or certified check. As many of the stores in this book wait for a personal check to clear before delivering goods, it is faster to use a card than a personal check.

Note: *Letters given after catalogue listings represent the charge and credit cards accepted: AE = American Express, DC = Diners Club, MC = MasterCard (Access in Britain), V = Visa (outside of the United States, often known by the name of the issuing bank, e.g., BarclayCard).*

Unfortunately, some stores won't accept payment by credit card for smaller orders. Other stores put a surcharge on smaller payments charged to a credit card.

For information on choosing and using a card, and other ways of paying, see appendixes.

Shipping

Firms must send ordered goods within 30 days. If they don't, they must let you know so that you can cancel the order and get a full refund. If you don't ask for a refund within 7 days of notification, the firm is allowed another 30 days to deliver.

Parcels weighing up to 70 pounds are sent either through the United States Post Office or by United Parcel Service. Firms are increasingly using UPS because, although it is more expensive, it is considered faster and safer. However, UPS deliveries can not be sent to a post office box. In addition, deliveries require a receipt, so if no one is at home to sign, packages are returned to the sender (UPS claims that parcels are returned only after three tries).

Returns

Always keep the receipt, box and wrapping materials until you are certain you want to keep whatever you have bought.

Almost nothing is sold without a manufacturer's or store's warranty against defects. If something you have bought is defective, check with the store for instructions before returning it. Include a photocopy of the receipt with whatever you are returning.

Most stores will accept the return of goods that are not defective, but if the return is your fault rather than the store's, there is sometimes a "restocking" charge. Watch out for that and for stores that only make exchanges or give credits on returns rather than money back. The descriptions of stores in this book include information about their returns policies.

BUYING FROM ABROAD

There are great bargains to be had by buying from abroad, even after paying postage and duty. It is slow, but quite easy—especially if you pay by credit card.

If you want to telephone Europe, remember that European time is several hours ahead, so call before 7 A.M. our time and get the AT&T night rate (40% off morning rates as I write).

Catalogues

Never pay for a foreign catalogue with a personal check. It drives the stores mad, because after bank charges they get nothing at all. I recommend paying with dollar bills. It may be slightly risky, but it's so simple. If you want to play it safe, get International Reply Coupons at the post office.

Most of the catalogues listed as free will come by surface mail and take at least four weeks to arrive. Do remember to send your request by airmail if you are in a hurry. Airmail letters to and from foreign countries take between 4 and 14 days each way. Surface mail letters take between 1 and 2 months each way. Airmail parcels take roughly 1 to 2 weeks; and surface mail parcels, roughly 1 to 2 months. And, as you know, everything takes longer before Christmas.

Ordering

Many overseas stores will give you the price of their goods in U.S. dollars if you ask. If you want a very rough idea of exchange rates, there is a conversion table at the back of this book. If you want an up-to-date exchange rate, telephone the foreign exchange company DeakInternational toll-free at 800-635-0515. Be sure to ask for DeakInternational's *selling* (not buying) rate for the foreign currency. If you are lucky, the person you talk to will not only give you the exchange rate but also tell you what the exact sum you are converting will come to in dollars. Banks and newspapers will also have the current exchange rate.

Once you have the exchange rate, multiply the price of the goods by the dollar equivalent of one unit of the foreign currency.

Paying

The easiest way to pay overseas firms is with a credit card. If a store accepts the card you have, you simply give it your card number, its expiration date and your signature. You are charged according to the going exchange rate, not on the day you make the purchase but on the day the shop's bank logs the transaction into its computer. If you pay with MasterCard or Visa, you will get a more favorable rate than banks give (see credit card appendix).

You can also pay with a personal check, but that holds matters up for several weeks while your check clears. A faster way is to buy an international check at the bank. In some countries sending actual currency by registered mail is allowed. But do this only if you are a gambler; when you send money through the mail, you have no proof that it has been sent or received. More information on these methods of paying can be found in the appendix.

Duty

Duty isn't as high as you may think. In the United States it is charged on what you actually paid for whatever you bought (not what it would sell for in the United States). Gifts worth less than $25 are exempt from duty, but only when bought by someone outside the country, so the very common practice of asking stores to mark parcels "gift" is, in fact, illegal. However, I have found customs officers to be rather lenient with parcels; only about one in six of mine seems to be charged.

There is a guide to various rates of duty at the end of this book, but the rules for applying them are sometimes complicated, so you can't be sure what the exact charge will be until you receive the goods. If you ever think you have been overcharged, either refuse the parcel and write a protest to your postmaster or accept the parcel and pay the duty, but send copies of the receipt for the duty and the shop's bill to the address given on the receipt. You may be able to get a refund, though not of the $2.50 post office handling charge called "postage due." If you ever want to return goods you have bought from abroad, write to the address on the receipt for duty to see whether and how you can get a refund.

READERS OUTSIDE THE UNITED STATES AND CANADA

Catalogues

When there is a charge for a catalogue, you can assume that the charge for sending it abroad is double the U.S. price. You can also assume that most catalogues will come by sea, which means a delay of several weeks.

The most sensible way of paying for catalogues is with bank notes, because, even though there is a chance of loss, you do avoid the charges involved in paying through a bank or post office, which are high on small sums. I am afraid that American firms insist on being paid in dollars for their catalogues, so serious mail-order shoppers should stock up on dollar bills ordered through their bank or the nearest bank that deals in foreign currencies. Though unpopular with stores, another possible way of paying for catalogues is with International Reply Coupons, which you can get at the post office.

Paying

Shops in other countries generally don't mind which currency they are paid in, so you can pay with a personal check (adding $4 for bank charges). American firms, I'm sorry to say, usually insist on being paid in dollars. The easiest way of doing this is with a credit card.

Your country may allow you to make out an ordinary personal check in American dollars, in which case you mail the check with your order exactly as though you were ordering within your own country. But a personal check will delay the arrival of your goods, as most firms will wait for the check to clear (roughly three weeks) before filling the order.

If your country does not allow you to write out a personal check in dollars, go to your bank for a transfer or draft in dollars.

Duty

If duty is charged by your customs department, it must be paid when you receive whatever you bought. It cannot be included in the sum you send the store.

APPLIANCES AND ELECTRONICS

Krups coffee-making machine makes up to ten cups of coffee in a few minutes and keeps them warm. When the list price for model 150 was $75, the Whole Earth Access price was $39.

RCA's first lower-priced convertible VCR VLP800 can be used with a video camera and also as a home VCR. When the list price was $729.95, the Comp-U-Store price for the same model delivered to my home was $474. (Prices vary according to where you live.)

APPLIANCES AND ELECTRONICS

Consumer Reports magazine and *Buying Guide Issue* (see page 4), with their independent testing and rating, can be invaluable when you are choosing appliances and electronics (and just about anything else). If you find, as sometimes happens, that by the time you get around to buying a *Consumer Reports*–rated product, it has been discontinued, the manufacturer may be able to help. When I have telephoned manufacturers as a consumer, I have sometimes managed to find someone who is willing to be informative about different models, their features and in which ways they differ from past and future models.

Many manufacturers have illustrated brochures of their products. These are extremely helpful when you are choosing an appliance, especially if your nearest stores don't have much on display. See the list of manufacturers at the back of this book.

To help you zero in on likely stores when looking for something specific, I have divided this chapter into three sections. But please notice that there is a good deal of overlap (especially on television and video equipment, which all the stores sell).

Firms in the Telephone Buying Services section are another main source of appliances and electronics.

LARGE KITCHEN APPLIANCES, AIR CONDITIONERS, VACUUM CLEANERS AND SO ON

Where and When to Buy

You can get large appliances at lower prices at low-price stores than at most local sales. Appliances are normally discounted only by about 25% at local sales (although there are certainly exceptions where discounts are higher). However, if you find that shipping costs to your area are too high, or if you want to buy locally for any other reason, here are hints about when you are likely to find sales near you.

Seasonal Sales of Large Appliances

The following guidelines are rough, because sale dates vary in different parts of the country. In addition, department stores and other retail stores are fighting back at low-price stores by increasing the number of sales. Watch patterns in your own area. Sales are now held not only at the end of selling seasons to get rid of inventory, but also at the beginning of buying seasons, to convince dawdlers to buy and to woo customers away from competitors.

Air conditioner and refrigerator sales are held either before June 1 or after September 1. It is definitely best to buy both air conditioners and refrigerators at preseason sales, when there is a wider selection and you have time to buy thoughtfully. (Most refrigerators are bought during the summer, when old models have been overloaded and break down—an emergency that is *not* conducive to sensible buying.)

Clothes washers and dryers are bought mostly in the fall, when, because of the weather, people stop hanging clothes on the line and object to taking clothes out to coin-operated machines. Look for high-season sales in October and November and postseason sales from January to April.

Dishwashers are not seasonal items, as they are usually bought as part of a remodeling project. Any sales are part of store promotions.

Microwave ovens are bought as gifts before Christmas, so there are promotional sales in November and December and postseason sales from January to April.

Mail and Telephone Sources

"Nobody pays list price anymore," one store owner said to me. And I, for one, certainly haven't paid full price for any appliance or piece of electronic equipment for the last ten years. There are now perfectly respectable firms in most urban centers that specialize in selling at lower prices. They do this by cutting overhead and, often, by increasing turnover. Some of the stores work from small premises in low-rent districts; others that sell by telephone have no retail space at all. Prices at these stores tend to be up to 45% off list price and so well worth buying from. Low-price large-appliance stores get their merchandise from American manufacturers or their authorized distributors, just as list-price stores do. This means that you get exactly the same manufacturer's warranty that you'd get from regular stores. Repairs are handled by your local authorized servicer, exactly as they are if you buy from any store that does not service.

If you want to pay the *very* least possible, it is worth calling, or writing to, several of the listed stores. I have found that prices do vary slightly among these stores. For instance, when I was buying a clothes washer (retail price: $680), the discounted prices I was quoted by the stores below went from $486 to $515, including tax and delivery. On a steam iron (retail price: $60), prices quoted went from $42 to $48. And I haven't found any one store that consistently has the lowest prices on everything.

To order an appliance, you'll need a model number. You can get it from another store or the manufacturer (see list at the end of the book).

Coles Appliance and Furniture Company, ***4026 Lincoln Avenue, Chicago, IL 60618. Telephone 312-525-1797.***
Write or telephone Monday through Saturday, except for Wednesday, 10 A.M. to 5 P.M., for prices in the U.S. and Canada.
MC, V.
Sells furniture, large kitchen appliances, televisions, audio and video equipment.
Returns: none.
Established 1946.

Coles was started by Al Krasney in 1946 and is still run by Mr. Krasney and his son Barry. It is a walk-in store that sells to several Chicago unions, including those of employees of the major hospitals and the Marriott hotels, and to members of the Chicago police department.

Coles, besides selling large appliances and some electronics, also sells furniture and will ship all over the country. I have found it to be good at giving price quotes, either by mail or long-distance telephone (like many discount stores, it won't quote prices on local calls).

Dial-a-Brand, ***110 Bedford Avenue, Bellmore, NY 11710. Telephone 516-783-8220 or 718-978-4400.***
Write or telephone for specific prices.
Sells major kitchen appliances, air conditioners, television and video sets.
Returns: money back if there is a valid reason.
Established 1967.

Dial-a-Brand claims to have been the first firm to sell appliances by telephone, and it is somewhat snooty about "imitators." Be that as it may, Dial-a-Brand is certainly well established. I, and several of my friends, have bought large appliances through this firm and have always found its prices and service to be good. (I bought a Friedrich air conditioner there for $395, whereas the firm I used to buy from was charging the list price of $559 for the same model.)

Stanley Gross, co-owner of Dial-a-Brand, says he uses his own trucks to deliver in New York, New Jersey and Connecticut. Outside that area he delivers by common carrier, and shipping costs are likely to be high on large appliances. Unless you live in a hick town where you are paying "super list" prices, or are buying several appliances at once, you will probably save more by buying from local discount stores.

Foto Electric Supply Company, ***31 Essex Street, New York, NY 10002. Telephone 212-673-5222.***
Prices given by mail only; send name and model number.
AE, MC, V.

Sells large and small appliances of all sorts: kitchen, television, video, radio, and photographic equipment and calculators.
Returns: credit.
Established 1962.

Foto Electric sells big and small appliances of just about every kind and also some of the more expensive brands: some Braun appliances, Chambers stoves and Subzero refrigerators that you don't often find in discount stores.

LVT Price Quote Hotline, ***Box 444, Commack, NY 11725-0444. Telephone 800-645-5010.***
Free leaflet lists brands; write or telephone Monday through Saturday, 9 A.M. to 6 P.M., for prices.
Sells an especially wide range of major appliances for the kitchen, air conditioners, televisions and video equipment, radios, telephones and answering devices, vacuum cleaners, radar detectors, electronic keyboards, calculators and typewriters.
Returns: none.
Established 1976.

Richard Levitt, founder and president of this small firm, swears that he treats his customers like his family. He shares a cooperative warehouse with other dealers and says that if something ordered is not in stock, he immediately telephones rather than writes to his customer.

He sells to every state that UPS serves, but things weighing over 70 pounds go by common carrier and on these you have to work out your own shipping costs. Customers who pay with cashier's checks, certified checks or postal money orders get their goods usually within 10 to 15 days. Richie waits for personal checks to clear, so if you pay with one, delivery will take about 20 days.

Richie has sold to Radio Free Europe, Showtime, the Coast Guard, the Forest Service and me. A friend and I both bought air conditioners from him and got excellent prices and speedy service (but then we live in New York City, just next door).

Percy's TV and Video, ***315 Grove Street, Worcester, MA 01605. Telephone 617-755-5334; in Massachusetts, 800-922-8194.***
Send stamped, self-addressed envelope or telephone Mondays only, 9 A.M. to 6 P.M., with brand and model number for price.
MC, V. Money order (no personal checks).
Sells audio, television and video equipment and kitchen appliances in standard brands.
Returns: exchanges; no refunds.
Established 1928.

New England's largest independent appliance dealer, Percy's has a walk-in store and an "outside" sales department to deal with telephone questions and orders. Although the salespeople prefer make-and-model-number orders, this is one of the few places that you can telephone with vaguer questions such as, "I like Sony, and I want a 19-inch color television. What do you have?" They will try to give a thumbnail sketch on the telephone or send literature.

Percy's also says that it is willing to special order and has "quick access" to stuff that has to be ordered.

Vacuum Cleaners

AAA-All Factory Vacuum Cleaner Service Center, ***241 Cedar, Abilene, TX 79601. Telephone 915-677-1311.***
Write for brochure ($2 in the U.S. and Canada) or telephone, 9 A.M. to 5 P.M. on weekdays, 9 A.M. to 3 P.M. on Saturdays, for prices.
MC, V.
Sells vacuum cleaners, floor polishers/shampooers, ceiling fans. Brands: Compact, Eureka, Filter Queen, Hoover, Kirby, Panasonic, Rainbow and others.
Returns: money back if goods returned within ten days.
Established 1975.

Although AAA says it charges $2 for the brochure, I have found that it will send one for free if you write for a price.

If you call up to ask for a price, you'll be asked where you got the model number and what price you have seen locally. I checked prices on two Panasonics. AAA didn't stock one, and on the other the price was the same as at my local discount store. I had better luck on two Eureka machines: they were 27 and 30% off the regular prices at Macy's department store and 10 and 15% off Macy's *sale* prices.

BONDY and COLES (described in this section) and COMP-U-STORE (see General section) sell vacuums at prices comparable to those of the above store.

Used Vacuum Cleaners

Electrolux vacuums have a tip-top reputation and seem to be many people's favorite. New models start at $399 as I write and aren't available at a discount, although Electrolux does sometimes sell models it is discontinuing at lower prices. Electrolux distributors also sell reconditioned models at lower prices, and these start at $199. **THE VERMONT COUNTRY STORE, 657 Main Street, Weston, VT 05161,** telephone 802-362-2400, sells an old ("classic, classic" they call it) reconditioned and rechromed Electrolux for about a third of the price of the cheapest new model. It has runners instead of wheels, and a cloth bag.

Repairs

Everyone knows how infuriatingly expensive repairs on household appliances are. If you've got the guts to try your own repairs, GE and Whirlpool will help. Both companies publish do-it-yourself repair manuals for their products and have toll-free telephone numbers you can call to get a diagnosis of your problem. If necessary, company representatives can also talk customers through almost any repair, depending on the skill of the caller. Powell Taylor of GE says many repairs are so simple that they can be done by almost anyone (unclogging the drain of a leaking refrigerator, for instance). Other repairs ("screwdriver deals," as GE calls them) are necessitated by mechanical problems that many people can manage (changing a belt on a washing machine is a common one). High-level repairs involve such things as playing with wiring and are only for the knowledgeable. Contact:

GENERAL ELECTRIC ANSWER CENTER ***800-626-2000.***

WHIRLPOOL COOL LINE ***800-253-1301.***

SMALL APPLIANCES FOR THE KITCHEN AND FOR PERSONAL CARE (HAIR DRYERS, SHAVERS AND SO ON)

There are no seasonal sales for electronics alone, but as the market is so competitive, there are odd sales all year round. Promotional sales at the usual times—before Christmas and on public holidays—are especially likely. However, small appliances and electronics are especially easy to buy by telephone or mail (shipping costs aren't high), and prices at the stores below are good all year round, better than prices at most local sales.

Bernie's Discount Center, ***821 Sixth Avenue, New York, NY 10001.***
Telephone: questions, 212-564-8582; orders, 212-564-8758.
Send self-addressed, stamped envelope when writing for specific prices.
Sells top brands of small electrical appliances, including Braun and Salton; major appliances, including vacuum cleaners by Eureka and Hoover; electronics, including less common brands such as Hitachi and Mitsubishi.
Returns: must include sales slip and be within seven days.
Established 1948.

Bernie's is a walk-in store that does mail-order business, although it doesn't have a special mail-order department. It has a good selection of small appliances and is prompt about giving written price quotes, but usually won't quote by telephone. This is one of the few low-price stores that sell Mitsubishi television sets. Mitsubishi is a favorite of modern design enthusiasts because of its sleekly designed sets. I also notice that in a 1985 *Consumer Reports* survey, Mitsubishi television sets were rated second-best (after Sony) on number of repairs needed.

I ordered the top-of-the-line GE F440 steam iron from Bernie's for $44.50 plus $2.50 shipping (I had seen it the day before selling at Macy's for $60).

It arrived four days after I sent in my order—the store hadn't waited for my personal check to clear.

Bondy Export Company, ***40 Canal Street, New York, NY 10002. Telephone 212-925-7785.***

Send name and model number with stamped, self-addressed envelope for price quote.
AE, MC, V.
Sells all kinds of small appliances, photographic equipment, cordless telephones, answering machines, tape recorders, clock radios, shavers, calculators, watches (Casio and Seiko), shavers, pens, Ray-Ban sunglasses, vacuums.
Returns: none; manufacturer's guarantee only.
Established 1955.

Bondy, a tiny shop, keeps a selection of small appliances in stock and will send only things weighing 70 pounds or less (the UPS limit) out of state. In spite of insisting on a stamped, self-addressed envelope, Bondy doesn't answer questions at all if it doesn't stock what you are asking about. If it does stock it, you'll get a postcard.

I bought two appliances from Bondy (with certified checks), and they were both delivered immediately. Prices have sometimes been a dollar or two lower here than at other stores in this book.

Focus Electronics, ***14523 13th Avenue, Brooklyn, NY 11219. Telephone 718-871-7600; orders only, 800-223-3411.***

Write or telephone with model number for prices.
Telephone hours: Sunday to Thursday, 10 A.M. to 6 P.M.; Friday, 10 A.M. to 3 P.M. (closed Saturday, open Sunday).
AE, MC, V.
Sells air conditioners, small electric appliances, computers, photographic equipment, typewriters, video equipment.
Returns: money back if merchandise returned within 14 days.
Established 1967.

Focus sells a very wide selection of appliances. Major kitchen appliances are not stocked but can be ordered. Small appliances such as personal-care Water Piks, hair dryers and shavers are usually in stock. There are even pots and pans for the kitchen. The most popular lines are, as with most of these stores, television, video and photographic equipment. Focus "parallel" imports photographic equipment—"we have to, to remain competitive"—and gives its own one-year guarantee for anything that doesn't have a manufacturer's warranty.

Focus is a large firm (it has contracts with major organizations, including New York City) and has a full-scale mail-order department.

I have bought here by mail many times. When I paid with a credit card, service was prompt; when I paid with personal checks, my parcels took over three weeks to arrive.

AUDIO, TELEVISION, VIDEO AND OFFICE EQUIPMENT

Firms listed here are good places to look for audio, video, photographic and "office" equipment (calculators, copiers, telephones and typewriters). They won't have the less common brands of video equipment, nor high-end audio equipment (see the Audio Equipment section for that), but they do sell the most popular midpriced brands.

This kind of equipment is now so complicated that if you are not gadget-minded you may not know how to work all the features when you get a new piece of electronic equipment home. Several times I have not known whether my new unit was defective or whether I am. It has always turned out to be me. I have found that assistants in most stores, including full-price ones, don't know each piece of equipment well enough to be able to help over the telephone (they tell you to bring it in or take it to a repair center, a huge nuisance). Furthermore, they can't imagine that you haven't done something obvious, so they don't even ask whether you have or not. At this stage I have found the manufacturers to be much more helpful. First find out whether the manufacturer of your new unit has a toll-free number by dialing 800-555-1212. If not, the address and regular number will be in the instruction manual (they don't seem to put the 800 number in). Then telephone and ask for "technical support." Technical support has always solved my problems by being thorough, patient and soothing.

If you have trouble getting through, insist. When the manufacturer of my computer tells me to call its eastern regional distributor, I say, perfectly truthfully, that the technical support department of its regional distributor will take calls only from stores now. Also insist on getting someone who knows your model. When I called up Sony's hotline to ask why I couldn't get any stations on my new world band radio, my "technical support" consisted of a woman who just read me the instructions from my manual in a loud voice.

Sales

In highly competitive urban areas, there seem to be frequent promotional sales of one sort or another. Sales are also likely to happen at the classic times—at the end of summer, after Christmas and on public holidays. But my spot-checking in New York shows that year-round prices at the firms in this book are almost always quite a bit lower than sale prices at full-price stores.

Mail and Telephone Sources

East 33 St., ***42 East 33rd Street, New York, NY 10016. Telephone 800-223-3201; in New York State, 212-686-0930.***

Write or telephone for prices.
MC, V.
Sells audio equipment, computers, televisions and stereos, typewriters, office machines.
Minimum order $50.
Returns: none, except for defective equipment, which will be exchanged if returned with original carton and packing within seven days.
Established 1975.

This large, comfortable midtown store doesn't look like a discount store—goods are on display, there is lots of sales help (*two* people tried to serve me when I went in on a Monday in January) and there is plenty of space. Nevertheless, two different loyal customers (one of them Arnold Bob, editor of the now defunct *Discount America* newsletter) have told me that prices here are really good. The drawback is that the excellent prices that are advertised are mainly cash prices. On mail orders there is a 6% "shipping" charge for checks, and there is a 10% "shipping" charge if you pay with a credit card. That mounts up on more expensive goods.

47 St. Photo, ***36 East 19th Street, New York, NY 10003. Telephone 800-221-7777; in New York State, 212-398-1410.***
224-page catalogue, $2 in the U.S. and Canada, or write or telephone with model name and number for specific prices. Closed Saturday, open Sunday.
AE, MC, V.
Sells audio and video equipment; office equipment: calculators, computers, copiers, telephones and answering machines, typewriters; jewelry and watches.
Minimum order $25.
Returns: money back if merchandise returned before 5 or 15 days (depending on what is returned).

I have been buying for years at the famous 47 St. Photo, which has expanded over the years to four stores and the mail-order offices. 47 St. has actually become more of an electronics supermarket than anything else and is said to have over 5,000 items in stock, take in around $50 million a year and have cozy relations with manufacturers, who grant large product allowances, even on scarcer goods. There is a very wide choice here, and I've always found prices to be among the very lowest.

However, be warned: the May 6, 1985, issue of *City Business* ran a story headlined 47 ST. PHOTO LEADS IN COMPLAINTS telling how 47 St. had 60 complaints registered with the Department of Consumer Affairs between January of 1984 and February of 1985. The leading cause of complaints was that refunds are not returned promptly; other complaints were about the unavailability of things featured in the mail-order catalogue and differences between advertised and actual prices.

I consider the above problems annoying but not disastrous. I myself have suffered from the difference between advertised and actual prices. I once turned up with the catalogue to buy a shortwave radio and was told that the catalogue price was wrong—the radio was $2 more than the printed price. I also suffered from the slow refund, but I was grateful to get a refund at all. I bought two ribbons that snapped when I put them in my printer. In spite of the ferocious notice in the computer store saying something like "no refunds on ribbons and disks," I returned them, and several weeks later 47 St. replaced them. Meanwhile, I found to my embarrassment that it was my printer's fault—not the ribbons'.

One problem with the size and popularity of the stores is that, as with many discount stores, you get little attention. The stores are almost impossible to reach by telephone if you live in New York (although I have had some luck reaching the newer Nassau Street branch on the telephone). If you live outside the state, you can use the toll-free 800 number. Replies to mail queries are speedy—you'll get your own letter back promptly with the answer to your question scribbled in.

J & R Music World, ***3CC, 23 Park Row, New York, NY 10038. Telephone 800-221-8180; in New York State, 212-693-0396.***
Catalogue, $2.
MC, V.
Sells audio equipment and tapes, CB radios, computers and accessories, radios, telephones and accessories, television and video equipment, scanners, security devices for the house, watches.
Returns: money back if goods returned in original packing within 30 days.
Established 1972.

This large and popular store sells a wide variety of electronics, although it's best known for its wide choice in midpriced audio equipment, records and tapes. Prices on electronics are almost always below those of full-price stores, although not the lowest among stores listed here. There is a large illustrated catalogue, which costs $2, but I have found that if you write and ask a price, instead of answering your question, J & R sends a free catalogue.

S and S Sound City, ***58 West 45th Street, New York, NY 10036. Telephone 800-223-0360; in New York State, 212-575-0210.***
In Canada and the U.S., write or telephone Monday through Saturday, 9 A.M. to 6 P.M., for specific prices.
MC, V.
Sells audio equipment, computer parts and accessories, televisions, video equipment, video movies, radios, tape recorders, telephone-answering machines.
Returns: seven-day money-back guarantee providing that merchandise is returned in original factory carton with all packing intact and is "not abused."
Established 1975.

S and S Sound City belongs to two brothers, Kenneth and Mel Tillman, who say it's a plus that one of them is *always* on the premises (employees can't say, "the boss isn't here"). The busy walk-in store is in the very center of Manhattan and displays a slightly wider range of television and video brands than sold in most discount stores. The mail-order department is on the second floor. Prices are low, but not the lowest, *except* on their "specials." Periodically, they choose two or three items from each department, lower the prices and advertise them in the video magazines. If you haven't seen the ads, you can call in and ask for their specials. (When I was comparing prices on a Toshiba VCR, S and S had the lowest price of all, because it was on special sale.)

I bought an Aiwa personal stereo here. The price wasn't the lowest I found—it was $130 when a full-price store was selling it for $169—but I wanted to try S and S. The assistants were informative and easy to deal with. When I first called, the model I wanted wasn't in stock; they told me they were expecting it a couple of days later. I checked back on the day—sure enough, it had arrived. I ordered and received it promptly.

Stores listed under Computers and Photography also sell electronics.

AUDIO EQUIPMENT

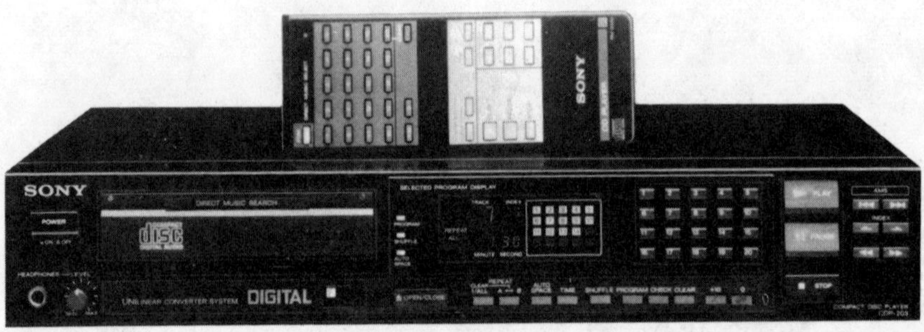

Sony CDP-203 compact disc player with remote control. When the suggested list price was $500, the price at Audio Unlimited was $375.

AUDIO EQUIPMENT

WHAT TO BUY

This chapter has been written with Clement Meadmore, author of *All Sound and No Frills.*

Intense competition among hundreds of manufacturers is resulting in the constant improvement of audio equipment sound quality. Lifelike clarity at all audible frequencies and at all volume levels is being achieved along with lower prices for a given quality level. As I write, it is possible to put together a truly excellent system (record player, receiver and speakers) in the midprice range ($800 to $2000) and a decent system for about $600. Components in price ranges above these are really only for fanatics.

But no manufacturer makes all components equally well. To get best value, it is essential to choose components carefully from among different manufacturers' specialties. To help with this task, buying hints for the various components and the names of manufacturers who produce best-buy equipment, i.e., equipment that is noticeably better than other equipment in the same price range, are given below.

Prices will most likely continue to drop as manufacturers compete in finding simpler, more economical solutions to audio equipment problems.

Compact Sets

Compact sets—consisting of record player, tape deck and radio in one unit plus two speakers—cost under $200. But if you are tempted to buy a compact set, please note that the bad bearings in the turntable and high stylus pressure of the tone arm will spoil your records; the amplifier will be of such low wattage that it will distort music played at any reasonable volume and the speaker enclosures will probably be of plastic or masonite and will therefore resonate unpleasantly.

Matched Systems

To make things easier for the bewildered buyer, several midprice manufacturers have recently started producing components specially designed to work well together and match visually. Matched systems can give far better sound than compacts, although not as good as the better component systems. Most matched sets have rubbishy speakers (the most expensive element), although the other components may be decent. But as no manufacturer makes all components equally well, you can get a far better set for a couple of hundred dollars more by choosing best-buy components from several different manufacturers.

If, for simplicity's sake, you want to buy everything from one manufacturer, NAD is a good one to choose. Although it does not promote and sell its components as matched sets, it is, as I write, the only manufacturer that makes each and every component, even speakers, at a decent standard. The speakers are good quality but not the best value for money, whereas the other NAD components are best buys. As I write, the cheapest complete NAD set costs $555 at a 20% discount, and a medium-priced system costs $950 at a 20% discount.

Components

If you want value for money, buy the best components you can find made by specialist manufacturers. By choosing carefully from among midpriced components, you can put together an excellent system. And if you can't afford better quality at the moment, an advantage of buying components is that you can replace the separate units with better ones when you want to.

Turntables and Tone Arms

Turntables have improved in recent years, and it is hard to buy a really bad one. Nowadays most of them turn smoothly and evenly and differ mainly in how much motor noise is allowed through. There is a dispute in the audio world as to whether belt-driven or direct-drive turntables are best; we think that belt-driven turntables work better because the belt isolates the motor vibrations from the record. Direct-drive turntables may have greater speed (pitch) accuracy, but we never met anyone who could hear the difference. The best buy among the reasonably priced belt-driven turntables is the NAD. The very cheapest Dual is acceptable, and it's far better than the turntable you are likely to get in a matched set. About 20 of the Japanese firms make turntables for $100 or less, but we would feel safer with the Dual because its platter is isolated from the base with springs (important for bumps and feedback protection), which is not true of most Japanese turntables.

As for tone arms, there is no point in buying a separate tone arm unless you are a total perfectionist. Arms on the better turntables are of excellent design. The one thing that is death to records is an automatic record changer. If you have one, get rid of it.

Cartridges

Cartridges and speakers have a more noticeable effect on sound quality than all the other components in between them. When upgrading your system, you can make the most dramatic change for the least amount of money by changing the cartridge. Among cartridges the absolute best buy is the Grado MTE +1, which costs $18 as I write. Any improvement beyond that would involve spending at least $300 (on a Grace Ruby, for instance).

Compact Disc Players

A dramatic new development in the last few years has been digital recording. The sound is recorded as a series of bits (like a newsprint photograph only infinitely finer) rather than as a series of waveforms (like a painting or real photograph), and records are played by a laser beam. One advantage of digital reproduction of sound is that the discs are hardier than analog records. Dirt and dust are far less harmful to them, so there is no surface noise when even old discs are played. Another sonic advantage is that digital recording captures a greater dynamic range (i.e., can convey both very soft and very loud sounds) and gives the correct contrast between, say, a single instrument and a full orchestra. This is more useful with certain sorts of classical and modern music than it is with jazz and chamber music.

Digital sound is said by most experts to be superior. Others say it is about equal to that of an analog record in very good condition played on a very good analog system. Wayne A. Schuurman of Audio Advisor (below) feels that in the midprice range (around $500) compact disc players, besides being much more convenient (easier to operate and maintain), have definite sonic advantages such as cleaner sound and better bass. However, in the top-price range ($1000 for the turntable or compact disc player alone) Wayne Schuurman still prefers the analog unit. Some models have an advance I approve of: a disc-changing feature (it doesn't hurt the disc) that enables you to get six hours of music without jumping up once.

The problem with compact disc players at the moment is that the discs are more expensive than analog records and the variety is nowhere near as great.

Price differences among compact disc players reflect, by and large, the number of features rather than dramatic differences in the quality of sound produced. However, it is generally agreed as I write that the English Mission and Meridian sound best (they are available at lower prices in England; see below), with the Japanese catching up fast. Sanyo makes a best buy at less than half the price of the English beauties, and the inexpensive Yamaha models have had good reviews. In fact, the Yamaha CD X2 (list price $299 as I write) won a coveted *Audio Video International* magazine citation.

Receivers

The receiver includes an amplifier, turner, pre-amp and radio. These can be bought as separate components for about three times the price. If you are a perfectionist and want each part made by a different specialist, pay the extra price; otherwise a receiver makes more sense.

The more watts a receiver has, the louder it can play before it distorts the sound. Unless you are destitute and/or have a very small room, don't buy a receiver with less than 30 watts per channel. With under 30 watts there will be distortion at even reasonable volume, and the radio section will have difficulty picking up stations clearly. NAD makes best-buy receivers.

Cassette Tape Decks

These have improved greatly recently. The background hiss has been reduced and the frequency response has been increased in both directions—higher and lower sounds can be captured more clearly. With cassette tape decks it is the frequency response that you pay for; the wider the response, the more high notes and low notes are recorded. Choose a deck with a range of 20 to 20K (20,000) Hz (cycles per second) if you can afford it.

Aiwa and Harman/Kardon are best-buy recorders. Among the very cheapest, Sanyo makes a marginally acceptable recorder.

Speakers

Speakers, like cartridges, are traducers; they translate electronic signals into mechanical movement. It is a hard thing to do well and there is a significant difference in quality among speakers. By upgrading your speakers, you can make a noticeable difference in the sound of your system. Most speakers perform well with high notes, but the farther down the scale they go, the larger and more expensive the speakers tend to be. Infinity is among those manufacturers who make speakers at all prices, from cheap to expensive. Acoustat is a best buy among medium-priced to expensive speakers.

Recently there has been a great improvement in very small bookshelf-sized speakers. A few years ago small speakers couldn't transmit low notes well, but now several manufacturers make good small speakers that do well on bass. When shopping for good low-cost speakers ($300 to $400), look for good bass and clean midrange. Speakers with polypropylene cones tend to be cleaner in the midrange, so look for polypropylene cones and bass down to 35 or 40 Hz. These requirements can be found in this price range in speakers by Apature, Audio Pulse, BES, Ego, Fried, Heybrook, Image, Infinity, Mitom, MTX, Paisley and RCA.

In addition, Clement Meadmore, who has provided the information for this audio section, has designed, in conjunction with an acoustical engineer, speakers that he considers an absolute best buy among shelf-sized speakers. (See Facsimile, described below).

SOURCES

These stores have reasonably well chosen audio equipment that they sell at a discount. Furthermore, most of the stores that sell midpriced and high-end equipment are helpful with information. When we called them to test their advice, we found that it tended to be sensible and useful on what they stock. If you have nowhere to turn for help on choosing equipment, we don't think you'll go far wrong if you go by these stores' recommendations. However, don't expect the unbiased information you'd get from a totally independent expert. These stores are knowledgeable about the lines they have decided to deal in, but are sometimes overly dismissive when it comes to equipment they don't know as well.

If you read equipment reviews, you'll find that most of the commercial magazines are afraid of offending advertisers and are therefore mealymouthed in their reviews. *Audio* is the most outspoken of the big magazines. **$ENSIBLE SOUND,** ***403 Darwin Drive, Snyder, NY 14226,*** is a small quarterly that gives independent reviews of less expensive equipment with an eye on value for money. **STEREOPHILE,** ***P.O. Box 1948, Santa Fe, NM 87501,*** reviews mid-priced equipment. **ABSOLUTE SOUND,** ***2 Glen Avenue, Sea Cliff, NY 11579,*** reviews high-end equipment for perfectionists.

Audio Advisor, ***225 Oakes SW, Grand Rapids, MI 49503. Telephone 616-451-3868.***
Free quarterly price lists, or call or write for specific prices.
AE, MC, V.
Sells mid- to high-quality audio and video products and accessories; sells and integrates visual with audio systems (sells Harman/Kardon, Yamaha and Mitsubishi VCRs, Proton and NAD monitors; can order Mitsubishi televisions).
Returns: returns accepted on products that do not perform as promised, but check first.
Established 1979.

This is one of the few firms that give discounts on high-end audio equipment. Discounts are mainly 15 to 20%, although Audio Advisor says they can reach 50% on accessories.

If you don't know what to buy, Audio Advisor will be very helpful. First the people there ask you what you want to spend (as I write, complete systems start at about $600), then they ask about room size and listening habits. They keep an extensive library of product literature and reviews, so they can send you information on anything they recommend. Whenever I have called anonymously, my questions have been answered carefully and informatively, especially by Wayne (I have found around 6 P.M. EST the easiest time to get through).

I bought the excellent Proton table radio here (model 300) at a 15% discount off list price. Few stores carry the radio. Audio Advisor charged only $4 for shipping, so I saved an extra $16 on the sales tax I would have paid had I bought it in New York.

However, Audio Advisor, besides selling directly to consumers, is a broker and sells units through other retail firms around the country. The assistant I spoke to assumed the Proton was in stock at his source; it actually wasn't and I had to wait four weeks for delivery.

Audio Unlimited, ***1203½ Adams Avenue, LaGrande, OR 97850. Telephone 503-963-5731.***
Occasional free flyers, or write or telephone for specific prices.
AE, MC, V.
Sells low- to high-priced audio equipment, car stereos, video equipment (all VCRs except Mitsubishi; monitors by Proton and NEC).
Returns: money back minus a 20% restocking charge if goods returned in new condition within ten days with original packing and paperwork.
Established 1976.

Audio Unlimited has a selection of well-chosen less expensive to most expensive components at discounts that varied between 21 and 25% off list price on the four midpriced components I checked. It seems to sell units in all price ranges. It offered a 20% discount on the Proton 300 radio but did not have it in stock (and gets good marks for telling me it wasn't in stock instead of leaving me to find out later). About 100 different brands are either stocked or can be ordered. When I telephoned pretending to be a possible customer, the salespeople helpfully gave me information on the units they sell and tried to supply what I wanted without steering me to more expensive units.

Community Audio, ***318 West Duval Street, Philadelphia, PA 19144. Telephone 215-843-9918.***
Ask for an "Audio Profile" (questionnaire).
MC, V.
Sells audio equipment.
Returns: seven-day at-home trial; money back (except for your return shipping costs) if you are not satisfied.
Established 1982.

John Adams, a social worker, sold audio equipment as a hobby before taking it up full-time in 1982. He now has a personal service, which he runs with part-time help, giving recommendations and selling midpriced and high-end audio. He sends out a rather messily reproduced questionnaire on which you give details of your current equipment and tell him which components you want to change or add. He makes one or two suggestions. He stocks a little in a couple of rooms in his home; other units he orders and says that he can get them within three weeks. The prices I checked were a few dollars higher than at other firms in this section.

John Adams also sells used equipment with a 90-day warranty and says that occasionally you can get a used system for as little as $150. It will look old-fashioned and worn but will play reasonably well.

Facsimile, ***9 Deer Hill Lane, Briarcliff Manor, NY 10510. Telephone 914-769-6358.***
Free information page.
Sells one speaker model so far: Facsimile II.
Returns: money back if merchandise returned within 30 days.
Established 1983.

Bookshelf-sized speakers have been designed by Clement Meadmore (who provided the information for this section) and an engineer who several years ago designed a legendary speaker (both the engineer and the speaker must remain nameless for contractual reasons). The speakers have extremely clean sound down to 35 cycles, and Clem is certain they are a best buy at $425 a pair. Although many small speakers cost the same or less, Clem says that none have such low bass and accurate sound.

Illinois Audio, ***12 East Delaware Place, Chicago, IL 60611. Telephone: questions, 312-664-0020; orders, 800-621-8042.***
Free price list, or write or telephone for specific prices.
MC, V.
Sells midpriced audio equipment by Akai, JVC, Kenwood, Onkyo, Sansui, Sony, Technics, others; cassette, reel and video tape recorders.
Returns: manufacturer's guarantee only.
Established 1970.

I find Illinois Audio impossible to get hold of by telephone—its people are *always* busy (they work 10 A.M. to 5 P.M.). But they do answer written price questions. They sell mostly less expensive Japanese audio equipment—brands that are fairly easy to find at a discount in any city that has discount stores.

International High Fi, ***6330 Frankford Avenue, Baltimore, MD 21206. Telephone 301-488-9600 (weekdays, 9 A.M. to 9 P.M.; Saturdays, 9 to 4).***
Free flyer (50 cents in Canada).
MC, V.
Sells midpriced audio and video equipment by Bose, Hitachi, Infinity, Jensen, JVC, Mirage, Onkyo, Sanyo, Sony.
Returns: five-day home trial on some speakers; money back on other goods if unopened.
Established 1970.

International High Fi sells less expensive audio and video equipment, the kind that is often discounted in the United States. Its range is small but discounts are respectable, and the people there boast that if you telephone, they will tell you honestly whether what you want is in stock or not (instead of holding on to your check and then offering a substitute as they say some other dealers do).

Lyle Cartridges, ***115 South Corona Avenue, Valley Stream, NY 11582. Telephone 800-221-0906; in New York State, 516-599-1112.***
Price list available; send stamped, self-addressed envelope, in Canada and overseas an International Reply Coupon.
MC, V ($25 minimum).
Minimum order $15.
Sells phonograph cartridges (Audio-technica, Grado, Ortofon, Pickering, Shure, others), factory-original replacement needles, record-care accessories.
Returns: defective items are replaced; no refunds unless there is an error in shipment.
Established 1971.

This firm specializes in cartridges. I bought my Grado cartridge here and was very pleased with the prompt service. Lyle also sells Discwasher, one of the best record cleaners.

Stereo Cost Cutters, ***P.O. Box 551, Dublin, OH 43017. Telephone 614-889-2117.***
Free catalogue.
Sells Dynaco parts, kits and tubes.
Returns: defective parts replaced if returned within the year.
Established 1976.

When Dynaco went out of business, SCC bought the entire inventory—kits, complete sets and parts. As long as supplies last, they *are* Dynaco and their prices are reasonable. The catalogue has good, honest descriptions.

Twenty First Century Audio, ***5041 Rising Sun Avenue, Philadelphia, PA 19120. Telephone 215-324-4457.***
Telephone or send self-addressed, stamped envelope for specific prices.
CB, DC, MC, V.
Sells audio equipment by small firms such as Audible Illusions, Apt Holman, Argent, Audio Pro, Bells Research, Beveridge, DCM, Dynavector, Grado, Spectrum, Stax.
Returns: defective or damaged units replaced.
Established 1979.

Twenty First Century specializes in high-end audio equipment made by small companies that often even audio afficionados haven't heard of. Owner Edward Smith looks for units that he thinks give good sound for the price. He says he has found several unknowns that later were well reviewed and acquired good reputations. I haven't seen the store, but it sounds like a small operation—the telephone rings in Mr. Smith's house as well as the store, so you may think you've got a wrong number when the telephone is answered in a homey way.

Local customers can listen to his wares. He recently sold a $600 pre-amp to a customer who thought it was as good (though not as good-looking) as an

$1800 pre-amp the customer had previously heard. If you are buying by mail, Edward Smith suggests that you try to hear his components locally. He can give you manufacturers' addresses if you want to get the names of local dealers. Otherwise try to read reviews in the more reliable journals such as *Audio, Absolute Sound* or *Stereophile.*

When comparing prices, don't miss EAST 33 ST. (Appliances and Electronics section), which sells the better midpriced audio brands such as NAD and Nakamichi that are not often sold in discount stores. Less expensive audio equipment is also sold by other firms in the Appliances and Electronics section.

OVERSEAS SOURCES

Audio T, ***P.O. Box 152, Enfield, Middlesex EN2 0PL, England. Telephone 1-366-5015.***
Price list: three $1 bills or equivalent International Reply Coupons.
AE, MC, V.
Sells high-end audio equipment, including better British manufacturers known in the United States such as Dunlop and Linn Sondeck (turntables), Basik (tone arms), Goldring (cartridges), KEF, Lentek, Meridian, Mission, Quad, SME, Syrinx.
Returns: credit, but only if previously agreed upon.
Established 1968.

In England, most English audio equipment costs just under half what it does in the United States, so if it is English equipment that you have set your heart on, it is well worth ordering direct from there. Small things such as tone arms and cartridges can come by airmail to your door. Even speakers can be worth ordering, if you can pick them up yourself at a port of entry. The excellent Quad Electrostatic ELS 63 speakers cost $2600 plus freight collect if you buy them from the U.S. discount firm Audio Advisor, but you can get them for $1570 including sea freight to New York from Audio T.

Intersonics, ***P.O. Box 113, Toyohashi 440-91, Japan. Telephone 532-88-4773.***
Cable INTERSONICS TOYOHASHI.
Free price list.
Sells high-end Japanese audio and video equipment.
Returns: goods are replaced or repaired free of charge under a one-year warranty.
Established 1980.

David F. Staples, an American painter from Salem, Massachusetts, went to Japan to study the art and culture, and stayed to become a calligrapher and seal engraver. He arrived in Japan with lists of audio components his American friends wanted if prices were reasonable. Prices *were* reasonable and David Staples soon found himself getting requests from perfect strangers. At that point he organized a business and now specializes in selling Japanese audio components and accessories. He handles only "hi-fi" (not "low-fi" or "mid-fi," most of which is heavily discounted on the western market), so all the prices are very much lower than the prices for the same components bought in the United States. The prices that David Staples quoted me were mostly 50% of U.S. prices or lower for cartridges by Accuphase, Audio Note, Denon, Dynavector and others and tone arms by Dynavector, Audio Technica and Micro Seiki. He also sells the handmade, limited-production Koetsu components at prices just above half of U.S. prices.

David Staples will also give advice about components, so Intersonics is a really marvelous source for audio perfectionists who want Japanese components.

Japan Audio Trading, ***Saikaen Building, 4-33-21 Kamimeguro, Meguro-Ku, Tokyo 153, Japan. Telephone Tokyo 3-715-0533.***
Price list, $1 bill or equivalent International Reply Coupons.
Sells Japanese audio equipment small enough to be airmailed. Carries Accuphase, Audio-Note, Audio Technica, Denon, Dynavector, Entre, Fidelity Research, Grace, Sony, Supex, Technics, Victor, Yamaha, other manufacturers.
Returns: merchandise repaired or replaced under warranty.
Established 1973.

This firm, which sells midpriced as well as top-priced Japanese components, is just for the electronically minded who also love comparing prices. I did find several prices that were 10 to 30% lower than U.S. discount prices (and the Japanese prices included postage, whereas the American didn't). But other prices, on less expensive equipment, were higher than U.S. discount prices. Another problem is that, as President Akio Hashimoto explains, "One thing we would like to get your understanding in advance is that the units we deal with are domestic models made for and distributed in Japan at present and for this reason some of them may be sent to you without instructions in your language. However, you do not have to worry—all wire connections are clearly marked L, R and Ground or color coded which are all the same internationally."

M. O'Brien, ***95 High Street, Wimbledon Village, London SW 19, England. Telephone 1-946-1528 or 1-946-0331.***
Write or telephone for specific prices; some manufacturers' brochures are provided (if you ask).
Sells audio equipment by manufacturers such as Dual, KEF, Meridian, Mission, Ortofon, Quad, Thorens.
Returns: money back if goods are damaged or lost in transit.
Established 1968.

I have had bad luck, or rather lousy service, trying to get price quotes. I have written for three price quotes, and the firm has never answered my first letter—

only my second letter asking why I hadn't received an answer to my first. But a sound equipment reviewer wrote in the American magazine *Absolute Sound* that he has had excellent success with Michael O'Brien and considers his combination of price and shipping to be the best he's found in England.

Reader Charles Flynn bought the Quad SM4 tuner here for $318, including postage and insurance, a few years ago when it was $625 at his local dealer (and not even in stock). His local dealer was amazed at the price and said it was 10% below what he pays.

O'Brien gave me the price of the superb B and W DM14 speakers including airfreight as $530 (this was a couple of years ago when a friend was buying them). As the U.S. list price at the time was $1000 (I found only a 15% discount in the United States), it should be possible to save $300 to $400 on these speakers if you live near an international airport. If you don't, you'll have extra costs, such as customs brokers. If you can get them for a final price, including duty and any extra costs, of 30 to 40% off U.S. list price, they become a great buy.

DO IT YOURSELF

You can buy kits to make speakers for about 30% below the list price of assembled units. As you can get about 20% off assembled units—and nothing off kits—you will save about 10%.

Stereo Cost Cutters (described above) sells Dynaco kits.

BUYING SECONDHAND

As audio equipment has been at the same time improving and going down in price, this is not a field in which buying older, used equipment makes much sense, especially as repairs are so expensive. Most used equipment is sold at 50% off the list price, and most discounts are about 20% off, so we are talking about a savings of about 30%. If you consider that improvements in technology and lowering prices probably mean that you can get an equivalent newer model for 15% below that, and take into account possible costly repairs because of used equipment containing parts on the verge of breakdown, there is not much to be gained.

Specifically: the bearings are likely to be worn on used turntables; new developments in receivers make older models a dubious bargain; old speakers have paper cones, which are obsolete, whereas newer speakers have polypropylene cones.

Q Audio, ***95 Vassar Street, Cambridge, MA 02139. Telephone 617-547-2727.***
Free price list, or write or telephone for specific prices.
AE, MC, V.

Sells new and used audio and video equipment.
Returns: unconditional money-back guarantee on used equipment if returned within 21 days; limited warranty on parts and labor for 30 days to three years, depending on units.
Established 1975.

Q was recommended to me as a source of used equipment by reader Charles Flynn. He bought a used Apt Holman pre-amp in mint condition with a three-year guarantee for almost 24% off the going list price, meaning he saved $140. Apart from the used equipment, Q sells full-price high-end audio equipment.

CARS

1986 Ford Aerostar. When the typical price of this miniwagon was $14,890, the price at Nationwide Auto Brokers was $13,293.

CARS

Never pay list price on a new car; suggested list prices on cars, tires and parts are meaningless. Real prices vary around the country—some areas are much more competitive than others. There are several ways of paying less: one, obviously, is to do a thorough search in your own area for the distributors with the lowest prices; another is to arm yourself with the dealer's invoice price and do some serious haggling; another is to buy through a discount broker; and, when the dollar is strong, another is to import your own car or buy an import on the gray market. The last three methods are described in this chapter.

CHOOSING A CAR

Several publications give helpful information for anyone choosing and buying a car.

The annual car issue of *Consumer Reports,* published in April, judges new car models, gives repair records and crash test results, advises on how to price shop for a new car and suggests good bets in used cars. Issues are available in libraries, on newsstands or by mail from *Consumer Reports* (address on page 4).

The Automotive Information Council will send a free brochure called ***Car Buying Tips*** to anyone who sends a stamped, self-addressed envelope. Write to: **AUTOMOTIVE INFORMATION COUNCIL,** ***29200 Southfield Road, Southfield, MI 48076. Telephone 313-559-5922.***

Each year in December or January, the government publishes a ***Gas Mileage Guide*** that tells how much gas each model of American car consumes. One free copy is available to anyone who writes or telephones: **U.S. DEPARTMENT OF ENERGY,** ***Technical Information Center, P.O. Box 62, Oakridge, TN 37830. Telephone 615-576-1301.***

The cost of collision insurance claims differs widely according to the car model. Each September the Institute for Highway Safety publishes information on collision losses and injury claims for different car models. The injury claims are an indicator of the safety record of the different models. Contact: **THE INSTITUTE OF HIGHWAY SAFETY,** ***Communications Department, 600 New Hampshire Avenue NW, Washington, DC 20037. Telephone 202-333-0770.***

The Car Book by Jack Gillis (Harper & Row) contains highly useful information for any economy- or safety-minded person about to buy a car. For new and used car models there are comparison charts on gas mileage ratings, cost of routine maintenance, price of replacement parts, insurance premiums, tire tread wear costs and the effect of different tires on fuel economy. There are also crash-test results, tips on buying used cars and a lot of other information. The book was originally compiled for the U.S. Department of Transportation, but the Reagan government would not continue funding. Now Jack Gillis, the author, updates the book annually. It is sold in bookstores for $8.95 and by mail from the nonprofit Center for Auto Safety for $8.95 postpaid. Contact: **CENTER FOR AUTO SAFETY,** ***2001 S Street NW, Washington, DC 20009. Telephone 202-328-7700.***

BUYING A CAR LOCALLY

To get the best price on a new car from a local dealer, you must negotiate. *Consumer Reports* suggests that you should pay no more than $150 to $400 over the dealer's "invoice" price. The invoice price is theoretically the price the dealer pays. In fact, the dealer pays less than the invoice price, as he gets an extra 2 to 3% off the price of each car he actually sells. Before negotiating, get the dealer's invoice price of your prospective car plus the optional accessories you want. It is easy to get prices from the discount brokers listed later. Or try one of the publications listed here.

For first-rate and very specific advice on how to get the best deal possible from your local dealer, see the *Consumer Reports* April car issue.

Consumer Reports will sell you a printout of the cost to the dealer and list price of one or more cars. The printout lists standard equipment, gives prices for all the available options and gives Consumers Union's own recommendations for desirable options. As I write, the printout costs $9 for the first car (and less for additional ones). Write to: **CONSUMER REPORTS AUTO PRICE SERVICE,** ***P.O. Box 570, Lathrup Village, MI 48076.***

A division of the H. M. Dousha Company publishes the ***New Car Cost Guide,*** which is used by professionals in the field. It is an excellent resource book, with very detailed listings of invoice prices and options for every American car and light truck. Ten mailings throughout the year keep it up to date. However, it is very expensive ($70 per year) so only worth consulting if you can find it at a credit union or bank. **AUTOMOBILE INVOICE SERVICE,** ***2001 The Alameda, P.O. Box 6227, San Jose, CA 95150. Telephone 408-296-2211.***

The Edmunds Publication Corporation publishes very inexpensive paperback books giving dealer and list prices for new and used American and foreign cars. They are available in bookshops or from the publisher: **EDMUNDS PUBLICATION CORPORATION,** ***515 Hempstead Turnpike, West Hempstead, NY 11552. Telephone 516-538-3030.***

CAR BROKERS

If you don't like haggling, you can avoid it by buying through an auto broker. Although brokers, like private customers, order through dealers, they buy in quantity and can get lower prices. When you buy through a broker, you pay the dealer invoice price plus the broker's markup of about $150 and probably a few other charges such as delivery and preparation fees. The total price will most likely be roughly what *Consumer Reports* thinks you should aim for when making a deal on your own—$150 to $400 above dealer invoice.

If you buy through a broker, you either collect the car from the broker or have it delivered (for an extra charge) to a dealer in your state. The dealer checks the car and prepares it for the road. This dealer also adds any "after market" products you have ordered, such as rustproofing, paint sealant and burglar alarm. The car comes with full warranties, exactly like cars bought from local dealers, and the broker can also arrange financing for Chrysler, Ford and GM cars.

American Auto Brokers, ***24001 Southfield Road, Suite 110, Southfield, MI 48075. Telephone 313-569-5900.***
Send self-addressed, stamped envelope or telephone Monday through Friday, 9 A.M. to 6 P.M., for a specific price.
Sells American cars, trucks and vans and most imports.
Returns: none.
Established 1972.

American Auto Brokers is a small firm, started in 1972 by Mel Palmer, who had been a Lincoln-Mercury dealer for 15 years, and Betty Fagin, who was just out of business school. They keep a list of the lower prices that they can get on domestic and imported cars, and they will give one free price quote. But they don't give you a complete list of options and accessories as the other firms listed here do. First choose your car and decide on any optional extra features; then write to them. If you want more than one quote, you'll be charged $3 for each of the others. If you decide to buy from them, they will write out a purchase agreement, at which point you pay a deposit of $300. They then order the car through one of their dealers, and in roughly eight weeks (it depends on the car) the car will be delivered to a dealer in your state. The full payment for the car is due when you are given the car registration number and told that it is ready to be picked up.

Betty Fagin refuses to generalize about how much you can save by buying through them. She says it depends on prices in your area and how good you are at haggling. But she did say that she was pleased to have saved a customer

$1000 on an Oldsmobile recently. She thought that his saving was so big because his local dealer, noting that he was a nice old man, had decided to take advantage of his gullibility.

Car/Puter International, ***1603 Bushwick Avenue, Brooklyn, NY 11207. Telephone 800-221-4001; in New York State, 718-455-2500.***
Write or telephone for descriptive leaflet.
AE, DC, MC, V.
Sells discount price information on cars and equipment plus dealer recommendations.
Returns: none.
Established 1964.

Car/Puter sells price quotes (for higher prices than the other two firms listed). But instead of selling you the car, the company recommends a dealer who will sell directly to you at the quoted price. And it says that, unlike the books of prices, it can tell you about manufacturers' rebates, special sales and freight costs.

Nationwide Auto Brokers, ***17517 West Ten Mile Road, Southfield, MI 48075. Telephone: questions, 313-559-6661; quotation orders, 800-521-7257.***
MC, V.
Sells cars and small trucks, all American makes and some foreign.
Returns: money back when check has cleared (out of state this may take two to three weeks).
Established 1967.

This large firm sends out between 2,000 and 3,000 price quotes a week. It works for several consumer groups such as Comp-U-Card buying service, as well as firms like Prudential Bache. It has been written up in the press—by *Forbes, Money* and *Newsweek,* among others.

Kenneth Tompor, the 36-year-old president, signs annual contracts with dealers to buy several thousand cars at lower "fleet" prices. According to Mr. Tompor, private customers who haggle on their own can usually get a discount of 5 to 8%, whereas his discounts range from 8% off the sticker price on less expensive cars to 18% on the most expensive cars.

To get a price quote from Nationwide, you telephone with the make and model of the car or cars you are interested in. You are sent a computer printout of all the available optional equipment and accessories. You check off what you want and return the list with $5.95 per quote. If you want to buy through Nationwide, you sign a purchase agreement and pay a $100 deposit. You pay the balance to Nationwide when you are told that the car is ready for pickup. You can either collect the car from Detroit or have it delivered to any dealer you choose, in which case there is an extra fee of about $125 for the "courtesy delivery."

Kenneth Tompor told me about the recent case of a man who bought a Blazer truck from him. The bad news is that one year later the truck was stolen. The good news is that the original price was so low that the first year's depreciation was offset and the insurance company paid him back all but $114.

IMPORTED CARS

When the dollar is strong, there are three ways you can save money on imported cars. One is by ordering a car through the official U.S. dealership and picking it up abroad. Another is by avoiding the official dealers and buying through a private importer. (As I explain elsewhere, this is sometimes called the "gray" market, but I don't like the term as it sounds unnecessarily murky.) A final way is to import a car yourself, and that is the most profitable.

European Delivery

When the dollar is strong, overseas delivery programs can save you a few hundred to a few thousand dollars on more expensive cars, and if you use the car while on holiday instead of renting a car, you can save a little more. In 1986 my friend Ed Koren saved $2,700 after paying all costs on a Saab by picking it up in Gothenberg. Savings change according to the strength of the dollar, but in 1985, a very strong dollar year, Volvo told me that, depending on model and accessories, savings were a clear $800 to $2000 after you paid additional charges such as shipping, brokerage and duty. With Mercedes-Benz savings went up to about $4185 on the 500SEL sedan—$47,615 total if picked up abroad, $51,800 plus tax in the United States.

Most foreign manufacturers have well-organized overseas delivery programs working through their regular dealers. Before you order your car, you can find out exactly how much the various charges will add up to and exactly how the program works.

Details vary according to manufacturer, but this is roughly what happens: You contact a U.S. dealer about two months before you want the car, put in your order and pay a deposit (the amount varies with the firm; it typically might be $500). The car will, of course, be manufactured to conform to U.S. specifications. You give the date and place where you will collect the car. Any car can be picked up at the factory, and many can be picked up at more convenient places (Volvo, for instance has 14 delivery centers such as London, Paris and Stockholm). The order will be confirmed within a few weeks, at which point you pay the entire balance. When you collect the car, there will be forms to complete, but the dealer will have taken care of all the arrangements, including shipping and so on. After using the car, you drop it off at a specified port (you can pay an extra charge and leave it somewhere more convenient if you want). The car is then delivered to your closest U.S. port, where, as arranged by the dealer, it is seen through customs and duty is paid (2.07% of the car's value). You will be notified when you can collect the car from the dealer.

For more information and the exact charges, contact the overseas delivery department of whichever manufacturer you are interested in:

BMW, ***Campus 3, Montvale, NJ 07645. Telephone 201-573-2000.***

MERCEDES-BENZ, ***One Mercedes Drive, Montvale, NJ 06545. Telephone 201-573-0600.***

PEUGEOT, ***One Peugeot Plaza, Lyndhurst, NJ 07071. Telephone 201-935-8400.***

PORSCHE NORTH AMERICA, ***Att. Tourist Delivery, 200 South Virginia Street, Reno, NV 89501. Telephone 702-348-3000.***

SAAB-SCANIA, ***Saab Drive, P.O. Box 697, Orange, CT 06477. Telephone 203-795-5671.***

VOLVO, ***P.O. Box 913, Rockleigh, NJ 07647. Telephone 201-768-7300.***

Dealers that specialize in overseas delivery for several manufacturers are listed below.

Europe by Car, ***9000 Sunset Boulevard, Los Angeles, CA 90069; telephone 213-272-0424. One Rockefeller Plaza, New York, NY 10020; telephone 212-581-3040.***
Write or telephone for a price quote.
Sells Audi, BMW, Citroën, Mercedes-Benz, Peugeot, Saab, Volkswagen, Volvo for overseas delivery. Also arranges overseas rentals.
Returns: none.
Established 1954.

This firm arranges European delivery for people who have no willing dealer in their area. If you buy through Europe by Car, you must get your own information about options and so on from the manufacturer or a local dealer. When you've decided exactly what you want, you pay a $50 deposit, and Europe by Car sends you completed order forms. You sign and return the forms with a $500 deposit. The manufacturer will confirm in writing the details of your order. Full payment for the car is due 30 days before you leave the country. The rest of the procedure is standard.

Martin's Manhattan, ***1274 Second Avenue, New York, NY 10021. Telephone 212-249-6700; out of state, 800-223-0552.***
Write or telephone for a specific price.
Sells BMW, Volvo for delivery overseas.
Returns: none.
Established 1934.

Martin's is an authorized dealer with two Manhattan showrooms, a service department and a parts distribution business. It specializes in organizing overseas distribution of Volvos and BMWs, which they do for travel agents and private customers. Paul Morris of the overseas department says that savings run from $1000 to as much as $5000 on the BMW 633CSi.

You should decide what model you want first, then contact Martin's at least six weeks before you need the car. Paul Morris will give you a price that includes all costs, including shipping and duty on the Volvo and everything but duty (2.07%) on the BMW. He, or his assistants, will also make all the arrangements. At the time that your order is written up, you pay a $500 deposit. The rest is due within 30 days of delivery. The BMWs can be picked up at the factory in Munich, and the Volvos in Gothenburg, and both at other places for an extra charge. The car will be shipped back to your nearest port in the United States, and you will pick the car up from a local dealer who will have seen it through customs.

Nemet Auto International, ***153-12 Hillside Avenue, Jamaica, NY 11432. Telephone 800-221-0177; in New York State, 718-523-5858.***
Free 32-page brochure, "Tom Nemet's Car Book," or telephone or write for specific prices.
Sells Audi, BMW, Mercedes-Benz, Nissan/Datsun, Peugeot, Saab, Volvo, Volkswagen for overseas delivery.
Returns: "in accordance with manufacturers' warranties and appropriate state laws."
Established 1916.

Tom Nemet, owner of Nemet, has been named "Dealer of Distinction" by *Sports Illustrated* and awarded *Time* magazine's "Quality Dealer Award." He has been chairman of a couple of car dealers organizations and advised a couple of presidents on the auto industry. Altogether he sounds like just the man you'd want to buy a new, or even a used, car from.

His franchised dealership specializes in overseas delivery and direct shipment. The direct shipment is for people who go abroad and want to buy a foreign car at lower overseas prices but don't want to drive it abroad. The car is delivered to the United States after the customer has presented him- or herself at a U.S. consulate or embassy for a certificate showing that he or she has been out of the country. This system is not particularly popular with manufacturers, and only a few cars, such as Peugeot and Saab, are available this way.

Direct Importing

There are two other ways of saving on the more expensive foreign cars. One is importing the car yourself, and the other is buying through a direct importer.

Joseph Normandy of the Automobile Importers Compliance Association, a trade group for those involved in the direct importing business, points out that on higher-priced cars you can save more if you avoid the U.S. dealers, go straight to a foreign dealer and import the car yourself. He says that in the strong-dollar year of 1985 you could have saved a clear $4000 by importing your own baby Benz 190E and $8000 by importing your own Mercedes 5000SEL sedan. With a weaker dollar, savings can only be realized on higher-end cars such as the Mercedes 500SEL and 560SEL, and savings are lower. In 1986, as I write, Mr. Normandy claims that on these higher-end cars you can still save $4000 to $6000.

Importing your own car involves arranging shipping, finding a broker to see the car through U.S. customs (unless you want to do this yourself), paying a bond while the car is modified to meet U.S. Department of Transportation and Environmental Protection Agency standards and choosing someone to make the modifications. Joseph Normandy says that it is important that anyone importing his or her own car research what is needed *before* going; this includes finding out the U.S. agency requirements and choosing a mechanic to do the modifying. The more you know about costs and so on beforehand, the more control you'll have of the prices you pay. The Automobile Importers Compliance Association produces a booklet, ***Handbook of Vehicle Importation,*** which explains the whole process.

If you are not going abroad at all, you can still sometimes save some money on an imported car by going to a professional direct importer. I talked to one member of the Automobile Importers Compliance Association, Paul Wain of **BIMMERS AND BENZ,** ***10 Shore Road, Glen Cove, NY 11542, telephone 516-671-7300,*** who imports to order and also keeps popular models on hand. He said that in 1985, when the dollar was strong, he imported a Rolls-Royce Cornisch Convertible for a customer who paid him $100,000 all told, whereas the U.S. price for the same model at the time was around $150,000. Now that the dollar is weaker, Mr. Wain says that savings on cars he imports are not as dramatic.

If you want to import a car yourself, you'll need the ***Handbook of Vehicle Importation*** which costs $22.95 including postage. It explains importing procedures, details U.S. requirements and lists AICA members in the United States and abroad whose services you can use, whether you import yourself or have someone else do it. **Automobile Importers Compliance Association,** ***12030 Sunrise Valley Drive, Suite 201, Reston, VA 22091. Telephone 703-476-2340.***

Many makes of cars have owner clubs that provide information exchange through newsletters. This is especially helpful for the owners of the less common foreign cars. Addresses of clubs are listed in the Encyclopedia of Associations, *which almost all libraries have. Most librarians will look the address up for you over the telephone if you don't want to go in yourself. The manufacturers' representatives listed under European Delivery above will also give you club addresses.*

TIRES

Tire prices do vary around the country. If you live in a highly competitive area, you may be lucky enough to have local stores with prices that equal those of these mail-order firms. (When I compared prices, for instance, prices at Washington, D.C., area stores chosen for their low prices were about the same as those at the mail-order firms below.)

The government annually grades tires, testing for treadwear, traction, and resistance to heat. A free copy of the gradings brochure ("Uniform Tire Grading") is available from: **U.S. DEPARTMENT OF TRANSPORTATION,** ***National Highway Traffic Safety Administration, Distribution Department, Office of Public and Consumer Affairs, Room 6123, 400 7th Street, Washington, DC 20590. Telephone 202-426-0874 (ask for Publications Department).***

Mail and Telephone Sources

The stores listed below sell tires and wheels at 25 to 30% below the prices of the average tire store. The stores have toll-free numbers and are efficient and pleasant about giving price quotes, so it is easy to call and find out whether you can do better by mail. When I compared prices on two high-performance radial tires that had done well in a December 1985 *Car and Driver* test, I found that the mail-order prices were very good. The Goodrich Comp T/A cost $104 plus tax in New York, yet only $75 delivered by mail; the Michelin MX L cost $67 plus tax in New York, yet only $46 delivered by mail. But onto the price of tires bought by mail you must add the cost of having them installed and balanced at a garage (unless you buy them at the same time as wheels, in which case there is no charge). Mounting costs about $4 to $12 per wheel, and it's worth shopping around on that too.

Incidentally, salespeople at these firms will advise you as to size and type of tire to buy, if you like.

Dick Cepek, ***17000 Kingsview Avenue, Carson, CA 90746. Telephone 213-217-1314.***
Catalogue, free in the U.S. and two U.S. $1 bills in Canada, or telephone for specific prices.
MC, V.
Sells off-road tires, wheels, lights and accessories.
Returns: only with prior approval.
Established 1964.

Dick Cepek was recommended to me by reader Ed Henson, who says that he bought tires here after comparing prices at several dealers. He says the stock for four-wheel-drive vehicles is extensive, and prices and service are good.

Euro-Tire, ***567 Route 46 West, P.O. Box 1198, Fairfield, NJ 07007. Telephone 800-631-0080; in New Jersey, 201-575-0080.***
Free catalogue in spring and fall, or telephone for specific prices.
AE, MC, V.
Sells tires (including the hard-to-find such as Fulda, European Uniroyal, and some Pirelli), wheels, shock absorbers.
Returns: money back minus shipping costs if goods returned in brand-new condition within 60 days.
Established 1974.

Car and Driver ordered seven sets of tires from Euro-Tire for the test mentioned earlier and comments, "Their telephone-ordering, mounting and balancing, and shipping services were exemplary." When my assistant called asking for tires for her four-year-old Saab, a salesman cheerfully and clearly explained the benefits (better handling) and disadvantages (shorter mileage life) of buying a larger, wider and more expensive tire. The Euro-Tire people are also happy to give more specific advice on tires (based, they say, on tire tests, customer feedback and personal use).

Offshore Imports, ***3674 East Noakes Street, Los Angeles, CA 90023. Telephone 800-421-8561; in California, 800-227-9276.***
Write or telephone 8 A.M. to 5 P.M. Monday through Friday for specific prices.
MC, V.
Sells tires by Fulda, B. F. Goodrich, Goodyear, Kleber, Michelin, Pirelli, Semperit, Yokohama; wheels by BBS, Centra, Epsilon, Exim, Ronal, Shelby; shocks by Bilstein, Koni, KYB; suspension techniques by Exhausts, Pace Setter; car covers, brake pads, steering wheels, sway bars.
Returns: money back if the goods are defective or unused.
Established 1939.

Salespeople at Offshore are helpful but don't offer advice unless you ask specific questions, in which case they are thorough and patient. I found the lowest prices here on the tires I priced.

Teletire, ***17622 Armstrong Avenue, Irvine, CA 92714. Telephone 800-835-8473; in California, 714-549-1191.***
Free brochure, or telephone for price information and advice.
MC, V.
Sells automobile and light truck tires by Bridgestone, Continental, Kelly Springfield, Michelin, Pirelli, Semperit, Quantum, Yokohama; alloy-type road wheels by Ronal, Weds.
Returns: if merchandise returned within 30 days for an exchange, customer is charged shipping cost; if customer wants money back, shipping cost and 10% restocking fee are charged.
Established 1939.

Jerry Firman of Teletire says that the parent company, which also has 35 retail "4-Day Tire Stores" stores around the country, started its mail-order business five or six years ago to service customers who couldn't find major-line tires at good prices. Most of the mail business is concentrated in the East, where foreign-car owners in particular run into this problem. Firman says that customers can save as much as 60%, but most savings are about 25%. I found prices here among the lowest.

When I called, anonymously, to ask for prices, the salesman was very friendly and suggested that I buy a narrower, less expensive tire that would meet my needs and last longer than a larger, more expensive tire.

Retreaded Tires

Another way of saving money on tires is to buy retreaded ones. The National Tire Dealers and Retreaders Association points out that the tires are safe (98% of the world's airlines use retreaded tires) and cost 30 to 50% less than new tires, yet last almost as long (they'll do 30,000 to 35,000 miles, as opposed to new tires' 35,000 to 40,000). However, all this applies only to the best retreaded tires, so get yours from reputable firms such as Sears or Montgomery Ward. Or go to one of the 500 retreaders who have been A-rated by the Retreaders Association. For names of A-rated dealers in your area, write or telephone: **NATIONAL TIRE DEALERS AND RETREADERS ASSOCIATION,** ***1343 L Street NW, Washington, DC 20005. Telephone 800-368-5757.***

DO-IT-YOURSELF PARTS

According to a study run by *Consumers' Checkbook,* a Washington-based consumer publication, you can save up to almost two-thirds of your costs if you buy your own supplies and do easy routine maintenance and repairs yourself. *Consumers' Checkbook* found that at a time when a 5-quart oil change plus filter cost about $22 in a repair shop, it would have cost only $8 to buy it yourself. A starter motor that would have cost $116 installed at a dealership would have cost you only $40, and it can be installed with a crescent wrench.

If you are not up to even minor repairs, do what the New York State Consumer Protection Board advises—save money by buying the parts yourself and supplying them to a repair shop. Two firms that sell parts at low prices are listed here.

Edgewood, ***6603 North Meridian, Puyallup, WA 98371. Telephone 206-927-3388.***
No catalogue.
MC, V.
Sells auto parts for four-wheel-drive vehicles.
Returns: call for permission; restocking charge on some goods.
Established 1984.

Edgewood has no catalogue but can take telephone orders if you know what you want. The firm sells heavy-duty performance parts and parts for four-wheel-drive vehicles. It is the top supplier for jeeps and stocks such things as transmission parts for World War II jeeps. Manager Jim McConnaughhui tells me that 90% of the stock is discounted and that discounts run up to 30%. Edgewood was recommended by customer Ed Henson, who says it has excellent service and probably the best prices.

J. C. Whitney, ***1917 Archer Avenue, P.O. Box 8410, Chicago, IL 60680, or 1104 South Wabash, Chicago, IL 60605. Telephone 312-431-6000.***
Free catalogue.
MC, V.
Sells parts for cars.
Returns: money back if goods returned within 90 days.
Established 1916.

A well-known firm that sells a multitude of car parts and accessories, many unobtainable elsewhere, at low prices. But reader Ed Henson tells me that the quality is sometimes disappointing. Best if you know the brand you want and are already familiar with whatever you are buying.

CIGARS

Macanudo Cigars. When the typical price for a box of 25 No. 1 (6-inch) cigars was $51, the price at Famous Smoke Shop was $35.95, including shipping.

CIGARS

MAIL AND TELEPHONE SOURCES

What with toll-free telephone numbers and credit cards or charge accounts, it is easy to order cigars from these stores. Almost any cigar is available, and discounts can reach up to 35% off regular prices.

Famous Smoke Shop, ***55 West 39th Street, New York, NY 10018. Telephone 800-672-5544; in New York State, 212-221-1408.***
Catalogue, free in the U.S. and Canada.
Sells cigars and tobacco; brands handled: Ramon Allones, Dominique, Don Diego, Hoyo de Monterrey, Macanudo, Montecruz, Montesino, Partagas, Primo del Cristo, Primo del Rey, Te Amo, El Triunfador, H. Upmann.
Minimum order one box of cigars in the U.S., four boxes in Canada.
Returns: call immediately if cigars are not satisfactory for authorization to return.
Established 1939.

This is the place to buy cigars. My cigar-smoking, price-watching reader Allen Pasternack reports that Famous consistently has the best price on cigars. Yes indeed, when I last checked, Nat Sherman on Fifth Avenue was selling 25 Upmann Lonsdales for $45, J-R was charging $29.95 and Famous was charging only $22.75. Nat Sherman was selling Partagas Coronas 898 for $58, J-R was charging $45.95 and Famous was charging $38.85.

Cigars are kept in a 3,000-foot humidor in the basement and are tracked by computer. Newly added house brands are made to order for the owner, Mr. Zaretsky, and, he says, undersell the well-known brands by $4 to $6 a box.

Famous won't accept credit cards ("just an extra overhead that we would have to build in to our prices, as our competition does") but does welcome charge accounts.

J-R Tobacco Company, ***277 Route 46 West, Fairfield, NJ 07006. Telephone 800-572-4427; in New Jersey, 201-882-0050.***
Free catalogue.
AE, MC, V.
Sells "almost 3,000 varieties" of famous brand name cigars.
Minimum order $10.
Returns: "unconditional money back."
Established 1961.

This popular store is run by wisecracking cigar expert Lew Rothman, who publishes a catalogue filled with irreverent and irrelevant copy—one of my old catalogues announces a "Business is Stinky Poo Sale" and begs loyal cigar smokers to "puff faster, chew harder, and lose more frequently the cigars you get from us."

J-R has been recommended by cigar-smoking reader Allen Pasternack, who points out that cigars are sold at discount prices that almost match those of Famous (above) and that there are plenty of sale items. Also available are J-R substitutes for brand name cigars. "Trust us! We'll send you a comparable cigar," says J-R, which means the closest cigar in "size, taste, and origin that J-R has been able to purchase from one of the seven internationally famous manufacturers who jointly produce one of the free world's best-known premium cigars." Prices for these cigars are about a third to two-thirds of the price of the originals.

CLOTHES AND SHOES

New larger lined Aquascutum trenchcoats. When the price of "Bogart" for men was $525 in New York, it was $381, including postage, from Selfridges, London. When the price of "Brookfield" for women was $600 in New York, the price, including postage, was $416 from Selfridges, London.

CLOTHES AND SHOES

There are several ways of buying better clothes for less. One way is to shop at factory outlet and retail clearance stores around the country. At these off-price stores you can find great bargains—brand name clothes often cost 50% or less of the original price. But you have to search for the bargains, as good-quality stuff is mixed in with bad.

Another approach is to do at least part of your buying at sales, which for clothes are regular and can be planned for. Clothes are seasonal—stores have to clear each season's clothes to make way for the next season's, so you'll find genuine reductions and great bargains at the end of a season. You'll get real value for money if you go to sales at the better stores. Go in with an open mind, ready to pounce on whatever looks particularly good.

There are also many mail-order sources that give exceptional value, and some of those firms reduce their prices even further during sales.

SEASONAL SALES

Fine specialty clothing stores start their summer clearance sales the last weekend of June and carry on through July and even August. They start their winter clearance sale the first weekend in January and carry on for a month or more. These are times when clothes that have been offered for the current season are reduced by 20 to 30% to make room for new stock. Better clothing stores also have smaller sales throughout the year to clear lines that haven't sold well or lines in which only a few sizes are left. If you buy something at one of the better clothing stores in your area, make sure you are on the mailing list, because you'll then be notified of sales before the general public and even sales that aren't generally advertised.

Department stores start their seasonal clothing sales before the clothing stores, often at the beginning of June and on the day after Christmas, and the sales last for up to two months. These sales usually work on a two-tier pricing system: for the first weeks goods are reduced by 25 to 30%; later they are reduced by 40 to 50%. Department stores bring in new styles five or six times a year and have a faster turnover than other stores, so there are often additional small sales with a few racks of clothes to clear.

Most stores also now have sales on all the high-traffic holidays: Memorial Day, Labor Day, Veterans Day and so on. At these times they sell a mix of clothes that are reduced for clearance and clothes that have been brought in for special promotions to attract customers.

HONG KONG

Having a "little" dressmaker knock off copies of expensive haute couture creations is an old European practice, even among the rich who can afford originals. If you can't find a "little" dressmaker—try Hong Kong. The tailors of Hong Kong are famous, and stopping off to buy a tailor-made suit has been de rigueur with male tourists for decades.

I have found the workmanship to be very fine (see below), and many clothes by well-known designers are now made in Hong Kong. I noticed Liz Claiborne being quoted in the *Washington Post* after checking factories in Hong Kong and Shanghai, saying that it's not just the lower price of manufacturing overseas that makes it so appealing but the superior quality of the workmanship as well. "In all honesty," she said, "there are certain things not made well here [in the United States]; we don't have the 'hands' for it, it takes a certain expertise and patience, for example, to work in silk or fine filament fabrics."

At best, a successful shopper can get a man's suit that is better than American ready-made at about half the price. The tailors are especially useful if you have trouble finding what you want ready-made. The safest way to go is to have something you own and like copied, perhaps in a different fabric or color (although you can also have clothes from magazines reproduced). I am rather picky, so I much prefer to send my own fabric (it's cheaper too), but Hong Kong tailors have fabrics of every sort, including British and Italian imports, so you will probably be able to find something you like. Always see swatches before choosing, even for something that is being copied from your own clothes, and don't stint—the wrong fabric can make your creation look disastrously cheap.

Apart from Sitlani, I have chosen to include only tailors who are members of the Hong Kong Tourist Association. The maintenance of ethical standards is a condition of membership and so, I hope, an indication of reliability. If you have comments or complaints, write to: **HONG KONG TOURIST ASSOCIATION,** ***Membership Department, 35th floor, Connaught Centre, Hong Kong. Telephone 5-244191.***

Ascot Chang Company, ***2/F Block D, 41 Man Yue Street, Hung Hom, Kowloon, Hong Kong.***
Catalogue, three $1 bills (airmail).
Sells made-to-measure shirts for men and women, made-to-measure underwear and nightwear for men.

Minimum order three shirts.
Returns: credit given if merchandise returned within 30 days.
Established 1953.
Member of the Hong Kong Tourist Association.

This 33-year-old firm is said to be the best custom shirtmaker in Hong Kong and one of the best in the world. It has thousands of mail-order customers and also sends representatives to the United States with swatches and measurement charts. Knowledgeable American shoppers such as Stanley Marcus (of Neiman-Marcus) and Bob Sakowitz (of Sakowitz, I presume) are said to buy here.

At reasonable prices (about the same as "better" American ready-made and half the price of American made-to-measure) you can have shirts made here in any fabric, from fine English Sea Island cotton to crepe de chine, pongee silk, shantung and suchlike luxurious fabrics. Buttons are all pearl-type. Details such as extra pockets are free, although there is a small charge for monogramming and, say, white collar and cuffs on a colored shirt.

The Hutton Shop, ***125 Tai Shan Gallery, Ocean Terminal, Kowloon, Hong Kong. Telephone 3-673439.***
Free measurement charts and fabric swatches.
AE, DC, MC, V.
Sells made-to-measure suits for men and women, Pierre Cardin accessories, brand name accessories from Italy and France.
Minimum order $50.
Returns: objections considered if "so arises within 10 days"; credit but no money back.
Established 1965.
Member of the Hong Kong Tourist Association.

Although not the cheapest, this is one of the best-known Hong Kong tailors. It has been written up in the *Times* of London and has a good, solid reputation. The Hutton Shop works with fabrics imported from England, France, West Germany, Italy and Spain.

Jen's Fashion, ***Shop 114, First Floor, Hotel Regal Meridien Hong Kong, Tsim-sha-tsui East, 71 Mody Road, Kowloon, Hong Kong. Telephone 3-679950.***
Free measurement charts and fabric swatches.
DC, MC, V.
Sells made-to-order suits, coats, trousers for men and women; skirts, blouses, dresses for women.
Returns: none; only free alterations.
Established 1982.
Member of the Hong Kong Tourist Association.

When I asked Jen's for linen samples for a skirt, they sent me four good samples. However, as the charge was $100 for a fully lined skirt made out of their fabric and only $50 for one made out of mine, I decided to send my own. By mistake I sent the fabric by sea and uninsured, but it arrived safely in eight weeks, and Jen's wrote immediately to say that "our men has started working on it." The skirt arrived via airmail three weeks after that.

The six-paneled skirt, made from a drawing I sent, is more than satisfactory—made skillfully and exactly to the measurements I gave. The zipper has been sewn in by hand and the hem has been finished with a tape, as is done by better dressmakers. The seams are straight, the hem is invisible, hanging tabs have been added and the skirt has been correctly pressed. The only fault is that the inside of the side seams has not been overstitched.

Sitlani Custom Tailors, ***10 Humphrey's Avenue, First Floor, Kowloon, Hong Kong. Telephone 3-685644 or 3-663744.***
Free measurement charts and fabric swatches.
AE, DC, MC, V.
Sells made-to-measure clothes for men and women.
Returns: credit.
Established 1933.

Sitlani owner Prakash Advani writes, "The most unusual service is our very personal touch to all our customers and our own undue honesty which nowadays is frightfully rare!" A few months ago, I airmailed Sitlani 1½ yards of fabric, with instructions, measurements and a drawing by me of a six-paneled skirt I wanted made. I also asked for a price quote. Mr. Advani said it would cost $42, including postage, and he'd airmail the skirt as soon as he got my bank check. As he had my fabric, he had the skirt made right away, without waiting for the money. Five weeks later the skirt arrived, and I did not have to pay any duty. As I had paid $10.60 to airmail the fabric, the skirt cost me $52.60 plus the price of the fabric. The skirt is beautifully made, exactly the same way as the Jen skirt (above) is. I showed it to a professional dressmaker and sewing teacher, who was impressed. One of my readers, Bernice Lanspa in Nebraska, also tried Sitlani. She had a hand-beaded red dress copied from a magazine illustration. She was very pleased with the service and quite happy with the dress, although because it had been made to her exact measurements and was lined, it didn't have much give. She also found the pinkish red beads and rhinestones a bit garish and thought that she had not been specific enough about the color. Her dress cost $120, which is, of course, extremely low for hand beading.

Men Only

Allan Tom and Co. Burlington Arcade Shop "L", ***92–94 Nathan Road, Kowloon, Hong Kong. Telephone 3-666690.***
Free measurement charts and fabric swatches.
V.

Sells made-to-measure clothes for men.
Returns: credit.
Established 1964.
Member of the Hong Kong Tourist Association.

To test Allan Tom I decided to have one of my (reluctant) husband's old linen jackets copied. I asked Tom to match a swatch of the old jacket, and the firm replied with four linen swatches, one a perfect color match. As the cloth was a little lighter in weight, however, I decided to send my own linen. On September 4 I sent them the old jacket, my linen and a personal check for $121 (the price of tailoring a man's jacket plus airmail postage for the return of the two jackets). I didn't hear a word, but exactly 7½ weeks after I had sent the parcel and check, the new jacket and old jacket were delivered (there was $6.41 duty to pay). The new jacket was an almost perfect copy of the old one, and so well made that even my husband (who has a strong anti–Hong Kong tailoring prejudice) was won over and didn't mind that the new jacket was an inch narrower at the waist. Normally I would have taken the jacket down to be altered by our local tailor (who said he'd do it for $12), but for the sake of scientific investigation I sent it back to Allan Tom. I didn't hear a word, but once again seven weeks later the two jackets arrived back. This time the new one was a perfect match of the old jacket. The parcel had been marked by Allan Tom, "Jacket for alterations—Duty has been paid," and I wasn't charged.

W. W. Chan and Sons, ***A2 Burlington House, 2nd floor, 94 Nathan Road, P.O. Box 96115, Kowloon, Hong Kong. Telephone 3-669738 or 3-662634.***
Free measurement charts and fabric swatches.
Sells made-to-measure clothes for men.
Returns: free alterations or money back.
Established 1946.
Member of the Hong Kong Tourist Association.

The proprietors of W. W. Chan sent me a flowery letter in which they assured my good self of their meticulous attention and top-quality custom tailoring at all times. But I didn't try them because the samples they sent to match my husband's linen jacket swatch, although perfectly all right, were synthetic mixes; they said that they stocked no linen. Their tailoring charge was also higher than elsewhere, so I tried Allan Tom instead.

MAIL AND TELEPHONE SOURCES

Antartex Ltd, ***Lomond Industrial Estate, Alexandria, Dunbartonshire, Scotland. Telephone 389-52393.***
24-page catalogue, $1 bill in the U.S. and Canada.
AE, MC, V.

Sells sheepskin coats and jackets for men, women and children in standard sizes and made to order; sheepskin mittens and slippers.
Returns: money back if goods are returned clean and unworn within a month.
Established 1954.

Antartex, the best-known and most respected British manufacturers of sheepskin clothes, have a mail-order catalogue with extraordinary values for American customers. About 20 sheepskin jackets and coats are shown at prices that are half to one-third those of similar clothes sold in the United States. (When I checked, Antartex coats and jackets cost $130 to $210 in Scotland, whereas clothes of equal quality were around $400 here.) If you are worried about fit, remember that Antartex gives a no-questions-asked money-back guarantee. If you are still worried, how about a pair of pigskin gloves at a third of the U.S. price, or moccasin slippers at half the U.S. price? Duty on sheepskin clothes is 11%.

Charlie's Place, ***61 Orchard Street, New York, NY 10002. Telephone 212-431-8880.***
Send self-addressed, stamped envelope or telephone Monday through Thursday, 9:30 A.M. to 4 P.M., for specific prices.
AE, MC, V.
Sells shirts, pants, raincoats, underwear for men; raincoats for women. Brands handled: Arrow, Aquascutum, Christian Dior, Farrah, Gant, Haggar, Jaymar, London Fog, Misty Harbor, Sansabelt, Stratojac, Van Heusen, Zero King.
Minimum order $50.
Returns: credit if goods are in selling condition.
Established 1948.

This is *the* place to stock up on brand name clothes for men, and the best times to do it are in January and after Father's Day in June and July, when an extra 20% is taken off to clear everything and make way for the new season's stock. The owner, Kurt Lichtenstein, says that the most popular clothes with mail and telephone customers are Arrow and Van Heusen shirts, Haggar slacks and London Fog and Misty Harbor raincoats. Write or telephone with the brand name, model number, size and color of what you want.

I tested prices during the summer sale and found the Van Heusen "417" button-down shirt—usually $22 at Macy's department store but on end-of-season sale at Macy's for $16—cost $14.70 at Charlie's. Izod Lacoste mesh shirts cost the usual list price, $27.50, at Macy's, while they were normally $19.95 at Charlie's and now were on special sale at $14.95. Misty Harbor's "Tioga" raincoat, which cost $215 regularly at Macy's and $160 at Macy's end-of-summer sale, was $140 at Charlie's. Christian Dior's "Monsieur" raincoat cost $185 at Macy's but only $140 at Charlie's.

Deva, ***303 East Main, Box CC6, Burkittsville, MD 21701. Telephone 301-663-4900.***

10-page catalogue, $1 (refundable) in the U.S. and Canada.
MC, V.
Sells cotton clothing.
Returns: money back so long as goods are in resalable condition.
Established 1978.

"The dream that started with three of us in a garage has grown to include a bunch of us in a barn and homes all over this part of the country," say the owners. Deva produces casual clothes in pure cotton. Everything made here is loose and simple. "The clothes from Deva are the most comfortable I have ever worn," writes one customer. "Why did it take me so long to discover you?" writes another. Sizes range from small to extra large, and prices are low (almost everything costs under $40 as I write).

The Edinburgh Woollen Mill, ***COC 1, Langholm, Dumfriesshire, DG13 OBR, Scotland. Telephone: inquiries, 541-80611; orders, 541-80092.***
Free 30-page color catalogue.
AE, DC, MC, V.
Sells coats, skirts, jackets, sweaters for women made by Romanes and Patterson; Lyle & Scott and Pringle sweaters for men and women.
Returns: refund if goods mailed within two months in as-new condition.
Established 1808.

This is an extraordinary source for very classic clothes. It is the catalogue division of a Scottish mill that has outlets all over Britain to sell its own clothes, plus knitwear by Pringle and Lyle & Scott. Fabrics are mostly natural, shapes are simple (lots of pleated skirts, some flared), colors are subtle (sage green, bue-gray, dark heather, cream, beige and so on) and skirts and jackets are fully lined. And prices are astonishingly low, roughly a quarter of what you'd pay for the same sort of clothes in the United States. I bought a skirt to see whether the bargains are as good as they look, and I found that my skirt, at least, certainly is. It fits properly and is neatly made of a light wool. It's fully lined, with tabs for hanging, well-finished seams and none of the puckered seams that I have found on some American clothes, even designer clothes. The catalogue shows a couple of coats, several suits, jackets and skirts, sweaters and blouses.

Icemart Mail-Order Department, ***235 Keflavik Airport, Iceland. Telephone 800-431-9003.***
36-page color brochure, two $1 bills in the U.S. and Canada.
AE, DC, MC, V.
Sells Icelandic woolen clothes.
Returns: unconditional money-back guarantee.
Established 1970.

A beautiful collection of knits in typical Icelandic color combinations—lots of white with pale gray and pale blue designs. Most are machine-knitted, but there are some hand knits in Lopi wool. Prices are up to 40% off those of the same kind of knits in the United States. There are sweaters, jackets, mittens, caps and scarves, stoles and blankets. The store now has a U.S. toll-free number to speed orders.

Kathleen's, ***Upper Main Street, Mountcharles, Co. Donegal, Ireland. Telephone 73-35108.***
Free brochure.
AE, MC, V.
Sells hand-knit Aran sweaters (any size can be made to special order), Jimmy Hourilon tweeds, Avoca capes, bedspreads, and other things are carried also.
Returns: money back.
Established 1976.

Kathleen has the lowest prices I have found on *hand-knit* Aran sweaters (many Arans are now "hand-loomed"). When I checked, her prices were between 10 and 20% below those of other Irish stores. Another nice thing is that everything is available for the same price in the natural black (actually gray) sheepswool that is absolutely lovely, increasingly popular in the United States and horribly expensive here.

Kathleen herself lived in New York for 12 years and says her American customers are her "bread and butter," so they get her personal attention. In fact her mail-order business started with U.S. customers writing for repeat orders once they got home.

Lands' End, ***Lands' End Lane, Dodgeville, WI 53595-0001. Telephone 800-356-4444.***
Free 100-page color catalogue.
AE, MC, V.
Sells slightly sporty clothes for men, women and children, foul-weather gear, luggage.
Returns: unconditional guarantee.
Established 1963.

Lands' End is my favorite among the preppy-clothes-by-mail stores because its prices are sometimes lower, its colors are better and its range is wider than at its competitors. For instance, when I checked, some of its poplin pants were half the price of the ones in the L. L. Bean catalogue, others were a third off, and they came in eight colors instead of four. The cotton mesh knit shirts were 25 cents more expensive than Bean's but came in 14 good colors instead of 10 boring ones. (The same shirts were half the price of the Izod Lacoste shirts *and* didn't have the annoying little alligator.) The lisle sport shirts were $1.75 to $3 below the Bean equivalent.
Sales: Lands' End has significant sales at the end of each season, when it reduces prices of overstock by 15 to 50%.

Monaghans, ***15–17 Grafton Arcade, Grafton Street, Dublin 2, Ireland. Telephone 1-770823.***
Free color leaflet.
AE, V.
Sells very large stock of knitwear by manufacturers that include Barrie, Glen Abbey, Glenmac, Gaeltarra, Lyle & Scott, Alan Paine and Pringle. Men's sizes up to 56-inch chest.
Returns: money back.
Established 1960.

Monaghans stocks sweaters by more manufacturers than most (you can get Alan Paine knitwear here). A few of the sweaters, mainly Pringle cashmeres, are shown in the swish brochure, but not all, so this source is best for people who know what they want.

Padraic O'Maille, ***Dominick Street, Galway, Ireland. Telephone 91-62696.***
Color leaflet, $1 bill or equivalent International Reply Coupons. Prices given in dollars.
AE, MC, V.
Sells traditional Irish knitwear, tweed jackets and hats.
Returns: unconditional money back.
Established 1938.

A small color leaflet shows inexpensive hand-loomed Aran sweaters, patterned sweaters, one or two cashmeres, and tweed jackets that cost about half the price of tweed jackets on sale in the United States. Tweed jackets are made to measure, and you can send for swatches.

Reekies of Grasmere, ***Old Coach House, Stock Lane, Grasmere, Cumbria, England. Telephone 9665-221.***
Price list published in January. $1 bill or equivalent International Reply Coupons.
AE, MC, V.
Sells hand-woven clothes and travel rugs, local knitwear and sheepskin gloves.
Returns: none.
Established 1950.

This small family firm sells a mixture of knitwear, including mohair sweaters, sheepskin gloves and slippers, mohair and cashmere coats and capes, all at reasonable prices. There are also good presents, such as hand-woven mohair travel rugs and stoles and alpaca travel rugs—all at prices that are much lower than those in the United States. The company sells its own hand-woven mohair goods, as well as things produced by other firms. Reekies has been warmly recommended by New York couturier Shirley Salerno. The only problem is it will send you just a few line drawings—no color illustrations or samples.

W. S. Robertson, ***41 Bank Street, Galashiels, Scotland. Telephone 896-2152.***

Color brochures, $5 bill or equivalent International Reply Coupons.
Sells Scottish knitwear by Kinloch Anderson, Barrie, Braemar, Lyle & Scott, Pringle, Peter Scott.
Returns: money back if merchandise mailed immediately.
Established 1930.

One of the firms that has been selling by mail to U.S. customers for years. Brand name cashmeres sell for just over half of American prices, lamb's wool for about a third off. Robertson also has a far bigger stock of Scottish knitwear than any American store—more styles, many more colors and more sizes (there are a few "outsize" sweaters for men). If you send $5, you'll receive about four assorted manufacturers' brochures unless you say what you want specifically (e.g., brochures for men or women, particular brands).

A. Rubinstein and Son, ***63 East Broadway, New York, NY 10002. Telephone 212-226-9696.***
Send self-addressed, stamped envelope for specific prices.
AE, DC, MC, V.
Sells men's clothes, including shirts, ties, slacks, suits, coats, raincoats; handles brands such as Armani, Damon, Givenchy, London Fog, Nino Cerrutti, Oleg Cassini, Pierre Cardin, San Remo, Stanley Blacker, Yves Saint Laurent.
Returns: none on altered clothes.
Established 1922.

This small shop sells at small discounts, but owner Sam Rubinstein says that he will special order clothes by designers, including the Italian designers. To buy, you must provide brand name, model number, size and color. The staple items that he has in stock are Damon shirts, London Fog raincoats, Stanley Blacker sport coats, and Lord West tuxedos. I compared prices on two raincoats: Misty Harbor's "Tioga" raincoat cost $179 instead of Macy's regular price of $215 (but *on sale* Macy's was selling the coat for $160—less than Rubinstein). The price of Christian Dior's "Monsieur" raincoat was $176, as opposed to Macy's $185. *Sales:* are in July and January/February.

Skye Crotal Knitwear, ***Muileann Beag a' Chrotail, Camus Chros, Isle of Skye 1V43 8QR, Scotland. Telephone 47-13-271.***
Color brochure, $1 bill or equivalent International Reply Coupons.
MC, V.
Sells sweaters for men and women.
Returns: money back.
Established 1974.

These sweaters are recommended by a friend of mine who bought some when she was on the Isle of Skye. She says they are the best she found. This small firm started making knitwear in local wools and traditional Hebridean patterns to provide employment on the island. The business has expanded and now also makes specially designed sweaters. I like the traditional ones better, but they are all bargains, especially the heavy, rough-tough Harris wool sweaters, which cost half of what outdoor sweaters cost in the United States.

Sweater Market, ***15 Frederiksberggade, 1459 Copenhagen, Denmark. Telephone 1-152773.***
Free color leaflet.
AE, DC, MC, V.
Sells hand-knitted pure wool knitwear for men, women and children.
Returns: credit.
Established 1964.

Sweater Market sells hand-knitted ski sweaters with wide bands of snowflake designs on a white or gray background. The colors are mainly blue, gray and white and appealingly soft and subtle. When I compared prices with those of similar (imported) sweaters in New York, I found that at one shop prices were about the same and at another prices were 30% higher than at Sweater Market. So you may save money by buying from Denmark, but check prices with your U.S. source first.

Le Tricoteur, ***Pitronnerie Road Estate, Saint Peter Port, Guernsey, Channel Islands. Telephone Guernsey 26214***
Free leaflet and yarn samples.
AE, DC, MC, V.
Sells heavy sweaters in weather-resistant worsted wool for adults and children.
Returns: money back.
Established 1964.

The Guernsey fisherman's sweater is the best outdoor sweater you can buy. The design is an ancient tunic shape, which happens to be very flattering; the wool is an oiled worsted, which is warm, hard-wearing and slightly rain-resistant; the knitters are Guernsey women. Guernsey has a long tradition of knitting, although it used to be the men who did it. (They are said to have knitted the stockings Mary Queen of Scots wore to the scaffold.) Prices are about a third to half off prices charged for Guernseys in the United States, if you can find them here.

R. Watson Hogg, ***Auchterarder, Perthshire, Scotland. Telephone 7646-46-2151.***
Free Ballantyne leaflet.
AE, DC, MC, V.
Sells tweed jackets, cashmere sweaters and skirts by Ballantyne, many other woolen goods, including cashmere and wool ties; socks and scarves are also sold but not illustrated in the brochure.
Returns: money back if merchandise mailed within a month.
Established 1940.

"Those things called dear are, when justly estimated, the cheapest," announces the Watson Hogg letterhead. I don't know about that, but certainly Ballantyne cashmere sweaters for men and women and skirts for women are somewhat less dear if bought direct from Scotland. They cost about a third to half of the U.S. price. Ballantyne is considered by some to be the finest Scottish manufacturer of knitwear.

Westaway and Westaway, ***62–65 Great Russell Street, London WC1B 3BL, England. Telephone 1-405-4479.***

Westaway and Westaway hasn't answered my letters and doesn't always have a catalogue. However, if you *can* manage to pry a catalogue out of this store, you'll see why it is always jam-packed with customers. Basic (no brand names) sweaters, kilted skirts, scarves, stoles and so on are sold at the lowest prices in London. (Typically, earlier this year Viyella shirts for men cost $25 here but $35 at an Oxford Street department store.)

Whole Earth Access, ***2950 7th Street, Berkeley, CA 94710. Telephone 415-845-3000, 800-845-2000.***
458-page catalogue, $5 (refundable) plus $2 postage. ($6 in Canada).
MC, V.
Sells small collection of durable work clothes: jeans by Levi and Lee Riders, overalls by Oshkosh, shirts by Woolrich, leotards and tights by Danskin, boots by Frye and Herman, shoes by Timberland, Wolverine, Clarks and Rockport, other brands in the above categories; cotton clothing, sweaters, socks. (See main listing for complete list of goods.)
Returns: money back.
Established 1969.

The Whole Earth Access store concentrates on finding goods that are practical and durable. The splendid general catalogue has a good selection of classic work and casual clothes and shoes, mainly by well-known manufacturers, at lower prices (see partial list above). Clothes for men, women and children are stocked, so this is a terrific one-stop source for basics. Toni Garrett, who is in charge of the catalogue, told me that the policy is to keep prices low so that customers can be confident they are getting the best price. She says that shoe prices are especially "competitive" and that Levi's on which the store makes only $2 a pair are also a good buy. I spot-checked Levi's 501s for men and Oshkosh children's overalls; both were selling at 15% below other stores. Rocsports walking shoes were selling for 25% under what Eddie Bauer outdoor clothes catalogue was selling them for.

Women

Clothkits, ***24 High Street, Lewes, East Sussex, BN7 2LB, England. Telephone 273-477111.***

Free 44-page color catalogue in February and August.
MC, V.
Sells ready-made knitwear and ready-to-sew kits for women's and children's clothes.
Returns: money back.
Established 1969.

Strikingly colorful and handsomely designed English Clothkits clothes for women and children. Some tights, sweaters and shirts are ready-made; others are ready to cut out and sew. If you like sewing, you can make rather sophisticated and unusual things and pay less than you'd pay for the dullest and most predictable clothes in the stores.
Sales: during November and June sales, an extra 15% or more is deducted from the price of some of the clothes.

Moffat Woollens, ***Mail Order Department, Benmar, Moffat, Dumfriesshire, DG10 9EP, Scotland. Telephone 683-20134.***
14-page color catalogue published in March and September.
AE, DC, MC, V.
Sells woolen skirts, jackets and sweaters in American sizes 10 to 20, made-to-measure kilts.
Returns: money back if goods returned promptly in good condition.
Established 1940.

Pure wool sweaters, skirts and jackets cost roughly one-third of what similar clothes cost in the United States. Several less classic skirts that have stripes, gathers and checks are available, and there is a good choice of fully lined classic blazers that are special bargains considering what they cost in America.

Pitlochry Knitwear, ***Scottish Woollens House, P.O. Box 8, East Kilbride, Glasgow, G74 5QZ, Scotland. Telephone 3552-42080.***
16-page color catalogue, $1 bill.
AE, DC, MC, V.
Sells women's clothes in sizes 12 to 44, made-to-measure women's skirts in tartan or tweed.
Returns: money back if clothes mailed within five days unworn.
Established 1969.

Another Scottish firm that sells classic skirts, jackets, blouses and sweaters at prices that are about a third of what you'd pay in the United States. Besides the smart pale gray and camel-colored matching skirts and jackets, there are less traditional pieces such as patterned Viyella blouses, velvet waistcoats and, in one catalogue, a Chanel-type mohair blend jacket. Skirts can be made to measure in any size.

Recommended by my reader Mrs. Lanspa, who, after ordering a suit successfully, has gone back for a skirt and a sweater.

Kits

Edith Kressy Designs, ***R.F.D. 1, Plymouth, NH 03264. Telephone 603-536-1785.***
Brochure and samples, $5.
Sells kits to make dresses cut to customer's measurements, women's sizes only.
Returns: money back if kits returned unworked within 14 days.
Established 1979.

Edith Kressy designs some attractive clothes for women and sells them ready-made or as kits. She calls her clothes "classic," but they in fact change with the fashions even though they remain basically understated. Fabrics are all natural and of high quality. With some (but not all) of these kits you can make clothes that are far cheaper than their equivalent ready-mades would be in the stores. For instance, in the last brochure I looked at, a kit to make a reversible quilted coat cost only $65.

Children

Cotton Dreams, ***2962 Northwest 60th Street, Fort Lauderdale, FL 33309. Telephone 305-977-0148.***
Catalogue, free in the U.S. and Canada.
MC, V.
Sells children's clothes in natural fibers.
Returns: money back if within 30 days.
Established 1979.

This firm sells only natural fiber clothes—mainly for babies and children up to the age of 6—at reasonable although not discount prices. However, in each issue of the catalogue there are two pages of leftovers sold at about 25% off.

Mothercare, ***P.O. Box 145, Cherry Tree Road, Watford, Hertfordshire, WO2 5SH, England. Telephone: inquiries, 923-33577; orders, 923-40366.***
Free 164-page color catalogue.
MC, V.
Sells clothes for pregnant women, babies, and children up to age 10.
Returns: money back if clothes returned within two weeks.
Established 1962.

This terrific English chain has opened stores in the United States and already gathered some very devoted customers. The American branch doesn't do mail order, so if you don't live near a store it is well worth buying direct from England.

The catalogue has almost everything you'd need for babies and young children. Probably the simplest things to mail are the clothes, which are well made (mostly in blends or synthetics), good-looking and sold at the lowest possible prices. Some of the clothes (for instance, babies' dresses and girls' nightdresses) cost about half Sears's prices, yet the designs are far classier. There is a special section of safety goods, such as safety film for glass, catches for drawers and doors and a rail to protect children from hot pots on the stove.

Young Idea, ***Dept. 919, 9 Kingsbury Street, Aylesbury, Buckinghamshire, HP20 2JA, England. Telephone 296-24013.***
30-page color catalogue, $1 bill.
MC, V.
Sells clothes for babies and children to age 10, by Ladybird, Banner, Trutex and own brand.
Returns: credit if merchandise returned within a month.
Established 1968.

Young Idea is a marvelous source of children's clothes at very low prices. It used to sell only leftovers by the well-known English firm Ladybird, but now it has added its own line and clothes by other manufacturers. A few of the clothes are of natural fiber, most are at least partly artificial, but all are well made, sturdy and pleasing. I've bought lots for my own children, and they have worn well. Furthermore, prices are usually half those at Sears and similar stores, or even less.

Rachel's Boutique, ***4218 13th Avenue, Brooklyn, NY 11215. Telephone 718-435-6875.***
Send stamped, self-addressed envelope for specific prices.
MC, V.
Sells children's clothes by Carter, Dan Jean of France, Dijon, Health-Tex, Izod Lacoste, Oshkosh, Petit Bateau of France, Pierre Cardin.
Minimum order $10.
Returns: credit if clothes returned within 14 days.
Established 1972.

Rachel Krausz has a large stock of better brands (see list above) but no catalogue. She won't give price quotes over the telephone, and although she has claimed each time I've talked to her about it that she does give price quotes by mail if you give the model number, size and color, the store has not answered my query letters. I think it is probably best, if you know exactly what you want, to send in an order giving brand, model number, color and size of child with your credit card number and expiration date. But note that there is a $20 minimum for Visa and MasterCard orders and a $40 minimum for American Express orders.

Miss Krausz says that she gives a 20 to 40% discount off list price.

Underwear

If you are organized enough to know which brands and sizes of underwear and hosiery you want, you can save time and money by buying from the New

York discount stores. In fact, it's well worth getting organized and finding brands and models you like. Once you've done that, you can very easily order and reorder from the stores below and forever avoid the boredom of shopping for socks and so on. I've been a happy woman since I collected brand names and model numbers and started ordering my underwear (and my family's underwear) by mail.

Everything is sold at about 20 to 25% off list price. Prices vary by a few cents at each store, but I haven't found one that is consistently lower than the others. And I have found service very prompt at my two favorites, Louis Chock and D & A Merchandise.

Louis Chock, ***74 Orchard Street, New York, NY 10002. Telephone 212-473-1929.***
Catalogue, $1.
MC, V.
Sells Hanes, Mayer and Berkshire hosiery and stockings; Carter, Vassarette, and Duofold underwear for women; Bill Blass, Munsingwear, BVD and Hanes underwear for men; Carter underwear and nightwear for children; Supp-Hose, Christian Dior and Burlington socks; terry cloth robes for men and women; Oscar de la Renta and Botany 500 pajamas for men.
Returns: money-back guarantee on returns within 30 days.
Established 1921.

I buy huge batches of underwear here for all my family. There is a small catalogue, and service is really fast. Furthermore, the staff is friendly (if you walk into their store with a foreign accent, they'll pull out a visitor's book for you to sign) and helpful (I once forgot to sign checks I sent them, and they telephoned immediately so as not to delay the order). They've even been helpful to me when I telephoned on a Sunday, their busiest day.

They don't sell bras and girdles but do have some stuff for women, such as Hanes pantyhose (in large and small sizes with the Hanes sizing chart). They also stock things that are hard to find anywhere in New York, such as hosiery, underwear and pajamas for big and tall men and pure cotton boxer shorts (by Hanes).

D & A Merchandise, ***The Underwear King, 22 Orchard Street, New York, NY 10002. Telephone 212-925-4766.***
Brochure, $1.50; or write or telephone for specific prices.
MC, V.
Sells underwear and hosiery for men, women and boys: men's underwear by BVD, Camp, Duofold, Hanes, Jockey; boys' underwear by BVD and Hanes; hosiery and socks by Bonnie Doon, Burlington, Camp, Dior (socks only), Interwoven, Trimfit, Wigwam; women's underwear and foundations by popular manufacturers such as Danskin, Bali, Christian Dior, Lily of France, Maidenform, Olga, Playtex, Vassarette, Warner's.

Returns: money back if wrapping is unopened.
Established 1946.

Possibly the only store on the Lower East Side to sell underwear and hosiery for men, women *and* children. Owner Elliott Kivell says he sells no imports but does sell all major U.S. brands (including with-it Anne Klein and Perry Ellis socks for women and Thorlo sports socks). It may be just luck that D & A happens to stock the brands, models and colors I want, but I have always had an amazingly fast response here on anything I have ordered and anything I have asked about.

L'eggs Products, ***P.O. Box 100, Rural Hall, NC 27098-1010. Telephone 919-744-1170.***
L'eggs Showcase brochure and Active Wear brochure, free.
MC, V.
Sells Underalls and Bali underwear; L'eggs, Sheer Energy and Hanes stockings; Gitano active wear.
Returns: satisfaction guaranteed; money back so long as receipt is enclosed.
Established 1969.

Imperfect L'eggs underwear and pantyhose, Hanes pantyhose, Bali bras and active wear are available at savings of up to 40%. A friend told me about this firm; she reckons she saves $2 a pair on colored, patterned L'eggs pantyhose here. On some things, prices go down if you buy more, so if you buy in quantity you can get prices that are even lower than those at the other stores in this section. With Hanes pantyhose, for instance, if you buy 12 slightly imperfect pairs at once, you can get prices that are about 12% lower than those at the other stores. Colorful all-cotton underwear is shown in the catalogue too.

Roby's Intimates, ***1905 Sansom Street, Philadelphia, PA 19103. Telephone 800-631-1610; in Pennsylvania, 215-751-1730.***
Send self-addressed, stamped envelope or telephone Monday through Friday only for specific prices.
MC, V.
Sells women's underwear, stockings, loungewear and bodywear; brands include Bali, Danskin, Dior, Goddess, Hanes, Lejaby, Lily of France, Maidenform, Olga, Playtex, Eve Stillman, Vassarette, Warner's.
Returns: money back if merchandise not tried on; tickets must be on.
Established 1985.

Roby Rosenthal worked in her father's New York store for many years—"since she was born," she says. When he retired, she brought the business to Philadelphia, where she continues to sell underwear at a discount (and she sounds just as cheerful in Philadelphia as she used to in New York). The unusual thing about this store is that Lejaby from France is stocked, as are the more common U.S. brands.

Roby is very willing to special order, but in that case there is a minimum of a boxful (which is about three of most things). If you write, be patient. Responses used to be slow in New York; I don't know whether they are faster from Philadelphia.

Notable Sales

Damart, ***1811 Woodbury Avenue, Portsmouth, NH 03805. Telephone 800-258-7300.***
Produces free sales brochures, January to March and June.
AE, MC, V.
Sells discontinued and "seconds" underwear at 10 to 40% off regular prices.
Returns: money back if within ten days.
Established 1971 in the U.S., earlier internationally.

Several people I know swear that wearing Damart's insulated underwear is the best way to keep warm. As the advent of winter is inevitable and predictable, buy early and take advantage of the reductions (up to 40%) during Damart's spring sales.

Victoria's Secret, ***P.O. Box 16589, Columbus, OH 43216. Telephone: questions, 212-276-3131; orders, 800-821-0001.***
Produces sales catalogues, January/February and May/June.
AE, MC, V.
Sells lingerie and stockings at a 10 to 40% discount.
Returns: money back if goods unworn and unaltered.
Established 1980.

The provocative lacy underwear and nightwear sold by Victoria's Secret are reduced by 10 to 40%, but mainly by 20%, in two catalogue sales each year.

SHOES

Mail and Telephone Sources

When I checked prices on national brands at these stores, prices hovered around 20% below list.

Aly's Hut, ***85 Hester Street, New York, NY 10002. Telephone: questions, 212-226-5475; orders, 212-226-5555.***
Will quote prices by mail only; send self-addressed, stamped envelope.
MC, V.
Sells Bass penny loafers and tassel loafers in medium and wide.
Returns: credit if shoes returned within seven days.
Established 1970.

Although Aly's has mainly walk-in customers, it does ship Bass loafers. I have checked several times and found that discounts are a steady 20%. So if you definitely want Bass, and you know the list price, I think you are safe in ordering without writing for prices first. When I compared prices on Weejun penny loafers and tassel loafers for men, they were selling for $14 below what list-price stores were charging, and in this case tax exactly equaled postage costs.

Baker's Shoes of Cambridge, ***751 Massachusetts Avenue, Cambridge, MA 02139. Telephone 617-492-8783.***
Free leaflet in March and September.
AE, MC, V.
Sells Rocsports and Clarks.
Returns: money back if shoes returned as new within 60 days.
Established 1951.

Bernard Short took over his father's 33-year-old shoe shop, moved it, jazzed up the interior and started selling first-quality brand name shoes at a 20% discount. He also does something unusual for a discount shoe store—he produces leaflets with line drawings of some of his most popular Clarks and Rocsports shoes. A few shoes are stocked in three widths and Bernard Short says he will give "helpful advice on shoes and feet."

Hill Brothers, ***99 Ninth Street, Lynchburg, VA 24504. Telephone 804-528-1000.***
46-page catalogue, free in the U.S. and Canada, published in January and July.
AE, DC, CB, MC, V.
Sells house brand women's shoes in sizes 3 to 13 and AAAAA to EEEE widths.
Returns: 14-day wear trial, money back if not completely satisfied.
Established 1968.

This firm has been recommended to me for good values by two readers. One of them, Shirley Salerno, writes, "Leather shoes in every size and width you can think of. Discount coupon. Shoes wear very well, beautiful styles from dress to sports."

Leslie's Bootery, ***36 Orchard Street, New York, NY 10002. Telephone 212-431-9196.***
Write (self-addressed, stamped envelope appreciated) or telephone on any day except Sunday for specific prices.
MC, V.
Sells shoes for men by Bally, Clarks, Cole Haan, Freeman, Rockport, Sperry, Topsider; for women by Bally, Caressa, Nickels, Mr. Seymour, Reebok.
Returns: exchange or store credit if shoes returned within three weeks.
Established 1969.

This well-known store is sometimes hard to get through to by telephone, but when you do get through the staff is cheerful about quoting prices (though with one written query I had to write twice before getting an answer). Leslie's gives a 20% discount on the shoes it stocks.

WHOLE EARTH ACCESS (main listing in General section) sells Clarks, Frye, Rocsports and Timberland shoes at a similar discount. Stores in the Sports section sell running shoes at a discount.

COMPUTERS

IBM PC computer. When the typical price for this model with monochrome monitor, 256K RAM (memory) and dual 360K drives was $2520, the price at stores in this section was $1495.

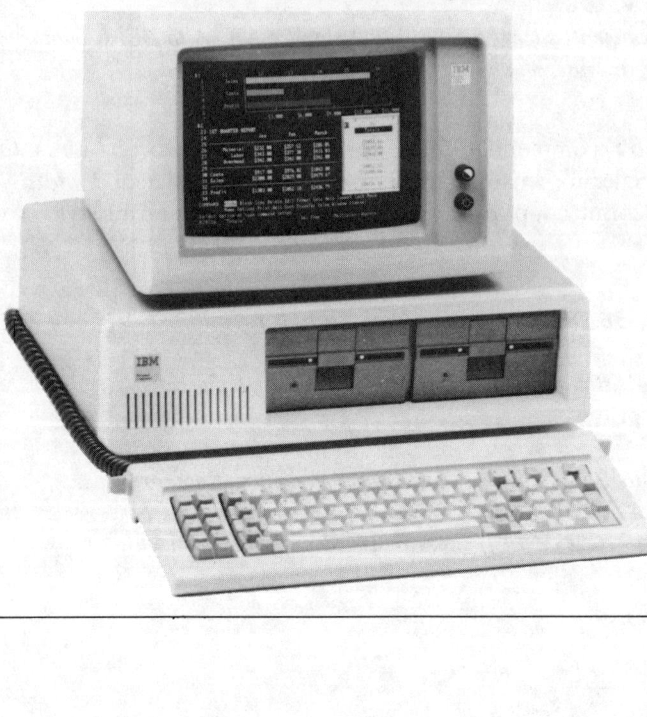

COMPUTERS

HOW TO FIND OUT WHETHER YOU NEED A COMPUTER AND WHICH ONE YOU NEED IF YOU DO

If you don't know anything about computers, don't know whom to ask and don't even know whether you want or need a computer, you'll probably have a hard time finding out what you need to know. Computer salespeople know how to work the machines they are selling, but they are rarely able and willing to give you an honest, careful and detailed account of what a computer can really do for you and your particular needs. I think the answer to this problem lies in books and one amazing person.

The books I like I describe below. The amazing person is Russ Walter, an independent, full-time computer buff who writes and publishes his own computer books and gives computer seminars and courses when he is not playing with his computer. He also does something extraordinary—he answers computer questions 24 hours a day from anyone who calls him. He has answered many of mine very helpfully, both when I was buying a computer for myself several years ago and, more recently, in a professional capacity for this chapter. (When I was buying my computer I learned far more from him than from the four different salesmen I made appointments with in smart New York stores.) He usually sounds rather morose when he picks up the phone, but as he warms to the subject he tells you more and more useful stuff. He says that he gives more time to people who have bought one of his books than to people who haven't.

Russ Walter, ***22 Ashland Street, Somerville, MA 02144. Telephone 617-666-2666.***

If you are a beginner, buy *Skills,* the first volume of Russ Walter's three-volume *Secret Guide to Computers.* Among other things, this volume makes specific suggestions on what to buy. It compares and teaches you about popular word-processing, data-management and spreadsheet programs. Russ Walter is frank, he names names.

Thrills, the second volume, teaches computer art, music, games and advanced programming. Volume 3, *Chills,* is about exotic programming languages and computer hassles, history and future. Each volume costs $8 postpaid from the above address.

If you want to find out what you need to know to buy a computer setup with the minimum of intellectual effort, read **THE PERSONAL COMPUTER BOOK** ***by Peter McWilliams, published by Doubleday, 501 Franklin Avenue, Garden City, NY 11530, telephone 516-294-4400.*** It is easy to understand, explains what computers can do for you and what they can't and, like Russ Walter, comes through where other books get coy—with an outspoken brand-name buying guide. *The Peter McWilliams Personal Computer Buying Guide,* from the same publisher, consists of evaluations of hardware, software, printers and peripherals. *The Whole Earth Software Catalog,* also from Doubleday, is packed with invaluable information and evaluations. The problem with the evaluations in these books is that there are only a few for each type of product, and even though both books are updated annually, they get out of date. I have, for instance, just bought a second printer and a friend of mine is buying a computer, and neither the printers nor the writing software recommended to us by salesmen were listed in these books.

Consumer Reports runs informative reports with ratings of computers and some software.

CHOOSING

These points are important in choosing a computer *if you are not a buff* but a normal person who just wants to use a computer with minimum fuss and is not interested in experimenting or programming.

1. The computer must run the best programs for your needs. (This is an argument in favor of the biggies such as IBM and IBM-compatibles, as more and better programs are constantly being written for them.)
2. The computer should be compatible with the computer of any institution or person that you work with (and, if possible, anyone you play with so that you can get advice, borrow a printer if yours breaks and share programs).
3. The manufacturer should have staying power. Otherwise your model may become totally obsolete, without available parts and repair people.

Which One?

As I write, the Leading Edge Model D seems to be a favorite home computer with people in the know (Russ Walter, Peter McWilliams and *Consumer Reports* all consider it good value). An IBM copy, it can run the IBM programs yet, as I write, costs very roughly 60% less than the equivalent IBM. Russ Walter also suggests the Tandy 1000, which is even cheaper, although it doesn't imitate IBM as closely.

If you want to get a whole computer setup for less than $1000, you'll have to sacrifice many conveniences, but Russ Walter has lots of ideas. First, he says, it is important to know what you'll use the computer for. When I talked to him in early 1986, he made these suggestions: If you want to use ready-made programs, the Commodore 64 is the cheapest available computer that is still having new software developed for it. If you want to share programs with friends, then the Apple IIc is a promising choice because there are lots of them around and lots of programs for them. If you want to write programs, the Atari 65XE is inexpensive and satisfactory if you supplement it with the Microsoft BASIC cartridge.

But please try to check the above specific recommendations; they may be out of date by the time you read this book.

WHEN TO BUY

With antiques the best time to buy is always yesterday, when whatever it is went for a song. With computers the best time to buy is always tomorrow. The longer you wait, the more you get for your money. Computers, and computer programs, get cheaper and more efficient every day. If you feel you ought to get a computer but don't especially need or want one now, then wait. On the other hand, if you need or want a computer now, don't worry about future improvements. What computers now on the market can do is tremendous. Most computer owners, once they have learned to use their new machines, are so pleased that they either ignore new developments or are perfectly delighted to pay more to bring their computers and programs up to date.

WHERE TO BUY

Buying a computer is not like buying any other machine—you'll need a little or a lot of help in learning how to use it. Ideally, you have a friend with the same computer and the patience to answer foolish questions. Otherwise you may be lucky enough to find a good computer store in your area. If you find a first-class store, with assistants who can work out an integrated system with the programs you need, lead you through the instruction manuals and advise you as you learn to use the system—buy from that store. However, if there are no really good computer stores in your area, you might as well buy from a low-price store and save several hundred dollars. As a computer professional told me, the average computer shop is staffed by know-nothings who send the machine back to the manufacturer for repairs anyway, so there's not much difference in buying by mail or in person, except for the savings (of at least 20%).

Buying a computer is rather like playing the stock market, because prices are always changing. Almost all walk-in stores normally charge full list price, although you may be able to haggle them down by 10% by showing or quoting another store's lower price. And they do have special sales that may be good.

If you buy by mail, you'll have to get help from books, instruction manuals, the manufacturer (some manufacturers have a telephone line for questions), a user group or, best of all, a friend with the same computer.

If repairs are needed (rare with computers, more likely with printers), you send the machine back to the shop or manufacturer via UPS while it is under warranty and do the same or find a local repair person when it's out of warranty.

MAIL AND TELEPHONE SOURCES

Mail-order computer stores and low-price stores routinely sell computers, related equipment and supplies at prices that are roughly 20 to 30% below prices at walk-in stores. However, if you want to find the *very* lowest price for something you are about to buy, always compare the prices of the stores listed in this book, and check out the prices in computer magazine advertisements for current specials.

EAST 33 ST., FOCUS AND 47 ST. PHOTO (in the Appliances and Electronics section) and OLDEN (Photography section) all have active computer departments. I didn't include them in this chapter because I don't want to repeat myself, but when buying computers, peripherals and software, always consider them. Their prices are even lower than those of most of the specialized firms in this chapter. COMB (in the General section) sells inexpensive reconditioned machines.

Computer Plus, ***435 King Street, Littleton, MA 01460. Telephone 800-343-8124; in Massachusetts, 617-486-3193.***
Free catalogue, or write or telephone for prices.
AE, MC, V.
Sells Tandy (Radio Shack) computers, peripherals and supplies.
Returns: money back if returned within ten days; there may be a 5% restocking charge.
Established 1973.

Computer Plus is an authorized Tandy (Radio Shack) dealer that sells hardware at roughly 10% off, and software at roughly 15% off, list price.

Conroy-Lapointe, ***12060 Southwest Garden Place, Portland, OR 97223. Telephone 800-547-1289; in Oregon, 503-620-9878.***
Telephone for prices.
AE, MC, V.
Sells IBM PCs, Apples, peripherals and software for those machines, supplies such as diskettes, ribbons and paper.

Returns: defective merchandise replaced or fixed if returned within 60 days.
Established 1978.

This is one of the largest, oldest and most reputable mail-order stores in the country. A good source for people who know what they want, the firm doesn't give help and so it is not good for people who are floundering.

Harmony Video and Computers, ***2357 Coney Island Avenue, Brooklyn, NY 11223. Telephone: questions, 718-627-1000; orders, 800-441-1144.***
Write or telephone for prices.
MC, V.
Sells computers, peripherals, supplies.
Returns: "depends on circumstances."
Established 1981.

Harmony was suggested to me as a store that sells lower-priced computers such as the Commodore 64 and Atari. In fact, it also sells Apple and IBM. Harmony sells good products and has excellent prices, but it does not have a full line by each manufacturer.

Logic Soft, ***110 Bi-County Boulevard, Farmingdale, NY 11735. Telephone 800-645-3491; in New York State, 516-249-8440.***
Telephone for prices.
AE, MC, V.
Sells IBM PC series (PC, XT, AT), Compaq, AT&T peripherals and software for IBM.
Returns: anything that arrives damaged will be replaced if returned within three weeks.
Established 1978.

Logic Soft guarantees that it will sell any item that it stocks costing over $100 for $10 less than its competitors, if you can find an ad in a national magazine or a written price quote that is lower than the Logic Soft price. It also provides all sorts of fancy services. It sends smaller things (not machines, monitors and printers, obviously) by Purolator overnight service at no extra cost. It has an active special-order department and will hunt down anything costing over $200 and sell it to you for 20% off list price. It also gives a free 90-day service contract with Sorbus, who in many parts of the country will come to your home. Logic Soft says it doesn't want people to be afraid of mail order.

Logic Soft has a European branch based in Amsterdam. Far Eastern and South American accounts are handled at this office.

WCB Computers, ***14 West 3rd Street, Suite 4, Santa Rosa, CA 95401. Telephone 707-575-9472.***
Spring and fall price lists, free in the U.S. and Canada. Product cards available at other times.
MC, V.

Sells IBM PCs, Zenith and Columbia computer systems, most printers, modems, monitors and other hardware. Stocks, or can order, most microcomputer software available.
Returns: manufacturer's warranty on all products; totally dissatisfied customers may return products within 14 days for credit toward other purchases, minus a 15% restocking fee.
Established 1983.

A *San Francisco Chronicle* columnist nominated WCB his first choice as a mail-order firm because of its nearly unlimited range of products, its reputation for integrity and praise heard all around for its excellent service. *The Whole Earth Software Catalog* praised the firm for the same reasons (could it have been the same writer?). When I compared prices of software, WCB was higher than other firms in this section (by 20% in one case), but I include it because of the recommendations.

Software

Commercial Software

As John Jainschigg at Family Computer said to me, "No one in his right mind buys software at the manufacturer's suggested list price." Even beginners who don't want to risk buying machines at a discount can confidently buy programs by mail.

Since users who know how to make software copies by defeating manufacturers' protection systems try to return the original for a refund, some manufacturers do not supply refunds (but will replace a defective copy with a working copy).

The following are good sources of information:

THE WHOLE EARTH SOFTWARE CATALOG, *published by Doubleday, 501 Franklin Avenue, Garden City, NY 11530, telephone 516-294-4400.*

This book (mentioned above) by the Whole Earth people describes and evaluates popular programs for each computer activity. It's updated annually and is, as you'd expect, informative, well written and easy to read.

MICRO INFORMATION PUBLISHING, *4730 Dakota Street, Prior Lake, MN 55372, telephone 612-447-6959. Write or telephone for free information.*

Publishes and sells catalogues of all software available for IBM PCs and compatibles. Prices range from $20 to $100 each. Updated quarterly.

Eastcoast Software, *49 Derrytown Mall, Hershey, PA 17033. Telephone: inquiries, 717-533-8125; orders, 800-233-3237.*
Price list, free in the U.S. and Canada, or telephone, 10 A.M. to 5 P.M. EST, Monday through Saturday, for prices.
MC, V.

Sells educational and business software and games for Apple, Commodore, Macintosh and Omega computers; "non-machine specific" supplies such as disks and printer ribbons.
Returns: money back if requested within 30 days.
Established 1982.

The prices I have been quoted at Eastcoast have been good—usually the same as, and a couple of times lower than, prices at New York discount stores. I twice bought floppies here. The first time I was told they'd arrive "within the week," and they arrived in four days. The next time I ordered on Friday afternoon, they said they'd ship Monday and I received the disks on Wednesday. The only problem I've had is that the salespeople were impossible to get through to in December. When I reached them on January 8, the woman I spoke to giggled apologetically, blamed it on Christmas and said things were easing up now.

800 Software, ***940 Dwight Way, Berkeley, CA 94710. Telephone 800-227-4587.***
Summer and fall/winter software price lists, free in the U.S. and Canada, or telephone for prices.
AE, MC, V.
Sells hardware, business software, peripherals.
Returns: all products are guaranteed against manufacturing defects and will be replaced if they don't perform as warranted; some programs may also be returned if you are unsatisfied.
Established 1982.

800 is recommended for good service in *The Whole Earth Software Catalog* because of having been praised by readers. It is a large firm that sells to dealers and has corporate customers such as Coca-Cola, General Electric and Ford, but it also sells to individuals. Prices of the programs I checked were good, but the firm was out of Wordstar just before Christmas. It produces posh printed price lists with feature comparison charts for popular programs, and, best of all, it has a number you can call for "technical support" when you are befuddled by a new program.

Firms in the Appliances and Electronics section that sell computers and OLDEN (Photography section) are a main source of commercial software at excellent prices. I am told that the manufacturers of the Lotus 1-2-3 program decided as a publicity stunt to give a car to whichever U.S. dealer sold the most Lotus 1-2-3s. They were so embarrassed to find that a discount store, 47 St. Photo, was the winner, that the stunt fizzled and they presented the car very quietly.

Public-Domain and User-Supported (Shareware) Software

Public-domain software has been written by government or business institutions or computer buffs and, instead of being copyrighted, has been donated for anyone to use. Programs are available for little more than the cost of the disk they are on (about $10) and are similar to programs that cost ten times as much, or more.

User-supported software *has* been copyrighted and it sells for the same sort of price as public-domain software, but the program contains a message asking for a voluntary contribution.

There are thousands of programs for every conceivable use, from the mundane to the very peculiar. Patrick Cox of PC Software Interest Group is especially enthusiastic about public-domain and user-supported software. He says their current tremendous growth in popularity will pressure the commercial software producers into lowering their sky-high prices (on some of which there is a 10,000% markup) until commercial programs cost as little as books do now. Find out what is available through user clubs or from the sources below.

For Apple: **APPLE/BOSTON,** *% Richard Bloom, 215 Hartman Road, Newton, MA 02159.* Free price list.

For IBM: **SOFTWARE EXCHANGE,** *% Proteus Software, 363 The Great Road, Bedford, MA 01730. Telephone 617-275-3610.* Catalogue, $10 (make check out to Boston Computer Society).

or

PC SOFTWARE INTEREST GROUP (PS/SIG), *1030 East Duane, Suite D, Sunnyvale, CA 94086. Telephone 408-730-9291.* This is a company, not a user group. If you pay $15, you get a catalogue of IBM software plus newsletters describing new releases. If you don't pay the $15, you can buy just the catalogue for $8.95. One very important advantage of buying here is that the firm offers technical support. You can call in with questions on the programs you have bought.

For Macintosh: **BOSTON COMPUTER SOCIETY,** *% Macintosh Group, One Center Plaza, Boston, MA 02108. Telephone 617-367-8080.* Catalogue, $2 (make check out to Boston Computer Society).

For Apple, Atari, Commodore, IBM, Radio Shack and Texas Instruments: **NATIONAL SOFTWARE LENDING LIBRARY,** *507 Race Street, Cambridge, MD 21613. Telephone 301-221-0051.* Free price list of software for loan to members and sale or rent to nonmembers; user guides to individual computers with list of software, $1 each.

Supplies

It makes sense to buy supplies such as disks, paper and ribbons in bulk. You save more money, it's less trouble and they are there when needed.

As for choosing disks, both Russ Walter and Steve Weinberg of Village Computers, a New York City store, say that as long as you buy double-sided, double-density disks, price is not an indication of quality. When comparing prices, note that some firms sell house brands without envelopes and/or without labels.

Communications Electronics, ***P.O. Box 1045, Dept. HR, Ann Arbor, MI 48106-1045. Telephone 800-872-3475; in Michigan, 313-973-8888.***
Price list, free in the U.S. and Canada, available only September, October, November.
MC, V.
Sells disks by Superdisc, Wabash, BASF, 3M, Memorex, Burroughs, TDK, Fuji, Dysan, Nodak, Maxell, Verbatim, Ultramagnetics; scanners, satellite receivers, shortwave receivers.
Returns: money back minus handling charge if merchandise returned within 31 days.
Established 1971.

Recommended by John Jainschigg (of Family Computer) as having the lowest-priced disks that he has found. When I compared, prices were low, but not the lowest. There is no minimum order requirement. Inexpensive house brand disks are sold without labels and without envelopes.

Disc World, ***629 Green Bay Road, Wilmette, IL 60091. Telephone 800-621-6827; in Illinois, 312-256-7140.***
Write or telephone for specific prices.
MC, V.
Sells disks, disk storage units, ribbons, other supplies.
Minimum order $35 or 20 or 50 diskettes (depending on brand).
Returns: money back; lifetime guarantee on magnetic media; on other goods there is a 30-day time limit, and in some cases only a manufacturer's warranty.
Established 1983.

This firm was mentioned by Russ Walter as having the best prices and seems to me to be the place to buy basic supplies. Owner Jerry Saperstein sounds genuinely interested in providing good products at lower prices. He sells Kodak, 3M, Sony, BASF and Athana disks and also his own house brand. The house brand is made by firms such as BASF and is at least 50% over the American National Standards Institute's minimum standard. The brands he sells have been tested by an independent laboratory. By buying in quantity and sticking to in-demand, rather than specialized, products, he keeps prices on his disks and ribbons very low.

When I talked to him, Jerry Saperstein told me that he is planning to add paper to the list of supplies he sells. As paper is so expensive to ship, he has been looking for manufacturers with warehouses around the country in order to cut shipping costs.

QUILL (Office Equipment and Stationery section) sells computer supplies at excellent prices and produces a catalogue.

Used Equipment

Now that computers have been around for a while, a secondhand market is developing, mainly at "conventions" small and large. Buying secondhand is one way for enthusiasts who know what they are doing to save money. It is not a good way for untutored beginners. The equipment might be obsolete, in which case you'll have trouble finding repair people and parts, and there is no guarantee of its integrity.

Stan Veit, editor of *Computer Shopper*, points out that use doesn't damage computers, so if you *do* know what you are doing, there are bargains to be had. But, Stan Veit warns, most owners ask too much for their used equipment. Computer prices are going down all the time, so you should pay only 40 to 60% of the current price of a piece of equipment (the original price paid has nothing to do with it). However, Dan Delmar of Comp-Used points out that supply and demand also affect the price, as there are more would-be buyers than sellers for some popular equipment. He says that goods in most demand can go for as much as 75% of the lowest discount price of exactly the same new equipment with the same add-ons.

Remember: if you want to buy used equipment through these brokers, prices are negotiable.

Boston Computer Exchange Corporation, ***Box 1177, Boston, MA 02103. Telephone 617-542-4414.***

Telephone for information on computers and peripherals you want to buy or sell. Boston Computer Exchange doesn't sell anything but acts as a broker between people who are buying and selling computers and peripherals.
Returns: none.
Established 1981.

Boston Computer Exchange provides a useful service. It has a list of people who want to sell used computers, printers, modems, software and so on. If you want to buy, you can get information in the form of a printout or through your modem, or you can be put in touch with a seller directly. The company may be able to introduce you to sellers through affiliates located around the country and in major cities of the world. If it can't find you a person close enough for you to deal with face-to-face, it will try to give you the name of someone who has what you want in another part of the country and who will ship. When I telephoned asking for an Epson computer, Boston Computer Exchange gave me the name of two sellers in New York, where I live. When I asked for a Comrex printer, it gave me two sellers in Boston.

If you do buy from someone in another part of the country, Boston Computer Exchange can keep your check in an escrow account and pay the buyer only when you are satisfied with your purchase. The company charges the seller 10% of the selling price, but only when a sale is made. Otherwise there is no charge.

Sellers promise that whatever they are selling is in complete working condition, and Computer Exchange president Alex Randell says that in the 10,000 sales that have been organized there have been only about five cases in which the buyer was seriously dissatisfied. In such cases the buyer, seller and Boston Computer Exchange have a three-way telephone conversation and negotiate to (a) undo the deal, (b) have the seller repair the equipment or (c) lower the price.

The Boston Computer Exchange people (there are 12 of them) try to be as helpful as they can in advising buyers about what might suit their needs and telling sellers about going prices. Prices tend to be about 20 to 40% off list price.

Comp-Used, ***85 Rivergate Drive, Wilton, CT 06897. Telephone 203-762-8677.***
Send self-addressed, stamped envelope for a list of sellers and what they are selling in one category, or $9 for a complete listing of all categories.
Comp-Used doesn't sell anything; it acts as a broker between people who are buying and selling computers and peripherals.
Returns: none.
Established 1984.

Tell Comp-Used what you want to buy—mainframe or personal computer, monitor, modem, printer or whatever—and you will be sent a list of everyone who has something to sell in your category, his or her telephone number and the asking price. Or you can get a complete listing in all categories for $9. Most sellers are in the Northeast, according to owner Dan Delmar. For an extra $20 or 1% of the buying price (whichever is greater), when you buy something, you can send Dan Delmar a certified check that he will not release to the seller until you have checked out your purchase. If you have something to sell, for $8 Comp-Used will give you an estimate of what it will fetch, based on prices in the data bank. The estimate is free if you put your unit up for sale with Comp-Used within 30 days.

Another way of finding used equipment is through the small ads in *Computer Shopper.* It also has ads from discount mail-order firms and inventory-reduction ads from firms going out of business or changing their products, so it's a good place to look for bargains. It's on sale at newsstands or available by subscription from: **COMPUTER SHOPPER,** ***407 South Washington Avenue, P.O. Box F, Titusville, FL 32781. Telephone 305-269-3211.***

USER GROUPS

Computer owners get together with other owners of the same brand to exchange information. Through a user group you can save money by buying secondhand machines, exchanging software, buying software at a discount and getting free advice. Find out whether there is a group near you through a local store or the manufacturer of your computer. If there isn't, there are groups around the country producing newsletters with advice, exchange and for-sale columns.

The Boston Computer Society, ***One Center Plaza, Boston, MA 02108. Telephone 617-367-8080.***
Annual membership costs around $30 as I write; ask for up-to-date information.

If you don't have a user group near you, you might be interested in BCS, which says it is the largest organization of its kind in the world and has members in all 50 states and 20 countries. Benefits for far-from-Boston members include a magazine and a monthly newsletter from two user groups of your choice (there are groups for 20 different brands of machines and 4 different special interests such as business and databases). I'm told the newsletters have telephone numbers of people you can call for "support" (advice), which is marvelous if true (although the people are mainly in the Boston area, so calling them involves a long-distance telephone call). You also get access to public-domain software and a bulletin board through your modem.

FABRICS AND FIBERS

FABRICS

Mail and Telephone Sources

New York couturier Shirley Salerno has very generously told me about some favorite discount stores where she and other professionals buy. For outstanding fabrics and prices that are often as much as 50% below those of other sources, try these highly recommended firms.

Art-Max Fabrics, ***250 West 40th Street, New York, NY 10018. Telephone 212-398-0755, 212-398-0754 or 212-398-0756.***
Write only with request for specific samples and prices.
AE, MC, V.
Sells fabrics for women's dresses; specializes in evening and bridal fabrics: satins, swiss embroideries, imported laces, beaded chiffons, metallics.
Returns: no returns on cut fabrics.
Established 1947.

Shirley Salerno describes this store as "three floors crammed with A1-quality fabrics at wonderful discounts." Everything is stocked, including luxury fabrics such as Abrahams silks and cashmeres. The shop is always crowded, mainly with professionals, so it is best to telephone before 10 A.M. Shirley Salerno says she always asks for Marcial Negron, who is especially helpful. She cites bargains such as silk and worsted at half price, exquisite laces at almost half price and tissue faille and French wools at 30% off. When I checked, I found Irish handkerchief linen at 25% off usual U.S. prices, *and* it was in a wider width.

Britex by Mail, ***146 Geary Street, San Francisco, CA 94108. Telephone 415-392-2910.***
Swatches, $2 in the U.S. and Canada.
AE, MC, V.

Sells natural fiber fabrics, mainly silks, wools and cottons.
Minimum order: ½ yard.
Returns: none on cut merchandise.
Established 1935.

Write and ask for samples of whatever fabrics you are looking for. Britex stocks and sells by mail beautiful fabrics at about two-thirds to half the price they'd cost in department stores and regular fabric shops. For instance: silk crepe de chine for $15 when a similar quality cost $22 elsewhere; wool jersey for $10 a yard when it cost $20 elsewhere; all wool tweed for $15, $30 and up elsewhere.

Laces of the World, ***P.O. Box 1118, Bellmore, NY 11710.***
Catalogue, $2.50 (refundable).
Sells lace.
Minimum order $5.
Refunds: money back.
Established 1984.

Lace manufacturers sell to designers and also direct to the public at large discounts. All kinds of polyester laces for underwear, blouses, dresses, wedding dresses and bedspreads are available.

Reekies of Grasmere, ***Old Coach House, Stock Lane, Grasmere, Cumbria, England. Telephone 9665-221.***
(Main listing in Clothes and Shoes section)

Reekies sells hand-woven fabrics but specializes in mohair. Shirley Salerno, who likes this firm a lot, bought beautiful hand-woven mohair here at well under half the U.S. price (under $20 per yard at a time when mohair cost $50 to $100 in the United States).

Thai Silk, ***252(c) State Street, Los Altos, CA 94022. Telephone 415-948-8611.***
Price list, free in the U.S. and Canada.
MC, V.
Sells silks of all kinds and a few imported cottons; new additions: wool gabardine and flannel.
Returns: full refund.
Established 1961.

Deanne Shute imports her own Chinese, Indian and Thai silks and sells them at extra low prices. Couturier Shirley Salerno tells me that discounts are great on beautiful silks from the Orient: brocades, pongees, Indian silk and Thai silk all at big discounts. When, for example, crepe de chine silk was selling for $22 in the stores, it was selling for $10.40 at Thai Silk. Other fabrics, such as cotton and gabardine, are being added.

Utex Trading, ***710 9th Street, Suite 5, Niagara Falls, NY 14301. Telephone 716-282-4887.***
Price list, free in the U.S. and Canada; swatches roughly $3 a set.
Sells imported Chinese silks, blouses, scarves; French dyes for hand painting silk fabrics.
Returns: only on defective merchandise.
Established 1980.

Utex has an enormous collection of silks imported direct from China at very low prices. Silks come in "haute couture" colors and all weights—good for underwear, wedding dresses, even sportswear (there is a wool-silk mixture too). There are also silks for curtains, cushions and wall coverings. The owner, Patrick Au, writes, "We sell to fashion designers and couturiers who in turn service customers with names such as Elizabeth Taylor and the Queen Mother."

Warren of Stafford, ***99 Furnace Avenue, Stafford Springs, CT 06076. Telephone 203-684-2766.***
Catalogue with swatches, $3 (refundable) in the U.S. and Canada.
MC, V.
Sells cashmere, camel hair, fine woolen fabrics.
Returns: money back if within 30 days.
Established 1853.

This old mill makes extraordinarily lovely classic fabrics from imported camel hair and cashmere. Warren has supplied fabrics to the fancier clothing manufacturers for years and has recently started selling directly to the public. Shirley Salerno tells me that the fabrics are first-rate and the savings are big. I checked prices on a couple of fabrics, and they were 10 and 20% lower than those in a New York fabric store.

Fabrics from Abroad

Natural fabrics from abroad cost up to 40% less than similar fabrics bought in the United States. The stores listed here stock superb fabrics, of a quality it's hard to find in this country, and some of the stores are willing to send samples for free.

Cleo Ltd, ***18 Kildare Street, Dublin 2, Ireland. Telephone 1-761421.***
Color brochure and prices, two $1 bills.
Sells clothes and tweeds, yarn to match tweeds.
Returns: credit if goods returned within reasonable time.
Established 1936.

Cleo sells wool fabric with heavy knitting yarn to match in five dyed colors and four natural. I find all the shades unusually handsome. The dyes are brick red, very dark blue, a sort of loden green, a purplish heather and a medium blue. The naturals are a creamy white and three subtle gray-browns.

Dublin Woollen Company, ***Metal Bridge Corner, Dublin, Ireland. Telephone 1-775014.***
Write with a description of what you want for prices and samples.
AE, DC, MC, V.
Sells clothes and pure wool tweed made in Ireland, by the yard.
Returns: money back.
Established 1888.

Cloth merchants since 1888, the owners of this popular shop now sell Irish clothes, "dry goods" and hand-woven tweeds. If you tell them what kind and color of tweed you are looking for, they'll send you swatches. Prices are excellent. When I checked, many 54-inch-wide tweeds cost around $15 a yard.

Kevin and Howlin, ***31 Nassau Street, Dublin 2, Ireland. Telephone 1-770257.***
Write for swatches with a description of what you need.
MC, V.
Sells tweeds by the yard for men and women, many specially woven for Kevin and Howlin.
Refunds: none.

This is a very well-known store that sells traditional-style tweeds, mainly for men's clothing but also for women's.

Anne Thomas Fabrics, ***274 Canongate, Royal Mile, Edinburgh EH8 8AA, Scotland. Telephone 31-557-1503.***
Samples, two $1 bills or equivalent International Reply Coupons.
AE, MC, V.
Sells natural fabrics: cotton, linen, silk, wool, etc.
Returns: credit.
Established 1978.

When her children started school, Anne Thomas, who had always loved sewing and fabrics, decided to open a fabric store. Her small store is on the Royal Mile, Edinburgh's most historic street, so she has lots of foreign customers and is used to mail order (a customer in Australia recently sent a gift of cashmere to her sister in Japan). She says that American customers most often buy 100% wool crepe, silk and wool mixtures made in Scotland, as well as Irish linen that she gets from the manufacturer used by Perry Ellis and Ralph Lauren. When I compared prices, her Moygashel linen (in 17 different colors) was 40% off U.S. prices.

CLERY'S and PETER JONES (in General section) sell fabrics and will send swatches. Prices are especially good on European natural fibers (for instance, when I checked, they were selling Irish linen at about half the U.S. price).

SEWING SUPPLIES

Newark Dressmaker Supply, ***6473 Ruch Road, P.O. Box 2448, Lehigh Valley, PA 18001. Telephone 215-837-7500.***
Free 44-page catalogue.
MC, V.
Sells everything needed for making clothes, dolls, drapery and upholstery; a few fabrics for clothes by Springmaid, Dan River and Desire Mills.
Returns: money back if merchandise returned within two weeks.
Established 1981.

Newark has a catalogue that is invaluable for anyone who sews. It displays anything you might need for sewing crafts, clothes or curtains. Apart from a much wider choice in all the basics, such as needles, bobbins, elastics and fasteners of all sorts, this firm sells pressing accessories, name labels and measuring tools, not to mention tapes, appliqués and interfacings. I checked prices, and on Coats and Clark's thread prices were the same as at my local Woolworth, but on the other things I checked, such as elastics, zippers and needles, prices were up to 60% off. Don't miss this one.

KNITTING YARNS

Here is a list of some of the more unusual yarns and their characteristics.

Alpaca. Soft hair of the South American animal of the same name. Available in natural shades—golden beiges, grays, browns and subtly dyed Peruvian shades. Wears especially well, as it doesn't "pill."

Angora. Fluffy wool from the Angora rabbit. It is wonderfully soft, even nicer than cashmere. Angora tends to shed, must be washed carefully and must not be dry-cleaned with heat.

Aran. Yellowish cream sheepswool. For hundreds of years it has been used for fishermen's sweaters. Untouched by chemistry, it is naturally waterproof.

Camel. From the fine down wool of the camel's undercoat. Warm, soft and everlasting, it tends to stretch when worn and so should be knitted tightly.

Cashmere. Soft down from the undercoat of the Kashmir goat. It gets softer each time it is washed but is liable to mat if it is not washed in lukewarm water.

Cotton was forgotten when man-made fibers hogged the market, but it is now fashionable. Modern Turkish industries, Italy and England are producing fine-quality cotton yarns.

Lopi. From Icelandic sheep "intermarried" with the Merino sheep of the North African Atlas Mountains, originally brought home from Europe by Icelandic spice traders. It is the longest and softest sheepswool. Because of its quality, it does not have to be twisted spun but is "straight laid" spun. It excels in every quality needed for skiing, sailing and outdoor knitwear.

Mohair. Long silky fiber from the Angora goat. Stronger and less expensive than angora, it does not wrinkle or "pill," but will mat if rubbed when washed.

Shetland. Sheep on the Shetland Islands are a hybrid of native-grown and Merino sheep. The Merino sheep were said to have come from the shipwrecked boats of the Spanish Armada, where they were kept on board as a meat supply. The climate and island conditions make Shetland sheepswool a superior blend, and the dyed shades of Celtic-Viking-Byzantine origin are outstanding. Available in two-ply (knits to three-ply), lace-ply and one-ply for featherweight lace knitting.

Care of Knits

Two American yarn firms strongly recommend washing woolens in the liquid soaps used for dishwashing, such as Ivory. They say that these are better than cold-water products advertised as being especially for wool because they contain no harsh ingredients and are easy to rinse out.

Silk and "hair" (alpaca, angora, camel and cashmere) have a tendency to stretch, especially if knitted loosely. Never pull knits made from silk or hair out of the water so that the water drags them down—squeeze *before* lifting out. Wash very gently, with no rubbing, in lukewarm water (no sudden changes of temperature) and dry flat on a towel.

Mail and Telephone Sources

Prices of really beautiful yarns are lower outside the United States, especially in the traditional wool-spinning countries. The most amazing buy I know of is the Shetland wool from Jamieson & Smith, which costs, after postage, half of what Shetland normally costs in the United States and a third off the price at U.S. discount stores. Shetland is a lovely basic wool that can be used for any pattern that doesn't call for one of the exotic yarns. Aran yarn from Britain also costs half the U.S. price, and Lopi from Iceland costs half of the usual U.S. price and a third off the discount price. You can save on other yarns by buying from B and M in New York or whichever of the foreign stores has the best price on the yarn you want.

It is easy to buy from abroad. These firms are all set up with sample cards or catalogues, and they already have mail-order customers around the world. Furthermore, a knitting Washingtonian, Judy Smith, tells me she has ordered about enough yarn from Britain to start a shop, yet hasn't been charged duty once.

B and M Yarn Company, ***151 Essex Street, New York, NY 10002. Telephone 212-475-6380.***
Write or telephone 9:30 A.M. to 4:30 P.M. on weekdays for specific prices.
Sells embroidery and macramé supplies and knitting yarns.

Returns: money back on yarn left over from a knitting project, if untouched.
Established 1954.

One American source that matches, or beats, many foreign prices on exotic yarns. B and M isn't as geared for mail order as some, but if you ask for samples, Miss Edith will carefully stick pieces of yarn and write out prices on a piece of paper for you.

Briggs and Little Woollen Mills, ***York Mills, Harvey Station, New Brunswick, E0H 1H0, Canada. Telephone 506-366-5438.***
Free yarn samples.
Manufactures and sells pure wool yarns for hand knitting or weaving.
Returns: money back if skeins are unopened.
Established 1857.

A small collection of pure wool yarns for knitting and weaving, including some pretty heathery yarns, are sold. Prices are very low—below U.S. discount (and about the same as Jamieson & Smith's). The firm was recommended by Judy Smith.

Creativity Yarns, ***15 Downing Street, Farnham, Surrey, GU9 7PB, England. Telephone 252-714856.***
Price list, three $1 bills or equivalent International Reply Coupons; complete samples, $18 (refundable upon return).
Sells yarns by well-known British manufacturers Emu, Jaeger, Sunbeam, Wendy and its own yarns spun to order.
Returns: money back.
Established 1976.

A supreme source of luxury yarns, Sylvia and Peter Owen specialize in British-spun natural yarns and have an abundant stock of rarer yarns, such as angora, camel, cashmere and mohair. They also have many silks and cottons and sturdier British wools, such as Aran, Cheviot and Jacob. The stock changes and there are glamorous specials.

The Owens have annoyed me by being slow about sending me samples and by not answering my questions, but I hope they'll treat proper customers better.

Holmfirth Wools Ltd, ***Briggate, Windhill, Shipley, Yorkshire, BD18 2BS, England. Telephone 274-586943 (24-hour service).***
September catalogue and sample cards, two $1 bills or equivalent International Reply Coupons.
MC, V.
Sells woolen and synthetic knitting yarns and patterns.
Returns: merchandise that is not satisfactory may be returned for credit within three months.
Established 1964.

Holmfirth has a tidy and easy-to-use catalogue with bright yarn samples (baby wools, wool-synthetic mixtures, and plain wool—no exotics), illustrated knitting patterns and reasonable prices. It sells buttons in matching colors. This is a good source for anyone who likes synthetics and one-stop shopping.

Jamieson & Smith, ***90 North Road, Lerwick, Shetland Isles, 2E1 0PQ, Scotland. Telephone 595-3579.***
Free sample card; three $1 bills or equivalent International Reply Coupons for airmail.
Sells one-, two- and three-ply Shetland wool.
Returns: money back if wool returned immediately.
Established 1952.

An absolutely marvelous direct source of Shetland wool at the lowest prices. Samples in over 200 colors and four weights are pasted into a handy booklet. Jamieson & Smith was found and recommended by Judy Smith, who knows about lots of sources but says that it is number one on her list. Her (multiple) orders arrive by surface mail in five to six weeks, and she has never been charged duty.

Snowflake Kits, ***N- 1315 Nesoya, Norway. Telephone 472-847078.***
Children's sweater leaflet, $1 bill or equivalent International Reply Coupons; complete catalogue, $5 bill.
Sells kits to make traditional Norwegian sweaters.
Returns: "faulty or wrong deliveries (virtually nonexistent) we replace at no cost and dispose of the yarn or kit in the country of destination" to avoid postage costs.
Established 1969.

With Snowflake's kits you can make traditional Norwegian-design, snowflake-patterned sweaters in "the very best, soft and lovely" Norwegian wool with pewter buttons and clasps. Directions are in English. Snowflake says that long-time customers have learned from experience that "no other sweater lasts so well, retaining both shape and bright colors—even after years of wear and washing." The catalogue shows forty models, for adults and children. Prices of kits for sweaters for children are mostly $30 to $36 as I write.

St. John's Knitting Wool, ***P.O. Box 55, 55 Parkside Mills, Bradford West, Yorkshire, BD5 8DZ, England. Telephone 274-729031 (24-hour service).***
12-page color catalogue and samples, $1 bill (surface mail).
Sells woolen and synthetic yarns for hand and machine knitting.
Returns: credit given on receipt of returns.
Established 1964.

Another easy-to-use catalogue, offering a small, practical collection of yarns (mostly pure wool) for family knitting. Everything you need is sold here: needles, matching buttons and rather nice patterns. Inexpensive wool fabrics by the yard are also available (solid colors and tartans only), as is yarn on the cone at rock-bottom prices.

Texere Yarns, ***College Mill, Barkerend Road, Bradford, BD3 9AQ, England. Telephone 274-722191.***
Prices and samples, two $1 bills or equivalent International Reply Coupons.
Sells yarns for knitting and weaving.
Returns: none.

Texere used to send messy sheets for weavers but has been adding tidy cards with samples for knitters. The yarns are often special offers and odd lots, with surprises such as bouclés, cotton-silk mixes, mohairs and spun silks. Prices vary from good to terrific. Texere is always worth trying for the very lowest prices, but only if you are going to buy a lot, as its lowest mailing charge to the United States is $14 for any quantity up to 11 pounds.

Do-It-Yourself Designer Sweaters

Coulter Studios, ***118 East 59th Street, New York, NY 10022. Telephone 212-421-8083.***
Send sweater or photograph and measurements for a price quote.
Sells yarns and custom-made knitting patterns.
Returns: money back on yarn returned with receipt; no returns on custom-made patterns, but patterns are guaranteed so Coulter will change pattern and help with problems on knitwear that is unsatisfactory.
Established 1975.

If you long for designer knits but don't want to pay the astronomical prices, you can knit it yourself. The more expensive the original, the more you can tell yourself you are saving—several hundred dollars if you are copying one of the really expensive sweaters, the ones that cost $400 and up.

Coulter will make you a knitting pattern based on any magazine photograph, drawing or actual original. Mail whichever you have with your measurements; Coulter will tell you how much the pattern will cost and also send you suitable yarn swatches (you must buy the yarn from Coulter). As I write, patterns cost $10 to $25, depending on the complexity.

FOOD

Soft cheeses made simply and quickly with instructions from *Cheesemaking Made Easy* by Ricky and Robert Carroll. When a lactic cheese of the Boursin type cost about $5.16 a pound in a store, the same amount cost about $2.60 to make at home (the price includes rennet and starter culture from New England Cheesemaking Supply Co. and a gallon of milk bought locally). Photo by Tommy Elder.

FOOD

FOOD CO-OPS

One way to save money on food is to join (or start) a food-buying club. According to Art Rasch of the Truman College Co-op Center, you can save an average of 20 to 30% on food bills by buying wholesale. Foods that you can really save on include fruits and vegetables, which cost half the retail price bought by the crate. In fact, fruits and vegetables are main attractions because they are almost always much fresher bought this way. Cheese and meat can be bought at about 15% off; bread and cookies, about 20% off.

Co-ops present other advantages. Many people find shopping with a group of friends and neighbors more agreeable than shopping at a supermarket. People who have no supermarket nearby prefer buying everything in one place over schlepping around to different stores. Retired people living alone (who are increasingly forming co-ops) like to order canned foods in smaller sizes.

But clubs are definitely for sociable rather than busy people. Members have to put time—probably about one to four hours a month—into doing such tasks as ordering, pricing, picking up food, sorting, cashiering and distributing any extra food. Although as families increasingly have two working parents, with little time for food shopping, that is changing: clubs are becoming less time-consuming, buying in bigger quantities and meeting less often (perhaps once or twice a month).

If you don't have a food club near you, you can always start one. You'll need about 10 large families or 20 families of three or four before you can comfortably buy in wholesale quantities. Bigger clubs will not necessarily get lower prices, but they will be able to provide a much wider choice of foods. Small clubs usually stick to popular basics that everyone wants. You do need one or more places to distribute the food, often a basement or garage in someone's home or else the public area in an apartment house, a day-care center, a school or a church.

Buying clubs are just one kind of food co-op. There are also co-op retail stores with paid help. You may not have to help out at these professionally run storefronts, but savings at them are smaller, about 10 to 15%. There are also supermarket co-ops, often started to service areas that the chains have left; at these there are no savings, but extra consumer services and information are provided.

To find out whether there are any food co-ops in your area try the Chamber of Commerce or contact Central States Co-operatives, the organization that coordinates the co-op wholesalers. It can put you in touch with your nearest wholesaler, who in turn can give you the names of your closest co-ops. Wholesalers tend to know about smaller groups that are not so easy to trace. **CENTRAL STATES CO-OPERATIVES,** ***2412 University Avenue SE, Minneapolis, MN 55414. Telephone 612-376-8357.***

The National Co-operative Business Association can also help you to find local co-ops and can give you general advice on setting one up. Call or write to: **NATIONAL CO-OPERATIVE BUSINESS ASSOCIATION,** ***Box 8293, Ann Arbor, MI 48107. Telephone 313-665-2667.***

The best source of information on starting a food club is the Co-op Center at Truman College. The center specializes in training people to start co-ops, and the director, Arthur Rasch, meets with groups in Chicago and gives free telephone consultations. He's very helpful. The center also has pamphlets for sale. Contact: ***Arthur Rasch,*** **TRUMAN COLLEGE CO-OP CENTER,** ***1145 West Wilson, Chicago, IL 60640. Telephone 312-878-1700.***

For pamphlets and brochures on how to set up and organize a co-op, ask for a publications list from **NASCO,** ***Box 7715, Ann Arbor, MI 48107, telephone 313-663-0889.***

MAIL AND TELEPHONE FOOD SOURCES

Zabar's, ***2245 Broadway, New York, NY 10024. Telephone: questions, 212-787-2000; orders, 800-221-3347.***

(Main listing under Kitchen Equipment)

Zabar's is famous for its overwhelming selection of exotic foods at reasonable prices (cheeses, for instance, are generally 20 to 30% cheaper than at stores such as Bloomingdale's). Unfortunately, Zabar's ships only a few of its foods, so only New Yorkers can benefit from the low prices on most of its goodies. There are luxurious exceptions though—caviar (Zabar's and Macy's go into a much-publicized price war every year before Christmas and New Year's) and smoked salmon are always good buys here. Other things, such as their delicious first-pressing California olive oil, vinegars, mustards, salamis and chocolates, may be worth your while, depending on your local prices and shipping costs.

Natural Foods

Natural food prices are often 20 to 50% lower at these mail-order firms than at local health food stores. (There are exceptions, however; price differences aren't big, for instance, on bottled cooking oils, juices and ketchups.) The problem is the cost of shipping. It really pays to buy in bulk from these companies, either with friends or just to store at home. For instance, when I checked, if I had bought 7 cans of Walnut Acres clam chowder direct from Walnut Acres instead of my local health food supermarket, I would have saved a pesky 74 cents. But if I had bought 24 cans, I would have saved a very respectable $11 after paying postage. Incidentally, I would have saved $11.72 if I had bought 24 cans of Walnut Acres clam chowder by mail instead of Pepperidge Farm's clam chowder soup at my local supermarket.

Country Life Natural Foods, ***Box 86 D, Chisholm, MN 55719. Telephone 218-254-4286.***
Spring and fall catalogue, $1 ($2 in Canada).
Sells natural grains, flours, nuts, fruits, juices, cereals.
Minimum order $200.
Returns: credit on request only.
Established 1978.

Country Life has a basic list of nuts and nut butters, dried fruits, beans, grains, flours, juices and honeys. The prices I checked were around 15% lower than those at the other stores listed here, but you must order in bulk (nuts, for instance, come only in 30-pound boxes). This firm is good for a group of families that wants to stock up.

Jaffe Brothers, ***P.O. Box 636, Valley Center, CA 92082. Telephone 619-749-1133.***
Brochure, free in the U.S. and Canada.
MC, V.
Sells dried fruit, nuts, grains, seeds, beans, oils.
Returns: money back if merchandise returned within ten days.
Established 1948.

This small business, run by two brothers, one wife and one son, sells unsprayed and some organically grown nuts (including macadamia nuts in the shell), dried fruits, whole-grain cereals and nut butters (peanut, almond and macadamia). It's a good place to get smallish quantities of nuts and dried fruits—prices are low, and you can buy in quantities of 5 pounds.

Walnut Acres, ***Dept. CC, Penns Creek, PA 17862. Telephone 717-837-0601.***
44-page color catalogue, 50 cents (85 cents in Canada).
MC, V.

Sells very wide choice of natural and organic foods.
Returns: money back but notify Walnut Acres within two weeks of receiving order.
Established 1946.

A wonderful resource for anyone who is interested in foods grown without pesticides and treated without preservatives, Walnut Acres was started by an ex–mathematics teacher and his wife, Paul and Betty Keene, who got interested in agriculture when teaching in an Indian school run by Mahatma Gandhi. On returning to America, they went to an organic farm school and bought Walnut Acres in 1945.

The farm has flourished, a friendly and informative catalogue has appeared and expanded and this is now the top source for an enormous variety of naturally grown foods. Furthermore, the Walnut Acres people are not just commercially minded but have an interest in nutrition and agriculture. The Walnut Acres Foundation does nonprofit work, contributing to and raising contributions for world hunger, child sponsorship and similar groups. A couple of pages of some of the catalogues report on these interests.

Besides mixes, breads, cakes, cereals, dried fruits, nuts, juices, honeys and jams—a dizzying choice in each category—there are canned vegetables, meats and soups. By buying carefully, if you live in parts of the country where shipping costs won't be too high, you should be able to save around 20% off local health food store prices.

Customer relations are good too. Last year I bought some olive oil from Walnut Acres that seemed to me (and my ma) to have a rather odd taste. After six months of dithering about whether to use it or not, I decided to return it. Walnut Acres turned up trumps, refunding my money and agreeing that the oil "tasted bad," while gently pointing out that oil should be kept for only three or four months and asking me to notify them within two weeks in future.

Make-It-Yourself Cheese

New England Cheesemaking Supply Company, ***Box 8549, Ashfield, MA 01330. Telephone 413-628-3808.***
Catalogue, $1 in the U.S. and Canada.
MC, V.
Sells home cheese-making equipment.
Returns: money back.
Established 1978.

Ricky Carroll of New England Cheesemaking says that 1 gallon of milk makes about 1 pound of hard cheese, and about 2 pounds of soft. Cheese lovers who live near a farm and can get cheap milk can save lots by making their own cheeses. Soft cheeses such as mozzarella, feta, cottage and Boursin types (which can be flavored with garlic and herbs) are easy to make. They require no special equipment (just cheesecloth and thermometer), take only about as long as it takes to heat milk and can be eaten after draining on the kitchen counter for a few hours. Hard cheeses such as cheddar, Swiss, Gouda and the Welsh Caerphilly need more equipment: a cheese press and a cool basement or an old refrigerator (often bought secondhand). But with about four hours' work you can make up to 10 pounds of hard cheese (it has to age for 60 days to develop good flavor). Cheeses of the Camembert and Brie variety need a special cavelike environment for ripening and are therefore only for fanatics or professionals.

If you are interested in trying cheese making for yourself, New England Cheesemaking is just the place you need. Bob and Ricky Carroll, the owners, started out by making cheese with extra milk from their own goats. Then they went to England, France and Holland to learn more and eventually progressed to teaching cheese making, writing books, publishing a newsletter and selling the equipment and ingredients. Lots of help and information here for beginners.

Smoked Salmon

Smoked salmon from Scotland (not "Scotch-smoked," which can be any kind of salmon smoked in the Scotch manner) is generally considered better than Salmon from Norway, Nova Scotia and the Pacific. The best Scotch salmon available in the United States is very expensive, and often it is bred on farms—salmon connoisseurs sneer at the texture of farmed salmon. George Campbell sells wild salmon.

Smoked salmon ordered direct from Scotland is less expensive than the best salmon bought in the United States—*how* much less depends on the strength of the dollar. You can stock up ahead of time, as the salmon freezes beautifully. You can also have it mailed as a gift (I have never been charged duty).

George Campbell, ***18 Stafford Street, Edinburgh, EH3 7BE, Scotland. Telephone 31-225-7507.***
Free price list.
Sells smoked salmon and other smoked fish.
Returns: money back if fish delayed or lost.
Established 1872.

An absolutely extraordinary buy is smoked salmon direct from George Campbell, "By appointment to Her Majesty the Queen Suppliers of Fish and Poultry." These fishmongers smoke salmon caught specially for them (they don't deal with wholesalers), and it is done exquisitely (I have ordered it myself).

I compared prices with regular New York prices (not with low special-sale prices), and this is what I found: If you buy it unsliced, after postage, the salmon costs about the same as the cheapest western or Nova Scotia smoked salmon available in New York; and it costs half the price of the best smoked salmon in New York. If you order the salmon already sliced from Campbell, savings aren't as great, but they are still pretty good.

Mermaid Fish Supplies, ***Clachan, Isle of North Uist, Outer Hebrides, PA82 5ET, Scotland. Telephone 8764-209.***
Free price card.
Sells peat-smoked salmon.
Minimum order ¼ pound.
Returns: money back; "only value of fish would be compensated—not postage and packing."
Established 1976.

I discovered this peat-smoked salmon at the Osprey Hotel, Kingussie. The Osprey owners, Duncan and Pauline Reeves, tried ten different oatmeals before choosing their porridge, so you can imagine how carefully they chose their salmon. But unless you are as discerning as the Reeves, you may not be able to tell the difference. To me, this salmon from the Outer Hebrides simply tasted liked very good smoked salmon, perhaps rather more richly flavored than the blander cures I have tasted in New York.

Spices and Flavors

The Spice House, ***1102 North 3rd Street, Milwaukee, WI 53203. Telephone: questions, 414-272-1888; orders, 414-272-0977.***
21-page spice price list, $1 in the U.S. and Canada; flavors price list, free.
Sells spices, herbs, seasonings and flavors.
Returns: 30-day return policy, no questions asked.
Established 1957.

Spices and herbs from the Spice House cost under half what they cost in supermarkets, if you buy them 4 ounces at a time. Besides that, you'll be buying from a specialist source, with a wide choice of first-rate herbs and spices (I buy saffron here at $1.75 a gram, whereas it costs $3 to $9.95 a gram in regular shops). The owners, Bill and Ruth Penzey, say that they "work hard and hold to old-fashioned ways"—mixing by hand and grinding small lots in stone mills. The price list includes descriptions and helpful background information on the different spices sold.

Nuts and Chocolates

Durey Libby, ***Box 345, Carlstadt, NJ 07072. Telephone 201-939-2775.***
Price list, free in the U.S. and Canada.
MC, V.
Sells raw, roasted, unsalted and salted nuts.
Minimum order 3 pounds.
Returns: exchanges if customers complain.
Established 1950.

This fruit and nut wholesaler, which has a mail-order division, has the lowest prices I have found on nuts—they are mostly 30 to 50% below supermarket prices for raw nuts, even after you pay postage, and about 25% below supermarket prices for roasted salted nuts. Nuts come in 3-, 4- and 5-pound cans that are rather ugly, so they are not much good as gifts but are perfectly fine for home consumption.

J. Wolsk and Company, ***87 Ludlow Street, New York, NY 10002. Telephone 212-475-7946.***
Telephone for prices preferably Monday or Tuesday.
Sells dried nuts and fruits, chocolates by Droste, Lindt, Perugina, others.
Returns: credit given on returned goods.
Established 1940.

A recent *New York Times* write-up recommended this store for low prices and noted, "The quality of Wolsk's roasted nuts is very high, as indeed it is for the shop's raw nuts and sweets."

Nuts from Wolsk cost 35 to 40% less than at my local fruit and nut shop. It is well worth buying here if the nuts are a gift that will be mailed anyway, or if you can buy in quantities big enough to offset shipping costs. Seven pounds of roasted cashews plus postage, for instance, cost 25% less here than at my local fruit and nut shop—$39.40 here and $49.70 at the nut shop when I checked. Superior imported chocolates are also sold at a discount; Perugina Baci, for instance, are almost 40% less than in my neighborhood.

Coffee

Zabar's, ***2245 Broadway, New York, NY 10024. Telephone: questions, 212-787-2000; orders, 800-221-3347.***
(Main listing under Kitchen Equipment)

Zabar's imports and roasts its own coffee beans (and has an excellent decaffeinated expresso roast). Prices are about $1 a pound below the average in New York. There is a 5-pound minimum and high postage charge, but buying from Zabar's may be worthwhile for you if coffee prices are especially high in your area.

Tea

Whittard and Company, ***111 Fulham Road, London SW3, England. Telephone 1-589-4261.***
Free price list.
AE, DC, MC, V.
Sells coffee and tea.
Returns: money back; but "our teas and coffees obviously deteriorate after a while, so returns after four to six weeks, though dealt with efficiently, are thought to be a 'try on.' "
Established 1886.

You can save 50% on tea. This reputable shop blends fine teas that cost half the price of Twinings' even after you pay for postage. I buy here with a credit card. Whittard was originally recommended to me by an enthusiastic U.S. customer who loves its dozens of teas from China, India and Sri Lanka and its coffees from the best farms in the best places "at their peak and 100% true." As the customer points out, the company handles mailings like "masters of old" and sells to the world's most "respected select."

Make-It-Yourself Tofu

Mountain Ark Trading Company, ***120 S. East Avenue, Fayetteville, AR 72701. Telephone 501-442-7191; orders only, 800-643-8909.***
Catalogue, $1.
MC, V.
Sells whole foods by Mitoku and others, a very good supply of Japanese ingredients, some cookware.
Established 1982.

Mountain Ark, among many other things, sells soybeans and the coagulant nigari, the two ingredients you need to make tofu.

Soyfoods Center, ***P.O. Box 234, Lafayette, CA 94549. Telephone 415-283-2991.***
In the U.S. and Canada, send long self-addressed, stamped envelope for price list.
Sells books on making tofu.
Returns: credit if merchandise returned in good condition.
Established 1976.

To *really* save money on food, eat tofu. Tofu is made by pressing soybeans, is used in Chinese and Japanese cooking and is a wonderful protein food—it has minimal calories, and is very inexpensive. It is even cheaper if you make your own (a third to half the price of store-bought tofu). It is also cleaner (tofu is usually sold from water-filled basins into which customers dip their hands). Owner Bill Shurtleff sells copies of his own book *The Book of Tofu,* which Craig Claiborne says is the best book he knows on tofu making. Besides instructions it has 500 recipes.

Make-It-Yourself Drinks

Beer

As the Berkeley-based firm Wine and the People says, "Home brewing is so easy these days that we don't understand why every beer drinker isn't doing it." You save money: homemade American-style beer costs about half what store-bought costs, and imported-style costs about one third of the price of store-bought. As I write, imported beers generally cost 80 cents to $1 a bottle (plus tax) to buy, yet imported-type beer costs only about 20 to 31 cents a bottle to make. You can make a tastier brew with a good hoppy, malty flavor and without the corn or rice that American brewers use to cut beer for what some call a "lighter" flavor (and others call the "carbonated horsewater" flavor). If you make your own beer, you also make sure the stuff you drink has no coloring or artificial preservatives—American brewers are suspected of using additives.

You need a minimum of equipment for beer making. The stores listed below sell everything you need and can advise you on what to get. The method is simple: You boil water, hops and malt extract on the stove, strain it and add yeast. Leave it to ferment for about three months. After that, you siphon the clear beer of the yeast dregs, add sugar for carbonation and bottle. Two weeks later you can drink it.

Wine

A friend of mine who loves wine and has a wife and three (grown) children who all love wine makes his own in order to save money. He makes a just drinkable bottle from juice concentrate that costs him between $1 and $2 a bottle. He and his family drink it happily as is, but if he wants to posh it up a bit for friends, he mixes it with Côte du Rhône or some other robust wine.

Wine making need not be much more complicated than beer making. If you make wine from concentrated grape juice, you can make 5 gallons in a 14-inch-diameter tub you keep in the closet. Making the wine involves mixing the ingredients, "racking" (siphoning) the mixture twice and bottling it. If you want to make a better wine, you can use real grapes, in which case the quality of the wine depends on the quality of the grapes you buy and how much time and trouble you take over it. The stores listed below claim that with whole grapes and practice you can make wines that are as good as professionally made $20 wines. The grapes cost slightly less than concentrate, if you can find them locally, but you do have to invest about $200 in a grape crusher and a press to make 5-gallon batches of wine (or about $500 for equipment to make quantities of up to 200 gallons).

Fresh wine juice grapes can be bought from about September 10 through the end of October from wholesalers, mainly in the East and in cities such as Detroit, Chicago and Pittsburgh. Frozen wine juice grapes can be bought from Great Fermentations and Wine and the People. Orders are taken in August, and grapes are distributed in November.

Great Fermentations, ***87C Larkspur, San Rafael, CA 94901. Telephone 415-459-2520.***
16-page brochure, free in the U.S. and Canada. Noirot information brochure, free. AE, MC, V.
Sells beer- and wine-making equipment, liqueur and soda drink flavors, vinegar cultures.
Returns: money back.
Established 1978.

Great Fermentations has a nice, simple brochure that lists kits for beginners and ingredients for inexpensive liqueurs and soda pops. It has a page of advice on how to make fruit wine—almost free if you have fruit trees. The company also ships frozen grapes and grape juice (order in August).

E. C. Kraus Wine and Beer Making Supplies, ***9001 E 24 Highway, P.O. Box 7850, Independence, MO 64053. Telephone 816-254-7448.***
Free 16-page catalogue.
MC, V.
Sells home beer-, wine-, liqueur- and soda pop–making supplies.
Returns: "full refund if we made error, refund less 15% restocking charge if customer made error."
Established 1965.

This catalogue of supplies has an extremely helpful booklist for beginners. The booklist actually describes the how-to books sold (other catalogues just list them). The owner, Mr. Kraus, advises any novice to start by buying *First Steps in Wine Making,* which, among other things, tells what equipment is needed.

Ridgewood Wine and Beer Supplies for the Home Brewer, ***60-48 Linden Street, Ridgewood, NY 11385. Telephone 718-456-4329.***
Free price list.
MC, V.
Sells equipment, supplies and books for making wine, beer and soda.
Minimum order $10.
Returns: credit minus 15%.
Established 1978.

This small firm has a sketchy and somewhat primitive catalogue, but owner James Miegel is very helpful to customers. If you telephone with a problem, he'll try to help with advice. During the grape season (September-October), he sells fresh grapes to local home wine makers.

Wine and the People, ***948 3rd Street, Napa, CA 94559. Telephone 707-252-9555.***
30-page catalogue, 75 cents ($1 in Canada), in February and August.
MC, V.
Sells wine-making supplies.
Returns: none except for defective merchandise, which will be replaced if returned immediately.
Established 1970.

At the top of the scale is Wine and the People, catering to serious hobbyists and small commercial vineyards. It is run by Peter Brehm, once a Peace Corps worker, now a wine afficionado.

For wine makers, Wine and the People ships via UPS ready-pressed grape juice in 5-gallon quantities for Riesling and Gewürztraminer wines. It also provides grapes from the better vineyards (from the Stags Leap area of the Napa Valley, for instance), which it says are far superior to the varieties normally available to the home wine maker. Orders are taken from July through September (there is a 125-pound minimum), and the grapes are delivered frozen in November. Peter Brehm says that freezing grapes in no way harms the wine. Indeed, wines made from his frozen Chardonnay grapes and from his Pinot Noirs have won "Best of Show" awards at American Wine Society conventions.

GARDENING

Hybrid tea rose "Neue Revue," created and sold by W. Kordes' Sohne, West Germany. When the U.S. price was $7.85 per bush, the W. Kordes' Sohne price was $3.06.

Narcissus variety "Amor." When a typical price for 25 bulbs was $22.97, the price at Peter De Jager Bulb Company was $14.50. When a typical price for 100 was $84.95, the price at Peter De Jager was $40.

GARDENING

By Peter Schneider

When buying for the garden, you can have everything—price, quality and service. Peter Schneider, an experienced amateur gardener, has written this section. He has chosen the firms listed below for their excellent prices and stock and good service. You will be able to get almost anything you want at prices that can reach 65% off prices at other sources, both local and mail-order.

However, there are a few exceptions. One is plant specialties (dahlias, orchids and sedums, for instance). The leading growers offer such variety and quality that serious collectors would be foolish to order from anywhere else, even though prices at the leading specialized nurseries are not low.

Another thing not worth buying by mail is granular lawn and garden fertilizer. Because of shipping costs, you'd do better to buy this at a local discount center.

Seasonal Price Reductions

Many garden centers have fresh seed at a discount in January and February—we have found Burpee seeds at 50% off. But remember that the selection at garden center seed racks is puny compared to the choice in catalogues.

Around June all unsold seeds are routinely discounted at excellent savings. Most seeds can be safely stored in a cool, dry place for a year or more.

Watch for potted nursery stock to be discounted slightly in July and significantly in August. But there may be a reason why these items remain unsold (an outdated variety, a sickly plant), and no one saves money by buying poor quality.

Fertilizers go on and off discount all summer, often as part of national sales campaigns. Watch the local newspaper's garden section for announcements, and when there are sales be sure to stock up. Fertilizer will keep indefinitely so long as it is dry.

Many garden centers clear out all chemicals each October. Be cautious of compounds that will not keep (such as benomyl) and never store any liquid chemical where it could freeze.

NURSERIES

General

Buying nursery stock by mail is advantageous not only because you save money but also because there is a much wider variety to choose from and, if you buy from a reliable nursery, a stronger likelihood that trees will live and grow.

Blackthorne Gardens, ***48 Quincy Street, Holbrook, MA 02343-1898. Telephone 617-767-0308.***
Catalogue in July, $2.
Sells bulbs, lilies, small fruits, perennials.
Returns: replacement to half purchase price if productivity not satisfactory.
Established 1957.

Although Blackthorne Gardens is sometimes grouped with the well-known nurseries Wayside Gardens and White Flower Farm as a firm catering to a clientele with grounds instead of yards and employees to do the gardening, its prices are actually quite reasonable—often 30% below Burpee's and as much as 45% below Wayside's. Blackthorne has an outstanding selection of all kinds of lilies, one of the very few lists of *named* tree peonies still published, Japanese iris, assorted perennials and small fruits.

Royal W. Bemis, the proprietor, has devoted a lifetime to popularizing clematis, an easy-to-grow and greatly rewarding plant that is not nearly so widely grown in this country as it deserves to be. Mr. Bemis's enthusiasm is infectious, making his one of the best catalogues for bringing spring to life on a cold wintery night. It is hard to resist ordering from the Blackthorne catalogue, and when stock finally arrives with the spring it will invariably be first-rate. This is a superior source for nearly everything it chooses to carry.

Krider Nurseries, ***P.O. Box 29, Middlebury, IN 46540. Telephone 219-825-5714.***
Free 32-page catalogue with some color in January. Free flyer in August.
MC, V.
Sells plants, shrubs, trees.
Returns: money back if returned immediately; otherwise see catalogue.
Established 1896.

Krider is a general, nonspecialist nursery with a wide variety of plants at very low prices. Most of what Burpee offers in the way of shade trees and shrubbery can be found here at 40% savings. Other examples: at the time of writing, Krider had the outstanding new dwarf Korean lilac Miss Kim for $4, while the well-known Wayside Gardens was charging $11.25; and Krider had a 2- to 3-foot specimen of the beautiful Rivers Purple-leaved beech for $13.45, while Wayside Gardens was charging $37. The firm lists both old favorites and well-tested new introductions and is an excellent alternative for people new to gardening or anyone, such as the owner of a new garden, who wants to construct a complete and varied (although not exotic) landscape at a minimal price. Quality and service are very good.

Note: you receive 75 cents worth of merchandise of your choice for each $5 you spend on orders of $15 or more during January and February only.

Park Seed Company, ***Cokesbury Road, Greenwood, SC 29647. Telephone 803-374-3341.***
Free flower and vegetable catalogue in December, free fall flower catalogue in July.
AE, MC, V.
Sells bulbs, plants, seeds, garden accessories.
Returns: money back.
Established 1868.

It is a poorly kept secret but still not common knowledge that Wayside Gardens is now owned by Park Seed. So although Park seeds are no great bargain, gardeners can get Wayside quality at Park prices through the Park nursery catalogue. (I don't think that Park honors separate requests for the nursery catalogue, but even the smallest order from the Park seed catalogue will bring it to your door.)

Park offers only a fraction of Wayside's stock, but if it has what you want, you can take advantage of considerable savings. Perennials through the two catalogues are fully equal in size and quality, yet they are consistently 20% cheaper through Park (and Park charges a third of what Wayside charges for postage and handling). The only difference is that orders from Park don't get the "custom" information card that Wayside sends with its perennials.

Some Wayside plants, such as azaleas, camellias and viburnum, appear in smaller pots in the Park catalogue a year earlier. If you don't mind slightly smaller stock from Park and are a competent gardener, you can save up to 55%. For instance, a White Swan azalea in a quart container from Park cost $9.95 when a larger one in a gallon container from Wayside cost $24.

Note: you get free seeds of Park's choice on orders of $10 or more and free seeds of your choice on orders of $20 or more. The offer is good during January and February only.

Bulbs

A few years ago you could save money, and get better and more varied bulbs, by ordering direct from Holland. Now the bigger firms are moving to New Jersey, and that is the place to buy. In every case the best selection, and in most cases the best prices, can be found in catalogues published in America.

The bulbs themselves are still from Holland, so they are protected by the Dutch government's rigid and exacting export standards.

Dutch Gardens, ***P.O. Box 400, Montvale, NJ 07645. Telephone 201-391-4366.***
Free color catalogue in April, November.
MC, V.
Sells Dutch-grown bulbs.
Minimum order $20.
Returns: money back on complaints received within the growing season.
Established 1956.

The lowest prices we know of anywhere for bulbs (in most cases they are from 10 to 50% below others) can be found here. Because of the cost of postage and handling, as well as the firm's bonus system, savings are bigger on larger orders. So this is a really useful source for a group of neighbors with similar tastes sending in a common order, or municipalities, hospitals and other institutions.

However, the stock is limited in variety. Anyone who wants to construct an extensive spring-flowering border, with a succession of blooming and harmonious colors, will be restricted by the small selection. And you won't find anything different from what your neighbors are growing—or even were growing ten years ago.

Peter De Jager Bulb Company, ***188 Asbury Street, South Hamilton, MA 01982. Telephone 617-468-4707.***
Free catalogue in June.
MC, V.
Sells imported Dutch flower bulbs.
Returns: money back.
Established 1952.

This firm is the best choice for most gardeners—the selection is extensive, the quality is unquestioned and the service is excellent. *On average* it is 10% more expensive than Dutch Gardens these days, but De Jager's prices are up to 40% lower than those of some domestic sources and on a par with those stragglers still back in Holland. (One example: when De Jager was charging $4.25 for three *Allium gigantum,* Dutch Gardens was charging $6.75; Burpee was charging $9.95; Park, $8.95 and Royal Gardens, $12.70.)

Cacti and Succulents

Mesa Garden, ***Box 72, Belen, NM 87002. Telephone 505-864-3131.***
Price list, 44 cents in stamps (one International Reply Coupon in Canada).
Sells cacti and succulents, both seeds and plants.
Returns: money back "at customer's request, none ever happened in the past."
Established 1976.

Mesa Garden was recommended by reader Jacob Adler, who says, "seeds and plants very reasonably priced . . . less than in most supermarkets. I ordered some plants last summer, and was thoroughly pleased with them."

Fruit Trees and Plants

The important thing to remember when buying trees is to pay attention to what size is offered. The ideal size for a newly planted tree has long been considered to be 8 feet. Since mail-order trees reach only 7 feet, the gardener who goes for the biggest mail-order tree he or she can get will be best served. (The exception is dwarf trees, which are sold at under 3 feet, yet still should be sturdy, branched and well rooted.)

It may be a consolation for mail-order buyers to know that smaller transplanted trees start to grow before larger ones. There is a direct relationship between trunk size and the time it takes a newly planted tree to "get up and grow," as opposed to just being alive and in leaf. A 14-foot tree with a 3-inch trunk should not be expected to grow normally for three years, by which time an 8-foot tree planted at the same time will usually have surpassed it.

The ever-increasing cost of shipping means that more and more nurseries will be pre-pruning the trees they send. Nurseries in England have done this for years. The 5-foot tree you order may arrive pruned to, say, 3 feet, and you will have to take the nursery's word that it was 5 feet tall to begin with. Examine the tree carefully. It should be sturdy, neither willowy nor stunted. (If you are not sure whether the tree is stunted, prune into it and count the rings. If there are three, you have an old, stunted tree, but this is rarely a problem with mail-order firms—it's more common at local "backyard" nurseries.) The tree should have a well-developed root system. If it doesn't, send it back.

J. E. Miller Nurseries, ***5060 West Lake Road, Canandaigua, NY 14424. Telephone: questions, 716-396-2647; orders, 800-828-9630; in New York State, 800-462-9601.***
Free catalogues.
AE, MC, V.
Sells food-producing plants and trees, including very hardy fruits.
Returns: money back on any stock that is not as represented; any stock that fails to grow replaced free of charge if reported before August 1 and at half price if reported after August 1 but within a year of shipment.
Established 1935.

A fine nursery in every way, with an extensive and excellent stock of modern fruit trees, grapes and berries, it emphasizes varieties that will stand extreme cold. Service is excellent, and although the prices aren't the very lowest, they are the lowest among nurseries with large lists of fruits suitable for severe winter conditions. Prices are, on average, 30% below those of Burpee and 15% below those of other nurseries such as Stark's. When a 3-foot Bartlett

Dwarf pear sold for $10.75 at Miller's, it was selling for $13.95 to $16.95 at the other nurseries.

For many years this pleasant little nursery relied primarily on repeat orders from a small but loyal clientele for such favorites as Reliance, "the 25-below-zero peach" and Hardy Worden, "the king of the short-season grape." Recently there have been changes. Miller's has started to grow larger without (so far) any diminution of quality or service. The pace of new introductions has accelerated and, most interestingly, three or four antique apples are being reintroduced each year. As I write, Miller's lists 30 heirloom varieties, including Sops of Wine from medieval England, Summer Rambo from 16th-century France and Sheepnose from colonial Connecticut. The firm's interest in these is logical: many are much more winter-hardy than modern varieties. Some of them are real treats to taste, and unlike heirloom vegetables they can be improved for suitability in the home orchard. All of the antique apples sold here are grafted onto a dwarfing understock, which keeps them, if planted properly, to a reasonable size. However, because in many cases both yields and resistance to disease will be lower in antique than in modern varieties, no one should rely on these for their primary source of apples.

Extra discount: Miller's issues a reduced-for-clearance brochure in March featuring overstocked varieties at half off. Shipping continues through May. This is a huge bargain, but since there is no telling which varieties will be in surplus in a given year, it is risky to wait until March to order. What you want could be sold out then.

Patrick's Nursery and Sun Garden Seeds, ***Box 159C, Ty Ty, GA 31795. Telephone: questions, 912-382-1770; orders, 912-382-1122.***
Free 32-page catalogue in October.
Sells fruit trees, nut trees, berry plants and grape vines for the South.
Returns: money back if complaint is filed within 15 days.
Established 1836.

Patrick's seems to be the absolute price leader in fruit trees, nut trees and berries for the South. Last year it included a price comparison in its catalogue, showing that nine of its fruit trees were one-third to two-thirds less than those of Bountiful Ridge, Hastings and Stark Brothers during the two previous years.

Southerners will delight in the countless fascinating fruits, ranging from regional exotics such as Cavendish bananas and Ogeechee limes to the latest USDA introductions for southern states. The catalpa tree is of special interest; although this is only one of several nurseries to list it, it is the first to latch on to its use in attracting a steady supply of worms for fishermen.

There is some stock that is suitable for northern climates but, with one or two exceptions, it is quite ordinary.

Patrick's seems to be knowledgeable, abreast of new developments and eager to please. I placed a small order with the firm and was satisfied.

Ground Cover

Park (above) is the clear price leader on ground cover. For instance, 100 vinca minor cost $24.25 at Park when they were $44 at Krider and $57.95 at Burpee. The Park perennial catalogue has a bigger selection of ground cover than the seed catalogue.

IMPORTING

Some first-rate sources are outside Canada and the United States. No permit is needed to import seeds or bulbs, although you do need a permit to import plants. It is not hard to get a permit, but begin at least two months before you plan to order. Telephone your local department of agriculture, animals and plants or write to the address below. Send a short note explaining what you want to import, and you will receive the necessary forms and instructions. For plants such as buddleias, camellias, magnolias and viburnum, you simply list the plants you want to order. When you return the form, you will be sent a mailing label, which you forward to the nursery with your order.

Other plants, such as roses, must be quarantined in your garden for 24 months. This involves more initial paperwork and about four visits a year from government inspectors. Peter Schneider reports that the visits are an agreeable chance for a chat about gardening rather than an annoyance.

U.S. residents should contact: **PERMIT UNIT,** ***U.S. Department of Agriculture, PPQ Federal Building, Room 638, Hyattsville, MD 20782.*** Canadian residents should contact: **PERMIT OFFICE,** ***Plant Health Division, Agriculture Department, Ottawa, Ontario, K1A 0C6.***

Bodnant Garden Nursery, ***Tal-y-Cafn, Colwyn Bay, LL28 5RE, North Wales.***
24-page price list, $1 in bills or equivalent International Reply Coupons.
Sells trees and shrubs.
Minimum order $25.
Returns: none.
Established 1947.

Considering the worldwide reputation of Bodnant Gardens, run by Britain's National Trust, the nursery catalogue is surprisingly modest. It is modest in scope, which is a shame—many more plants must be grown than are listed. It is also modest in tone, even though the writers would certainly have every right to be boastful about much of what they do list. The new plants that Bodnant introduces have a way of turning up in the American Wayside Gardens and White Flower Farm catalogues. For instance, the Dawn viburnum was featured as a novelty in one Wayside catalogue, in which the price was listed as $19.75, while during the same season it cost roughly $6.30 from Bodnant, including postage. The Bodnant prices are as modest as the rest of the catalogue, which makes the nursery an excellent high-quality, low-cost source of the sort of ornamental trees and shrubs that the posher U.S. nurseries, Wayside and White Flower, seem to have a monopoly on here.

Buddleia, camellia, magnolia and viburnum can all be imported quite easily if you apply for a permit (see above). Other stock is either forbidden entry to the United States (for example, jasmine, lilacs and maples) or requires quarantine (for example, hydrangea, eucalyptus and willow).

Roses

It is impossible to save money by buying roses by mail from American rose nurseries. The advantage of domestic mail-order firms is that they offer a wealth of plants that you can't find at local garden centers. But you can buy the latest English roses for about 25% less, even after paying postage, than you would pay for the latest American ones. You can save considerably more if you buy a ready-made collection from these English growers and even more from the German one. All three are outstanding firms.

R. Harkness and Company, ***The Rose Gardens, Hitchin, Hertfordshire SG4 OJT, England. Telephone 462-34027 and 462-34171.***
46-page color brochure in May, $2 surface, $3 air.
MC, V.
Sells rose plants.
Minimum order 15 plants.
Returns: replacement in event of loss.
Established 1879.

Jack Harkness is England's leading rose breeder, and no one could be more helpful to the would-be importer than Peter Harkness. In addition to its own roses, the firm distributes new introductions from Cockers in Scotland and Dicksons in Northern Ireland, so this is a great place for one-stop shopping. But order early—many varieties are sold out by the end of October.

As with all British nurseries, postage and packing charges are high compared with German charges.

W. Kordes' Sohne, ***rose-nursery, D 2206 K1 offenseth-Sparrieshoop, Holstein, West Germany. Telephone 4121-8688.***
Free color catalogue.
Sells bare-root rose plants—over 300 varieties bred here and by breeders around the world.
Minimum order DM 100.
Returns: money back.

The best source for getting roses and getting them cheap from overseas is W. Kordes' Sohne. Wilhelm Kordes created the great rose Crimson Glory in 1935, and since the early 1960s his son Reimer's roses have been winning awards and acclaim all over the world. The catalogue is 30 oversize pages in dazzling color, and something I still can't believe is sent out for free. In it are hundreds of roses from all over the world, including Kordes's own Esmeralda, the most sought-after new variety today. Unavailable in America, it costs about DM 7.30 (which equaled $3.54 in September 1986) here. Older varieties are even less. When all charges including air parcel post are included, Kordes roses cost about DM 12.25 each when ordered in quantities of 12 to 20 of the same or mixed varieties. With new roses from American growers such as Jackson and Perkins and Armstrong hitting the streets at close to $10, not including postage and handling or local taxes, this represents incredible savings. It is also fun to have varieties that your neighbors won't be able to get for years to come.

E. B. LeGrice Roses, ***Norwich Road, North Walsham, Norfolk, NR28 ODR, England. Telephone 0692-402591.***
24-page color catalogue in June, 1 pound sterling money order.
V.
Sells rose plants.
Minimum order $30.
Returns: credit if informed within six months of planting.
Established 1920.

This is where to go for green, brown, gray, purple and speckled roses. LeGrice specializes in these "arranger" types and has a very solid selection of more traditional kinds as well, at prices much the same as those of Harkness.

SEEDS

Where vegetables are concerned, a gardener saves a little by buying seeds at lower prices and a lot by producing more from a given space. To save money through bigger crops, stick to hybrid rather than open pollinated seeds. They are bred for increased vigor and yield, uniformity, resistance to stress and disease and, yes, flavor. The gardener who chooses among hybrid seeds for those bred specially for tenderness and flavor, and who grows crops well, will enjoy the tastiest vegetables on earth.

Lindenberg Seeds, ***803 Princess Avenue, Brandon, Manitoba R7A OP5, Canada. Telephone 204-727-0575.***
Free 60-page catalogue.
V.
Sells vegetable and flower seeds.
Minimum order $8.
Returns: "never run into this, would exchange if we made a mistake."
Established 1935.

Lindenberg Seeds was started during the depression by Hugo Lindenberg, a farmer, and is still a small firm, now run by his son. Eric Lindenberg says that they try to stock regular seeds at "fair" prices, and indeed, the seeds are almost always 25 to 65% below what the biggies (Burpee, Harris, Park and Stokes) charge. Thirty seeds of the excellent new Celebrity tomato, for instance, cost 60 cents from Lindenberg when the other seedsmen were charging from 95 cents to $1.15. Half an ounce of Early Jersey Wakefield cabbage cost 94 cents from Lindenberg when they were between $1.50 and $2.75 from the others.

We endorse the quality and variety of the vegetable seeds without hesitation. The flower seeds are also of good quality, but more European than American. This is also the only remaining alternative to Thompson and Morgan for named, unmixed sweet pea varieties.

Stokes Seeds, ***7064 Stokes Building, Buffalo, NY 14240. Telephone 416-688-4300. Canada: Stokes Seeds, Box 10, St. Catharines, Ontario L2R 6R6.***
Free catalogue in November. No catalogue available May through October.
MC, V.
Sells flower and vegetable seeds, some supplies.
Returns: money back on unopened seed packets returned within 30 days.
Established 1881.

A Canadian gardener, Richard Allen, tells me he gets together with neighbors to have a seed-ordering jamboree when the Stokes catalogue comes in, because the bulk prices at Stokes are so low. He sent me the example of pea seeds, which, when he made the calculation, cost 60 cents for 2 ounces—in other words, $4.80 per pound. At 5 pounds, the peas cost only $1.60 per pound. The seeds are good, and the catalogue is meticulously detailed and a valuable reference work. Legend has it that every word is written by one man, John Gale.

The Urban Farmer, ***P.O. Box 444, Convent Station, NJ 07961.***
Free 40-page catalogue in December.
Sells imported vegetable seeds from international seed houses such as Clause, Daehnfeldt, Hurst, S & G, Skata, Takii, Vilmorin.
Returns: money back if complaint is received during growing season.
Established 1980.

Lately there has been a proliferation of new small seed houses. Some of them offer smaller seed packets at bargain prices but have uninteresting varieties, often the same varieties sold at hardware stores at the same prices. Other seedsmen introduce foreign seeds, especially French and Japanese, but with prices as exotic as their seeds. The Urban Farmer walks the line between these two unpleasant extremes—and walks it well.

The catalogue is chock-full of both new and interesting vegetable varieties from abroad and quite practical cooking advice. The seed packets are small, making this a good place for gardeners who want to try novel varieties at the lowest possible cost and also for people gardening in small spaces. (But there is no price advantage at all if you want regular quantities.)

The Urban Farmer says that it will special order any seed—so long as it can meet the minimum order requirements of the suppliers.

DO IT YOURSELF

Growing Plants from Seeds

A very good way of saving a lot of money in the garden is to increase production by starting your own plants from seeds indoors. If you start seeds indoors rather than outside, you'll have greater control and can be sure that the seeds aren't parched, washed away, trampled on or eaten by birds as they sprout. With vegetables, you can time your planting to get one or even two extra crops in. You'll also have a much wider choice than if you buy plants at a garden center.

Once adept at starting seeds, you can make tremendous savings (and possible profit) by starting things like African violets, tuberous begonias and New Guinea impatiens from seed. You can also produce more vigorous plants this way, as they will not have been forced to bloom unnaturally and then transplanted when already blooming—two problems that afflict the flowering seedlings sold through garden centers, supermarkets and local nurseries. Seed-to-transplant time varies from 6 weeks for asters and marigolds to 12 weeks for begonias, geraniums and snapdragons. Flowering houseplants such as African violets and primroses usually take 6 months from seed to flower.

An easier and more productive approach than the old Styrofoam-cup-on-a-sunny-windowsill method is to buy flats and plant lights from Mellinger's (below). Or, better still, get the eight-tray Sunlighter plant stand, which only takes up a 20-by-24-inch area of floor space. (At the time of writing, it cost $159.75 at Mellinger's but $214.95 from Burpee.) Mellinger's has everything you need for seed starting at the best prices. But if you want to use soilless seed-starting medium instead of sterilized earth, buy that locally because of transportation costs.

Here are three firms that are particularly good for seed starting. Prices are not especially low at the American firms.

W. Atlee Burpee Company, ***300 Park Avenue, Warminster, PA 18974. Telephone 215-674-4900.***
Free spring seed catalogue in January, free spring bulb catalogue in March, free fall garden catalogue in July.
AE, MC, V.
Sells flower and vegetable seeds, fruit and ornamental nursery stock, perennial plants, flower bulbs, garden tools, kitchen aids.
Returns: money back.
Established 1876.

Burpee's prices are about equal to those of Park, but it has a much smaller selection. It's a good choice for beginners, as more instructions and seed-starting hints are given on the packages.

Note: there is a famous 5% discount from January 1 to February 28.

Chiltern Seeds, ***Bortree Stile, Ulverston, Cumbria, LA12 7PB, England.***
194-page catalogue, $2 (airmail).
Sells seeds for flowers, shrubs, trees, houseplants and a few unusual vegetables.
Returns: money back.
Established 1976.

Hundreds of dollars can be saved by gardeners willing to start their trees and shrubs from seed. A nursery bed or cold frame outdoors is needed, and the gardener must have patience but needs no particular skill.

Chiltern has seeds for almost 3,000 different plants (including houseplants) and trees; and it stocks many dozens of varieties that are simply unavailable as plants. The owner, Mr. Bowden, points out that some of the plants will be flowering within the year and the vast majority of his stock will be "interesting specimens of, or approaching, flowering size within four years."

The Chiltern catalogue is engaging, well written, and reasonably well organized. Furthermore, prices are about 24 to 40% lower than prices at Park and Thompson and Morgan, the only big seed houses that sell shrub and tree seeds in the United States. We haven't tried Chiltern, but it looks like a really first-class source, and a particularly good source of houseplant seeds.

Park Seed Company, ***Cokesbury Road, Greenwood, SC 29647. Telephone 803-374-3341.***
Free 124-page color flower and vegetable catalogue in December. Free fall catalogue in July.
AE, MC, V.
Sells bulbs, seed, plants, garden accessories.
Returns: money back.
Established 1868.

If you want to save money by starting your own marigolds and petunias, try Park. It is absolutely excellent for new flower seed introductions and it gives top quality and service.

Feeding the Lawn

A lawn is often the most expensive part of the garden to keep up. The cheapest ways of feeding the lawn are organic. If you mow with an old-fashioned reel-style mower, leaving the clippings to decompose, you won't need to add any phosphorus or potassium. Just add a high-nitrogen product such as Nitro-10 or all-organic 10-0-0 (available locally or from Mellinger's).

Another organic method is to use sludge. Many municipalities make activated sewage sludge available to gardeners for a nominal charge, or even free. It helps to know someone in the water department or to send a "get acquainted" present of flowers or vegetables from your garden. If you can get sludge, you have a nearly perfect lawn fertilizer. You need a lot—50 pounds will feed only 1,500 square feet—but it is applied only once a year, when the garden is frozen in winter. Activated sludge does not smell and it's perfectly safe to use.

For people really keen on saving money, the cheapest lawn of all is the bluegrass and white clover lawn first described by Ohio conservationist Louis Bromfield. The white clover makes nitrogen in the soil available to the bluegrass, so if clippings are left on the lawn, no fertilizer whatsoever is needed. Weeds must be removed by hand. White clover is sold by Lindenberg Seeds (above).

TOOLS AND SUPPLIES

Mellinger's, ***2310 W. South Range, North Lima, OH 44452. Telephone: questions, 216-549-9861; orders, 800-321-7444.***
Free 112-page catalogue in November.
MC, V.
Sells tools, seed-starting equipment, grafting supplies, organic plant food and pest controls, chemical controls, hydroponic plant food, plant-light fixtures, accessories of all kinds.
Returns: money back, but there is a 15% handling charge.
Established 1927.

An outstanding place to get garden supplies, Mellinger's is the quintessential mail-order source of better-quality goods at lower prices. Service is swift, and the wares never disappoint.

Prices are the best in mail order and better than almost all local prices, even those in highly competitive districts. On seed-starting equipment Mellinger's prices are 10 to 35% below the *closest* mail-order competitors. Savings are particularly good (15 to over 50%) on bulk quantities of pesticides; specialty fertilizers (such as orchid food, organic compounds and time-release fertilizers) and water-soluble fertilizers such as Peter's, Schultz and Hyponex; rooting hormones and herbicides (especially Roundup).

Note: Monthly ads in *Organic Gardening* magazine feature selected items at even lower than catalogue prices. A uniform shipping charge makes these especially valuable advertisements for West Coast residents.

Sotz, ***13600 North Station Road, Columbia Station, OH 44028. Telephone 216-236-5021.***
(Main listing in Hobbies section under Tools)

Sotz sells a few garden tools (such as True Temper's top-of-the-line "Finest" quality, which is better than its "American Made" and "True Temper" qualities sold in many discount, hardware and garden centers). It also has tractors, mowers, vacuums, leaf blowers, gas-driven trimmers, power hoes, edgers and so on—all at a discount. (I note that I would have saved a clear $4 if I had bought my new hose from Sotz instead of in New York *and* I could have bought one 100-footer, which I wanted, instead of the two 50-footers that I settled for.)

The Sotz garden cart was recommended in *The Next Whole Earth Catalog* by a farmer who said the metal wheels are tougher than the rubber wheels on the popular Garden Way cart and better for rough ground (but they wouldn't be as easy to push on a garden with lawns). Sotz has an annoying pricing structure for the cart, consisting of a list price and a "special" price. At the "special" price it is almost 30% cheaper than the Garden Way cart, and it is available as a kit at another 15% off.

Wiggle Worm Haven, ***7802 Spring Street, Racine, WI 53406. Telephone: questions, 414-886-2665; orders, 414-886-2484.***
Write or telephone 8:30 A.M. to 4:30 P.M., Monday through Friday, for prices.
MC, V.
Sells worm castings.
Returns: none.
Established 1970.

Worm castings are one excellent organic fertilizer not offered by Mellinger's. They are good scratched right into the soil but most economical and wonderful used as part of the potting mix when you grow vegetables in tubs or flowers in pots. No other fertilizer will be needed and the plants thrive.

WHOLE EARTH ACCESS (General section) has a carefully chosen stock of garden tools.

GENERAL:
LARGE STORES OVERSEAS

Royal Worcester "Forget-me-not." When the U.S. list price for a five-piece place setting was $65, it cost $48.75 at New York stores in this section and $33 at Selfridges in London. Shipping and insurance costs at the New York stores depend on where you live. Shipping and insurance from Selfridges is about $9 a place setting.

GENERAL:
LARGE STORES OVERSEAS

Amsterdam Airport Shopping Center, ***P.O. Box 7501, 1118 ZG Schiphol Airport, Holland. Telephone 20-51-72-49. Watch shop telephone number 20-17-59-36.***
Occasional free catalogues; otherwise write and ask about whatever you are interested in.

The dream of the thrifty shopper with expensive tastes, Schiphol is hands down the best airport shopping center in the world. Shop after shop is stuffed with better brand names as well as humbler goods, all at bargain prices. It's well worth a visit—you can stock up on caviar and smoked eel at the food shop; Aquascutum, Burberry and Gucci at the fashion shop; Carrera Porsche sunglasses and Cartier wallets at the men's shop (those stores won't sell by mail, unfortunately) and, of course, an international collection of electronics and small appliances.

If you can't visit Schiphol in person, you'll have to work a bit harder, because the catalogue isn't detailed enough for easy mail-order shopping. You'll have to write and ask about anything you are interested in. Small expensive things are such astounding bargains, and mailing costs are so low, that they are well worth buying by mail or even telephone: Mikimoto cultured pearls that started at $460 at Mikimoto in New York started at $100 at Schiphol when I compared. Lighters, pens and especially watches are also amazing buys (see Watches section for details).

A. Andrews and Co (Mail Order), ***38–44 D'Aguilar Street, 1/F (GPO Box 2983), Hong Kong. Telephone 5-266471.***
Catalogue in February, two $1 bills (one $5 bill airmail).
V.
Sells electronic and photographic equipment, household appliances, furniture, table linens, general goods of all sorts such as musical instruments, sports equipment, toys.
Returns: refunds upon receipt of goods "but such cases are rare."
Established 1962.

An enormous illustrated catalogue is aimed at U.S. forces overseas with full and clear instructions for ordering from any country. The catalogue contains just about anything you'd need to continue an American-style life abroad: appliances, electronics and practical equipment for the house and office—not forgetting necessities such as men's Jockey brand pure cotton underwear and ladies' Po Po–style synthetic wigs.

Most of the prices I checked hovered around U.S. discount prices—some were slightly more, some slightly less—and I can't see any reason for U.S. residents to order goods from abroad that are on sale at discount stores in America. (There are exceptions—you can save on watches. See under Watches.) More likely to be of interest to U.S. residents are Chinese porcelain and linens. I couldn't find exactly the same linen in New York in order to compare prices, but the linen at Andrews seems to cost about a third of the price of roughly similar linen sold in New York. For instance, a round cotton crochet lace tablecloth measuring 90 inches across cost $33 at Andrews when a similar but not identical, slightly smaller cloth cost $100 at Bloomingdale's.

China Products Company, ***Lok Sing Center, 31 Yee Wo Street, Hong Kong. Telephone 5-7908321.***
Catalogue, free by surface mail, $6 airmail.

This mainland government store is very popular with tourists, and the windows often flaunt letters from satisfied mail-order customers. This is how it describes itself: "a big-scale department store with a long history . . . dealing exclusively in general merchandise made in the People's Republic of China. A large variety of selected and exquisite Chinese products are available. The Overseas Service Department offers services for overseas mail orders. . . . Best service and high reputation are assured."

The lavish color catalogues printed on shiny paper display goods from mainland China: oddly named "Bodiless Lacquer Ware from Foochow," flowery cloisonné ware, jade flowers and fruit, embroidered satin cushions, linen handkerchiefs and numerous vases and figurines. None of that appealed to me, but there is at least one incredible bargain—a 70-by-90-inch cashmere blanket that cost about $125 at the time of writing. In New York the same sized cashmere blanket cost from $560 (lightweight) at Harris Levy (see under Linen) to about $900 (also lightweight) at Bergdorf Goodman. China Products also had a camel-hair blanket for $95 (I couldn't even find one in New York in order to compare prices, though the salespeople at Bergdorf's said they might be able to order me one and they'd call back, which they didn't). A long amethyst necklace cost $100 at China Products, but I didn't try to compare prices on this because of possible size and quality variables.

Buying from China Products is not simple. The catalogue sheets don't give prices, so you have to write and ask for them and the people there don't seem to understand complicated questions. I had best results when I returned the catalogue sheets with the items I wanted marked "How much?" But it is very annoying then not to have the sheet to refer to. Perhaps the best idea is to keep a photocopy of the catalogue page.

Clery's Department Stores, ***Post Department, P.O. Box 26, O'Connell Street, Dublin 1, Ireland. Telephone 1-786000.***
Write for specific prices.
AE, MC, V.
Established 1941.

Clery's calls itself the foremost store in Ireland, and the general manager told me in a letter what Americans go for. The only surprise is lace curtains; he writes: "We have discovered that American tourists are extremely interested in our lace curtains, of which we carry a very large selection." Apart from that, it's Irish linen, tweed and Aran wool, Aran knitwear and Irish fine bone china and crystal.

At the moment there is no catalogue, although "it is hoped that at some time in the future Clery's will undertake a mail-order brochure." So write only if you already know what you want.

Den Permanente, ***Vesterbrogade, DK-1620 Copenhagen V, Denmark. Telephone 1-12-44-88. Mail order: Ole Romer Svej 2, DK 8670, Lasby, Denmark.***
Very occasional brochures. Write for specific prices.
AE, DC, MC, V.
Sells furniture, china, glass, flatware, textiles, jewelry.

Of great appeal to anyone interested in design, Den Permanente sells only products designed in Denmark. Worst luck—the catalogues are produced only occasionally. So this firm is really for people who know Danish design. They will find glass by Holmegaard; china by Bjørn Wiinblad, Dansk (dinnerware Bistro, Generation) and Royal Copenhagen; Kaj Bojeson wooden toys, Cylinda-Line stainless steel holloware designed by Arne Jacobson (the same as sold at the Museum of Modern Art in New York), Stelton thermoses and ice buckets designed by Erik Magnussen; flatware by Gense, Georg Jensen, and Dansk.

Harrods, ***Knightsbridge, London, SW1 7XL, England. Telephone 1-730-1234, Export Office extension 2750.***
Write for individual prices, or buy a 230-page magazine/catalogue from British Publications, 11-03 46th Avenue, Long Island City, NY 11101. Telephone 718-937-4606. One issue, $6.50. Annual subscription to three catalogues, $18.
AE, MC, V.

Harrods, the most famous department store in the world, runs fabulous January and July sales which may well be worth crossing the ocean for if you are in the habit of buying British goods. Otherwise buy by mail—Harrods exports over 40 million pounds worth of goods a year, writes 10,000 letters a week and has 140 incoming telephone lines manned (or more likely womaned) by 17 operators. In spite of, or because of, all that activity, I have found Harrods efficient about giving prices on glass and china (nicely quoting in dollars) but not so good about answering odd requests for small, less standard items. When I ordered with a credit card, I didn't get any acknowledgment of my order—it just arrived.

An article in the English journal *New Society* accused Harrods of being a "flash" (showy) rather than smart store and mentioned a Lady Hartwell who used to say it was such a pleasure going to Harrods; it was the only store in London where she never felt tempted to spend her money on anything. Nevertheless, there is plenty of good-quality brand name stuff. You can get the usual British goods for sometimes as little as half of their U.S. price (as I write, leather-covered Filofax agendas that cost about $150 in New York cost about $80 at Harrods).

Peter Jones, ***Export Department, Sloane Square, London, SW1W 8EL, England. Telephone 1-73-3434.***
Write to the Export Department for specific prices.
Gerald Whiting, Chief Information Officer.

Peter Jones, which was founded in 1877, belongs to the renowned John Lewis Partnership (renowned in England at least). The chief information officer tells me that the Partnership is unique in British retailing in that "it is owned, in effect, by the 27,000 people working in it, managed and management alike." This store is strongest on household goods such as china and glass, furnishing fabrics and linens. Although the store isn't as practiced in export as Harrods and Selfridges (Peter Jones quotes prices in sterling and doesn't take credit cards), I had excellent service when I bought English flatware here by mail.

The same article that complained that Harrods is "flash" rather than smart said that smart people buy their household goods at Peter Jones in Sloane Square "for the excellent reason that it is cheaper than most other places."

Nordiska Kompaniet, ***Customer Service, S-103 74 Stockholm, Sweden. Telephone 8-762-80-00.***
Write for prices.
AE, DC, MC, V.

NK, as it's known throughout Scandinavia, is Stockholm's largest and smartest department store. In the heart of the city's downtown, its large, airy building offers a wide range of merchandise from all over Europe. The strongest selections, of course, are of Sweden's own specialties, particularly the fine glassware made by Kosta Boda and others. Stockholm lacks the rich variety of specialized stores found in Copenhagen, so NK makes sense as a source of most Swedish products. Prices can be slightly higher than elsewhere. Pub, the city's co-op department store, tends to be less expensive and has some of its own brand specialties. For furniture, IKEA is best known for inexpensive, tasteful modern, the northern equivalent of Conran. Letters to Sweden, however, may be referred to the Canadian outlet, **Ikea Mail Order, 1224 Dundas Street East, Mississauga, Ontario, Canada V6X2C3,** which now services North America.

Selfridges, ***Export-Letter Order Department, Oxford Street, London W1A 1AB, England. Telephone 1-629-1234.***
Write for specific prices.
AE, DC, MC, V and overseas accounts accepted.
Sells most things—Selfridges is a department store.

Selfridges was founded by an American born in Wisconsin, Harry Gordon Selfridge, who started his retailing career at Marshall Field in Chicago. According to the Selfridge official history, Harry Gordon brought "many new ideas into retailing by introducing annual sales, the bargain basement, and the idea" (lousy idea in my opinion) "of fashion rather than durability in ladies' clothing." When Marshall Field kept rejecting his other go-getting ideas, Mr. Selfridge took his family off to London, where he was "appalled" by the shopping conditions. Shops were dimly lit and badly ventilated, merchandise was kept in drawers and customers were not allowed to browse but harassed to buy by assistants and shop walkers. Furthermore, "with the exception of Harrods and one or two others," department stores were unknown in London.

Mr. Selfridge put all that right with his big new store, all olive green carpets, mahogany fixtures and brilliant illumination. Vast amounts of money were spent on "serious and ethical in tone" advertisements in the newspapers, written by Harry Gordon himself and illustrated by artists from *Punch* magazine.

Still flourishing 77 years later, the store is now a full-scale department store with all the departments you'd expect and more (scissor sharpening in the basement, sun lamp treatment on the third floor). Although Selfridges has a more workaday image than Harrods, it sells by mail the usual British bargains in china, glass and woolens. This is also a good place for Burberry and Aquascutum raincoats and Daks trousers for men, all of which cost about a third less than in the United States.

Shannon Mail Order, ***Dept. CC, Shannon Airport, Ireland. Telephone 61-62610.***
44-page color catalogue, $1 bill or International Reply Coupons.
AE, MC, V.
Sells crystal, china, Irish linen, jewelry, perfume.
Returns: money back if returned within a month.

Shannon has been selling by mail to the United States for 30 years now. The (very low) color catalogue prices are all given in dollars, shipping costs are noted and everything is made easy. I would guess that travelers buy a lot of gifts at Shannon—on display are Royal Doulton figurines, Coalport cottages, Aynsley flowered lamps and vases, Belleek bowls and Peggy Nisbett collectors' dolls. Popular Irish goods include linen tablecloths, jewelry, Peterson pipes, Foxford rugs and pure wool blankets. From other countries there are Goebel and Hummel figurines and perfumes from France. As you can see, there is nothing unusual here but a profusion of the most in-demand goods at low prices.

Stetchers, ***27 Frederick Street, Port of Spain, Trinidad, W.I. Telephone 62-32585 and 32586.***
Write or telephone for specific prices.
Sells china and glass by most European manufacturers, including Val St. Lambert crystal and Capidimonte figurines; pens; pipes; lighters; watches.
Returns: money back "if we are at fault."
Established 1948.

Stetchers, which says that it is almost a landmark for Caribbean tourists, has been widely written up in the American press as a great spot for bargains. Internationally known brands of glass, china, watches and perfume are listed in a leaflet, but without prices, so write and ask about whatever you are interested in. Stetchers says that it will order anything not stocked.

Oy Stockmann AB, ***Export Service, P.O. Box 220, Helsinki 10, Finland. Telephone 8-176-181.***
Manufacturers' brochures $5 bills.
AE, DC, MC, V.

The department store Stockmann, the biggest show in Helsinki, is a wonderful source of modern Finnish design. The 15-member export staff is supremely efficient (and sells about $5 million worth of goods a year to Russia alone). I have been buying cooking pots, Iittala glass, Arabia china and Muurame furniture from Stockmann for years. Reader Charles Flynn bought an Alvar Aalto vase by mail from the Museum of Modern Art in New York for $90; it took three weeks and was broken when it arrived. He bought the same vase from Stockmann; it cost $45, took five weeks to arrive and was perfectly packed.

GENERAL:
DEPARTMENT STORES, MAIL-ORDER HOUSES AND TELEPHONE BUYING SERVICES IN THE UNITED STATES

Best Products, ***P.O. Box 26303, Richmond, VA 23260. Telephone: questions, 804-752-3129; orders, 800-221-BEST.***
500-page color catalogue in September, $1.
Sells jewelry and watches, housewares, furniture and appliances, electronics and photographic equipment, tools, sporting goods, automotive equipment, bicycles, toys and equipment for babies and children.
Returns: money back if goods returned within 30 days.
Established 1957.

There are two very good things about the mail/telephone catalogue of nationally known brand name goods put out by this group of southern catalogue showrooms. One is that it is one of the few discount catalogues that is fully illustrated with photographs in glorious color. This means that you don't have to send for manufacturers' brochures or search your neighborhood to see what your purchases will look like. The other thing is that prices are excellent. On the things I checked, prices were as low or even lower than prices at the specialized discount stores. So I highly recommend keeping this catalogue around (it's valid for a year and costs only $1) as a handy reference tool at the very least.

The disadvantages of this general source, compared with the specialized ones, are that the selection in each category is limited and that it usually has medium-priced brands rather than the very tip-top ones. Nevertheless, if you look at the list of types of goods they stock, you'll see that you are very likely to find this a convenient place to buy a few things each year.

Comb Company, ***14605 28th Avenue North, Minneapolis, MN 55441. Telephone 800-328-0609.***
Subscription mailing service to 40 price lists, $30 a year, or telephone for specific prices.
AE, MC, V.
Sells most consumer products except clothes and food.
Returns: money back if merchandise returned within 14 days, but there may be a shipping charge.
Established 1970.

Comb is a liquidation company that buys overstocks, year-old models and reconditioned goods from manufacturers, department stores and wholesalers, and sells them at prices it says are 40 to 70% off the original list price. Popular goods are appliances, computers, generators, electronics, stereos and power tools. A computer buff told me about this firm, saying that it had great buys on reconditioned Commodore 64s at one point.

You can either call to ask about whatever you want or subscribe to the "Insider Hot Line," which for $30 a year puts you on the mailing list for 40 price lists of new arrivals, limited-quantity goods, markdowns and so on.

Service Merchandise Company, ***Box 225130, Nashville, TN 37202. Telephone 800-251-1212.***
Free color catalogue in February, September. Catalogue costs $2. Seasonal and "clearance" flyers monthly at other times of year.
MC, V.
Sells electronics, household appliances and kitchen supplies, jewelry, luggage, health and beauty aids, photographic equipment, sports equipment, toys.
Returns: must be notified within 10 days, none accepted after 30 days.
Established 1960.

This chain of catalogue showrooms also produces catalogues and flyers for mail order, through which it sells brand name products with what is called "good market recognition" at below suggested retail prices. (Yes indeed, I saw the Franzus travel steamer, which I had paid over $20 for, selling at Service for $11.97. I also saw the Norelco travel steamer selling in a snazzy mail-order catalogue for $22.50, whereas at Service it cost $14.84.) As in the Best catalogue (above), there is a bit of almost every smaller thing for the house (no furniture or large appliances) plus a lot of jewelry, so unless you are looking for something special or something unusual, this is a good place to stock up. This is true especially for practical things—with more decorative objects, the taste is usually tacky.

Whole Earth Access, ***2950 7th Street, Berkeley, CA 94710. Telephone: 800-845-2000, 415-845-3000.***
458-page catalogue, $5 (refundable) plus $2 postage.

Sells baby goods, books, clothing, electronics, energy-saving products, gardening tools (hand and power), household goods, kitchen supplies, outdoor equipment, tools (hand and power).
Returns: money back if merchandise returned as new in original carton with all papers within two weeks.
Established 1969.

The Whole Earth Access store in Berkeley was inspired by, although it is independent of, *The Whole Earth Catalog,* and now it produces an invaluable mail-order catalogue. The stock is very carefully chosen for quality and value for money. In each category you are likely to find the most reputable brands, and sometimes brands that are harder to find at a discount. The Whole Earth Access people say that they price goods at below list price so that customers can be confident they are getting the best price around. I have found that discounts range from none at all on a few things to an average of about 20%. One especially good price I checked: a 24-inch Samsonite Kicks Traveller suitcase cost $53, almost 50% off the list price Whole Earth Access quoted and 25% below the price I checked at Ace (see the Leather and Luggage section). As well as being carefully chosen, the stock is fully described, with plenty of information and some advice about each product, which makes choosing and buying much simpler.

The stock is sturdy and no-nonsense but by no means blindly "back to the earth"; it is a sophisticated selection of stuff from the better manufacturers. Along with the wood-burning stoves comes the Wolf Restaurant stove, beloved of fanatical cooks around the land. And along with axes come chain saws by Homelite. There are particularly complete selections of kitchen equipment, hand and power tools and electronics (a Sony ICF 2002 shortwave radio was selling for $299 at the New York store Hammacher Schlemmer when it was only $179 here and $175 at 47 St. Photo) and smaller selections of things for the home such as Levolor blinds (the price I checked was 15% below the price at Pintchik, described under Paint), Wamsutta pure cotton sheets (10% above the price at Harris Levy, described under Linen) and Faribo pure wool blankets (25% above the price at Harris Levy).

NOTABLE SALES

Bloomingdale's by Mail, ***P.O. Box 13087, Roanoke, VA 24031. Telephone 800-368-3438.***
Subscription to one year of catalogues, $3. Includes sales catalogues in January, June, July and after Christmas.
AE, MC, V.
Sells by mail mainly clothes, housewares, bed linen, some furniture.

If you subscribe to catalogues from New York's expensive and fashionable Bloomingdale's department store, you also get occasional sales catalogues.

Sears Roebuck and Company, ***Sears Tower, Chicago, IL 60684.***
General merchandise catalogues cost $4 (refundable with a $20 purchase) or are free to anyone placing at least two catalogue orders of at least $30 each every six months; published January, June, early fall. Specialty catalogues, $1. Sale catalogues free to anyone who meets the above conditions or who picks them up from a selling unit.

The above catalogues can be picked up or ordered by telephone from your nearest Sears distribution center. Otherwise catalogues can be ordered by mail at the same prices from the following addresses:

Eastern U.S., Canadian and European customers order from Sears at 4640 Roosevelt Boulevard, Dept. 146, Philadelphia, PA 19132.

Southern U.S. customers order from Sears at 675 Ponce de Leon Avenue, NE, 95 Annex, Dept. 146, Atlanta, GA 30395.

Midwestern U.S. customers order from Sears at 925 South Homan Avenue, Dept. 146, Chicago, IL 60607.

Western U.S. and Far Eastern customers order from Sears at 2650 East Olympic Boulevard, Dept. 146, Los Angeles, CA 90051.

Sells just about everything that you would expect a department store to sell, and more—fashions, home fashions, appliances, electronics, home improvement equipment, sporting and automotive products—mainly made to Sears's specifications. Some nationally known brand names are carried in computers (Atari and Casio), clothes and shoes (Levi's and Wrangler, Adidas and Puma and others), and telephones (AT&T, Mura, Panasonic and Uniden).
Returns: unconditional money-back guarantee with no time limit. Receipt requested.
Established 1896.

Besides the huge catalogues, Sears now produces many useful specialized catalogues (of toys, office supplies, sickroom equipment and much more) and also sales catalogues that are sent to customers who buy a certain amount from the regular catalogues (see above).

Sears is as basic an American institution as you can find; our government used to love to send the Sears catalogues behind the Iron Curtain to show the Reds how rich our lifestyle is. The move was probably more effective than our government realized, since Sears epitomizes the fifties taste that still seems to prevail in the Soviet Union. Perhaps most Americans still furnish their houses in the taste of the postwar movies. To me, the clothing and furniture styles seem from a bygone era (for those looking for a good old-fashioned corset, there is an ample selection). It is those who are looking for lingerie who will be disappointed, for there is only one page of "special statements," featuring one of the few black women models in the whole book.

Forgetting taste and moving on to practicalities, Sears does far better. The "better" and "best"-quality tools and supplies are generally respected. If you're looking for a pool table or even a sauna, in which case design is less important than price or just availability, Sears is most useful. And when you come to home appliances, Sears was one of the first firms to learn the lesson of today's American industry: build abroad and sell here under your brand name. Kenmore consistently rates well in Consumers Union tests, in terms of both quality and price, often costing about the same as discounted nationally known brands. Basic appliances, such as home freezers, look utilitarian, rate well and may be cheaper than those available to you locally.

After examining the 1980 census figures, Sears realized that the 50-and-up market was the fastest-growing one. People of 50 and over represent about 25% of the market, yet they control 50% of discretionary income. So Sears started Mature Outlook Club, which offers discounts on products and services, including Sears's products, to people aged 50 and over.

Discounts for People over 60

Government and private industry together produce *The Silver Pages,* telephone directories of firms that give discounts and special offers to people over 60 years old. Directories are planned for over a hundred cities. To find out if a directory for your area is published and how to get one, telephone 800-252-6060.

TELEPHONE BUYING SERVICES

If you have the make and model number of what you want, a telephone buying service makes it easy to shop. You join the service either through a group or as an individual (usually paying an annual membership fee) and receive a membership number that you give when you call a central toll-free number to get a quote and/or order.

One good thing about buying through these services is that getting a price quote is easy and fast. Another good thing is that the exact shipping cost is given to you with the quote. An advantage for people living in remote areas is that shipping costs on larger appliances may be lower than they would be from, say, New York stores, if the service has a vendor near you.

However, don't rely on telephone services alone, because there are all sorts of things that they don't sell (only one of them sells small appliances), and their stock is limited to the most popular brands and models. You'll find a much wider choice, and sometimes lower prices, if you also shop at the more specialized stores.

Bankcard Holders of America (Consumer Action Agency), ***333 Pennsylvania Avenue SE, Washington, DC 20003. Telephone 202-543-5805.***
Free publication list.
Membership fee: $12 per year.
Established 1980.

This nonprofit organization is not a buying service. It is an independent organization that informs consumers about credit. BHA is in this section because as a BHA member you get the right to use a couple of telephone discount buying services to which it would normally cost more to subscribe. There is the added advantage that if you run into any trouble with your purchases, BHA will try to help you. (In two cases when comparing prices I found that the BHA-recommended organizations were the winners.)

BHA publishes informative pamphlets on credit cards.

Buy Phone America, ***1987 Utica Avenue, Brooklyn, NY 11234. Telephone 800-223-4060; in New York, 718-251-7700.***
Membership fee: $19.95 for three years.
Sells large and small appliances and stereo equipment.
Returns: exchange or credit given if goods returned within seven days in original box.
Established 1982.

This is one of the few services through which you can get small appliances as well as large ones. When I was comparing prices on the GE F440 iron, Buy Phone America had the lowest price of all—$43 when it was selling at Macy's for $60—and was ready to deliver the iron immediately. I advise joining through Bankcard Holders of America (see above), because you then get to use other clubs as well, and receive extra benefits.

Comp-U-Store International, ***777 Summer Street, Stamford, CT 06901. Telephone 800-843-7777.***
Membership fee: $30 per year. Monthly list of special offers.
MC, V.
Sells large appliances, cars and tires, china, glass, computers, electronics, furniture, luggage, watches.
Returns: membership may be cancelled with full fee refund within the year.
Established 1974.

This organization has 1.5 million regular members and 29,000 members who have access through their computer modems. Comp-U-Store negotiates prices with vendors around the country and files the information on a computer. As I write, Comp-U-Store says that it has 100,000 prices on file. When a member calls in for a price, the computer works out the lowest price, including shipping and tax (if any), for that particular customer. If and when the customer orders, an order number is given and then a written receipt is sent with the order details and the name of the vendor. Recently I ordered a telephone manufactured by Webcor through Comp-U-Store and found that the vendor was actually Webcor. I got the Webcor Zip 757 telephone for a total of $47.94 including shipping, when it would have cost me $63.86 including tax to buy it locally. Someone else in North Carolina ordered a television set, and the vendor turned out to be a New York City discount store (S and S Sound City). I called the store to see whether the Comp-U-Store customer was getting a break, and found that I, as an off-the-street customer, would get the set for $249 plus tax, whereas the Comp-U-Store customer had paid $232.71 total, including shipping. However, in spite of the large membership and the computer, I have not, alas, found in my price comparisons that Comp-U-Store consistently gets the lowest prices. It would be much simpler if there were one unbeatable source but, to my annoyance, the lowest price seems to come from a different store each time.

Two disadvantages of Comp-U-Store: One is that the assistants seem to work exclusively with model numbers, so you can ask almost no questions about what you are buying. The other problem is that they give a discouragingly long delivery date (perhaps to be on the safe side, because they don't check with the vendors as to whether what you are ordering is in stock or has to be ordered). I was told that my Webcor telephone would arrive in three to six weeks. In fact it took two weeks.

Consumer Thrift Club, ***P.O. Box 9394, Minneapolis, MN 55440. Telephone 800-328-0786.***
Membership fee: $34.95 per year.
Sells appliances, carpets, cars and tires, china and glass, computers, exercise equipment, furniture, luggage, men's clothing, pianos and organs, sewing machines, typewriters. Offers supermarket discount coupons, car rental discounts, hotel discounts.
Returns: you can cancel membership and have entire fee returned anytime within the year.
Established 1982.

This club, a subsidiary of ITT, has at the time of writing 200,000 members, and it supports itself only by membership fees (no kickbacks on sales). When you join, you get a membership number and a list of vendors that you call directly. The advantage of this system is that you can ask more questions about the product, delivery and so on.

Besides the usual products that you can order by telephone, there is an unusual shopping coupon program. Through it you can buy $16 worth of coupons for $5. Why pay for coupons when they are normally given away for free? Because this way you can order exactly the ones you want (coupons for 1,000 of the most popular nonperishable supermarket goods are listed). You can also sometimes get coupons not normally available in your part of the country. As the club spokesman pointed out to me, this is especially useful for people who live near stores that give double value on coupons.

Purchase Power, ***352 Cedar Lane, Teaneck, NJ 07666. Telephone 201-836-3200.***
Sells membership to buying organization through which you can buy major appliances, electronics and photographic equipment, furniture, carpets, lamps, power tools, typewriters, vacuum cleaners, men's clothes, watches, jewelry, cars, pickups, vans.
Returns: depends on vendor.
Established 1964.

Purchase Power doesn't accept individual memberships, but if you call, it will refer you to the affiliated groups that use its services and that you can join.

When you join one of the groups, you are given a list of vendors with toll-free numbers, and you deal directly with them. If a vendor does not carry a *major* brand you are interested in, it is bound by its contract with Purchase Power to refer you to a vendor who does carry the brand you want.

There is also a lowest-price guarantee. If you buy something from a vendor and then see it somewhere else at a lower price within 20 days, the vendor must refund the difference plus 20% of the difference.

Quota Phone National, ***2 Hamilton Avenue, New Rochelle, NY 10801. Telephone 800-221-0626; in New York State, 914-633-8745.***
Membership fee: $12 per year.
Sells large appliances, cameras, electronics, furniture (no small appliances).
Returns: depends on vendor.
Established 1980.

Instead of dealing with you directly, Quota Phone refers you to a vendor (a large store, mail-order company or distributor) that services your area. You then call the vendor either toll-free or collect. The advantage for Quota Phone is, I suppose, that it is less work. The advantage for you is that you can probably get a little more information from the vendor than you can from an organization that simply quotes prices.

The company belongs to David Blau, who says he left an excellent job to start this firm. He says that he is trying to take the risk out of buying by telephone. He guarantees that he'll get you the lowest price on anything costing more than $150, and will refund the difference if you find anything you bought through Quota Phone at a lower price elsewhere. He will settle any damage claims that the trucking company will not settle, and he will help his customers in any dispute with vendors.

Last year I bought a White-Westinghouse clothes washer through Quota Phone because it beat by $6 the next lowest price I got (I called seven discount stores). Service and delivery were perfectly fine.

If you join Bankcard Holders of America (see above), you can use Quota Phone plus other services for the same price.

HAIRCUTS

For an up-to-the-minute hairstyle that doesn't cost the usual exorbitant price, you can get a complimentary or very inexpensive haircut from a hair salon or beauty school that uses outside models for its trainee hairdressers.

The trainees are already licensed, which means that they have been training for at least a year, so you will not be the victim of anyone's first haircut.

As the trainees are learning new cuts, you do have to be willing to change your style, but the salons vary in terms of how rigid they are. Most say that the big decision concerning style is made after a consultation between you and the stylist.

Appointments are often given during normal working hours, but some of the larger salons and schools have regularly scheduled classes, often to concentrate on a particular new cut. And some will do perms and hair coloring as part of the deal.

Here, just to give you an idea, are a few outfits that, at the time of writing, give free or cheap haircuts. To find one that suits you, call the larger salons in your own area or the beauty schools that are listed under *Schools* in the yellow pages.

New York

Bumble and Bumble, ***146 East 56th Street, New York, NY 10022. Telephone 212-371-4100.***

This is the favorite hairdresser of several of my younger, with-it friends. They pay $30 to $50 per cut, but a licensed assistant will do the cut for a mere $5. Bumble and Bumble looks for men and women who are interested in changing their hairstyle and will be flexible about what the new style is. They promise not to do anything you positively don't want. Call for an appointment during the weekly supervised class or even during regular working hours.

Clairol Evaluation Salon, ***345 Park Avenue, New York, NY 10154. Telephone 212-546-2713 or 212-546-2715.***

Clairol sometimes needs people for hair color testings. If you have hair of a color and type that Clairol happens to be interested in, it may color your hair for free regularly. You must apply in person, Monday through Thursday.

Jingles Advanced Hair Training Center, ***350 Fifth Avenue, New York, NY 10118. Telephone 212-695-9365.***

This training branch of a fashionable and well-known London hairdresser gives men and women haircuts that they say are in the latest London styles for $5 each. Haircutters are practicing hairdressers who are taking a course to keep *au courant* with the newest looks. You can say what you want done, but must be somewhat willing to compromise. You can make an appointment for the usual business hours, and you will be turned away only if your hair is too fine or you are inflexible about what style you want.

New York and Chicago, Los Angeles, San Francisco, Toronto

Vidal Sassoon, ***834 North Michigan, Water Tower Place, Chicago, IL 60614. Staff training telephone 312-337-9497.***

Vidal Sassoon, ***405 North Rodale Drive, Los Angeles, CA 90210. Telephone 213-858-9795.***

Vidal Sassoon, ***767 Fifth Avenue, New York, NY 10153. Telephone 212-535-9200.***

Vidal Sassoon, ***130 Post Street, San Francisco, CA 94108. Telephone 415-987-0744.***

Vidal Sassoon, ***37 Avenue Road, Toronto, Ontario, M5R 2G3, Canada. Telephone 416-920-1333.***

On two evenings or mornings a week each Vidal Sassoon salon holds a class for assistants who are still in training. In that class hair is cut, colored or permed for prices that are about one-eighth of Sassoon's usual prices ($7 to $9 for a cut, as I write, as opposed to the regular prices of $37 to $65). You go to the salon on the right day and wait around for a couple of hours hoping to be chosen. Being chosen depends on whether your hair is suitable for whatever is being taught that night. Both men and women are needed.

Cut-Price Cuts

A friend of mine says that a slightly shady way of getting a cut-price cut, popular with the fashionable poor, is to ask your hairdresser whether he or she "free-lances." This means cutting hair at his or her home, or yours, outside working hours. You negotiate the price, which, depending on how much your hairdresser gets paid per cut at the salon, can be as little as half of what you'd pay there. This, of course, does not please the salon, which thereby loses a customer.

Cut It Yourself

Think how much you could save if you could cut your own and your family's hair. **Whole Earth Access** (described in the General section) says that a staff member learned so well from a book that her friends ask her where she trained. The book is *How to Cut Your Own or Anybody Else's Hair* by Bob Bent (Simon and Schuster, $8.95).

HEALTH

DENTAL WORK

One way of saving money on dental work is to have it done at a dental school—if you are lucky enough to live near one. Work at dental schools is done by dentists who are in the process of graduating or who have graduated and are now specializing. They do the work under the close supervision of a professor, and people seem to agree that the workmanship is meticulous. The main drawback is the time taken—there is a waiting period before you are assigned to a student, and the actual work may take longer than at a dentist's office.

If you are thinking of having work done at a dental school, you first go in for X-rays and diagnosis. There is a fee for this, which varies according to the school. The two New York schools charge $35 in cash. If you decide to go ahead, you are put on a waiting list to be assigned a dentist, which can take three weeks to three months, depending on what you need done.

A friend of mine had her daughter's cross bite fixed at the New York University dental school. First my friend and her daughter visited two private orthodontists and got estimates of $3500 and over $4000 for the work to be done. Then they went to an orthodontist who was "the best man in the trade," according to their regular dentist. He said he'd charge around $5000. My friend most certainly didn't want to pay that much, so the best man in the trade recommended New York University or Columbia University, where the only drawback, he said, is the time factor.

The long and the short of it is that my friend and her daughter went to NYU. After the first diagnostic visit (which involved a whole morning's waiting and rather bureaucratic behavior on the part of the NYU staff), there was a wait of three weeks before she was assigned an orthodontist. Exactly the same work that the top man in the trade had recommended was done for $1250. On every visit, her daughter was seen by the student *and* the teaching specialist, who discussed the progress together. My friend says that the treatment was really up to date, the practitioners very efficient, pleasant and helpful. Her only complaint is that the hours are 9:30 A.M. to 12 noon because the students have classes in the afternoons. But she made early appointments and they never had to wait.

I also talked to the sister-in-law of a friend, who several years ago had lots of gum surgery done at the Columbia University dental school. At that time a private dental surgeon had told her he'd charge $2000; Columbia did it for $250. Her complaint was that it was time-consuming (the whole thing took a year instead of the four months it would have taken if she had gone to the private surgeon). Apart from that and the nuisance of having multiple medical staff members peering into her mouth and demonstrating techniques, she was pleased, for she thought she got better care than she would have from a private surgeon. She says the facilities were incredible and the workmanship superb. She also said she was given the best injections she'd ever had, and she hates injections so she's a connoisseur.

If you don't know whether there is a dental school near you, contact this association for a list of schools in the United States and Canada: **AMERICAN DENTAL ASSOCIATION,** ***Commission on Dental Accreditation, 211 East Chicago Avenue, Chicago, IL 60611.***

DRUGS

Generic Drugs

Whether you buy locally or by mail, consider generic drugs. These are drugs on which the patent has expired, so all manufacturers can make them. Competition keeps prices down, even though the U.S. Food and Drug Administration has officially stated that "there is no significant difference in quality between brand and generic name drugs." About 40% of brand name drugs now have generic equivalents, and the prices of these are sometimes half the prices of brand names, or even less. The president of the Generic Drugs Association has quoted various dramatic comparisons taken from a national drugstore chain, including that of 100 Valium tablets selling for $23.38 when the same amount of the generic equivalent diazepam cost $13.89. And the authors of a Federal Trade Commission Report, "Generic Substitution and Prescription Drug Prices," say that the *average* saving on a prescription when a generic is substituted for a leading brand name drug is 25%.

A doctor can prescribe generic medicine either by giving the generic name or by giving a brand name and writing "generic if available."

Note that you almost always get extra savings by buying in larger quantities.

Short-term Drugs

To save money on antibiotics and drugs that you'll need suddenly, be prepared by researching the best prices in your neighborhood. The American Association of Retired Persons has found that "prices charged by pharmacists in the same locale may differ by two or three times for the same drug." In ***Prescription*** *for Action,* a booklet that describes ways that volunteers can help keep health costs down, the AARP gives instructions on how to compare drug prices and pharmacy services in a community. *Prescription for Action* is available from **HEALTH ADVOCACY SERVICES,** ***AARP, 1909 K Street NW, Washington, DC 20049.***

Maintenance Drugs by Mail

If you get a sudden attack of the flu, these firms won't help, but if you regularly take maintenance drugs (for allergies, arthritis, diabetes, high blood pressure, heart disease and so on), you can save up to 30% by buying from these firms. They fill huge quantities of prescriptions for organizations and for individuals, buy in quantity and pass savings on to customers. Nevertheless, they employ registered, licensed pharmacists who fill prescriptions exactly as doctors prescribe them.

I compared prices on five common maintenance medicines with brand names (Aldomet, Dilantin, Motrin, Tagamet and Valium) and discovered that I could find each one at 20 to 30% off my neighborhood price at one or more of these stores. *But* discounts do vary—some are much smaller than others—so it is very much worth shopping around to see which firm has the lowest price on the medicine you use. Prices of the generics I checked were a third to a half off those of brand name drugs at these firms.

To buy from these firms, just send a doctor's original prescription. If you don't have the prescription, send the prescription bottle label or a copy of the prescription, but include your doctor's telephone number, because in that case the firm must ask his permission. You can reorder by telephone.

Note that, by law, prescription drugs can not be returned.

America's Pharmacy, ***P.O. Box 10490, Des Moines, IA 50306. Telephone 515-287-6872.***
Free catalogue, or write or call for a price quote.
MC, V.
Sells medicines—prescription and nonprescription, brand name and generic; vitamins; health equipment.
Returns: except for prescription drugs, money back if merchandise returned unopened within 30 days.
Established 1963.

The catalogue lists mainly vitamins and beauty and health aids, but America's Pharmacy claims to also have a complete inventory of all brand name drugs and all generic drugs. Either send in your prescription or write or telephone first for a price quote. Your order will be sent out within 24 hours by UPS or parcel post. If you don't want to pay with a credit card, you can pay later even if you are a first-time customer. You can call during working hours (8 A.M. to 4:30 P.M.) to ask questions of the full-time registered pharmacists or to order a prescription refill. (You can order on a tape recorder at night.) Other perks include an automatic year-end statement of your purchases for tax purposes and the possibility of having medications mailed direct to holiday addresses. There is also a computer that will take note if at any time you ask for a drug you are allergic to, or order two drugs that shouldn't be taken together.

Prescription Delivery Systems, ***136 South York Road, Hatboro, PA 19040. Telephone 800-441-8976; in Pennsylvania, 215-674-1565.***
Free brochure for generic nonprescription drugs, health aids and vitamins.
MC, V.
Sells generic nonprescription drugs, health aids, vitamins, prescription medicines for arthritis and epilepsy.
Returns: credit given on nonprescription supplies.
Established 1962.

The manager of Prescription Delivery Systems tells me that the firm is especially strong on generic substitutes for nonprescription drugs. The brochure lists prices for national brands such as Bufferin, Tylenol, Contac and Dristan and then gives the prices of its own equivalents, which are at least half off and usually much more. The only prescription drugs that the firm sells at "competitive" prices are for arthritis and for epilepsy.

Retired Persons Services, ***1 Prince Street, Alexandria, VA 22314. Telephone 703-684-0244.***
Free pharmacy catalogue and membership information.
Sells prescription and nonprescription drugs.
Returns: nonprescription drugs unconditionally guaranteed.
Established 1959.

To buy here, you must be a member of the American Association of Retired Persons, but membership costs only $5 a year, is open to anyone aged 50 or over and entitles you to all sorts of benefits. This large organization fills 5 million prescriptions a year, and, although it doesn't accept credit card payment, you don't pay ahead but are billed with the order. Retired Persons Services had the lowest prices for three of the five medicines I checked.

HOBBY AND PROFESSIONAL EQUIPMENT

ART SUPPLIES

Seasonal Sales

Full-price stores and the stores listed below tend to have special sales in November or December and sometimes in January, when some goods are discounted by varying amounts. Almost all art supply stores, including these, have major sales in May that are worth watching out for.

Mail and Telephone Sources

These art supply houses are wonderful sources, with a far bigger and better stock than most local stores. Prices are all discounted, but no one house consistently has the lowest prices on the national brands. On paints and papers the price differences among listed stores are in cents, but on the furniture and more expensive equipment it is worth comparing prices.

Dick Blick Company, ***P.O. Box 1267, Galesburg, IL 61401. Telephone: questions, 309-343-6181; orders, 800-447-8192.***
Catalogue, $2 in the U.S. and Canada.
MC, V.
Sells art and craft materials.
Refunds: money back.
Established 1911.

Dick Blick produces a big, complete, well-organized catalogue of art and craft supplies, clearly aimed at schools (discounts are best on large quantities) but useful for any artsy-craftsy person or family. Besides the art supplies, you can find here such things as flowers, ribbons and papers to make decorations, as well as supplies for picture framing, ceramics, printmaking and woodworking. You can also get art and office furniture—files, computer tables, lights and so on. When I checked, prices of plastic box–type picture frames were only a few cents under my local stationer's prices (but then my local stationer claimed to be discounting the frames). Other things, such as Elmer's glue and Strathmore 400 watercolor paper, were 25 to 45% under my local prices.

Jerry's Artarama, ***117 South Second Street, New Hyde Park, NY 11040. Telephone 800-221-2323; in New York State, 212-343-4545 or 516-328-6633.***
114-page catalogue in May and November, $2 ($3 in Canada). Additional sale leaflets throughout the year.
Sells artist's materials, architect's supplies, engineer's supplies, picture frames. Stocks better brands such as D'Arches, Bainbridge, Grumbacher, K and E, Koh-I-Noor, Letraset, 3M, Strathmore, Winsor and Newton.
Minimum order $25 by mail, $50 by telephone.
Returns: money back if merchandise has not been abused.
Established 1968.

Jerry's has a good range of artist's supplies, including, of course, the better paints and papers. Equipment for picture framing, batik, stained-glass work and sculpture and studio furniture are all shown. Prices of some paints that I checked were a few cents lower than Pearl's, but Pearl has a bigger inventory.

Pearl Paint Company, ***308 Canal Street, New York, NY 10013. Telephone 212-431-7932.***
30-page price list, $1.
MC, V.
Sells art and graphic supplies by Advance, Grumbacher, Koh-I-Noor, Sauer, Stacor, Taka, Winsor and Newton; pens; house paint.
Minimum order $50.
Returns: credit if notified within two weeks, but written authorization is needed.
Established 1935.

Pearl Paint is *the* famous five-floor art supply store in New York, and any New York painter will recommend it unreservedly (except for a few grumbles about its popularity and its lines). It stocks a wealth of top names in paints (Winsor and Newton, Grumbacher) and other art supplies, which are listed in the catalogue. But the marvelous array of hobby materials is not listed—you have to telephone for details. Pearl says that it will be glad to answer any "specific product inquiries." Almost everything is discounted 20 to 40%.

Utrecht, ***33 35th Street, Brooklyn, NY 11232. Telephone 718-768-2525.***
Free catalogue.
Manufactures and sells canvas, paints and inks. Sells water colors and supplies by other manufacturers.
Returns: credit if merchandise returned in mint condition.
Minimum order $40.
Established 1949.

Another New York favorite, Utrecht makes and sells its own canvases, paints and inks at rock-bottom prices. The paints cost a third to half of what the better-known brands cost.

Richard Osterweil, a painter and enthusiastic customer, assures me that Utrecht quality is high on all its products. He uses the oil paints and says the whites are wonderful, the light colors are very good and the darker hues vary—each person should experiment and see which ones he or she likes. He also uses the Utrecht jessop and canvas (he recently saw a canvas size he had just bought for a third more at Pearl Paints—and Pearl has discount prices).

Utrecht stocks only Utrecht paint but has other art supplies by independent manufacturers at a discount.

TOOLS

Mail and Telephone Sources

There are several stores where you can get a wide choice of good tools at prices that are as much as 30% below local hardware store prices. For instance, when I checked out the Milwaukee Variable Speed Jigsaw Kit No. 6287 it was selling for $292 at a New York store but only $207 at Whole Earth. Prices of most mail-order tools that I checked were about 20% below local New York prices, which means respectable savings, even after you add shipping charges. Savings are especially good on more expensive tools. *But* a few prices were only 15% off, so if you are ordering a tool costing less than about $60, be careful to compare mail-order prices with local prices and include local sales tax versus shipping costs. Otherwise you may find you have saved nothing.

Best Products *(main listing in General section).* I found excellent (in fact, the lowest) prices here on the limited selection of less expensive brand name tools that Best carries. A particularly good buy was a Remington 14-inch electric saw that was discounted 40% below list, and other prices were 30% off list.

Cook Brothers, ***240 North Ashland, Chicago, IL 60607. Telephone 312-421-5140.***
Free catalogue.
Sells tools.
Returns: money back if merchandise returned within 30 days in original box and with invoice.
Established 1949.

Cook Brothers, which is not a specialist tool store but has a general catalogue, was recommended to me by a reader. He told me (a few years ago) that it carries conventional tools whose quality is superior or equal to that of tools carried by Sears and J. C. Penney for much lower prices. He also recommended an exceptionally compact kit of 20 pieces (eight socket wrenches, four screwdriver shafts, one socket wrench driving shaft, five hex key wrenches and a pistol-gripped universal handle, all in a zippered case). He bought the kit to carry on his bike but found it indispensable around the house—with it, he needed few other tools. Cook was selling the kit for half the price that other stores were charging.

Sotz, ***13600 North Station Road, Columbia Station, OH 44028. Telephone: questions, 216-236-5021; orders, 800-321-9892.***
Free catalogues in March, September, November.
MC, V.
Sells garden and workshop tools, machinery, other equipment.
Returns: money back.
Established 1956.

Sotz sells equipment and supplies for the farm, garden and workshop. People asked have had only good, complimentary things to say about Sotz—it stocks high-quality brands, and prices are consistently good. Prices are much lower than at hardware stores, power lawn tools have been about 25% less than at a local lawn mower dealer and a line of Poulan saws was about 10 to 15% less than at a local lumber yard. However, one K Mart had the same line of Stanley professional tools at the same prices. This is a fine source for the East, but shipping probably makes it too expensive for people west of the Mississippi.

U.S. General Supply Corporation, ***100 Commercial Street, Plainview, NY 11803. Telephone for orders only 800-645-7077.***
180-page catalogue, $2.
MC, V.
Sells most American brand name tools: Black and Decker, Crescent, Makita, Milwaukee, Proto, Skil, Stanley, Wen.
Returns: money back.
Established 1955.

U.S. claims to sell all brand name tools made in America at 20 to 50% off, but when I tried to compare prices on four tools, only one was stocked—a Makita sander. This firm was recommended to me by a customer who said prices were low, but when I compared I found that Best equaled or beat the prices *if* it stocked the tool.

Whole Earth Access, ***Mail Order, 2950 7th Avenue, Berkeley, CA 94710. Telephone 415-845-3000.***
(Main listing in General section)

Whole Earth has an excellent section of garden, carpentry, power and stationary tools. The stock has been carefully chosen and is informatively described, so this is a great source for anyone trying to decide what to buy. When I compared prices on a Makita saw and sander, they were 25% below my local prices (and 12% below a local *sale* price).

Buying Secondhand

Basic used tools are available in good condition for a third to two-thirds off the price of their new equivalents. Old cast steel saws, for instance, cost around $15, whereas new ones cost around $45. Ordinary old Stanley metal planes (Nos. 4, 5 and 6) cost around $15, whereas new ones cost around $25. The old Stanley 45 plane in good condition costs, as I write, around $175, whereas a new comparable Stanley plane sells for around $300.

Flea markets and garage sales are good places to find old tools; so are classified advertisements. Raymond Townsend, editor of the *Ohio Tool Box,* suggests visiting a hardware or tool store to decide which tools you want and how much they cost new before looking for used tools. Just make sure the tools are in working condition, as sometimes old tools are put together with various parts and look good but don't work. Most urban areas have tool shops that sell reconditioned hand and power tools.

Iron Horse Antiques, ***R.D. 2, Poultney, VT 05764. Telephone 802-287-4050.***
Fine Tool Journal, sample issue $3.
MC, V.
Sells used tools for collectors and for use.
Returns: cash if merchandise returned within five days, otherwise credit.
Established 1970.

Iron Horse Antiques sells mainly hand tools for collectors, and these are no bargain for the ordinary handy person. But it also usually has in stock common used hand tools such as Stanley metal planes and Disston and Atkins cast steel saws that cost only one- to two-thirds of what new ones cost. Telephone if you know what you want, or try the classified ad section of the Iron Horse magazine, *Fine Tool Journal.*

Tool Libraries

Some public libraries have started tool-lending programs. Tool borrowing obviously makes a great deal of sense, especially in the case of expensive tools that are not often used.

Tool libraries do not pay for themselves. Money is needed for repair and maintenance of the tools. And a competent manager who knows the tools and can give advice on their use is important. In low-income neighborhoods lending programs have sometimes been supported by federal funds. In other neighborhoods they are supported by local businesses.

Here are the telephone numbers of some tool libraries now in operation:

Berkeley, California: 415-644-6101

Detroit, Michigan: 313-267-6555 (Mark Twain branch of the public library)

Grosse Pointe, Michigan: 313-343-2074

Plainedge, New York: 516-735-4133

Canal Fulton, Ohio: 216-854-4148

Eugene, Oregon: 503-485-3075 (Hours are limited to Saturdays, 10 A.M. to 2 P.M.; Tuesdays and Thursdays, 5 to 7 P.M.; Wednesdays, 3 to 5 P.M.)

HOUSE

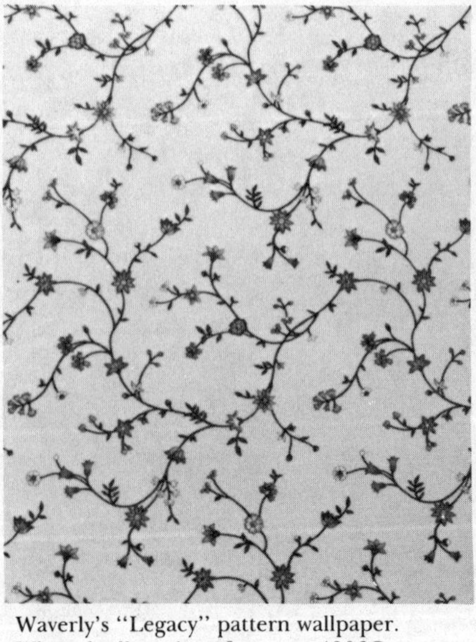

Waverly's "Legacy" pattern wallpaper. When the list price of pattern 4906C was $19 per roll, the price at Post Wallpapers was $14.37 per roll, including postage.

Oneida stainless steel "Julliard" pattern. When the list price for a five-piece place setting was $30, the price at Michael C. Fina was $18.95.

HOUSE

CHINA AND GLASS

No one but a reckless spendthrift should buy expensive imported glass and china in the United States. Most of it costs less than half the U.S. price in the country where it is made, so with little effort (but some patience) you can save quite a bit of money. The sister of a neighbor of mine bought "Bianca" pattern by Wedgwood by mail from London. She paid half the price "Bianca" was fetching at a reduced-price sale at her local Philadelphia department store. When I compared prices on a five-piece place setting of the same pattern, list price in the United States was $190 and the U.S. discount price was $140 plus shipping, while the price including shipping from England was only $73.

On glass, gifts, figurines and commemorative plates the price differences are also striking. The Bing and Grøndahl 1985 Christmas plate "Christmas Eve at the Farmhouse" cost $54.50 (list price) at full-price stores in New York and $43.60 (20% off) at U.S. discount stores (you'd have to add postage to both those prices). Yet it cost only $33.50, including surface postage, from A. B. Schou in Denmark. Lalique's candy bowl "Nogent" cost $200 and $181 plus postage or sales tax at two New York department stores but only $125 including surface postage from Schou.

The glass and china business seems to be one of the best organized foreign mail-order activities; several shops say they have been at it for over 20 years. Goods are expertly packed and on the rare occasions when something arrives broken, many of these shops will replace the article simply on your say-so. I have been ordering china and glass from Finland for years; nothing has ever arrived broken, and I usually have not been charged duty.

European Stores

Casselryds Gla o Porselin, ***Box 158, S 127 23, Skarholmen, Sweden. Telephone 468-7105116.***
38-page catalogue, two $1 bills.
AE, MC, V.

Sells china and crystal tableware by Kosta Boda, Orrefors, Rosenthal and Royal Copenhagen (only the Orrefors is illustrated in the catalogue).
Minimum order $50.
Returns: to claim on insurance, send copy of order, photograph of broken article and copy of claim to the local post office.
Established 1943.

This family business had the lowest prices I found when I compared prices. I found it a good place to buy even though service is a bit rough-and-ready, i.e., I had to get the exact model number of the knives I wanted and my second order wasn't acknowledged—it just arrived eight weeks after I ordered. I bought Kosta Boda knives here twice; 12 knives cost me $99 including surface postage, and no duty was charged. (In New York the same 12 knives cost $156 plus tax.) With my second order the company sent me a Rorstrand commemorative plate as a present.

D. J. Cremin and Sons, ***Kenmare and Moll's Gap, County Kerry, Ireland. Telephone 64-41597.***
48-page catalogue, one $1 bill; prices given in dollars.
AE, DC, MC, V.
Sells Waterford crystal, Belleek and Royal Tara china, Irish linen handkerchiefs, tablecloths and napkins.
Returns: unconditional money-back guarantee.
Established 1906.

"Who would ever have thought that a store sitting on the side of a mountain all by itself would give such excellent service," writes a very happy customer from Alabama. She praises Cremin's perfect packing and adds a dig at the London stores—"not as satisfactory, and that includes Harrods. . . ."

Fabrica Sant'Anna, ***Calcada da Boa Hora 96, Lisbon, Portugal. Telephone 1-638292 or 1-648035.***
52-page catalogue, prices on request, one $5 bill.
AE, DC, MC, V.
Sells handmade and hand-painted ceramics and wall tiles.
Returns: credit.
Established 1741.

The famous factory produces beautiful hand-painted pottery in traditional, somewhat rustic styles. Lamps, platters, bowls, vases and tiles cost well under half the U.S. prices—if you can find similar wares here. An 11-by-9-inch painted-to-order house name made up of several tiles, for instance, cost $125 in New York when a similar one measuring 16 by 11 inches from Portugal cost only $32, including postage and insurance. The illustrated catalogue comes without prices; you must write and ask about whatever you are interested in. After six weeks (at least that's how long it took them to answer me) you will be given a dollar price that includes postage and insurance. The firm was approved of by a reader who bought tiles to make a coffee table here.

Frosig, ***9 Norrebrogade DK 2200, Copenhagen N, Denmark. Telephone 00945-01399000.***
Brochures, two $1 bills.
AE, MC, V.
Sells figurines, dinnerware, crystal, glass Christmas and Mother's Day plates, steel kitchenware. Manufacturers: Bing and Grøndahl, Royal Copenhagen, Holmegaard, Lladró, Mats Jonasson, Orrefors.
Returns: money back, but "goods have to be returned not later than one week after receipt or we like an explanatory letter."
Established 1889.

Frosig has many American admirers, partly because of Mrs. Buddig, the mail-order manager, who has been corresponding with American customers for years. She says that Frosig has gained popularity not by advertising but by "the mouth-to-mouth" method (sounds exciting). One customer wrote to me that Frosig is an *outstanding* shop. He added that Mrs. Buddig "works hard to locate your order and is totally honest . . . one of the world's true sweethearts." This is one of the few places where you can buy Royal Copenhagen and Bing and Grøndahl seconds by mail.

Gered, ***173/174 Piccadilly, London, W1 0PD, England. Telephone 1-734-7262.***
Free color brochures; prices in dollars.
AE, DC, MC, V.
Sells china by Adams, Coalport, Masons, Minton, Royal Doulton, Royal Worcester, Spode, Wedgwood.
Established 1948.

This reputable shop is where the above-mentioned sister of a friend of mine bought her Wedgwood "Bianca" by mail for half the local price. She says that service was excellent and she got a personal follow-up letter from the manager, Barry Marcus. When she told him that three plates had arrived broken, the plates were replaced forthwith—no proof was asked for. She's only sorry that Gered doesn't sell Waterford crystal, her next purchase.

Although not all manufacturers are handled, prices of what Gered *does* handle are excellent, and chances are that what you want will be in stock.

Limoges Unic, ***12, rue de Paradis, 75010 Paris, France. Telephone 1-47-70-54-49.***
Color catalogue, four $1 bills.
AE, DC, MC, V.
Sells china by Raynaud, Ceralene, Haviland, Bernardaud, Royal Limoges; crystal by Baccarat, Daum, Lalique and St. Louis; silver plate by Christofle and Ercuis.

Minimum order $250.
Returns: money back.
Established 1932.

The color catalogue from this firm is not always available, but it is well worth writing for specific prices on crystal by Baccarat and Lalique, which is so expensive in the United States. I have not found that the famous Christofle silver plate is worth buying direct from France; in this case U.S. discount stores have better prices.

Hans Hansen, ***Baunegardsvej 3, Snogh/øj, DK 7000 Fredericia, Denmark. Telephone 5-94-35-01.***
Free brochure, published in January.
Sells china and porcelain for collectors: plates, figurines, bells, mugs by Bing and Grøndahl, Royal Copenhagen, Desirée, Goebel, Hummel, Lladró, Nao, Hutschenreuther, Rosenthal, Noritake, others.
Returns: money back; "might anything be lost in mail or arrive damaged, please inform us—and we will compensate."
Established 1958.

Recommended by a reader, Diane Arkins, who says the service is first-rate and the Hans Hansen people are friendly and really nice to deal with. When she ordered an out-of-stock figurine for a present, Hans Hansen wrote, "We hope and think that we will get it before September, at any rate you shall have the very first we get." Diane Arkins did some price comparisons for me on five Goebel Hummel figurines she had bought. Prices were generally a third off U.S. prices (one piece, "Mail Coach," was even more of a bargain—because of an extra Hansen 30% discount on the more expensive models, it cost only $154, while it was selling in New Jersey for $330).

Marechal, ***232, rue de Rivoli, 75001 Paris, France. Telephone 1-42-60-71-83.***
Free color leaflet, available anytime except February, when the store is closed.
AE, V.
Sells porcelain boxes by Limoges.
Returns: none.
Established 1934.

A marvelous address for collectors of miniature boxes, Marechal sells little hand-painted Limoges porcelain boxes for prices that are one-third to half the price (including airmail postage) of similar boxes bought in the United States at stores such as Tiffany's. The 2- to 3-inch boxes have delicate flower or country scenes hand-painted on the lids or are decorated with sculpted bird or animal figures. Wonderful as presents, the boxes cost mostly between $30 and $50.

Reject China Shop, ***Head Office, 13 Silver Road, Wood Lane, London, W12 7SG, England. Telephone 1-749-9191.***

16-page color catalogue, three $1 bills in the U.S. and Canada, or write for specific prices.
Sells china, pottery and crystal. China and pottery by Aynsley, Adams, Belleek, Beswick, Burgess and Leigh, Coalport, Caverswall, Crown Staffordshire, Denby, Elizabethan, Richard Ginori, Herend, Hummel, Hornsea, Johnson Brothers, Limoges-HRLND, Limoges Bernardaud, Lladró, Masons, Midwinter, Myott Meakin, Portmeirion, Paragon, Palissy, Poole Pottery, Royal Albert, Royal Grafton, Royal Worcester, Spode, Thomas China, Villeroy and Boch, Narumi, Mikas. Crystal by Atlantis, Baccarat, Edinburgh, Lalique, Orrefors, St Johns, Stuart, Waterford.
Returns: none; goods that arrive broken will be replaced (please send a photograph of any broken pieces).
Established 1960.

"Each year over 150,000 customers tread the steps of our quaint Victorian shops in their quest for beautiful bargains," says the Reject China catalogue. This group of shops is well known and popular, but, in spite of the name, all of the china sold by mail is of the first quality, not "reject" (you can buy the seconds only in person). The catalogue shows only a sampling, so if you know what you want, save $3 and simply write and ask for prices.

A. B. Schou, ***Skandinavisk Glas, 4 NY Ostergade, DK-1101 Copenhagen, Denmark. Telephone 1-138096.***
Catalogue in April, $4; prices in dollars. Or write for specific prices.
Sells porcelain and Christmas plates by Bing and Grøndahl and Royal Copenhagen, figurines by Lladró and Goebel, china by Herend (and several British manufacturers), glass by Baccarat, Kosta Boda, Lalique, Orrefors, Saint Louis, Schott-Zwiesel, Waterford.
Returns: satisfaction guaranteed or money back.

A. B. Schou specializes in low prices on certain "giftwares" such as porcelain figures, commemorative plates, bowls, vases and candlesticks by famous European glass and china manufacturers. The firm was originally recommended to me by the same reader who recommended Frosig. He wrote about Schou: "An OUTSTANDING firm. . . . I have had extensive dealings with A. B. Schou since 1969. Experience convinces me of their quality of integrity, attention to orders, willingness to help on items not featured in their regular catalogues and brochures. . . ." Another reader, Inge Friedmann in Virginia, who had bought Lladró figurines from Schou, told me that at one point when Lladró figurine #4807, "Geisha," was selling for $295 in the United States, it cost $155 at Schou.

Tierney's Gift Shop, ***72 Lower George Street, Dunlaoghaire, County Dublin, Ireland. Telephone 1-802898.***
Waterford brochure, free. Write with reference number for price on any of the china.
AE, DC, MC, V.

Sells Waterford, Coalport, Hummel, Lladró, Royal Doulton, Royal Worcester, Spode, Wedgwood.
Returns: refund or replacement.
Established 1951.

This shop doesn't look as prepared for mail orders as some of the larger stores, but it does have illustrated Waterford brochures. It will quote prices if you send a model number.

Watch out for British gift shops that advertise in the United States. I found some of their china and glass prices to be closer to U.S. discount prices. You'll find better prices at the above stores and at department stores such as Harrods, Selfridges and so on (see General section).

U.S. Firms

If the glass or china is inexpensive, or you are buying a single piece, it might be worth buying from an American source.

Always compare prices among these New York stores to find the lowest price on what you want, because I haven't found any store that consistently has the lowest prices on everything, and on large purchases the difference is significant. However, some stores deliver extra services such as gift wrapping, engraving and keeping bridal registries.

When comparing prices, notice that in the case of glasses and place settings some firms give a fixed discount however much you buy, while others give a good discount only on larger quantities (such as eight place settings). And remember to find out whether what you want is in stock or must be ordered.

All of the stores give prices by telephone, and a few will give prices *only* by telephone.

A. Benjamin, ***80–82 Bowery, New York, NY 10013. Telephone 212-226-6013 or 212-226-6014.***
In the U.S. and Canada, send self-addressed, stamped envelope, or telephone 9 A.M. to 3 P.M., Monday to Friday, for specific prices.
Sells crystal and glass; all brands of china (Franciscan, Gorham, Lenox, Mikasa, Noritake); silver (Gorham, Towle, Wallace, International, Oneida, Reed and Barton, Kirk-Steiff, Alvin, Lunt, Heirloom, Tuttle); sterling holloware; silver plate; pewter flatware and holloware.
Returns: none on special orders.
Established 1972.

Benjamin says it is "bombarded" with mail, which may be why the firm is organized enough to send out price quotes on informative (although messy) sheets, telling you how to pay, what to do about breakage and so on. On the five items I checked, Benjamin prices were among the lowest of the American firms, so this is a source to remember. It does have an order minimum (of $100 to $150) on certain things it has to special order.

Greater New York Trading, ***81 Canal Street, New York, NY 10002. Telephone 212-226-2808, 226-0809, 226-8850.***
In the U.S. and Canada, send self-addressed, stamped envelope or telephone (best hours: 1 P.M. to 5 P.M. any day except Friday or Saturday).
Sells electrical appliances, china, glass and silverware.
Returns: credit if merchandise returned within 10 days, unused and in original carton.
Minimum order $50.
Established 1929.

Greater New York Trading lives up to my picture of a classic discount store. Generations of enthusiastic handwritten notices, some yellowing, some fresh, crowd the windows and walls: "Terrific Prices!!" "All major appliances!!" "All silver manufacturers!!" Inside you can hardly move for the stacks of cardboard boxes, racks of dusty plate samples and huge catalogues and ledgers. None of it seems to faze the salespeople, who were exceptionally cheerful the day I visited. In fact, the store was a cheerful hubbub of neighbors and customers dropping in to chat, and in one case complain that a television had not arrived the day the deliveryman said it would (the woman was treated with great sympathy and told that the deliveryman had been taken ill).

Although the store is dedicated mainly to china and silver, Greater New York also sells appliances.

The Jompole Company, ***330 Seventh Avenue, New York, NY 10001. Telephone 212-594-0440.***
Write or telephone for specific prices.
Sells china, glass, silver by leading manufacturers.
Returns: no returns on special orders but credit is given for returns on patterns that are kept in stock.
Established 1919.

Jompole keeps the most popular patterns in stock and will special order anything not in stock—so long as you don't mind waiting. The manager, Mrs. Blank, says that they've been in business so long that they've learned how to please customers.

Robin Importers, ***510 Madison Avenue, New York, NY 10022. Telephone: questions and in New York State, 212-753-6475 or 212-752-5605; orders only, 800-223-3373.***
Send self-addressed, stamped long envelope or $1 for color brochure or write with self-addressed, stamped envelope or telephone for prices.
AE, DC, MC, V.
Sells any current pattern from any china or stainless steel flatware manufacturer; Galway and Val St. Lambert crystal.
Returns: money back if merchandise mailed within 10 days.
Established 1957.

The Robin color brochures that I have seen show more modern styles than other U.S. catalogues. Instead of being on silver, the emphasis is on stainless steel flatware and kitchen knives by Henkel and Sabatier. The firm carries glass and china by Arabia and Kosta Boda and newer designs by the traditional manufacturers. I checked five prices—three of them were not as low as those given by other stores in this section.

Rogers and Rosenthal, ***105 Canal Street, New York, NY 10002. Telephone 212-925-7557 or 212-925-7558.***
Send self-addressed, stamped envelope or telephone for specific prices.
Sells china, crystal and silver (all American brands of silver plate and stainless steel, most Japanese and Norwegian brands).
Returns: money back if goods not removed from original packing.
Established 1944.

Rogers and Rosenthal looks relatively staid, albeit less kempt than an uptown store, with silver samples in glass cases and suited gentlemen poring over catalogues. They haven't always answered my written inquiries, but they have always given me prices by telephone.

Rudi's Pottery, Silver and China, ***178 Route 17 North, Paramus, NJ 07652. Telephone 201-265-6096.***
In the U.S. and Canada, write or telephone for specific prices.
MC, V.
Sells all brands of china, stemware and giftware.
Returns: money back if within 10 days, credit if within 30 days.
Established 1969.

When I have checked prices by mail, Rudi's has answered quickly, and prices have been among the lowest. The price of the Wedgwood "Bianca" place setting was $117 no matter how few you bought.

Nat Schwartz and Company, ***549 Broadway, Bayonne, NJ 07002. Telephone 800-526-1440; in New Jersey, 201-437-4443.***
Color catalogue, free in the U.S. and Canada, or telephone for specific prices.
MC, V.
Sells china, crystal; flatware and holloware in sterling, silver plate and stainless steel; figurines and jewelry.
Returns: credit if goods returned within 30 days.
Established 1958.

This is a good place to shop if you are buying in quantity. For instance, when I checked, one five-piece place setting of Wedgwood's "Bianca" china cost $136, but if you bought eight place settings they cost only $117 each (several shops gave me this price, the lowest U.S. discount price I found). When I called, Schwartz had the pattern in stock ready to send, unlike some of the other stores. Other advantages of buying here are that the store does gift wrapping, will keep a gift registry, gives a money-back guarantee (even on special orders, although there is a handling charge for those returns) and has a color catalogue illustrating popular glass, china and flatware patterns and gifts. It also has a "Tabletop Coordination Service" and will give you expert advice on "setting the perfect table" and making a "statement of unsurpassed elegance" if that's your desire.

Schwartz also sells Seiko and Concord watches at 20% off list price.

Windsor Gift Shop, ***233–237 Main Street, Madison, NJ 07940. Telephone: questions, 201-377-7273; orders, 800-631-9393.***
Brochure in October, free in the U.S. and Canada, telephone for specific prices.
AE, MC, V.
Sells silver, stainless steel, china, glass, figurines and giftware.
Returns: credit if merchandise returned within two weeks, but there is a restocking charge on goods that have been special ordered.
Established 1933.

When I called Windsor to check Wedgwood's "Bianca," a rather genteel but cheerful lady told me that it was on special sale. The special sale price turned out to be $117, the standard lowest U.S. discount price, and I couldn't wheedle out of her how long the special sale price had been in effect. She also told me (and someone else confirmed) that in January, Christmas ornaments and Spode's "Christmas Tree" china are sold at 50% off.

FURNITURE

Brand name furniture in department or furniture stores is outrageously overpriced and takes just as long to deliver (six to ten weeks for wooden, three to four months for upholstered) as if you buy from the stores below. High Point in North Carolina has been a center for furniture manufacturers and wholesalers for decades. Many of the stores around there have expanded and now sell top American brands at cut-rate prices. As furniture is expensive, you can save hundreds of dollars even after paying for shipping.

I checked a lot of prices and found that these stores usually charged a whopping 40% less than department stores and 25% less than department stores having sales. In only one case I found that Macy's had a special sale on a discontinued line of Baker at about the same prices as those at the stores below. But this was very unusual. The southern stores have toll-free numbers and are eager to quote prices and shipping costs, so you can easily compare prices for yourself. Quite typical was the six-piece Baker mahogany "eighteenth-century-inspired" bedroom set, which, if you wanted to buy the whole thing, would normally cost $6974 at Altman's department store in New York or $5578 on sale at Altman's (both plus tax), yet only $3937 plus a $350 in-house delivery charge from the Furniture Annex.

How to Buy

The best way to compare prices and to buy is to get the model numbers of pieces you are interested in from a local department or furniture store or from a manufacturer's catalogue. If you have seen something you like but can't get the number, most of these stores will try to find it for you in their own manufacturers' catalogues. Certain lines of furniture (such as Baker) are easy to distinguish in the catalogues these stores have, but in the case of other lines, especially of upholstered sofas and chairs, there are too many similar designs and you really need a model number.

If you can't get to a furniture store, most of these stores will try to send you photocopies or brochures, if you can be fairly specific about what you want. When I called these stores asking for white aluminum and black wrought iron garden chairs, all of them (I had to insist with Annex Furniture Gallery) sent me photocopies or brochures.

After you have telephone estimates of the price of the furniture and shipping, you will get a written estimate from the store you choose to buy from. Ask for written descriptions of the different shipping methods, as well as instructions for what to do in case of furniture that is delivered damaged.

Shipping Methods

Some of the stores listed have their own trucks to deliver furniture to customers in nearby states. The great advantage of this is that if the furniture arrives damaged, the store is responsible; you do not have to file a claim with the trucking firm.

Over greater distances there are two ways that furniture is shipped, and it's important to know which one you want. Moreover, a few trucking firms have small extra charges; make sure the store you buy from tells you exactly how the trucking firm will operate.

Common carrier is the "no frills," cheapest way. The furniture comes in the manufacturer's cartons and is left outside your house. There may be only one deliveryman on the truck.

Although the driver is not supposed to, I have been told that he often agrees to bring, or help bring, the load inside if you tip him $10 to $20. When I received a "sidewalk" delivery of garden chairs, I gave the driver $5 for helping us to bring them up to the apartment. He said that most drivers are willing to do it.

Van line is the more expensive method. When it arrives from the manufacturer, the furniture is inspected and repackaged by the store. When it is delivered to you, the furniture is brought into your house, unpacked and set up by the van line.

Damages

If any furniture brought by a trucking company (not the store's own trucks) arrives damaged, it is the responsibility of the trucking company (not the store), so you must file a claim with the trucking company within 15 days. The shop you buy from will give you instructions about what to do in case of damage. Whichever trucking method is used, always inspect furniture in front of the trucker.

Mail and Telephone Sources

When I Bought a Mattress and Box Spring

I bought a mattress and box spring from Mallory's (below) and was very pleased with the whole business. I saved $325 off Bloomingdale's *sale* price quite easily. I think you'd have to be nuts to buy a mattress from a furniture or department store. The only problem is that it is hard to compare prices on box spring sets. If you look at box spring sets in several different stores, you'll think that each manufacturer makes hundreds of different sets in different qualities and at different prices. Not so. It is just that identical mattresses are given different names, at the request of stores, which would like to foil comparison shoppers.

Although each manufacturer does produce genuinely different lines (the box spring sets in some lines are better made and have more expensive innards than those in others), companies also change names around on lines and sets that are identical. If you are trying to compare prices of box springs by a manufacturer who changes the names around, stick to the top line, and remember that there are only about four basic models within that line.

What are you paying for when you buy a mattress in a manufacturer's top line? More and better materials. With each step up in price, you get more insulating material in the mattress and more and better slats in the box spring. Yet Sealy's Al Klancnik (vice president in charge of manufacturing, research and development), when asked, advises cost-conscious shoppers that they'll get the most for their money if they buy the second- or third-best set in a manufacturer's premium line. With the second- or third-best model, you'll be getting the best springs and a generous amount of high-quality insulating materials and padding. The only extras you'd get with the top-of-the-line model would be added padding for a more luxurious feel and a better grade of damask covering. Mr. Klancnik says all the sets within the premium line will last about the same length of time—15 to 20 years.

Annex Furniture Gallery, ***P.O. Box 958, High Point, NC 27261. Telephone 800-334-7391.***
In the U.S. and Canada write or telephone Monday through Saturday, 9:30 A.M. to 5:30 P.M., for specific prices. Free list of manufacturers handled.
Sells furniture by Baker, Century, Drexel, Heritage, Mastercraft, Thomasville and many other leading manufacturers; Sealy bedding and Brown Jordan and Tropitone outdoor furniture.
MC, V.
Returns: "depends on the situation."
Established 1949.

Annex Furniture Gallery started off as an annex selling the floor samples from a big High Point furniture market at very low prices. In the 1950s it developed mail and telephone sales of new and undamaged furniture by well-known manufacturers. It stocks most wooden furniture and some upholstered furniture. Whenever I have called, pretending to be a customer with questions, the salespeople have been incredibly helpful. In fact, one of them, Beth Enochs, answered all my questions about box springs and their innards in the greatest detail and even told me about her own mattress. I was really grateful.

When I was pricing garden chairs, I got the lowest price on the Meadowcraft chair I chose here ($13 below the next lowest price) as Annex gives an extra 5% discount on furniture that the manufacturer delivers directly to the customer (because it is saved manufacturer-to-Annex shipping costs). Before I ordered, Bill Barker of Annex called the manufacturer and gave me a shipping date (six weeks away) and shipping price ($100, to be paid C.O.D. to the manufacturer's trucker). I didn't wait for a written estimate but immediately sent in a check for six chairs. I was told that the chairs would be delivered in mid-July; they arrived on July 23. I was slightly annoyed that, without warning, they arrived by common carrier—the "sidewalk" delivery could have been difficult if the load had been heavier. As it happened, there were people around to help and even the driver helped, so it didn't matter. On the other hand, although I had been told that shipping would be $100 C.O.D., it was only $51.36.

Boyles Furniture Sales, ***727 North Main Street, High Point, NC 27261. Telephone 800-334-3185; in North Carolina, 919-889-4147.***
Manufacturers' brochures available.
Sells furniture by 300 American manufacturers, imported furniture and accessories such as oriental rugs and screens.
Returns: has a customer service department that works out problems of breakage and damage.
Established 1958.

Boyles has been a retailer and mail-order source of furniture for the last 26 years. The manager, Eddie Merrell, says that there are designers on staff who make an effort to help customers find what they want. If you call, for instance, and tell them you want an "eighteenth-century" dining room, they will find the right brochures to send you. Boyles also normally sends everything by private delivery trucks and sets the furniture up in your home.

When I called to ask about garden furniture, my saleswoman was very helpful, made recommendations based on her own experience and sent me photostats from her catalogues (these took six days to arrive). She gave me model numbers and list prices and worked out the 35% discount offered on furniture not made in the South (there is a 40% discount on furniture made in the South). A Brown Jordan "Quantum" chair that Bloomingdale's was just then offering "on sale" for $254 (regular price: $299) Boyles was offering for $194. She also found the telephone number of the manufacturer I was interested in so that I could call and ask where I could see the furniture in New York.

Loftin-Black Furniture, ***111 Sedgehill Drive, Thomasville, NC 27360. Telephone 800-334-7398; in North Carolina, 919-472-6117.***
In the U.S. and Canada write or telephone 8:30 A.M. to 5:30 P.M., Monday through Saturday, for specific prices. Free price list of Henredon, Thomasville and Stanton Cooper catalogues for sale.
Sells furniture by 300 manufacturers, including major ones such as Braddington Young, Brown Jordan, Century, Clayton Marcus, Drexel, Henredon, Heritage, Thomasville, Woodmark Chairs.
Established 1948.

This is another firm that makes an effort to help customers who don't know what they want. When I called about furniture I had seen in a department store catalogue, my saleswoman first tried to find it in her catalogues and then said she would call the manufacturer to trace it (I must admit I never called back). I called another time to ask about mattresses. A different saleswoman gave me a little talk on padding and springs and was generally quite helpful.

Loftin-Black has its own delivery trucks and sets up the furniture in your house.

Mallory's, ***P.O. Box 1150, Jacksonville, NC 28540. Telephone 800-334-2340.***
In the U.S. and Canada write for free leaflet listing furniture catalogues for sale, or telephone for a price quote.
Sells furniture from 40 to 50 manufacturers, including Drexel, Henredon, Heritage; lamps by La Barge, Chapman, Paul Hansen, Stiffel.
Returns: will repair or accept the return of pieces damaged in transit; if a customer returns a piece for reasons of his or her own, there is a 40% restocking charge.
Established 1949.

Mallory's, a furniture store near Camp Lejeune marine base, got into mail order because Lejeune customers who were transferred kept calling back with more orders. Mail order now makes up 50% of the business.

I bought a box spring set from Mallory because, after calling the firms I list (and one or two others) for price quotes, I found that Mallory's gave a 5% discount if I paid the whole price on ordering. That made its price the lowest. As I say above, buying here I paid $325 less (including shipping) than I would have paid Bloomingdale's department store for the same set on special sale, so I was very pleased. Mallory's sent me a helpful and informative brochure about shipping methods and what to do in case of damage. My only complaint is that my invoice said that delivery would be made in about four weeks or else I would be told a new delivery date. When I hadn't heard anything in five weeks, I telephoned my saleswoman. She immediately telephoned the manufacturer and cheered me up by telling me the box spring set was being picked up that day and would be delivered in a few days (it was) and furthermore was coming from a local warehouse so delivery charges would be unusually low (the delivery charge was $40 instead of the $80 I had expected). But I was left with the feeling that if I hadn't called, I could have waited several more weeks.

Mallory's says that if you have the name but not the model number of a piece of furniture, it can try to find it in its catalogues and send you a photocopied illustration. It also has designers who can plan a "total look" for your abode if you send a plan and your style preferences. There is no charge for the design service.

Rose Furniture Company, ***Box 1829, 214 South Elm Street, High Point, NC 27261. Telephone 801-334-1045.***
List of manufacturers stocked, or telephone for specific prices.
Sells furniture by 300 manufacturers.
Returns: money back or credit minus a 20% restocking charge if furniture returned within 60 days.
Established 1925.

When I called Rose about box spring prices, I was told that the firm carries only Sealy Posturepedic because it is "not happy with other brands." I considered that a "hard sell" answer as the explanation of why it carries only one brand, and it seemed unlikely. However, when I called other times, the salespeople were more straightforward, gave me prices, sent me garden furniture brochures promptly and, in one case when they didn't have the prices, telephoned a factory and got me the name of a New York outlet so that I could look at the furniture myself.

Do It Yourself

Well-made, good-looking, nontacky reproduction furniture is expensive. These firms sell furniture as kits ready to assemble and finish at prices that are 25 to over 50% off what similar finished pieces would cost. So you can see how much you would save if you furnished a house or apartment mainly with kits. You need a hammer and screwdriver but no special tools, and intelligence but no special skills. The furniture is well-constructed, with mortise-and-tenon joints and dovetailed drawers, and it is often delivered faster than it would be from a store.

One friend of a friend of mine had been scouring the shops for a simple narrow dining table for years. She found plenty of clunky, overshellacked maple tables, but anything more graceful started at $1000. She found exactly what she wanted for $300 at Cohasset Colonials.

Note that the price of kits depends partly on the type of wood used, and the type of wood used is an important factor in the appearance of the finished piece.

Cohasset Colonials by Hagerty, ***Cohasset, MA 02025. Telephone 617-383-0110.***
31-page color catalogue, $2 ($2.50 in Canada).
MC, V.
Sells kits to make reproduction seventeenth- and eighteenth-century American furniture; lighting fixtures; fabrics and made-to-order draperies and bed hangings.
Returns: money back if goods returned in original condition within 30 days.
Established 1936.

Cohasset sells kits to make simple and lovely seventeenth- and eighteenth-century American furniture in rock maple and almost knot-free eastern white pumpkin pine.

The friend of my friend, who had never made anything in her life, ordered and made a table and was delighted. She said the table was very easy to make, required no tools (it just involved gluing, sanding, staining and so on) and was quite manageable by one person, and the finished product was "amazingly terrific." The kit arrived very quickly and contained what was needed. Construction took her a whole day because of waiting for the stains and finishes to dry between layers. Her one complaint was that there was not nearly enough sandpaper, which was a major nuisance because she started the table on a Sunday. She says the table cost a third of what similar tables she had seen in New York cost.

Shaker Workshops, ***P.O. Box 1028CC, Concord, MA 01742. Telephone 617-646-8985.***
40-page color catalogue, $1.
AE, CB, DC, MC, V.
Sells reproduction and kit-form Shaker furniture.
Returns: money back if merchandise returned in original condition within 30 days.
Established 1970.

Kits to make beautifully graceful furniture, each piece copied from a specific Shaker original. Straight-back chairs, rocking chairs, a few tables and a bed are made of knot-free rock maple or pine. Prices are not low; as I write, chair kits start at $60 and candle stands (side tables) at $50, but they are still a steal compared to ready-made furniture of this quality.

Woodcraft Supply Corporation, ***Dept SD 1986, 41 Atlantic Avenue, Box 400, Woburn, MA 01888. Telephone: questions, 617-935-9278; orders, 800-225-1153.***
Woodwork tools catalogue, free.
AE, MC, V.
Sells woodwork tools and furniture plans.
Returns: money back if merchandise returned within 30 days with invoice.
Established 1928.

Woodcraft's main business is selling high-quality woodworking tools, but it also sells plans to make furniture. These are only for accomplished woodworkers, as they consist of measured drawings (some of them are full-scale so that they can be traced). Plans come with lists of building materials and hardware needed and with recommended construction techniques. Styles are basically early American.

Yield House, ***Route 16, North Conway, NH 03860. Telephone 800-258-4720.***
Free catalogue.
AE, MC, V.
Sells pine furniture and kits.
Returns: money back if merchandise returned within 90 days; Yield House pays postage.
Established 1947.

Yield House has inexpensive furniture in stained pine, mainly "olde" American styles adapted to new uses—for instance, swivelling TV consoles, message centers and filing cabinets—there is even computer furniture. Most pieces are available for 30% off as kits, already sanded; you assemble them with a hammer and a Phillips screwdriver and finish them.

HEATING

Firewood

You can get free or cheap firewood from most national and some state forests, and besides saving money, you get healthy exercise. One forester (call him a forestry technician, advised a telephonist) told me that people really enjoy collecting their own firewood, so there's a big demand in forests near urban areas. Rules of the game vary. You always need a permit, but the price, if any, times when you can collect, and quantities allowed change from forest to forest. You do usually need a station wagon and a chain saw.

Green Mountain National Forest in Vermont, for instance, allows people to collect up to 5 cords of "dead and down" firewood for their own use anytime between May and November, and there is no charge whatever. Enough wood falls after wind and ice storms so that everyone who applies gets a permit. Green Mountain also sells standing trees in wooded areas that need thinning. You are given a map, shown where the marked trees are and allowed to cut down 3 to 5 cords. This wood costs $6 a cord, but you are allowed to resell it—the same sort of wood delivered from a logging contractor would cost $40 to $50 a cord. Each year several hundred people apply for standing wood and Green Mountain picks about 40 names in an April lottery.

One state park whose forestry department I talked to, Long Island, allows about 900 people to collect wood that the department has cut and gathered.

Rules here are that you are allowed to do it on one day only sometime from November through February (though you can go in as many times as you like on that day). You can take only as much as will fit into a passenger car (no pickups or trucks allowed). There is a $10 charge and in recent years everyone who has applied has been given a permit.

To find out about firewood programs in national parks, contact your state district ranger, listed in the telephone directory under U.S. Government, Department of Agriculture, Forest Service.

If none is listed, ask for the National Forest Map and list of Forest Service field offices from: **PUBLICATIONS OFFICE, U.S. FOREST SERVICE, *Department of Agriculture, P.O. Box 2417, Washington, DC 20013. Telephone 202-447-7719.***

To find out about firewood programs in state parks, contact the administration headquarters of your state park, generally listed in the telephone directory under state or county government headings under Recreational Facilities.

Fuel

A good way of saving money on fuel oil is to join a fuel buyers group. How much money you save depends partly on the size of your group. Anthony Coates, director of a large New York group set up by Ralph Nader's NYPIRG (New York Public Interest Research Group), says that savings range between 10 and 20% of the fuel bill (and at one point when most households were paying $1.21 per gallon for No. 2 heating oil, NYPIRG members were paying 95 cents per gallon), with the average household saving between $100 and $300 a year.

The groups work by getting together a certain number of people and bargaining with local oil distributors for a better price. Once the group has been set up and members have been registered, members deal with the oil company just as though they were buying privately: they put in their own orders, arrange for their own deliveries and so on.

Larger groups not only get good discounts on the oil but also can use their clout to get better service for members than they would get individually. To make sure that members get preferential treatment, the NYPIRG Fuel Buyers Group staff calls distributors on members' behalf about any problems that arise. NYPIRG Fuel Buyers is also expanding to get discounts for members on insulating materials and Thermopane windows.

Smaller groups (50 households is probably the minimum needed) won't get such good prices. They *may* also have to deal with smaller distributors who can't give such efficient repair service. However, I talked to one small group, Flushing Fuel Consortium, which started with 40 households and has grown to 500 in three years; it asked for bids only from large, well-established firms that it knew would give good service, and immediately got a 10% discount on oil prices.

Fuel-buying groups are often run by neighborhood or civic groups, fraternal organizations and labor unions. If you can't find one locally, NYPIRG may be able to help you. It can certainly advise you on how to start a club within a neighborhood, at a workplace or school or through any other collection of people.

The NYPIRG Fuel Buyers Group started by sending a circular to NYPIRG members asking whether they were interested in joining a fuel-buying group. They got 300 yeses in one district and with just that information started negotiating with local oil distributors. The group now has 10,000 members and is self-supporting. All expenses and ten staff members are paid for by a $20 membership fee and 1% commission on oil sales to members, paid by the distributors.

To get the names of groups in your area or for advice on starting your own group, contact: ***Anthony Coates,*** **NYPIRG FUEL BUYERS GROUP,** ***9 Murray Street, New York, NY 10007. Telephone 212-349-6460.***

KITCHEN EQUIPMENT

These two stores have an outstanding stock of better kitchen utensils and small appliances. More common electric kitchen appliances and Farberware cooking pots are sold by the stores in the Appliances section.

Whole Earth Access, ***2950 7th Street, Berkeley, CA 94710. Telephone 415-845-3000; 800-845-2000.***
(Main listing in General section)
270-page catalogue in summer, $5 ($6 in Canada) (refundable) plus $2 postage. MC, V.
Sells KitchenAid, Kenwood, Cuisinart machines; Henckels, Russell Harrington knives; Acme, Champion, Sanyo juicers; Corona, Mil-Rite grain mills; Braun, Chemex, Melior, Melitta coffee makers; Braun, Krups, KitchenAid coffee mills; All Clad, Calphalon, Le Creuset, Revere Ware pots and pans; Wolf Restaurant stoves; Weber barbecues; a variety of everyday small utensils and specialized utensils for food preservation, cheese and yogurt making, sprouting, bread making.

Whole Earth Access, which was inspired by but is independent of *The Whole Earth Catalog,* sells the highest-quality products for basic living. There is a fine "food preparation" section in the catalogue with line drawings or photographs and detailed descriptions of the carefully chosen kitchen things. The stock is comprehensive and goes from the best hand can opener there is through several lines of good cooking pots to electric kitchen machines, juicers and coffee makers. Alongside these standards there are plenty of more specialized goods such as a tortilla press, a baker's tile and a food dehydrator. Don't miss this catalogue if you like cooking and are stocking up a kitchen.

Zabar's, ***2245 Broadway, New York, NY 10024. Telephone 800-221-3347; in New York State, 212-787-2000.***

Occasional free catalogues, or telephone for specific prices.
AE.
Sells kitchenware and foods.
Returns: money back on damaged goods if returned within two weeks.
Established 1938.

A New York institution, Zabar's has for years sold a wonderful array of foods and has now added an upper level of kitchenware at excellent prices. The pricing policy is combative—the windows are covered with notices shrieking, "Why pay more at Macy's?" and side-by-side price comparisons. But the catalogues show only a few of the goods available, so it's better to know what you want when you buy from Zabar's.

Just about every superior pot, gadget and small appliance you could want in the kitchen is sold: The widely distributed and reputable Mauviel copper pans from France cost 30 to 50% less here than at other cookware shops. You are also likely to find Braun electric coffee makers for 30% less than at other stores, Simac ice cream makers at 27% below other stores and West Bend stainless steel electric woks and electric skillets at 35% below other stores. Practically all the big names in kitchenware are displayed and discounted here: Le Creuset, Calphalon, Krups, KitchenAid.

LINEN

Seasonal Sales

I find that, unless you are looking for something special that you can't find at the stores below, it really isn't worth waiting for department store white sales. The stores in this section have lower prices all year round. For instance, Macy's New York store's regular price for the bath size of Fieldcrest's popular Royal Velvet pure cotton towels was $15 and the 1986 January white sale price was $12.99 when the usual price at these stores was only $10.

Mail and Telephone Sources

Blinds

Levolor makes the best-known custom blinds (in over 200 colors, various patterns and a number of materials, including wood) and also ready-made blinds in white and off-white aluminum. Most of the custom-cut blinds are available at about 30% off list price at the stores below, while the ready-made blinds are sold at paint stores such as Pintchik.

Eldridge Textile Company, ***277 Grand Street, New York, NY 10002. Telephone 212-925-1523.***
Write or telephone for specific prices.
MC, V.

Sells sheets and towels, comforters, dust ruffles by Burlington, Fieldcrest, Martex, Springmaid, J. P. Stevens, Dan River. (Carries Laura Ashley, Bill Blass, Perry Ellis and Marimekko.)
Returns: money back if goods returned within 10 days, exchange if within 30 days.
Established 1940.

Eldridge, like the other firms in this section, sells the towels, sheets and bedspreads of major manufacturers at prices that all year round are below most stores' white sale prices.

Owner Allan Leber (the firm was started by his father) says that his most popular line by far is Laura Ashley. He says he hasn't seen anything like it in the 20 years he has been working. Usually sheet patterns last a year at most, he says, whereas Laura Ashley's five-year-old first designs are selling better today than when they were first introduced. Ashley patterns aren't discontinued, they're just added to—unbelievable, says Mr. Leber.

Handart Embroideries, ***Room 106, Hing Wai Building, 36 Queen's Road Central, Hong Kong. Telephone 5-235744.***
Free illustrated photocopied price list.
Sells hand-embroidered tablecloths, place mats, napkins and pillowcases; crocheted place mats, tablecloths and bedspreads; acetate "satin" bedsheets; embroidered nightwear and shirts.
Returns: unconditional money-back guarantee.
Established 1952.

If your taste runs to satin bedsheets, you can save lots by buying here. When Macy's department store in New York was advertising satin acetate "shimmering sheets in ten dreamy shades," you could buy shimmering satin acetate sheets in 16 dreamy shades for under half Macy's sale price at Handart. One example: Macy's regular price for two queen-sized sheets and two standard pillowcases was $105 and the January white sale price at Macy's was $86.97, yet the Handart price was only $36 including surface postage (airmail cost $4 a pound extra).

Handart also sells handmade battenberg lace bedspreads; crocheted, embroidered, battenberg and Christmas tablecloths (these battenberg tablecloths in cotton cost roughly one-quarter of what cotton battenberg tablecloths cost in New York, and roughly one-tenth of what the finest battenberg and linen ones from Belgium cost); embroidered silk underwear and silk kimonos for men and women; embroidered and sequined blouses; embroidered or beaded angora cardigans and jade and ivory jewelry. Furthermore, Handart says that the illustrated price sheets represent only a very small portion of what it sells—"if you can not find what you want, write and describe your requirements."

Handart sends out only photocopied pages, but as it points out, "It would cost us too much money to have this catalogue printed in color, and for so doing we have to charge a higher price on our merchandise, which we do not want to do. . . . However, if you would like to see any item(s) more clearly, please let us know so that we can send you a colored photo of it/them free of charge." Careful instructions make me think that in spite of its only having black-and-white illustrations, this is a good place to order from.

Harris Levy, ***278 Grand Street, New York, NY 10002. Telephone: questions, 212-226-3102; orders, 800-221-7750.***
Write or telephone 10 A.M. to 4:30 P.M. on weekdays.
AE, MC, V.
Sells bed and bath linens. Carries both imported merchandise and most well-known American manufacturers and mills such as Burlington, Cannon, Dan River, Fieldcrest, Martex, Springmaid, J. P. Stevens, Wamsutta; Faribo and imported blankets; comforters, pillows, mattress pads, bathrobes, shower curtains and so on.
Returns: credit if returned within 30 days unopened and in original packing.
Established 1894.

Harris Levy has an amazing stock of luxury and better bed and bathroom linens at lower prices. I have checked many prices over the years, always getting careful answers. The firm seems to have almost everything: sheets by Conran for Dan River at 25% below Conran's own price and pure wool king-sized blankets—Faribo's "Melbourne" at 20% below and Northwood's "Pure and Simple" at 30% below Whole Earth Access (see General section) prices. It also has queen-sized Irish linen sheets and cashmere blankets at 25% below the uptown New York price. When I was comparing prices on comforters, the Levy price was not the very lowest, but its queen-sized comforter with 37 ounces of European goose down cost $200 at a time when a slightly smaller comforter with 36 ounces of European goose down cost $350 from the Brookstone catalogue.

When I have asked questions about pillow content and that sort of thing, Levy has informed me; once when I mistook manufacturers, the salespeople corrected me. I like this firm very much; the only drawback is slow shipping (10 to 14 days).

Limericks, ***Limerick House, 117 Victoria Avenue, Southend on Sea, Essex, SS2 6EL, England. Telephone 702-343486.***
Free 32-page catalogue in February and August.
DC, MC, V.
Sells household linens, blankets, fabrics by the yard to make sheets, towels, etc.
Returns: money back.
Established 1957.

The Limerick catalogue announces "postal shopping for everything in the linen cupboard" and hardly exaggerates, for there is an astonishing amount and variety to be found here. Most of the stock is not fancy (except for the pure Irish linen sheets, which in queen size cost exactly half the U.S. *discount* price), but you are certain to find something you need. There are extraordinary bargains and supplies for people who sew: Irish linen is available in three widths to make sheets; the widest, 103 inches for queen-sized sheets, cost (when I checked) $58 per meter (1 yard, 3 inches). Ninety-inch-wide pure cotton flannel to make double-bed sheets cost about $7 per meter. You can also get the ingredients to make down comforters and such things as curtain linings, waterproof-backed white cotton flannelette and all-linen tea toweling.

Ready-made basics, some of which are hard to find, are available: pillows in unusual shapes and sizes; all kinds of wool blankets, towels and tablecloths and cloths for cleaning (including window cleaner's "scrim").

Palmetto Linen Company, ***Box 109, Hardeeville, SC 29927. Telephone 800-833-3506; in South Carolina, 803-784-6692.***
Write or telephone 8 A.M. to 6 P.M. for prices.
AE, MC, V.
Sells sheets (including water-bed sheets) and dust ruffles to match, towels, blankets, comforters, pillows, tablecloths, place mats, shower curtains. Handles Cannon, Dundee, Martex towels; Springmaid and Wamsutta sheets; Riegel textiles.
Returns: credit if goods returned with sales slip and original wrapping within two weeks.
Established 1958.

Palmetto says that its most popular lines are beach and bath towels, and it also has a large department of kitchen accessories such as aprons, towels and oven gloves. But the easiest things to buy by mail are the standard lines of towels (by Cannon and Martex) and sheets (by Springmaid and Wamsutta).

F. Rubbrecht, ***23 Grand Place, B 1000 Brussels, Belgium. Telephone 2-5120218.***
14-page catalogue, $2; $3 airmail.
AE, DC, MC, V.
Sells Belgian linen and lace tablecloths and place mats, guest towels, handkerchiefs, doilies, wedding veils.
Returns: credit.
Established 1957.

Rubbrecht sells the finest Belgian linen and battenberg place mats, tablecloths with napkins, bun covers, coasters and tray cloths. I haven't been able to find lace of comparable quality in order to check prices, so I can only say that prices seem reasonable for these luxury linens. Linen and lace guest towels cost less than $5 as I write.

Wilco Trading Co, ***GPO Box 2225 (or 301 Wellington House, 3A Wyndham Street), Hong Kong. Telephone 5-230872 or 5-253457.***
56-page color catalogue, free; $2 airmail.
Sells table linens, Chinese crafts and jewelry.
Returns: "satisfaction or money back."
Established 1970.

Wilco's full-color catalogue has a multitude of lace and embroidered tablecloths, table mats and napkins of all kinds; embroidered guest towels and pillow slips. The catalogue also displays very simple jewelry in ivory and necklaces of semiprecious stones. What with the color catalogue and the really low prices, this is a particularly good place to order by mail. The firm was originally recommended to me by a reader who had had very satisfactory dealings with it. A friend of mine in Hong Kong paid Wilco a visit and reported that it had all the regular lines in linen, an active packing setup and a friendly staff.

PAINT

Seasonal Sales

If there are no discount stores in your area, don't pay the cost of shipping from the stores below; buy locally during sales, when prices typically go down by 25%. Look for sales (and special promotions such as "buy three gallons and get a fourth free") before Memorial Day (April and May), when shops are competing for customers at the beginning of the painting season, and also in September after Labor Day at the end of the season.

Paint stores are also used to giving discounts to professional painters and are often willing to give discounts to individuals or groups buying in quantity. According to a spokesman for the Benjamin Moore company, unless subjected to high heat (or, in the case of latex paint, freezing), paint has a shelf life of four to five years.

Mail and Telephone Sources

These stores sell brand name paint at about 35 to 40% below list price. If you are doing a big painting job, it will be worth your while to buy here, so long as your shipping costs aren't too high. Savings are more likely to be worthwhile on expensive paints, for which shipping costs are proportionately smaller. When I compared prices of a Benjamin Moore and a Pratt and Lambert paint, I found that a customer in upstate New York buying 15 gallons could still save 15% on an $18-a-gallon paint and 35% on a $23-a-gallon paint, even after paying for shipping. (I didn't include sales tax in my calculations, which would make the savings on out-of-state buys slightly greater.)

These are busy walk-in stores, so I find that writing is the most satisfactory way to get quotes.

Franklin and Lennon Paint Company, ***537 West 125th Street, New York, NY 10027. Telephone 212-864-2460.***
In the U.S. and Canada write or telephone 7 A.M. to 5 P.M. for prices.
Sells paint by Benjamin Moore, Paragon, Pentagon, Pratt and Lambert, Pittsburgh, USG, Rust-Oleum.
Returns: money back; "please show the original receipt."
Established 1933.

I was very pleased to find Franklin and Lennon several years ago during a telephone search for a genuine discount paint store. The company is businesslike, has consistent discounts throughout the year and also always quotes the lowest shipping charges. When I made a recent comparison, it was selling Benjamin Moore's Regal Aquavelvet for $13.95 a gallon instead of the $18 list, and Pratt and Lambert Accolade for $13.03 a gallon instead of the $23 list. The cost of shipping the 15 gallons to upstate New York was only $20.

Merit Kaplan Paint Supply, ***227 East 44th Street, New York, NY 10017. Telephone 212-682-3585.***
Send self-addressed, stamped envelope or telephone 7 A.M. to 5:30 P.M. for specific prices.
MC, V.
Sells paints by Benjamin Moore, Paragon, Pentagon, Pittsburgh, Pratt and Lambert (and has access to many others); lacquers, wallpapers, brushes and tools.
Minimum order 10 gallons for delivery.
Returns: money back if within 30 days.
Established 1918.

This is a shop in midtown Manhattan that is often listed in *New York* magazine for its paint sales. During my recent paint price comparison, which happened to take place during its spring sale, the store was selling Benjamin Moore's Regal Aquavelvet for $12.29 (list $18) and Pratt and Lambert Accolade for $15.95 (list $23). But shipping to upstate New York cost $50.

Pearl Paint Company, ***308 Canal Street, New York, NY 10013. Telephone: questions, 212-431-7932; orders, 800-221-6845.***
(Main listing in Hobby section under Art Supplies)
Sells Benjamin Moore and Pratt and Lambert paints at roughly 20% off regular prices (depending on quantity) and its own house brands at lower prices. Won't quote prices unless you are ordering.

N. Pintchik, ***478 Bergen Street, Brooklyn, NY 11217. Telephone 718-783-3333.***
Send self-addressed, stamped envelope or telephone 9 A.M. to 5 P.M. Monday through Friday for specific prices.
AE, DC, MC, V.
Sells paints and blinds; stocks ready-cut Levolor blinds.
Returns: must be within a week; money back if receipt is included, otherwise credit slip.
Established 1913.

I have compared paint prices several times and found that, in spite of its claims, Pintchik normally gives only the measliest of discounts on paints. However, it is one of the best places to get brand name ready-cut blinds. I compared prices being charged for the standard ready-cut Levolor blinds all over New York. The regular price for my size was $42 and my local store had them on special sale at $38, but Pintchik was selling them for $32.

WALLPAPER

Mail and Telephone Sources

Several firms sell wallpaper and the fabric that comes in the wallpaper books at a discount. Ideally, you should have the pattern number, the name of the book, the manufacturer and the price to give the store when you call. However, just the name of the manufacturer and the pattern number will usually do. If you have a sample of the paper or fabric but no other details, try American Discount Wallcoverings (below). It keeps patterns in the store, and the salespeople will do their best to find your sample in their books.

Post tells me that full-price stores are getting wise to discount buying and so are blacking out wallpaper pattern numbers and even page numbers. Post says that if you have only the manufacturer's name, the name of the pattern book and a description, it might be able to find the paper you want (although a page number is extra helpful).

American Discount Wallcoverings, ***1411 Fifth Avenue, Pittsburgh, PA 15219. Telephone 800-245-1768.***
Write or telephone 9 A.M. to 5 P.M. for prices.
Sells wall coverings, including murals, designer prints colored to order; fabrics, including brands such as Laura Ashley, Marimekko, Scalamandre and Schumacher; miniblinds and pleated shades by Bali, Delmar, Flexalum, Kirsch, Levolor, Nanik, and Verosol.
Returns: money back, minus 20% handling charge, on undamaged, uncut full rolls of wall covering; no returns on fabrics or blinds, as they are cut to order.
Established 1978.

Here is a helpful firm. The woman who answered the telephone was not worried by my having a pattern number but not the name of the sample book. She offered a 25% discount but added UPS charges (for my zip code it would have been $1.63 for a single roll). She also, nicely, told me that the pattern had been discontinued two months before, so I should make sure I ordered enough paper. Another time I called to ask about Marimekko fabric. A friendly woman said that if I didn't have the number I could send a sample from a wallpaper book and they would try to match it, as they keep some books there. They sell the fabrics in wallpaper books at 10 to 20% off list price.

Best Brothers Paint and Wallpaper Outlet, ***4900 5th Street Highway, Route 222, Reading, PA 19560. Telephone 215-921-8591 or 215-921-3566.***

In the U.S. and Canada write or telephone 9 A.M. to 6 P.M. for prices.
MC, V.
Sells all brands of wall covering and custom-made Bali, Delmar and Levolor window blinds.
Returns: money back, minus 25% charge, on wall covering returned within 30 days; no returns on blinds or cut rolls of wallpaper.

Another helpful although smaller company. When I telephoned with the number of a wallpaper but didn't know which book the paper came from, Sue called the manufacturer for me and got the price. (Other companies, eliminated from this chapter, insisted on knowing the book name.) Best Brothers takes 25% off the price (the list price Sue mentioned was, indeed, exactly what my local wallpaper store was charging) but adds 50 cents per roll for shipping.

Post Wallcovering Distributors, ***Bloomfield Hills, MI 48013. Telephone 800-521-0650; in Michigan, 800-482-2488.***
Telephone only, 9 A.M. to 5 P.M. Monday to Friday, for prices.
MC, V.
Sells all brands of wallpaper and covering, including hard-to-find designer brands.
Returns: defective paper will be replaced if not cut or hung.
Established 1969.

I discovered Post through *The Old House Journal* (a newsletter on restoration techniques for the antique house). The journal tested this firm by ordering a hard-to-find Schumacher wallpaper. The paper arrived in ten days, matched the same paper bought at a Schumacher distributor and cost only $11.64 postpaid (plus a 50-cent charge per roll for orders of under 24 rolls) instead of $16.15 per roll (plus sales tax) from the distributor.

Post sells papers at 27% off the suggested retail price and doesn't charge postage (but orders of less than 24 rolls have the added charge), so its prices are the lowest. It has wallpapers listed on a computer without prices, so you must call with the number of the wallpaper and the price.

Post also sells the fabrics that come in the wallpaper books at a 10% discount. You can order over the telephone with MasterCard or Visa. Post says that it can get any paper that is sold in the United States.

SILVER AND FLATWARE

Seasonal Sales

I can't see any reason for anyone to pay list price for silver and flatware by the well-known manufacturers, nor to wait for sales. There are plenty of shops selling at better prices all year round. The low-price stores keep popular patterns in stock, and some of them do gift wrapping and keep gift registries too.

Savings are huge. When I compared prices on Oneida's stainless steel

"Sheraton," a five-piece place setting cost $65 normally at Altman's New York department store and $36.90 on special sale at Altman's. Yet you could find it for $25 at one of these stores. When I compared prices on a four-piece place setting of Reed and Barton's very popular sterling silver "18th Century" pattern, the regular price at Macy's New York department store was $170 and the January *sale* price at Altman's was $118.75. The lowest (and most common) discount price I found was $93 (in other words, 20% below the *sale* price).

Mail and Telephone Sources

I have found discounts to be more consistent on silver than on stainless steel or china, but it is still worth comparing among these stores, because one or two (different ones each time) are likely to offer slightly lower prices.

Notice that some stores give the lowest price only for greater quantities. All of the stores give prices by telephone, and a few will give prices *only* by telephone.

A. Benjamin, ***80–82 Bowery, New York, NY 10013. Telephone 212-226-6013.***
(Main listing under China and Glass)
Telephone or send self-addressed, stamped envelope for specific prices.

Michael C. Fina, ***580 Fifth Avenue, New York, NY 10036. Telephone 800-223-6589; in New York State, 212-869-5050.***
Occasional free catalogues, or telephone for specific prices.
AE, MC, V.
Sells china, silver, giftwares, jewelry, watches.
Returns: china and silver is specially ordered, so no returns unless damaged or defective; credit or exchange of jewelry that is returned within ten days.
Established 1935.

A Fifth Avenue store, with Fifth Avenue services yet discount prices, Fina will order china and silver by major manufacturers. It will also wrap gifts, engrave and keep a bridal registry. It has a special-order department and a hard-to-find-patterns department, and it claims to have the largest collection of serving-piece silver in the world. It also has an antique silver department.

Some of the prices I checked were not the lowest, but Fina does run frequent special sales, when prices are as low as the lowest prices at other stores in this section.

Fortunoff, ***681 Fifth Avenue, New York, NY 10022. Telephone 800-223-2326, 212-671-9300 or 516-294-3300.***
Telephone for prices Monday through Saturday, 9 A.M. to 9 P.M., or Sunday, 11 A.M. to 5 P.M.
AE, DC, MC, V.

Sells silver and jewelry.
Returns: money back if merchandise returned in insured package with receipt within two weeks.

Fortunoff, which has been called one of the most successful jewelers in America, has described itself as "offering premium products in a premium setting at prices below those charged by the usual premium stores." Its prices on Gorham's "Chantilly" and Reed and Barton's "18th Century" were very good when I checked. The store sells other things that are rather unappealing in design, such as outdoor furniture.

Greater New York Trading, ***81 Canal Street, New York, NY 10002. Telephone 212-226-2808 or 212-226-2809.***
(Main listing under China and Glass)
Telephone or send self-addressed, stamped envelope for specific prices.
Sells all standard brands of silverware and stainless steel flatware, including Jensen and Christofle.

I found my best price here on the Oneida "Sheraton" I was checking. On Gorham's "Chantilly" the price was not especially good, and the discount was bigger for larger quantities.

Jompole Company, ***330 Seventh Avenue, New York, NY 10001. Telephone 212-594-0440.***
(Main listing under China and Glass)
Sells leading brands of china, glass and silver.

Has Christofle at 15% off list price and gives a bigger discount for larger quantities.

Robin Importers, ***510 Madison Avenue, New York, NY 10022. Telephone 212-753-6475.***
(Main listing under China and Glass)
Telephone or send self-addressed, stamped envelope for specific prices.
Carries stainless steel, not silver.

Prices are definitely discounted (the regular Oneida "Sheraton" price was below Altman's *sale* price), but I've not yet found the lowest price on anything here.

Rogers and Rosenthal, ***105 Canal Street, New York, NY 10002. Telephone 212-925-7557 or 212-925-7558.***
(Main listing under China and Glass)
Telephone or send self-addressed, stamped envelope for specific prices.
Carries all American silver, silver plate, stainless steel, Japanese and Norwegian stainless steel.

I've found this firm slow in answering written requests.

Rudi's Pottery, Silver and China, ***178 Route 17 North, Paramus, NJ 07652. Telephone 201-265-6096.***
(Main listing under China and Glass)
Write or telephone for specific prices.

Nat Schwartz and Company, ***549 Broadway, Bayonne, NJ 07002. Telephone 800-526-1440.***
(Main listing under China and Glass)
Telephone for specific prices.

Windsor Gift Shop, ***233–237 Main Street, Madison, NJ 07940. Telephone 800-631-9393; in New Jersey, 201-377-7273.***
(Main listing under China and Glass)
Telephone for prices.

INSURANCE

Insurance is a field in which you can save hundreds or thousands of dollars by buying well. If you are thinking of buying insurance and need help in this bewildering business, contact the National Insurance Consumer Organization. It's a nonprofit public interest group established by a former federal insurance administrator to "promote the interests of insurance buyers," and the organization actually doles out frank advice and makes recommendations. NICO produces a brochure, ***Buyers Guide to Insurance: What the Companies Won't Tell You.*** It gives general do's and, more important, don'ts for buying auto, homeowner or renter, life and health insurance. Send $2 plus a long self-addressed stamped envelope to: **NICO,** ***121 North Payne Street, Alexandria, VA 22314. Telephone 703-549-8050.***

AUTOMOBILE INSURANCE

NICO suggests that, as every $1 spent on insurance premiums returns 60 cents in claims, if you are an average driver you can save about 40% by "self-insuring" those risks you can afford to assume. As with all insurance policies, NICO suggests comparing prices, as identical coverage costs different amounts at different companies.

The two automobile insurance companies that NICO names as the best companies are both open only to certain people. **AMICA MUTUAL** policies ***(14 Corporate Woods Boulevard, Albany, NY 12211, telephone 800-732-6422)*** are usually available only to people who have been recommended by people who already have policies, and **UNITED SERVICES AUTO ASSOCIATION** policies (address on page 176) are only for present and former officers in the U.S. armed forces and the widows (and, presumably, widowers) of officers.

In its September 1984 issue, *Consumer Reports* published the results of a survey of their readers on how satisfied they are with the way their insurance companies handle claims. As *Consumer Reports* stated, "As far as the buyer is concerned, the crucial difference is this: some insurance companies are much more likely than others to provide satisfactory service." The report included ratings, and in this case *Consumer Reports* suggested that readers choose from among the top-rated companies, as "the company rankings have tended to remain stable over time."

HEALTH INSURANCE

Comparing insurance policies that supplement Medicare is no easy matter, because, apart from being priced differently, policies differ so much in terms of which benefits they provide. In fact, however, it *is* possible to compare policies for yourself using the brochures provided by the different companies in your state. Your state insurance commissioner may have a list of companies that provide Medigap coverage in your state. But if, like many people, you feel that you'll never understand all the complications by yourself, there are a few sources of help.

Clark County Coalition Health Systems Agency, ***1455 East Tropicana, Suite 530, Las Vegas, NV 89109. Telephone 702-798-1033.***

This innovative agency has a free comparison chart of the main Medicare supplemental policies for Nevada that includes all the major national plans. As I write, it is also preparing a brochure on long-term-care programs. In addition, it has a very unusual free information service. By telephone, representatives can help with questions about reading and interpreting medical bills and understanding Medicare and supplemental insurance. They can't provide legal or medical advice or recommend specific providers.

Allan Eckert, Bureau of Program Operations, Health Care Financing Administration, U.S. Department of Health and Human Services, ***Room 500 East High Rise, 6325 Security Boulevard, Baltimore, MD 21207. Telephone 301-597-3724.***

The Department of Health and Human Services has someone there especially to answer questions on supplemental health insurance.

The National Association of Life Underwriters, Public Relations Department, ***1922 F Street NW, Washington, DC 20006. Telephone 202-331-6000.***

This organization can refer you to your local life underwriters association, which may have a speaker's bureau with volunteers who are willing to come and talk to a group of people about health and/or life insurance. The volunteer comes to talk to you in "educational" rather than "commercial" terms and will not try to sell you a policy, but the volunteer *is* an insurance agent so surely not entirely impartial.

Consumer Reports published a very helpful study on Medigap insurance in the June 1984 issue. It has a detailed account of important issues involved in choosing insurance and a worksheet to help you make your own comparisons. It also rates Medicare supplemental policies but points out that the ratings should not be used as is, partly because policies change and partly because their buyer was hypothetical—your claims will probably be different. An insurance specialist also pointed out to me that other policies not examined by *Consumer Reports* may be as good as the *CR* top-rated policy.

James Hunt of NICO tells me that the **AMERICAN ASSOCIATION OF RETIRED PERSONS (AARP),** ***1909 K Street NW, Washington, DC 20049, telephone 202-728-4450,*** has good supplemental policies.

HOMEOWNER INSURANCE

"Why pay $3905 when you can pay $291?" asks the Kentucky Insurance Department. When surveying homeowner insurance rates, the department found that the prices quoted for one identical example ranged from $291 to $3905 per year. NICO points out that the more coverage you buy, the better off your agent and company are—so don't automatically go along with their suggestions for higher limits. A $120,000 policy costs about 20% more than a $100,000 policy, even though the extra risk for the companies is far less than 20% (because most claims are for partial losses).

Two firms to consider when looking at homeowner insurance are **USAA** and **AMICA MUTUAL** (mentioned above).

By the time this book is published, Milton Brown at **INSURANCE INFORMATION** (below) may have a homeowner insurance rating service.

The institutes listed below and your state insurance department are also sources of information on homeowner insurance.

LIFE INSURANCE

Doing your homework before choosing a life insurance policy can save you thousands of dollars. When, in 1979, the Federal Trade Commission studied life insurance, it found that costs for similar policies varied widely. More specifically, Consumers Union found that, while delivering similar benefits, the most expensive $100,000 term policy it looked at would cost $13,000 more than the least expensive over 20 years. The most expensive whole life policy would cost $33,000 more than the least expensive.

Furthermore, you may not even need life insurance. According to NICO, insuring your own life is a good idea if you are a wage earner who will leave dependents in financial difficulties if you die. But if no one is dependent on you, using insurance as a way of saving for retirement seldom makes financial sense; you'd get better value if you saved in other ways. And NICO recommends that you never buy cash value life insurance if otherwise you could invest in an Individual Retirement Account (IRA).

There are two main kinds of life insurance, *term* and *cash value* (which includes variations such as *variable life, whole life* and *universal life*).

Each term insurance policy lasts for only a few years, say up to five. When the policy is up, if you chose a term policy with an option to renew, you can renew. But if your dependents are now independent and you don't need insurance anymore, you can drop it. No more payments, no more possible benefits. And although you get no money back, you can thank your lucky stars that you are still alive to rue the money you spent on life insurance.

With cash value insurance you pay premiums at a fixed rate, usually throughout your life; then at your 95th or 100th birthday, you get the whole face value (face value is the basic amount to be paid when the policy holder dies) of your policy back. Furthermore, there are various ways of getting the money before the end, and at any time you can borrow against the policy if you need to. Sounds good? Well, NICO urges great caution in buying cash value life insurance, partly because it is too hard to tell good cash value policies from bad ones. It recommends annual renewable term policies as likely to offer better value than other forms of term life insurance, and it reminds consumers to shop around carefully to maximize savings. And Consumers Union, when studying life insurance, decided that term insurance with the option of renewing and the option of converting the term to whole life insurance is the best bet for most people. The main reason is that in the early years, when people earn less money, the premiums are lower. This means that families with children can afford better coverage at the time when it would be most needed.

Choosing a Policy

In 1979 the FTC found that the life insurance business is so complex that consumers can't evaluate the costs of different life insurance policies.

NICO has published an extraordinarily helpful booklet, ***Taking the Bite out of Insurance: How to Save Money on Insurance*** ($8.25 postage paid from the address above). It tells you, clearly, just about everything you need to know to make an informed choice of policy, including how to compare costs for yourself on both term and whole life policies. It also actually names companies that NICO considers to offer good-value policies.

As I write, NICO suggests that anyone shopping for term life insurance consider policies from these companies (the first two sell direct to consumers, the second two through agents):

USAA LIFE CO., ***USAA Building, San Antonio, TX 78288. Telephone 800-531-8000.***

BANKERS NATIONAL, ***1599 Littleton Road, Parsippany, NJ 07054. Telephone 800-631-8080.***

BERKSHIRE LIFE, ***700 South Street, Pittsfield, MA 01201. Telephone 413-499-4321.*** Not recommended for women, smokers or older people.

SECURITY MUTUAL LIFE, ***100 Court Street, Binghamton, NY 13092. Telephone 607-723-3551.***

Evaluating a Cash Value Policy

If you insist on disregarding its advice that term policies make more sense than cash value policies, NICO is still willing to help you by offering a computerized service that compares the rate of return in your own situation on any cash value policy to a program of buying annual renewable term life insurance (at NICO's maximum recommended rates) and investing the difference in some savings medium. The charge is $25 for the first policy and $15 for each additional policy submitted at the same time. NICO may also be able to provide the service on a policy you already have if you can get an "in force" ledger statement from your company. For details of what NICO needs for the comparison, send a self-addressed, stamped envelope to its Rate of Return Service at the above address on page 173.

Evaluating Term Insurance

If you want to avoid *all* investigation and calculation of term life insurance policies, there is one independent firm, recommended to me by James Hunt of NICO, that will do the work for you. Insurance Information keeps up-to-date computerized information on term policies. Give the organization the details that you would give an insurance company: birth date, state of health, whether you smoke or not, employment and so on, plus the amount of insurance you want to buy. It will send you a computer printout of the names and addresses of five companies that have policies with the lowest annual premium for your situation. It also gives the independent rating company A. M. Best's evaluation of the companies' financial stability. The charge, as I write, is $50, but if Insurance Information can not save you more than $50 on your first year premium, your $50 fee is refunded.

When I talked to Milton Brown, the owner of Insurance Information, he was planning to introduce similar advisory services for universal life insurance, automobile insurance and homeowner insurance.

Contact: **INSURANCE INFORMATION,** ***45 Palmer Street, Lowell, MA 01852. Telephone 800-472-5800.***

MORE SOURCES OF INFORMATION

One source of practical and unbiased information on insurance is **CONSUMERS UNION,** ***256 Washington Street, Mount Vernon, NY 10553,*** which has published articles and some ratings of companies in the magazine *Consumer Reports* as well as a book, *The Consumers Union Report on Life Insurance* by the Editors of Consumer Reports Books, first published in 1980. The book—available for $8.95 plus $2.15 postage from **CONSUMER REPORTS BOOKS, *540 Barnum Avenue, Bridgeport, CT 06608***—gives a clear and thorough rundown of the different kinds of policies and the advantages and disadvantages of each kind, practical advice on shopping for and buying a policy and calculating value for money and actual ratings of the insurance company policies. But while the general information in the book is useful, the specific data are stale and not to be relied upon.

The following two industry-supported organizations answer questions about insurance. They can tell you how much coverage they think you need, interpret incomprehensible contract terminology and give you the A. M. Best rating of a company's financial stability. They can also tell you what to do if you have a complaint against an agent, broker or company. But they don't get down to the nitty-gritty business of rating individual companies for value and performance.

AMERICAN COUNCIL OF LIFE INSURANCE, *1850 K Street NW, Washington, DC 20250. Telephone 800-423-8000; in Washington, DC, 202-862-4054.* This organization gives advice on life and health insurance. (Whenever I have called they have been busy.)

INSURANCE INFORMATION INSTITUTE, *110 William Street, New York, NY 10038. Telephone 800-221-4954.* This one answers questions about property and casualty (homeowner and automobile) insurance.

STATES THAT GIVE OUT USEFUL INFORMATION

Every state has an insurance department that gives out general advice on choosing insurance policies. Most of them have someone who answers questions (even quite specific questions on individual problems) and handles complaints against agents, brokers and companies. A few especially good departments do even more: they provide comparative information on named companies that is a tremendous money-saving help to anyone buying insurance. The **AMERICAN COUNCIL OF LIFE INSURANCE** (see above) can give you the address and telephone number of your own state's department of insurance.

Here is a list of states that, at the time of writing, provide really helpful specific publications that name companies and give actual prices.

STATE OF ARIZONA DEPARTMENT OF INSURANCE, *1601 West Jefferson, Phoenix, AZ 85007. Telephone 602-255-4783.* "Private Passenger Auto Premium Comparison," "Homeowner Premium Comparison," "Personal Lines Complaint Ratio."

STATE OF CONNECTICUT INSURANCE DEPARTMENT, ***165 Capitol Avenue, Hartford, CT 06106.*** "Auto Insurance Price Comparison Guide."

BUREAU OF CONSUMER RESEARCH AND EDUCATION, FLORIDA DEPARTMENT OF INSURANCE, ***Suite LL25, The Capitol, Tallahassee, FL 32301.*** "Medicare Supplement Insurance Shopper's Guide" (compares representative policies of Medicare supplement insurers), "Auto Insurance Shopper's Guide" (shows sample prices of Florida's largest volume auto insurance companies). Shopper's guides to life insurance, health insurance and health maintenance organizations are being prepared as I write.

FLORIDA HOSPITAL COST CONTAINMENT BOARD, ***Room 535 Larson Building, Tallahassee, FL 32301.*** "You Can Choose" (leaflets comparing costs in Florida hospitals).

STATE OF ILLINOIS DEPARTMENT OF INSURANCE, ***320 West Washington Street, Springfield, IL 62767.*** Annually publishes complaint ratios against all kinds of insurance companies: auto, homeowner, accident and health, life.

COMMONWEALTH OF KENTUCKY DEPARTMENT OF INSURANCE, ***P.O. Box 517, 151 Elkhorn Court, Frankfort, KY 40602. Telephone 502-564-3630.*** "Consumer Report on Automobile Insurance" (premiums quoted by eight companies). "Consumer Report Homeowner Insurance" (company rates).

MAINE BUREAU OF INSURANCE, ***State House Station 34, Augusta, ME 04333. Telephone 207-289-3101.*** "Automobile Insurance Premium Comparison Report," "Homeowner Insurance Premium Comparison Report," "Medicare Supplement Insurance Comparison Chart."

MICHIGAN INSURANCE BUREAU, ***P.O. Box 30220, Lansing, MI 48909.*** "Do Not Buy Car Insurance Until You Read This!" (a survey of car insurance premiums at 16 different companies).

STATE OF NEW JERSEY DEPARTMENT OF INSURANCE, ***201 East State Street, P.O. Box CN 325, Trenton, NJ 08625.*** Assorted guides.

STATE OF NEW YORK INSURANCE DEPARTMENT, ***Agency Building One, Nelson A. Rockefeller Plaza, Albany, NY 12257.*** "Consumers Shopping Guide for Automobile Insurance," "Consumers Shopping Guide for Homeowners Insurance," "Consumers Shopping Guide for Life Insurance," "Medicare Supplement Insurance in New York State" (all include cost-comparison tables).

STATE OF UTAH INSURANCE DEPARTMENT, ***Heber Wells Building, 160 East 300 South, 2nd floor, P.O. Box 5803, Salt Lake City, UT 84110-5803.*** "Medigap Shopping Guide" (a comparison of Medicare supplemental policies offered for sale in Utah).

STATE OF VIRGINIA BUREAU OF INSURANCE, ***Box 1157, Richmond, VA 23209.*** "Virginia Auto Insurance Consumer's Guide" (includes sample automobile insurance rate table for Virginia's 50 largest companies), "Virginia Homeowners Insurance Guide" (includes statewide average rates for Virginia's 50 largest companies).

STATE OF WEST VIRGINIA, INSURANCE COMMISSIONER, ***2100 Washington Street East, Charleston, West Virginia 25305. Telephone 304-348-3354.*** A comparison list of premium rates for homeowner insurance in five cities in the state.

OFFICE OF THE COMMISSIONER OF INSURANCE OF WISCONSIN, ***P.O. Box 7873, Madison, WI 53707. Telephone 608-266-3585.*** Assorted guides.

INVESTMENT

J. Michael Reid, the editor and publisher of the investment newsletter *Insider Indicator,* has written the following advice for beginning investors. He is bullish on investment as a hobby and advises young people to start early and think of themselves as investors rather than consumers. He also says that investing is an enjoyable way for retired people to remain productive members of society, which may be why some of J. Michael Reid's clients won't release the grasp of their portfolio management until the coffin lid closes.

LEARNING HOW TO INVEST

By J. Michael Reid

The stock market is not like a bicycle—"once you've learned you never forget." The problem with the stock market and basic investing is that you always have to keep learning, because the market is an ever-changing place. A good example of change is the U.S. Treasury bond. A favorite movie star may have been correct in telling you to buy in 1942. In 1972 you would have been losing money on them because of inflation. Now the downward drift of interest rates makes the guaranteed rate of the current Treasury offerings an interesting hedge against further declines.

How do you start a systematic investing program? The first investment you should make is one of time. You need to do some basic reading. There are many classics that are easily understood by both professional and first-time investors. To get on a par with professional investors, you must first learn the language. You can use a basic textbook with a good index and glossary, like *Personal Investing* by Wilbur W. Widicus and Thomas E. Stitzel, or you can use the introductory material of an investing service, such as Value Line's *How to Use the Value Line Investment Survey—A Subscriber's Guide.*

After becoming familiar with the terms used by investors, you can go on to some classic books with common-sense messages that have helped investors. Four you might consider are Benjamin Graham's *Intelligent Investor,* Norman

Fosback's *Stock Market Logic,* David Dreman's *New Contrarian Investment Strategy: The Psychology of Stock Market Success* and John Boland's *Wall Street's Insiders.*

What you want to read for is a system that makes sense to you. There are 20,000 different securities you can invest in. The average investor is lost in such a forest of choice. The first thing you have to build is a systematic way to sort the mountains of facts and figures you can see being reported by the traded companies to their investors.

Basically, there are three purely systematic ways of going after sound investing results. All have been subjected to many studies. All have many proponents.

The most widely followed method, which is also the most debated and modified, is an offshoot of Benjamin Graham's work and involves looking for values in securities. The market, a herd that is subject to psychological movement, tries to set the value of a security. Looking for undervalued investments in a systematic way requires the most training of the three methods. You have to continue to study stocks over the years to get to the point where you just may be a better analyst than some of the highly paid ones that frequent such popular shows as "Wall Street Week."

The next method involves finding an individual analyst or a company with analysts that will do some of the work for you. A professional analyst takes many factors into consideration in a consistent manner over time and uses a developed set of criteria to give you some sort of ranking system to view all the investing choices you might have. The firm that has the longest history of doing this in the most studied way is Value Line, publisher of *The Value Line Investment Survey* newsletter. (You can sample the service by writing to the address below. Most libraries that have a financial section also carry the service.) You will find that the Value Line analysts rank the stocks that they follow with a "Timeliness" and "Safety" rating. The point for your investing is that the systematic method used by the firm and reported to its readers each week has worked in beating the market averages.

The third method with a long history of success is following the corporate insiders and stock market specialists. The insiders you can follow are the officers, directors and certain beneficial owners of a stock representing the company for which it is their duty to advance the shareholders' interests. The specialists are the individuals whom all brokers must go to in order to trade securities listed on the New York or American stock exchange.

Most of the publications you will find follow the insiders. You can find weekly investment letters that provide you with a list of the most current activity (such as *Vickers Weekly Insider Report*), as well as ones that take into consideration all the transactions and report only signals of significant activity (such as my own *Insider Indicator*).

Research clearly shows that insiders outperform the market averages. There is nothing illegal about their transactions if they follow certain guidelines. One of those is that the insiders can not trade when they know a significant fact that would have an impact on the price of the stock. They can trade using what they know in general—such as what all the brokers and analysts are saying about the firm they know best. You can bet that if Wall Street is overlooking a firm, you will find some insiders with good reason to buy. If Wall Street earnings estimates are too high, an insider will be more apt to sell than borrow money against his or her holdings.

If you use insiders to be your initial screen of which stocks to look at, you will find you can use all three methods described here. You can see what the insiders are saying, balance that against what a ranking system is showing and apply your own judgment to come up with a group of stocks that will make you a portfolio that can meet your investing needs.

To get a feel for the current market, make a trip to the library to review a popular magazine on investing, such as *Money*. This would be a starting point to set your first area of study. It is a good idea to start modestly with tax-deferred programs, such as your own Individual Retirement Account (IRA), or others designed to fulfill a future goal, such as paying for a child's college expenses through instruments like striped Treasury bills. The point is that you should start with an immediate goal and then, as you learn more, you can get more ambitious.

Maybe, until you have spent several years in the investing field, you will want to rely on the advice of investing professionals. You can go to a full-service broker, which will allow you access to research done by the house. You may even want to have a mutual fund be your investing tool in the beginning. At the same time, you should spend ten minutes a day reading up on the market and watching how the management you picked performs.

Once you have enough money for a reasonable investment in the stocks you have studied—when the fee to buy or sell doesn't take all your profits!—you may want to put your money into several different investments until you are more experienced. Meanwhile develop your own system of investing, using the information you already receive daily. You grow slowly using such an approach, but you do progress at a pace that assures you that you will keep meeting your goals and adapt to changes in the investment market.

FURTHER READING

Many of the expensive research tools you need to use may be available at the local library, just waiting for the correct systematic use.

A DICTIONARY OF FINANCE AND INVESTMENT TERMS ***by Jordan Elliot Goodman and John Downes. $6.95 plus 15% plus $1.04 postage from the publisher. Order Department, Barron's, 113 Crossways Park Drive, Woodbury, NY 11797. Telephone 800-645-3476. AE, MC, V.*** An excellent dictionary, which is what most investors really need.

HOW TO USE THE VALUE LINE'S INVESTMENT SURVEY—A SUBSCRIBER'S GUIDE. ***$2.50 from the publisher. Value Line, 711 Third Avenue, New York, NY 10017. Telephone 800-633-2252.*** This is available at most libraries.

THE INTELLIGENT INVESTOR, ***by Benjamin Graham. $18.95 plus $2.50 postage from the publisher. Bookstore, Harper & Row, 10 East 53rd Street, New York, NY 10022. Telephone 212-207-7065 with AE, MC, V.*** This is available at most libraries.

THE NEW CONTRARIAN INVESTMENT STRATEGY: THE PSYCHOLOGY OF STOCK MARKET SUCCESS ***by David Dreman. $18.95 plus $1 book rate postage from the publisher. Order Department, Random House, 400 Hahn Street, Westminster, MD 21157. Telephone 301-848-1900 with AE, MC, V.***

PERSONAL INVESTING ***by Wilbur W. Widicus and Thomas E. Stitzel. $27.95 plus $2 UPS charge from the publisher. Order Department, Richard D. Irwin, Homewood, IL 60430. Telephone 312-798-6000.*** A good basic introductory text.

STOCK MARKET LOGIC ***by Norman Fosback. $30 paperback plus $2.40 postage from the publisher. The Institute for Econometric Research, 371 North Federal Highway, Fort Lauderdale, FL 33306. Telephone 800-327-6720 with AE, MC, V.***

WALL STREET'S INSIDERS ***by John Boland. $16.95 plus $1.50 postage (takes about five weeks) from the publisher. William Morrow and Company, 6 Henderson Drive, West Caldwell, NJ 07006. No telephone orders.***

Newsletters

As you become more independent, there are specific newsletters that can tell you about details and timely situations that are important to your investing. Some letters cover mutual funds. Many like to stay with hard assets of precious metals. Others are stock pickers. Most are expensive—you can expect to pay $50 to $300 for a good one—but remember that libraries, universities and investing clubs often share expenses for the smaller investor who doesn't need a personal copy.

There are services that let you sample a lot of different approaches before you pick which letter you want. One of these is **SELECT INFORMATION EXCHANGE,** ***2095 Broadway, New York, NY 10023, telephone 212-874-6408.*** Through SEI, a discount subscription service, you can sample up to 20 financial and business newsletters for $11.95. It has a free catalogue.

There are other services that quote and rate newsletters, for example, **THE HULBERT FINANCIAL DIGEST,** ***643 South Carolina Avenue SE, Washington, DC 20003, telephone 202-546-2164.*** It rates 76 financial newsletters. Sample current issue, $10.

Here are several newsletters that J. Michael Reid suggests are worth sampling (the list includes letters that discuss several different strategies for investing):

GROWTH STOCK OUTLOOK, ***Editor Charles Allmon, P.O. Box 15381, Chevy Chase, MD 20815. Telephone 301-654-5205.***
Two issues a month, $175 a year. Free sample: two recent issues. Looks for companies that need cash to expand and will produce capital gains through growth stocks.

INSIDER INDICATOR, ***Editor J. Michael Reid, 2230 Northeast Brazee, Portland, OR 97212. Telephone 503-281-8626.***
Subscription $145 a year. A signal format following corporate insider transactions with two monthly issues. Scope includes NYSE, Amex and OTC issues. Signals have been compiled since 1974, so current buys have comments about past timing of insiders. Charts show volume and percentages of past activity versus the appropriate market index. Signals are indexed quarterly by industry groupings. A portfolio of buy signals are followed for a full year after their publication.

INVESTMENT QUALITY TRENDS, ***Editor G. Weiss. 7440 Girard Avenue, La Jolla, CA 92037. Telephone 301-654-5205.***
Two issues a month, $195 a year. Trial subscription: four issues, $20. Looks for stocks that produce consistent dividends, follows a selected group of about 350 stocks.

MARKET LOGIC, ***Editor Norman G. Fosback. Institute of Econometric Research, 3471 North Federal Highway, Fort Lauderdale, FL 33306. Telephone 800-327-6720.***
Trial subscription: one month (two issues), free. Annual subscription includes above-mentioned book *Stock Market Logic,* $135. A well-run generalist letter that tries to cover all aspects of the market.

DISCOUNT STOCKBROKERS

The Securities and Exchange Commission abolished fixed brokerage commissions in 1975, whereupon discount brokerage firms emerged to compete with the established full-service firms. Discount firms do not have researchers or give advice—they merely execute transactions. If you use a discount broker, you have to make your own investment decisions. But the commissions discount brokers charge can be half or even a fifth of what full-service brokers charge.

The biggest savings are on very large trades. On very small trades "discount" commissions may be higher than those at full-service houses because most discounters charge a minimum commission rate that you have to pay if your trade isn't large enough.

In a 1985 report on discount stockbrokers, the Better Business Bureau of Metropolitan New York points out that the way to calculate your savings is to compare the fee schedules and other important terms of the different firms with your own trading patterns in mind. The Better Business Bureau's one-page report is very helpful. It describes significant ways (services and terms) in which discount stockbrokers differ so that you can ask the right questions in order to decide which one is best for you. The report, "Choosing a Discount Stockbroker," is available, free, from the **BETTER BUSINESS BUREAU OF METROPOLITAN NEW YORK,** ***257 Park Avenue South, New York, NY 10010, telephone 212-533-7500.***

Major Discount Stockbrokers

Here is a list of major discount stockbrokers, most of which have offices in cities around the country. In December 1985, I telephoned these major discount brokerage firms and asked them for their minimum commission, as well as the commission they charge on transactions of 100 and 1,000 listed stocks worth $40 a share. I chose those figures at random, and they are intended to give just a rough idea for comparative purposes, as the actual commissions may well have changed by the time you read this. The discount brokers were happy to quote commission fees and send written information; the full-service houses refused or were difficult about quoting.

At the time I got the figures below from the discount houses, the official commission at the major full-service stockbroker Shearson American Express was $87 for 100 listed stocks at $40 a share, and $543 for 1,000 listed stocks at $40 a share. But remember that if you are a very active trader, you can negotiate the commissions with your full-service stockbroker and so narrow the price difference between a discount house and a full-service one.

COMMISSION ON LISTED STOCKS TRADED

Brown and Company, ***20 Winthrop Square, Boston, MA 02110. Telephone 800-225-6707; in Massachusetts, 617-357-4410.***
A subsidiary of Chemical New York Corporation. Offices in New York, Orlando, Philadelphia.
Handles bonds, listed and over-the-counter stocks, index options; will take market orders for U.S. Treasury bills but will not quote on them.
Minimum commission $25 plus 8 cents per share. Commission on 100 $40 stocks traded, $33 ($25 plus 8 cents a share); on 1,000 $40 shares traded, $105.

Discount Brokerage Corporation of America (DBC), ***67 Wall Street, New York, NY 10005. Telephone 800-221-5084; in New York State, 212-806-2888.***
Offices in 14 cities around the country.
Handles listed and over-the-counter stocks, bonds, index options, municipal bonds.
No minimum commission. Commission on 100 $40 stocks traded, $37.50; on 1,000 $40 stocks traded, $136.40.

Fidelity Brokerage Services, ***61 Broadway, New York, NY 10006. Telephone 800-221-5338; in New York State, 212-422-6000.***

Offices in major cities.
Handles listed and over-the-counter stocks, corporate bonds, options, government securities, municipal bonds.
Minimum commission $30. Commission on 100 $40 stocks traded, $40; on 1,000 $40 stocks traded, $149.

Olde Discount Brokers, ***140 Cedar Street, New York, NY 10006. Telephone 800-524-3000; in New York State, 212-406-5555.***
Offices around the country.
Handles listed and over-the-counter stocks, bonds, options, government securities, municipal bonds.
Minimum commission $30. Commission on 100 $40 stocks traded, $45; on 1,000 $40 stocks traded, $125.

Ovest Financial Services, ***90 Broad Street, New York, NY 10004. Telephone 800-255-0700; in New York State, 212-668-0600.***
Office in Providence, Rhode Island.
Handles listed and over-the-counter stocks, corporate bonds, options, government securities, municipal bonds.
Minimum commission $35. Commission on 100 $40 stocks traded, $40; on 1,000 $40 stocks traded, $110.

Pacific Brokerage Services, ***5757 Wilshire Boulevard, Los Angeles, CA 90036. Telephone 800-223-3242.***
Offices in Chicago, Dallas, New York.
Handles listed and over-the-counter stocks, bonds.
Minimum commission $25. Commission on 100 $40 stocks traded, $25; on 1,000 $40 stocks traded, $78.

Rose and Company, ***Lock Box A3880, Chicago, IL 60690. Telephone 800-435-4000.***
Offices in seven cities.
Handles listed and over-the-counter stocks, corporate bonds, options, government securities, municipal bonds.
Minimum commission $25. Commission on 100 $40 stocks traded, $35; on 1,000 $40 stocks traded, $165.

Charles Schwab and Company, ***The Schwab Building, 101 Montgomery Street, San Francisco, CA 94104. Telephone 800-648-5300.***
Offices in over 90 cities.
Handles listed and over-the-counter stocks, corporate bonds, options, mutual funds, unit investment trusts.
Minimum commission $34. Commission on 100 $40 stocks traded, $49; on 1,000 $40 stocks traded, $164.

Muriel Siebert and Company, ***444 Madison Avenue, New York, NY 10022. Telephone 800-872-0444; in New York State, 212-644-2405.***
One of the very few brokerage firms founded by a woman.
Handles listed and over-the-counter stocks, corporate bonds, options, government securities, municipal bonds, IRAs, Keogh plans.
Minimum commission $30. Commission on 100 $40 stocks traded, $39; on 1,000 $40 stocks traded, $160.

LEATHER AND LUGGAGE

I remember traveling in Spain when metal-studded trunks and wooden boxes tied with rope were standard issue. Since then, as travel has grown popular and porters have disappeared, luggage has become lighter and softer. Soft and semisoft (cases with frames but soft sides) now account for 70% of all luggage sold. In fact, to avoid airport waits most people are now buying carry-on luggage—a garment bag that can be hung in the airplane closet or stored overhead and a soft case that will fit under the seat. The other popular piece with people who carry their own luggage is the large case with wheels.

MAIL AND TELEPHONE SOURCES

Ace Leather Products, ***2211 Avenue U, Brooklyn, NY 11229. Telephone 800-342-5223; New York questions, 718-645-3534; New York orders, 718-645-9713.***

Free brochure, or write or telephone 10 A.M. to 6 P.M., Monday to Saturday. MC, V.

Sells Dooney and Bourke handbags and wallets; attaché cases and briefcases by Atlas, Grace, Michael Scott, Scully, Schlesinger, Tumi, Ventura, others; luggage by American Tourister, Andiamo, Boyt, Hartmann, Lark, Samsonite, Ventura, Verdi, others.

Returns: credit or exchange.

Established 1919.

I do believe that this is the best place to buy luggage and attaché cases. Most major brands are stocked and so are some exotic ones (handmade cases by the French Company in California, for instance). When I have checked prices, Ace has answered quickly (returning my own letter marked up) and has had the widest range and the lowest prices—from 17 to 25% off list. Andy Lubell of Ace says that he will order any size that he doesn't stock, and he points out that shipping luggage is not expensive. Even the largest cases cost only a few dollars by UPS.

Al's Luggage, ***2134 Larimer Street, Denver, CO 80205. Telephone 303-295-9009.***
Illustrated price sheets of Samsonite luggage, $1, or write or telephone 9 A.M. to 5:30 P.M. for specific prices.
AE, MC, V.
Sells luggage by Samsonite, Lion leather goods, luggage carts.
Returns: money back if merchandise unused.
Established 1934.

Samsonite is the biggie in luggage, with 25% of the market, and it has moved with the times. Much of its stuff is now soft-sided, in fashionable styles in black and khaki inspired by the backpack/safari/military crazes. Incidentally, when *Consumer Reports* tested soft-sided luggage with wheels in July 1985, it top-rated a case from Samsonite's Series 2100 (which tied with Ventura 505026).

If you want Samsonite, this is the place to get it. Morton Lesser carries all the Samsonite lines that department stores and better luggage stores carry (not the lines that catalogue stores have). He says prices are 30 to 50% off. I checked two prices, and they were 35 and 45% off the list prices given by *Consumer Reports.* If you send Morton Lesser $1, he'll send nice clear photostats and complete price lists together with shipping information and an order form. If you talk to him on the telephone, he has a pleasant Colorado manner, and he's willing to answer any questions you have about what to buy.

Leeds Luggage Shop/Kay-Sherman Luggage, ***33 West 46th Street, New York, NY 10036. Telephone 212-719-2860.***
Free catalogue, November/December only. Write or telephone 9 A.M. to 5 P.M. for specific prices.
AE, CB, DC, MC, V.
Sells popular brands of luggage and briefcases.
Returns: money back if in reasonable time, but no returns on initialed goods.
Established 1936.

The best-known brands of luggage and briefcases are sold here at what they say is a standard 25% discount. Prices when I spot-checked were good, almost as low as at Ace.

MUSICAL INSTRUMENTS

WHAT TO BUY IF YOU ARE A BEGINNER

The two cardinal rules in buying musical instruments are:

1. Choose your teacher before your instrument—so that your teacher can help you choose your instrument.
2. Don't pay list price for anything.

An experienced player can tell a good instrument by playing it, but a beginner can't. If you buy an instrument without knowing much about it, you may find you've bought an instrument that doesn't play properly and doesn't sound as it should. If you have no one to advise you, avoid unknown and lesser-known brands, some of which are so badly made that they'll hold a student back.

A satisfactory instrument has good internal acoustics, notes that play evenly and moving parts that are well aligned and don't stick. The reputable instrument makers use better materials and keep a watch over workmanship so that consistent quality is maintained.

There are plenty of relatively inexpensive instruments that are more than adequate for the first few years of playing and will by no means hold a student back. The trick for a beginner is to find the best value for money. If you don't have a knowledgeable teacher or friend, then I hope the shops listed here will be able to give you honest advice. Most of them have been recommended to me by people working in the field.

BUYING SECONDHAND

Don't buy string, brass or woodwind instruments secondhand unless you find an unimpeachable source or have expert advice. (And keep away from pawn shops and jumble sales. Many is the music teacher whose heart has sunk as a proud pupil presented a great garage-sale find that, in fact, sounded terrible.) As with new instruments, used strings, brass and woodwinds may have flaws that spoil your playing.

However, it does make sense to buy used drums and cymbals. Depending on their condition, the popularity of the model and so on, used drums typically cost about 40% less than new ones. Cymbals cost about 35% less. Drums that are well cared for keep their good condition, and cymbals, unless they are cracked, don't change at all. They also keep their resale value.

Buying these instruments secondhand is a simple matter compared to buying cars or cameras, as there are no hidden mechanical parts. With drums, make sure that the brand name is on a metal tag on the shell, that the wood isn't warped and hasn't been clumsily refinished, that the metal parts are in good shape and that the set generally looks in good condition. Better-quality drums to look for are the Japanese Pearl, Tama and Yamaha. They have received respectable endorsements and are now the most popular drums of all. Good American brands are Gretsch, Premier, Rogers and Slingerland. Although some drummers debate the point, Nick Savene, who specializes in used drums and cymbals in his New York store, Stik's Place, thinks there isn't a great deal of difference in sound between the drums in the different grades that each manufacturer produces. If you want to save money, buy a good brand but the less expensive line he advises.

With cymbals, the only possible problems are hairline cracks; if they run along the grain, they are hard to see. Among cymbals, the American-made Zildjian and Swiss-made Paiste are the top brands and are excellent investments, as they don't lose their value. Just make sure that the brand name is engraved on the cymbal.

MAIL AND TELEPHONE SOURCES

When comparing prices, make sure you know what extras or parts you want to include in the quote; for instance, do you need the instrument's case? If you are buying a wind instrument or brass, is the mouthpiece included?

Instruments and Accessories

Sam Ash Music Stores, ***124 Fulton Avenue, Hempstead, NY 11550. Telephone 800-4-SAM-ASH; in New York State, 718-347-7757.***
In the U.S. and Canada telephone 9 A.M. to 6 P.M., Monday through Saturday, for specific prices.
AE, MC, V.
Sells major brands of musical instruments, amplification and sound systems.
Returns: money back or credit—"varies with circumstance."
Minimum order $25.
Established 1921.

The well-known Sam Ash has been recommended to me by musician and teacher Brian Coogan, who says that besides being reputable, the store has very good prices and will often special order anything you want that it doesn't have.

The firm was started by Sam Ash, father of the two brothers who now run the store, and has grown to be one of the largest mail-order houses in the industry, selling to customers around the world. The mail-order department has six full-time salespeople who take calls and answer letters and Telex communications. They will advise by telephone and follow up with price information and tear sheets.

Because of the large volume of business Paul Ash says that he buys in quantity and passes on the lower prices to customers. Also because of the volume, manufacturers offer the store closeouts and discontinued items so that each week there are specials at what Paul Ash calls "crazy low" prices. One particularly good recent special was a Hohner keyboard. Sam Ash took 500 of a discontinued model originally sold at $1700 and sold it for $295. The 500 sold out in two weeks because, although technological developments had made the keyboard obsolete at $1700, at $295 it was still an excellent value. There is an especially large stock here of the electric instruments used by rock groups.

Frank Richards, ***30 Chapin Road, P.O. Box 776, Pine Brook, NJ 07058. Telephone: questions, 201-575-5511; orders, 800-MA-MUSIC.***
Separate catalogues for band and orchestral instruments, accessories, gifts, supplies; or write or telephone 9 A.M. to 5 P.M. for specific prices.
MC, V.
Sells musical instruments and accessories of all brands, printed music by all publishers.
Minimum order $10.
Returns: depends on product.
Established 1967.

Frank Richards has a specialized service, 90% mail order, selling to schools, band directors and choral directors around the country. It sells mainly wind and percussion instruments and music books at discounts that go up to 40% for large-quantity orders. It has an extensive music library for schools and students (it deals with all U.S. and also foreign publishers) and will research music for music teachers trying to trace something. It also deals with private individuals who know what they want. Frank Richards was recommended by musician and teacher Brian Coogan, who likes the good discounts on instruments and music for schools, the reliable service and the fact that the firm will order anything.

Silver and Horland, ***170 West 48th Street, New York, NY 10036. Telephone 212-869-3870.***
Write or telephone for prices.
AE, MC, V.

Sells new and used musical instruments and accessories, vintage instruments. Has everything but acoustic pianos and harps.
Minimum order $15.
Returns: no returns on new equipment unless defective; used and vintage instruments must be returned in same condition received within 24 hours for money back, one week for credit.
Established 1930.

Silver and Horland sells over a million dollars' worth of musical instruments and equipment a year, especially guitars and amplifiers. Richard Silver suggests that customers first research what they want locally, through shops, friends or teachers, and then call with a brand and model number. If you can't do that, you can call in and say how much you want to spend, and the salespeople will suggest a few brands. Richard Silver suggests that customers in doubt telephone, rather than write, as there are so many different questions to be answered about most items—especially the used and vintage instruments on sale. As for prices, he told me about a family that had recently bought a Traynor amplifier from him for $90 when the same model cost $160 in their home town, Fort Lauderdale.

West Manor Music, ***831 East Gun Hill Road, Bronx, NY 10467. Telephone 212-882-8790 or 212-655-5400.***
Free price list, or write or telephone for specific prices.
MC, V.
Sells all musical instruments used in schools: brass, woodwinds, strings, percussion; limited number of standard music books.
Minimum order $25.
Returns: no returns, but instruments have a one-year warranty.
Established 1959.

One of the biggest mail-order suppliers in the country, West Manor Music sells and rents out almost any instrument used in schools, and guarantees that it has the lowest prices on all of them. It also has a workshop that checks new instruments, services violins before they go out and does repairs. The firm was recommended by musician Brian Coogan, who says that its prices are hard to beat.

World of Music, ***20015 Steven's Creek Boulevard, Cupertino, CA 95014. Telephone 408-252-8264.***
In the U.S. and Canada send self-addressed, stamped envelope for prices.
AE, MC, V.
Sells musical instruments, amplifiers, drums, microphones, PA systems and musical accessories and oddities. Band instruments by Armstrong, Benge, Boosey & Hawkes, Buffet, Conn, Gemeinhardt, King, Leblanc, Selmer, Schilke, Yamaha; guitars by Gibson, Guild, Hamer, Martin, Rickenbacker, Yamaha; amplifiers and electronics by Aria, Fostex, Ibanez, Music Man, Roland, Spectra.

Minimum order $50.
Returns: exchanges but no refunds.
Established 1985.

In 1985 Larry Sweet bought Currlin's Music Center, moved it to Cupertino and turned it into the World of Music. Mr. Sweet says that he still gives the same discounts of 10 (on sheet music) to 40% and that his is still a family-oriented store. Although he is obviously not as geared to mail order as the eastern firms, thrifty westerners might want to try him.

World of Music sells used instruments, as well as instruments on consignment.

Fretted Instruments (Guitars and Folk Instruments)

Elderly Instruments, ***1100 North Washington Avenue, P.O. Box 14210cc, Lansing, MI 48901. Telephone 517-372-7890.***
Free catalogue ($2 in Canada and abroad).
Sells mainly new and used stringed instruments: guitars by Gibson, Guild, Martin, Sigma, Yamaha; mandolins by Flatiron, Gibson, Kentucky, Stiver; banjos by Deering, Gibson, Goldstar, Wildwood; banjos by Reiter; dulcimers by Folk Roots; Boreal bodhrans; Heatwole concertinas.
Returns: all instruments may be returned but "we ask that customers notify us within 48 hours (after they've received their order) of their intention to return."
Established 1972.

Elderly Instruments was started by a couple who wanted to create a folk and bluegrass music store that was the kind of place they'd like to shop in. Judging by the appealing, informative newsprint catalogues, the store has succeeded in combining knowledgeable salespeople, high-quality merchandise and fair prices. Manager Raoul Mitts says that the focus of the store is on service—the staff believes in giving customers as much information as they need and want and then letting them go from there. Just about everyone at the store plays an instrument, so if you call with difficult questions you'll be passed on to someone who knows your kind of instrument.

There is a workshop with a staff of three that works on used instruments and checks out new instruments. The store claims to give 10% discounts off list prices and up to 40% discounts on Martin and other major guitars.

Mandolin Brothers, ***629 Forest Avenue, Staten Island, NY 10310. Telephone 718-981-3226.***
Free catalogue.
AE, MC, V.
Sells new and vintage guitars, mandolins and banjos and accessories; multitrack cassette tape decks; Casio keyboards. Manufacturers handled: Daion, Dobros, Epiphone, Fairbanks, Fender, Fostex, Franklin, Gibson, Gold Star, Guild, Hondo,

Kentucky, Macaferri, Martin, Ode, Ovation, Paramount, Oscar Schmidt Autoharps, Stelling, Yamaha and more. Also appraises, repairs and sells instruments on consignment.
Returns: 48-hour approval time on instruments.
Established 1971.

This nice small firm specializes in vintage American fretted instruments—guitars, mandolins and banjos made by the most esteemed workshops of the golden era, 1920 to 1946. Salespeople answer questions from around the country and around the world on those instruments. They also give free verbal appraisals (and written appraisals for $35) to anyone who sends in a photograph of an instrument with a description of its condition and then telephones.

Mandolin Brothers also sells new instruments at a discount, and this is a very good place to call if you want advice. Ask for the owner, Stanley Jay, if you are in a muddle about what to buy; speak to the technician if you have a question about repairs.

Stanley Jay, who has taught guitar at colleges for six years, points out that beginners must start on a nylon-string guitar until they build up calluses. He recommends the classic CG120 Yamaha. For more advanced students, there are various choices—C. F. Martin's new less expensive Shenandoah line (D2832 series), for instance, or used instruments. (To give you an idea of the savings if you buy a used instrument: as I write, the standard C. F. Martin D-28 with case costs $1490 if you pay list, $931 at Mandolin Brothers and about $749 used.)

Mandolin gives a 37.5% discount off list price on all new Guild, C. F. Martin and Ovation instruments and a 20 to 25% discount on other brands.

Percussion

Drummer's World, ***133 West 45th Street, New York, NY 10036. Telephone 212-840-3057.***
Free brochure in February, $2 in Canada (refundable).
MC, V.
Sells percussion instruments and equipment of all kinds, ethnic instruments and replacement parts. Repairs on premises. Brands handled include Evans, Gretsch, Ludwig, Paiste, Pearl, Remo, Slingerland, Zildjian.
Minimum order $15.
Returns: credit.
Established 1979.

Drummer's World sells acoustic rather than electronic drums to "a strong classical crowd"—students and symphonic players, as well as jazz players. Discounts on drum sets are usually 30 to 40% off list price, says owner Barry Greenspon. But, he adds, the whole music world is so discount-oriented now that that is not unusual. He says that out-of-town customers buy from Drummer's World because it has greater diversity than shops that haven't specialized. It also sells African, Brazilian, Syrian and other ethnic instruments.

Lone Star Percussion, ***10611 Control Place, Dallas, TX 75238. Telephone 214-340-0835.***
Free catalogue.
MC, V.
Sells all brands of drum and percussion equipment and accessories.
Returns: money-back guarantee on major instruments, but guarantee varies on small perishable things such as drum sticks.
Established 1978.

Lone Star was recommended to me by Philip Weinkrantz (see below) as a large firm with low prices. President Harvey Vogel says that Lone Star is the world's largest seller of percussion instruments, even though it never advertises. Mr. Vogel tells me that he sells to 500 stores around the world and has 20,000 customers, from beginning drummers to every major symphony orchestra from Singapore to Israel and from Boston to L.A. Furthermore, Mr. Vogel says that he has many customers in New York because his prices are lower than those of the New York discount stores (such as Sam Ash) and he has a far greater inventory. He says he stocks *everything.*

Pianos and Organs

Altenburg Piano House, ***1150 East Jersey Street, Elizabeth, NJ 07201. Telephone 800-526-6979; in New Jersey, 800-492-4588.***
Write or telephone 9 A.M. to 9 P.M. for specific prices.
AE, DC, MC, V.
Sells all makes of pianos and organs.
Returns: money back or credit—"depends on situation."
Established 1847.

Between the years of 1825 and 1875, around 30 piano makers came from Europe (Austria, England, Germany and Poland) and set up shop in North America. Of those companies, the only one still 100% owned by the original family is Altenburg's, which belongs to the founder's great-great-grandson, Otto Altenburg.

The firm is still making its own pianos and sending them around the world (the U.S. army recently bought 15, the city of Newark, New Jersey, bought 31). But it also sells pianos and organs by almost every manufacturer, and at prices that are sometimes as much as 40% off those of full-price stores. Otto Altenburg says that prices are low enough so that, even with shipping costs of roughly $200 to the West Coast, this is a good source for the whole country.

Most of the big buying clubs use Altenburg Piano House "because of our tradition of service," says Otto. The firm also has a toll-free number and will advise you over the telephone if you don't know what to buy.

Conn Music Centers, ***1385 Deerfield Road, Highland Park, IL 60035. Telephone 312-831-3250.***
Telephone for specific prices.

MC, V.
Sells pianos by Everett, Kimball, Seiler and Young Chang; organs by Lowrey and Technics; clocks by Howard Miller.
Returns: none.
Established 1974.

This firm was recommended to me by Otto Altenburg, who says that the owner, his frend Peter Wyclaff, is a "good man" and that his prices are competitive. Mr. Wyclaff says he gives a 20% discount on Howard Miller clocks and a 30% or higher discount on pianos and organs. Pianos and organs are sent anywhere by common carrier and then delivered and set up in your home by a local dealer or piano agent.

Stringed Instruments

If you want to buy an inexpensive new stringed instrument, it is important to buy from a store with a workshop. New violins must be adjusted before being played. By working on the fit of the pegs, the curve of the bridge and so on, a competent workshop can make even the most inexpensive mass-produced instrument perfectly playable.

Reliable student-quality violins are made by Juzek (Germany), Roth (Germany) and Suzuki (Japan). Reliable student-quality cellos are made by Roth and Juzek.

Metropolitan Music Store, ***Mountain Road, R.R. 1, Box 1670, Stowe, VT 05672. Telephone 802-253-4814.***
Free catalogue. Also quotes prices by mail and telephone.
Sells stringed instruments in the violin family including "John Juzek" violins, violas, cellos and basses; "Ibex" Luthiers supplies, tools and wood. Does precision wood turning for instrument makers.
Minimum order $15.
Returns: "If our fault, complete cash refund; if your fault, cash refund less shipping and minimal service charge. We must be notified immediately of any complaint."
Established 1925.

Recommended by violin maker Steve McGhee and musician Brian Coogan, Metropolitan Music Store divides its business between selling parts and tools to stringed-instrument makers and new instruments to individuals, schools and dealers. For many years, Metropolitan supplied the New York Board of Education.

Instruments are sold at a good discount, but owner Bob Juzek stresses that this is a lower-price, no-frills store. The typical Metropolitan customer knows what he or she wants or has a knowledgeable teacher to help. The people at Metropolitan don't give advice on what instrument to buy, and they don't make adjustments once the instrument is sold. But, says Bob Juzek, you can rely on the quality of the instruments—he doesn't sell the cheapest imports, and all instruments are adjusted and ready to play, so you won't get stuck with anything shoddy. You can also return anything you don't like.

Bob Juzek says that his instruments are more reliable than those from the general music stores around the country, where the assistants have no special knowledge of violins. On the other hand, if you really want advice and extra help, he advises you to go to local violin specialists, where you pay more but get more service.

Philip Weinkrantz Musical Supply Company, ***2519 Bomar Avenue, Dallas, TX 75235. Telephone 214-350-4883.***
Accessories price list, free in the U.S. and Canada. Write or telephone 9 A.M. to 5 P.M. on weekdays, 9:30 A.M. to 3 P.M. on Saturdays, for specific prices.
Sells instruments and accessories for the violin, viola, cello and bass family.
Returns: money back; "we guarantee all merchandise with the exception of strings once they have been installed on an instrument."
Established 1975.

Recommended by a New York wholesaler, Philip Weinkrantz claims he has the lowest prices in the country (about 30 to 35% off list price, he says). Mr. Weinkrantz sells, by mail and telephone, stringed instruments and all their accessories such as strings, shoulder rests, bows and cases. His violins range from Suzukis to better student instruments, and, although he doesn't have a workshop, he himself sets up the bridge and makes sure the sound posts are in the correct position.

Shar, ***2465 South Industrial Highway, P.O. Box 1411, Ann Arbor, MI 48106. Telephone: questions, 313-665-7711; orders, 800-521-0791; in Michigan, 800-982-1086.***
Catalogue, free in the U.S. and Canada, in March and September.
MC, V.
Sells musical equipment and accessories for stringed instruments—viola, violin, cello—and a large stock of music (9,500 titles) for string players.
Returns: "complete customer satisfaction."
Established 1962.

The firm was started by a man whose two sons played the violin. Now the sons have stopped playing and are running the business. The five-person workshop is headed by David Burgess, who has won first prize in many major violin-making competitions and several international ones. Besides doing careful work on instruments sold, the staff is ready with advice. Owner Charles Avsharian says that most of his customers don't know what they want, so the staff is quite used to helping.

Most things are discounted at about 15 to 20%, with extra discounts and specials during fall and spring sales.

Wind Instruments

Giardinelli Band Instruments Co., *151 West 46 Street, New York, NY 10036. Telephone 800-457-7200; in New York State, 212-575-5959.*
Free price list in January, March, June.
AE, MC, V.
Sells brass and woodwind instruments, including harder-to-find brands such as Paxman and Alexander tubas and French horns.
Returns: money back if not satisfied; shipping charges not refundable.
Established 1947.

For years Giardinelli has been the leading discount store and repair shop for brass and woodwinds, and it is a first stop for visiting overseas musicians. The store has recently been sold by the family that owned it, and a spokeswoman for the new owners says that everything is going to continue in the same way.

Wichita Band Instruments Company, *2525 East Douglas, Wichita, KS 67211. Telephone 800-835-3006.*
In the U.S. and Canada write or telephone for specific prices.
Sells musical instruments and accessories, including Loree oboes, Paxman horns, Heckel bassoons, Prima Sankyo flutes and harpsichords.
Minimum order $25 on accessories.
Returns: money back but depends on the condition of the item.
Established 1954.

This firm has been recommended to me by a recorder player who tells me that the prices are the best anywhere—phenomenal, in fact. Wichita says that it sells only the best, and it follows the unusual practice of sending one or two instruments out for customers to try before buying. All instruments have a 24-month service guarantee, and there is a repair shop to back it up.

A few used, demonstrator and closeout instruments are also sold.

Sheet Music

These stores sell mostly standard music in original versions (for music for schools and students, try Frank Richards, described above). They do not publish or sell their own catalogues but can tell you what is available and at what prices if you are looking for a specific piece.

Frank Music Company, *250 West 54th Street, New York NY 10019. Telephone 212-582-1999.*
Write or telephone Monday through Friday 9 A.M. to 6 P.M., Saturdays 12 noon to 5 P.M., for specific prices.
Sells classical music of all publishers at a 10% discount.
Returns: "we do not accept returns unless item is defective."
Established 1937.

Heidi Rogers tells me her customers say she has the largest inventory of classical music in New York. Instead of having 20 copies of one thing that sells well, like Patelson, she has one copy of 20 things that are in less demand. She will order music that she does not have in stock, but she does not sell out-of-print music.

Ms. Rogers at first told me not to say that she gives discounts, as she has more or less stopped it. When I told her my book is only for discount stores, she told me to go ahead and put the discount information in. So make sure she *is* still taking 10% off list prices when you write or telephone.

Music Exchange, ***151 West 46th Street, 10th floor, New York, NY 10036. Telephone 212-354-5858.***
Write or telephone; credit cards not accepted.
Sells all music by all publishers and out-of-print music.
Established 1936.

"All music by all publishers" is the motto of this store, and the owner tells me that the firm has been in the same hands (hers) since it was established. She sells everything—classical, popular, operetta, out-of-print—and will get anything you want. Telephone calls and orders come in from around the world.

When I talked to her, the owner was cagey about details. She says that some but not all of the music is sold at below list price.

Joseph Patelson Music House, ***160 West 56th Street, New York, NY 10019. Telephone 212-582-5840.***
Sells printed music, sheet music, music books and publications, music volumes by leading international music publishers—mainly classical music but also some old-time popular songs.
Established 1920.

This well-known and well-liked firm (it was recommended to me by three people) sells classical music, usually at 10% off list price. There are exceptions—music of certain publishers who won't give discounts is sold at full price. Patelson takes special orders on classical music not stocked.

OFFICE EQUIPMENT AND STATIONERY

Smith-Corona's word processor for use with computer-compatible electronic typewriters. When the list price was $499.99, the price at Typex Business Machines was $369. The electronic typewriter can be bought and used independently or serve as the keyboard and printer for the word processor. When the list price for typewriter model XD7000 was $519, the price at Typex Business Machines was $339.

OFFICE EQUIPMENT AND STATIONERY

MAIL AND TELEPHONE SOURCES

You can save up to 40% by buying computer, office and writing supplies in quantity from these two firms. It is well worth waiting to stock up during their January sales, when prices are even lower.

Frank Eastern Company, ***599 Broadway, New York, NY 10021. Telephone 800-221-4914; in New York State, 212-219-0007.***
Free 56-page catalogue in January and May.
MC, V (but minimum order with cards is $75).
Sells office supplies and furniture.
Orders under $40 carry $3 handling charge.
Returns: money back, but first call customer service department.
Established 1946.

If you are willing to buy a dozen or a hundred at a time, you can save up to 40% on writing and office supplies such as brown envelopes, Liquid Paper for typing corrections and Scotch transparent tape. As I write, film ribbons for the IBM Selectric II cost $2.98 each at my local stationer, whereas, if you buy 12, they cost only $1.58 each at Frank Eastern.

Quill Corporation, ***100 South Schelter Road, Lincolnshire, IL 60069. Telephone 312-634-4800. West of the Rockies: P.O. Box 92781, Los Angeles, CA 90009. Telephone 213-461-2707.***

This firm has a large free catalogue, a good assortment of office and computer supplies and an excellent reputation for good prices, service and speed. (I notice that the ribbon for my computer printer, which costs $9.98 locally and $10.10 in midtown Manhattan, costs $4.22 if you buy 12 from Quill.)

Quill says it sells only to businesses, not people, but I think that if you invent a company name you can get away with it. I certainly know a person, not a business, who has been buying here for years.

Typewriters and Copiers

Typex Business Machines, ***23 West 23rd Street, New York, NY 10010. Telephone 212-243-2500.***
In the U.S. and Canada send self-addressed, stamped envelope or telephone 9:30 A.M. to 5:30 P.M.
MC, V.
Sells typewriters by Olivetti, Olympia, Royal, Silver Reed, Smith-Corona, others; calculators; copiers and other office machines.
Returns: credit is given only on defective machines if returned within five days.
Established 1936.

Typex is a friendly shop—very friendly: one day when I was in there, the owners were trying to persuade a surprised customer that he was a relative, because he had the same name as a Typex aunt.

More important, this is a full-service shop with a repair department and well-informed staff. Several years ago I bought a Smith-Corona here for $184 when the list price was $263. More recently, after comparing prices at several discount firms, a reader, Allen Pasternack, bought a Smith-Corona Ultrasonic II Messenger here for $459 (including $20 worth of supplies). At the time it was selling for $625 in his area. Mr. Pasternack was very impressed with the company and said that the man who took his telephone order was unusually friendly and knowledgeable. I agree—when I was comparing typewriter prices by telephone this morning, I commented on how low the Typex price was on one model and the assistant frankly replied, "Yes, the manufacturer reduced the price. It didn't happen to be the best model."

Several stores in the Appliances and Electronics section and OLDEN CAMERA AND LENS COMPANY in the Photography section sell typewriters and small copying machines.

Printing

The U.S. Post Office will print 500 prestamped envelopes with your name and address in the top left-hand corner and deliver them to wherever you want. As I write, 500 regular-sized or number 10 (business-sized) envelopes cost $135. As the 500 22-cent stamps cost $110, the envelopes, printing and delivery cost only $25. The clerk at my post office claims that even professional printers have envelopes for their own use printed by the post office. Order forms for "Printed Stamped Envelopes" are available at post offices throughout the country.

Pens

Schiphol Airport (*main listing in General section*) has amazing prices on ballpoint and fountain pens, usually under half of U.S. list prices (and airmail postage is minimal on pens, of course). I got a letter this morning from one of my readers, Inge Friedmann in Virginia, telling me that she has just received the Montblanc No. 144 from Schiphol for $56.53, including shipping (no duty was charged). In the United States it now generally costs $150. "The difference in price was mind-boggling," adds Inge. When I checked prices, the largest Montblanc Diplomat (No. 149) was selling for $250 (or $175 discounted) in the United States; it cost $108 at Schiphol. The Lamy Safari *set* was $9.70 at Schiphol, whereas the ballpoint and pencil were $12 *each* and the pen was $20 in the United States.

Pens are listed but not illustrated in the catalogue, so you do need to know what you want. Rather than asking for the catalogue, ask for the price including postage of any pens you are interested in. A few pens by each of these manufacturers are stocked: Aurora, Pierre Cardin, Cartier, Cross, Dupont, Gucci, Lamy, Montblanc, Parker, Sheaffer.

Christmas Supplies

January is obviously the month to buy Christmas cards, wrapping paper and decorations, as many stores cut prices then. Some museum stores have Christmas card sales for walk-in customers then too. In New York, for instance, the **Museum of Modern Art** cuts Christmas card prices by 50%, the **Pierpont Morgan Library** takes 25 to 30% off card prices and the **South Street Seaport Museum** reduces boxed card prices by various amounts.

English cards are much less expensive than American cards (they cost about half the price) so are well worth buying if you are popular and need lots of cards. But buy ahead of time so that they can come by surface mail. One of the few British catalogues with illustrations of cards is the one published by **THE PUBLICATIONS DEPARTMENT OF THE VICTORIA AND ALBERT MUSEUM,** ***South Kensington, London, SW7 6371, England.*** The catalogue appears in August. The cards are charming and unusual.

Gift Wrap and Mailing Supplies

United States Box Corporation, ***1296 McArter Highway, Newark, NJ 07104. Telephone 201-481-2000 or 718-387-1510.***
Free color catalogue.
Samples, $2 plus cost of item.
Sells packaging materials of all sorts, boxes, padded mailing bags, wrapping paper, labels and tapes.
Minimum order $150.
Returns: none.
Established 1948.

Gift-wrapping paper is extremely expensive, and any family that goes in for birthdays and Christmas and/or other celebrations eats up wrapping supplies by the yard. You can save lots of money and make sure you have stock ready for any emergency by buying in quantity. United States Box sells mainly to businesses, but if you can make the minimum order of $150, perhaps with a friend or a small group, you can buy wrapping paper, boxes, ribbons and mailing supplies of all sorts. When I checked, wrapping paper at United States Box cost about 9 cents a foot instead of the 23 cents it cost at my local stationer, and size 5 padded mailing envelopes cost 21 cents instead of the 49 cents being charged by my local stationer.

Make It Yourself

You can make lovely and cheap greeting and gift cards and wrapping paper with colored paper, rubber stamps and colored inks (and, for extra effect, color the cards with markers). Here are some firms that sell everything but the paper. Paper is sold by the stores listed under Art Supplies in the Hobby section.

Bizzaro Rubber Stamps, ***P.O. Box 126, Annex Station, Providence, RI 02901. Telephone 401-521-1305.***
34-page catalogue, $1 (refundable) in the U.S. and Canada.
MC, V.
Sells rubber stamps and inks.
Returns: money back if merchandise returned within 30 days, "but we always try to satisfy the customer and will accept returns at any time."
Established 1969.

The catalogue features twenties- and thirties-style stamps, with two pages of Christmas designs and a page of them for Valentine's Day. There are also postcards and labels for stamping and a very large collection of inks, markers, brushes and dyes for stamping on fabrics.

Hero Arts Rubber Stamps, ***2998 San Pablo Avenue, Berkeley, CA 94702. Telephone 415-849-9633.***
30-page catalogue, $2 in the U.S. and Canada.
Sells rubber stamps.
Returns: credit.
Established 1971.

Cartoon figures of the forties and other nostalgic images are available. The catalogue has a page of Christmas stamps and half a page of birthday stamps.

Mary Alice Scenic Stamps, ***2453 Echo Park, Los Angeles, CA 90026. Telephone 213-663-2862.***
6-page folder, $1.50 ($2 in Canada).
Sells rubber stamps.
Minimum order $7.

Returns: credit.
Established 1978.

Turn-of-the-century images, four different alphabets, several decorative labels, and a few Christmas trees, candles and a Santa Claus.

Pigs and Fishes, ***676 26th Street, Richmond, CA 94804. Telephone 415-236-2217.***
18-page catalogue, $1.50 (refundable).
Sells rubber stamps.
Returns: money back.
Established 1979.

Rather simple stamps, mainly of animals, dolls and clowns drawn by the owner, Marcia Alpert. Also an Elizabethan and a floral alphabet and a page of holiday stamps for Christmas, Easter, Halloween, Thanksgiving and Valentine's Day. Recommended by a customer, Julia Hildebrand.

Rubberstampede, ***P.O. Box 1105, Berkeley, CA 94701. Telephone 415-843-8910.***
Free 30-page catalogue in March, September.
MC, V.
Sells rubber stamps and stamp pads.
Returns: unconditional guarantee.
Established 1977.

Sweet and cheerful animal and people stamps and a pageful of Christmas stamps. Colored inks including gold, silver and copper, as well as stamps made from customers' own designs.

PERFUME AND COSMETICS

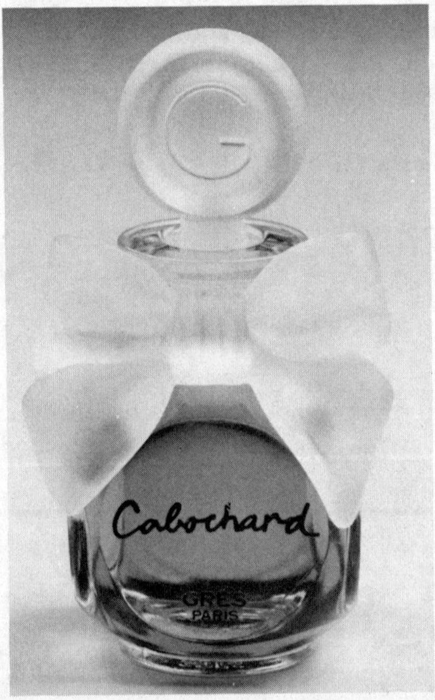

Cabochard perfume by Gres. When one ounce cost $119 in New York, it cost $60, including postage, from Anne Paree in France. At the same time, an American-made unauthorized copy of Cabochard cost $11.50, including postage, from Classique Perfumes.

PERFUME AND COSMETICS

MAIL AND TELEPHONE SOURCES

I am told by a wholesale drug house employee that the markup on perfumes and cosmetics is enormous—bigger than any markup except for that on drugs. So if you don't mind last year's colors, you can find great bargains and save up to 80% on cosmetics by buying from the catalogues listed below. They specialize in selling overruns and erstwhile "special offers" at ridiculously low prices—or rather, at reasonably low prices—it is the markups that are ridiculous.

Beautiful Beginnings by Spencer, ***Spencer Building, Atlantic City, NJ 08411. Telephone 609-645-5407.***
Free color catalogue.
Sells cosmetics.
Returns: money back.
Established 1945.

Really low prices on cosmetics, lotions and bath products. When 8 ounces of Mary Chess White Lilac Body Cream Massage cost $15 from Mary Chess, for instance, Beautiful Beginnings had it for $3.50. After Calvin Klein cosmetics went out of production, Beautiful Beginnings was stocking them for up to 44% off. (Incidentally, Calvin Klein cosmetics had been recommended to me by a television makeup person, so I was very pleased to find them here.)

Beauty Buy Book, ***810 South Broadway, Hicksville, N.Y. 11801. Telephone 516-576-9000.***
Free brochure.
AE, MC, V.
Sells cosmetics, men's toiletries, perfume, jewelry.
Returns: money back.
Established 1960.

Here's another firm that sells closeouts and the kind of goodies that are usually given away by cosmetic firms when you buy something. You can find great bargains here (and it's a good place to find presents) from manufacturers such as Germaine Monteil, Charles of the Ritz, Elizabeth Arden and Halston. In one catalogue I looked at, ¼ ounce of Charlie perfume was selling for only $5.95 when it was generally unavailable because production had stopped.

Perfume

The French stores listed below have been selling to American tourists and mail-order customers for years. They stock a wide choice of perfumes and cosmetics, including the unusual and the old and new that are not so easy to find in the United States. Their perfumes are made in France with superior French alcohol (some French perfumes sold in the United States are made here).

Prices are slightly lower than prices at French department stores, generally lower than at duty-free airport shops and on airplanes and very much lower than in U.S. stores. In fact, perfume prices at these stores are often 65% off U.S. prices. It is always well worth buying from Paris rather than in America, and if you are buying several things at once to offset postage costs, it is even worth buying by mail rather than waiting to go in person. The prices may come out even, but you'll avoid the irritating business of getting the French tax refund.

The last time I compared prices, ¼ ounce of Chanel No. 5 perfume cost $55 at a New York department store, $28 on board TWA and $28.60 including postage from Paris. In the case of Joy perfume by Patou, ¼ ounce cost $85 in New York, $49 on board TWA and $45.30 including postage from Paris. You can also save by buying French cosmetics by mail. As I write, for instance, Orlane's popular Classique Hydratante moisturizing cream costs $23 in New York, yet $15 including postage from Paris. Rigaud perfumed candles cost $50 in New York, yet $25 including postage from Paris.

Perfume companies have converted to milliliters. Most price lists still have quantities in ounces, but here, in case you need it, is a list of equivalents.

7–7.5 ml = about ¼ oz

13–15 ml = about ½ oz

28–30 ml = about 1 oz

50–60 ml = about 2 oz

100–125 ml = about 4 oz

200–250 ml = about 8 oz

Note: If you know what you want, don't bother to wait for price lists. They are not always in print, and it is easier to write and ask for the price, including mailing costs, of whatever you want.

Remember that you'll save a little more on postage if you buy two or three things at once.

Catherine, ***6, rue de Castiglione, 75001 Paris, France. Telephone 14-260-81-49.***
Price list, free in the U.S. and Canada.
AE, V.
Sells all French perfumes and cosmetics; gifts such as scarves, ties and handbags.
Returns: "if articles are returned within six months, we either replace them immediately or give the client a credit to be used with the next order."
Established 1955.

Here is a splendid place to buy a lot of presents easily. Catherine takes credit cards, so all you have to do is choose the gifts and send in a list of names, addresses, gift-wrapping instructions and "texts" for the gift cards. Although the printed list of perfumes is short (only one perfume is listed per manufacturer), more are stocked, and there is a long list of cosmetics (by Chanel, Dior, Lancôme, Orlane and Stendhal), bath oils, body lotions and candles for less pricey presents.

Anne Paree, ***10, rue Duphot, 75001 Paris, France. Telephone 14-260-03-26.***
Free price list.
Sells perfume by all the leading French manufacturers; cosmetics by Lancôme and Orlane; Rigaud candles; sunglasses by Ted Lapidus, Porsche Carrera and Vuarnet; silk ties and scarves; Limoges hand-decorated china.
Returns: unconditional guarantee.
Established 1958.

Recommended by my neighbor Alice Eckstein, who says that Anne Paree has the lowest perfume prices she has found. This is also the only Paris price list that includes the swanky brand name sunglasses. Its prices on sunglasses are up to almost 35% off U.S. prices.

Michael Swiss, ***16, rue de la Paix, 75002 Paris, France. Telephone 14-261-61-11.***
Brochure, free in the U.S. and Canada.
Sells perfumes and cosmetics, scarves, bags and umbrellas.
Returns: "replacement or credit if evidence is made of defection or breakage."
Established 1950.

The Michael Swiss perfume price list is the most comprehensive put out by these Parisian shops. This firm is recommended by reader Bernice Lanspa, who has ordered perfumes, men's ties and Rigaud candles. She says that response is quick and prices are low. However, my neighbor Alice Eckstein, who bought happily from Michael Swiss for many years, says she has now, sadly, switched to Anne Paree because her prices are lower and Michael Swiss's service has slowed up lately.

Perfume Copies

Over the last few years the business of copying expensive perfumes has taken off; the copies are sold at a fraction of the price of the originals. Some manufacturers say that it's because fashionable perfumes are now heavier and spicier—and easier to copy. I read about one woman in the *New York Times* who was wearing a Giorgio copy in a department store when the Giorgio representative came up and thanked her for wearing Giorgio.

It is perfectly legal to make these copies so long as the manufacturers don't use exactly the same formulas, and so long as they call their perfumes "versions" of the originals, rather than copies. The copycat firms insist that they use the same kinds of essential oils that are in the originals and that their ingredients are of similar quality. Prices are so low, they say, because they save on advertising, packaging and other overhead.

Here are three firms that make perfumes that cost roughly an eighth to a quarter of the price of the originals in New York and roughly a third of the price of the originals mailed from Paris. As I write, ¼ ounce of Chanel No. 5 perfume costs $28.60 from Paris, whereas the Classique version costs $7.50 including shipping; the same amount of Joy by Patou costs from $45.30 from Paris and $12.50 from Classique. The "versions" aren't exactly like the originals—and some are closer than others—but you may find that you prefer them. In a blind testing that *Shop* magazine ran, to everyone's surprise the testers preferred the reproduction in six out of nine cases.

Classique Perfumes, ***10-02 44th Drive, Long Island City, NY 11101. Telephone 718-392-1650.***
Free price list.
Sells perfumes, colognes, bath oils and face creams.
Returns: money back.
Established 1975.

In *Shop* magazine's blind testing of perfume reproductions by four manufacturers, Classique turned up trumps. Classique was judged closest to the original of four out of nine different perfumes (in three other cases there was no consensus as to which was closest). Furthermore, also blind, the judges *preferred* the Classique version to the original in four out of nine cases.

Essential Products Company, ***90 Water Street, New York, NY 10005. Telephone 212-344-4288.***
Free price list. If you send a long self-addressed, stamped envelope, perfume cards will be sent.
Sells 43 perfumes and 13 men's colognes.
Minimum order $17.
Returns: "merchandise completely refundable if returned within 30 days."
Established 1895.

Here there are "interpretations" of expensive perfumes and men's colognes, sold under the "Naudet" trademark. Each fragrance is numbered, and the price list tells you which original is being "interpreted." President Barry Striem says that mail-order customers are pleasantly surprised by the speedy shipping, which is done by UPS and usually the same day.

Tuli-Latus Perfumes, *P.O. Box 422, Whitestone, NY 11357. Telephone 718-746-9337.*
Price list, free in the U.S. and Canada.
AE, MC, V.
Sells perfumes.
Returns: money back if perfume is returned within 15 days and is unused.
Established 1971.

Tuli-Latus makes about 28 what it calls "exquisite renditions" of famous originals. Its versions of Joy by Patou and Bal à Versailles by Jean Desprez are steady best-sellers, and at the moment its version of Giorgio has "taken off" to become its biggest seller. Tuli-Latus also has high hopes for its new version of Calvin Klein's Obsession.

PETS

ADOPTING A PET

To save money and do the right thing, instead of buying, adopt a pet from an animal shelter as the ASPCA and American Humane Society recommend. Both organizations worry about the overpopulation of animals and the animals that have to live in shelters or be killed. "Do you really NEED a purebred?" asks the Humane Society, pointing out that some of the homeless puppies up for adoption "strongly resemble and have most characteristics of" an American Kennel Club breed. Most shelter dogs are mongrels between the ages of six months and a year, and they cost between $25 and $40. Shelter kittens are mainly mixed breeds, but some look quite superior and there are occasional pure breeds. Kittens are often free, but can cost up to $30 if they have already been neutered.

You can find a shelter in the yellow pages under Animal Shelters. There are public and private shelters. To minimize the chances of getting a neurotic or sick animal, make sure that you are dealing with a well-run shelter. Take a look to see whether the place is clean and the animals have room to move about freely, the cats have litter boxes and all the cages and kennels clearly and completely identify the animals inside.

Ask about specific policies of the shelter. In some, the animals will have been given all the shots they need and, if they are old enough, will have been neutered. Good shelters (unlike pet shops) will let you return a pet that doesn't suit you.

The ASPCA will send you a very helpful article on what's involved in adopting from a shelter. Write and ask for "Second-Hand Dogs" by Carol Benjamin. The address is: **ASPCA, *Education Department, 441 East 92nd Street, New York, NY 10028.***

BUYING PUREBRED DOGS

The best way of getting a purebred dog on the cheap is to find an adult. Not all of them cost less—some are valuable trained show or hunting dogs—but breeders do occasionally have good unwanted grown dogs for sale or to give away (show or breeding rejects or dogs that have been returned for family reasons such as divorce, the arrival of an elderly relative or a developing allergy). You will probably have to try several dealers, and you may have to wait. But it's worth it. Beverly Miller, who breeds as a hobby, bought her favorite dog for $25 as a 1½-year-old. At six months the dog would have cost $150 (that was several years ago—prices would be higher now). And besides saving money, you'll know what you are getting in the way of looks and character, and the dog will probably be housebroken, neutered and inoculated and may even be obedience trained.

In addition, many breed clubs have "rescue" programs that place adult dogs of their breed for little or no fee or a promise to neuter the dog. The American Kennel Club (address below) will give you the addresses of national and local clubs of breeds you are interested in. The secretaries of the clubs will put you in touch with rescue groups for the breed you want.

Don't try to save money by buying a dog through wholesale dog breeders, commercial kennels or pet or dog shops. Prices aren't lower, and the sellers know neither the characteristics nor the problems of the breeds they are selling. Problems can range from minor, such as a dog that does not look much like the breed, to major, such as congenital problems (allergies, deafness and so on) or an incubated infectious disease.

Besides, the American Humane Society has found that puppies from wholesale dog breeders (sold through pet shops) have often been bred with no interest in the animal's temperament or behavior and raised in overcrowded, unsanitary conditions. "You can't do better than adopt a homeless animal from a local shelter," says the Humane Society. But, it adds, "if your heart is set on having a purebred, don't buy a puppy unless you can meet one or both of its parents."

To find a rescue club or a breeder, telephone or write to the **AMERICAN KENNEL CLUB,** ***51 Madison Avenue, New York, NY 10010, telephone 212-696-8292.*** Tell them what breed you are interested in and ask for the name and address of the secretary of the breed club in your area. The secretary can give you the names of local breeders, and probably of any local rescue groups. If there are no nearby rescue groups, ask the American Kennel Club for the national secretary of the breed you are interested in; the national secretary may be able to help you find a group.

PET FOOD

Don't try to save money by buying no-frills foods. There have been published reports of their nutritional deficiencies. If you absolutely must buy your pet food in the supermarket, buy one that is labeled "complete and balanced." However, one of the problems with commercial foods is that to get that "complete and balanced" nutrition, many pets have to eat so much that they get fat.

People professionally involved with animals recommend the alternative foods used by dog breeders. These foods are made from better ingredients, the recipes are stable (they don't change according to what is cheapest on the commodities market) and the factories have better quality control. Although these foods seem expensive, two dog owners have told me that they cost about the same as, or sometimes less than, supermarket brands, because pets eat less.

Dr. Jane Bicks, a New York veterinarian who has specialized in, and lectures on, animal nutrition, prefers Iams brand foods. She says that the firm uses the best ingredients, buys in smaller quantities (just enough for one batch), filters meat material twice to make it more digestible and has excellent quality control. The company will give you the name of a local Iams distributor or will sell to you direct. It also answers customers' general questions about pets. Contact: **THE IAMS COMPANY,** ***Box 855, Lewisburg, OH 45338. Telephone 800-525-IAMS; in Ohio, 800-222-PETS.***

SUPPLIES AND EQUIPMENT

Mail and Telephone Sources

Don't buy supplies and equipment from a pet store, supermarket, discount drugstore or the pet section of a garden supply store. Many of the products are shoddy, and the better goods are way overpriced. The specialty stores listed here sell brand name products for roughly half of what local retailers charge.

The concessions that travel with dog shows also sell goods at prices that are below those of local stores, although not as low as mail-order prices, and they can usually give better advice on products than clerks in local pet or discount stores.

Animal Veterinary Products, ***P.O. Box 1267, Galesburg, IL 61401. Telephone 309-343-6181; orders, 800-447-8192.***
Free 80-page catalogue ($1 in Canada).
AE, MC, V.
Sells supplies for cats and dogs: furniture, feeders, litters, cages, toys, grooming and training aids, food supplements, medical supplies, books.
Returns: "which returns are accepted varies according to the situation."
Established 1975.

A large, easy-to-read catalogue illustrated with photographs shows and describes almost anything you are likely to need for a dog or cat—beds, feeders, grooming supplies and health-care products.

Ross Carson, ***3304 Appleton Road, Landenberg, PA 19350. Telephone 215-255-5348.***

Free catalogue.
MC, V.
Sells dog training equipment and supplies.
Returns: unconditional money-back guarantee.
Established 1978.

An excellent assortment of supplies and equipment for the serious trainer (obedience or hunting) as well as many sizes and styles of crates, pens, collars and so on. There are also a few dog obedience books. Beverly Miller, a breeder who recommended this firm, writes, "I have found their service and products to be excellent and their prices very reasonable." For example, a Sheltie-sized air crate (required for shipping dogs by plane, also popular for use at home) of the brand name Vari-Kennel cost $69.95 plus tax at Beverly Miller's local garden shop, whereas she bought the same model, same brand, same size for $39.95 including shipping from Ross Carson.

J and J Dog Supplies, ***P.O. Box 1517, Galesburg, IL 61402. Telephone 800-642-2050; in Illinois, 309-375-6944.***
Free catalogue.
MC, V.
Manufactures and sells dog obedience training equipment.
Returns: unconditional money-back guarantee.
Established 1965.

J and J is recommended by Beverly Miller, who writes that it is "another excellent source for the serious dog trainer. The specialty is latigo leads, some of which they created. They carry a good assortment of jumps and a nice sampling of supplies (but no crates or pens). A portion of their profits go to Hearing Dog Inc. in Henderson Co., which takes dogs from pounds and trains them to serve the hearing impaired—a nice touch I think. They are also one of the few sources I know of for Bob Self's obedience books and tapes, which are highly sought after." A good stainless steel collar here cost under half the price of collars sold in Beverly Miller's area, which were too big and heavy anyway.

Kennel-Aire, ***731 North Shelling Avenue, St. Paul, MN 55104. Telephone 612-645-3633.***
16-page color catalogue, free in the U.S. and Canada.
MC, V.
Manufactures and sells wire mesh dog crates, exercise pens and pet supplies.
Returns: money back if merchandise returned within 15 days.
Established 1958.

Probably the biggest supplier of stainless steel wire exercise pens, shipping crates, whelping boxes, car barriers and so on. It gives speedy service and has very fair prices.

Kennel Vet, ***1811 Newbridge Road, Bellmore, NY 11710. Telephone 516-783-5400.***
Catalogue, free in the U.S. and Canada.
AE, MC, V.
Sells equipment for cats and dogs, dishes and feeding equipment, housing and cages, health and grooming aids, books.
Returns: no returns on cutlery and crates; money back on other goods if in salable condition.
Established 1971.

Recommended by Margaret English for its very good prices and usually-same-day service. Prices here are among the lowest. I compared prices on a travel barrier, several sizes of Vari-Kennels, Johnson pet door and a large wagon barrier, and prices were several dollars lower than at other stores in this section, with the exception of R. C. Steele.

Petco Animal Supplies (Animal City Division), ***8500 Alvarado Road, P.O. Box 1076, La Mesa, CA 92041. Telephone 619-469-0188.***
128-page catalogue, free in the U.S. and Canada.
BA, MC, V.
Sells grooming supplies, watering and feeding supplies, beds, cages, antibiotics, vitamins and supplements, pest controls, toys and treats for cats and dogs; aquarium and bird supplies.
Minimum order $5.
Returns: money back if merchandise returned within 15 days.
Established 1953.

A large and well-known supplier of general goods for dogs, cats, birds and fish and their owners, this is Beverly Miller's regular veterinary supply source. She says it has "super service—very prompt" and "good prices." She quoted prices of some vitamins and an antiseptic that were 25 and 50% below her local prices even *after* she paid UPS charges (one week delivery time). A stainless steel teeth descaler cost $11 locally but only $5.95 at Petco. Prices are lower than at walk-in stores, but not the lowest in this section.

R. C. Steele, ***15 Turner Drive, Spencerport, NY 14559. Telephone 716-352-3230.***
Free 31-page catalogue.
Sells dog equipment and kennel supplies.
Minimum order $50.
Returns: no returns without authorization.
Established 1975.

Collars, leads, beds, gates, rubber bones and training and grooming equipment are sold here. Customer Margaret English told me about Steele's prices and, with a few exceptions, they have been the best prices I have found. Steele's largest Johnson pet door was 14 to 30% cheaper than at other firms in this section. Its Wagon Barrier, to keep traveling dogs away from the driver, although not the cheapest, cost 20% less than the same one at American Veterinary Products.

VETERINARIANS

Prices at some (but not all) colleges of veterinary medicine are lower than those at private clinics, and the medical care is reputed to be excellent. To find out whether there is an accredited veterinary college near you, contact: **AMERICAN VETERINARIAN MEDICAL ASSOCIATION,** ***Division of Scientific Activities, 930 North Meacham Road, Schaumberg, IL 60196.***

Friends of Animals, a nonprofit organization, has a low-cost spaying and neutering program. It will send you an enrollment form and a list of 600 vets around the country that spay and neuter for about half the price that vets normally charge. You fill out the form and send the money to Friends of Animals, and they send you a certificate that, when you present it to one of the listed vets, entitles your pet to spaying or neutering at no further charge. Contact: **FRIENDS OF ANIMALS,** ***11 West 60th Street, New York, NY 10023. Telephone 212-247-8077.***

Do It Yourself

If you are not too squeamish, you can save money by giving routine Parvo and distemper shots yourself—your vet can show you how. You can get surgical-quality stainless steel needles and syringes or plastic disposable ones with Parvo/distemper vaccine from Petco (described above). Besides avoiding an excursion to the vet, you can save almost 90% of the cost by giving the shots yourself (one home shot giver tells me that each shot costs her $3.95 instead of $18).

DOG TRAINING

Private training classes are a rip-off, says Margaret English, who used to train dogs herself. If your problems are the usual ones—a dog that chews up your furniture, barks too much or needs house training—you can do it all perfectly well yourself (in fact, trainers just train you to train your dog). All you need is advice from a knowledgeable person or a book.

The best book, says Margaret, is the classic ***Training Your Dog: The Step-by-Step Manual*** by Joachim Volhard and Gail Fisher, $12.95 from Howell Book House, 230 Park Avenue, New York, NY 10169.

The second-best, says Margaret, is her own book, and it's cheaper. ***Basic Guide to Dog Training and Obedience*** by Margaret English, $4.95 plus $1.50 postage and packing from Putnam Publishing Group, 200 Madison Avenue, New York, NY 10016.

On the other hand, obedience classes for dogs with problems such as shyness, unruliness or aggressiveness are another matter. Here, group obedience classes are the last great bargain left in dogs. At the moment an eight- to ten-week course usually will cost $40 to $50. Private training usually starts at $400 and isn't as good.

Before choosing a course, observe several classes. Notice class size (the smaller, the better, and there should be no more than 15 dogs) and find out how many people drop out of a typical beginner's course. If a school loses most of its students, it'll probably lose you too. Don't bother with anything under eight weeks, as it takes at least six weeks to make any permanent change in a dog's behavior.

Breeders may be able to recommend obedience classes, or write to the American Kennel Club (address above) for the names of obedience training clubs in your area.

LIVESTOCK SUPPLIES

These two sources of veterinary supplies for farm animals are recommended by farmer Orville Schell. He estimates prices to be 20% lower than at local suppliers such as veterinarians, but the price I checked (injectable penicillin G) was 35% lower at both places, even including shipping costs. He also says that service is reliable, efficient and quite fast. As both firms have toll-free numbers, Orville Schell says he finds buying from them easier than driving to the vet.

PBS Livestock Drugs, ***P.O. Box 9101, Canton, OH 44711. Telephone 800-321-0235; in Ohio, 800-362-9838.***
Free 58-page catalogue.
MC, V.
Sells commercial livestock pharmaceuticals and specialty supplies for dairy cows, beef, swine and sheep; has a licensed prescription-filling service.
Returns: unconditional money-back guarantee.
Established 1941.

A very complete supply of medicinals, vaccines, "supportives" and so on is illustrated and described in this catalogue. Also listed are instruments such as syringes and veterinary thermometers, dairy specialties such as udder supports and swine specialties such as a pig puller "to assist pig delivery."

About 30 prescription drugs are carried that can be sent out if your veterinarian telephones PBS with the prescription. PBS also has a veterinarian and veterinarian's assistant who will answer questions about animal problems and products.

Wholesale Veterinary Supply, ***P.O. Box 2256, Rockford, IL 61131. Telephone 800-435-6940.***

86-page catalogue of veterinary products, 86-page catalogue of grooming supplies for small animals and horses, both free in the U.S. and Canada.
MC, V.
Sells veterinary products for pets and meat-producing animals, grooming supplies for pets and horses.
Returns: money back if returned within 30 days, 20% handling charge.
Established 1971.

"No need to pay for a clinic," says Wholesale. A full-time professional veterinarian is on staff to answer customers' questions about diseases and products. The veterinarian won't diagnose but can advise on disease prevention, products and use of products. Wholesale also boasts of attending almost all major conventions and scientific meetings, subscribing to hundreds of publications and being in touch with the research staffs of major manufacturers; it says it is therefore able to keep customers informed about new products and new findings about diseases.

There are two catalogues. One is a large-animal and sheep catalogue listing pharmaceuticals, grooming aids and other small supplies plus equipment for raising rabbits. The other is a catalogue of pharmaceuticals and grooming supplies for pets and horses.

PHOTOGRAPHY

Nikon One Touch 35-mm compact camera with automatic focus, exposure, flash, film loading, film advance, film rewind, lens cover and more. When the list price for the One Touch was $226, the Sunshine Cameras price was $139.

Nikon N2020. Nikon's first totally automatic single-lens reflex camera. When the list price for the Nikon N2020 body was $479, the Sunshine Cameras price was $219.

PHOTOGRAPHY

COLOR PRINT PROCESSING

In the July 1982 issue, the editors of *Consumer Reports* wrote up their sampling of firms that develop film by mail. They found two firms that, in their judgment, "made 35mm color prints whose average quality was better than Kodak's—and for half the price."

Note that one of the dangers of sending film away to be processed is loss, but, according to a *Consumer Reports* reader survey, film is not more likely to get lost if you send it by mail than if you send it through a store. One *Consumer Reports* reader cleverly suggested starting each roll of film with a shot of your own name and address written clearly on a card.

I decided to try out the two laboratories that *Consumer Reports* found "clearly superior" in its tests, as well as two others that had been recommended by *CR* readers. I shot five rolls of photographs of my somewhat unwilling family and sent four to the firms listed below. The other roll I gave to my local camera shop to send to Kodak. Kodak was fastest (3 days) and, unlike *Consumer Reports,* I found that Kodak color was the most lifelike. However, considering that the other firms charge half of the Kodak price or less and will redo the entire roll for free, I think they are well worth trying.

Clark Color Laboratories, *P.O. Box 1018, Washington, DC 20013, or P.O. Box 4831, Chicago, IL 60680.*

Total cost (including the two stamps they asked for) was just below half Kodak's price. Prints came back within seven days. My family looked unbecomingly pale and pink, so I sent back the negatives and three sample prints and asked for a whole new batch. Clark was the only firm to ask for the rest of the prints and "the original correspondence" before retrying. (Clark never answered the three questionnaires I sent them.)

Custom Quality Studio, ***P.O. Box 4838, Chicago, IL 60680.***

This is my favorite firm, although I had to write twice before they sent their self-addressed envelopes and price list. The same thing happened to *CR* readers. (The company didn't return my questionnaires either.) Total cost was also just below half Kodak's price. Prints arrived in ten days. This time my family had a golden look, more flattering but not quite natural, so I sent negatives and sample prints back and asked for a retry. The samples came back with new versions in color as good as Kodak's. The studio asked for the other prints so that they could redo them all.

The two firms that were recommended by readers in the survey, but too late for *Consumer Reports* to test, are:

Mystic Color Lab., ***Mason's Island Road, Box 144, Mystic, CT 06355. Telephone inquiries 203-536-3411.***
Ask for mailing envelopes.
MC, V.
Develops and prints photographs and slides.
Returns: unconditional guarantee.
Established 1969.

Total cost was just under half Kodak's price. Prints took two weeks, and my family was very pale with a tinge of blue. I sent my samples for a retry and got back the whole roll redone. The color was a little intense, but perfectly acceptable.

Skrudland Photo Service, ***5311 Flemming Court, Austin, TX 78744. Telephone 512-444-0958.***
Develops and prints photographic negatives.
Returns: money back.
Established 1965.

The cheapest of the lot, this firm charged only a third of the price of Kodak. Prints took two weeks. Part of my family looked too pale, another part too yellow. I returned samples and got back the whole roll redone, but the color was still unnatural.

PHOTOGRAPHIC EQUIPMENT

The manufacture of photographic equipment is highly competitive and there is constant innovation and improvement in the field. Most cameras are now well designed and manufactured. Lenses, for instance, which used to vary in quality according to price, are now made with the help of computers and electronic equipment and meet a high standard in even inexpensive cameras. Nikon and Canon are leading manufacturers that make top-of-the-line "professional" models. These are for professionals or amateurs who take hundreds of rolls of film a year and need cameras that will endure heavy use. But excellent photographs can be made with moderately priced cameras, and, unless you intend to make 2-by-3-foot prints, you'll probably never notice any difference between one lens and another that costs twice as much.

So choosing a camera is not a question of finding "the best" so much as deciding which features you want.

Which Camera?

By Harvey V. Fondiller

If your main interest in photography is to record friends, family events and vacations as simply and easily as possible, get a fully automated 35mm compact "point and shoot" camera. Such cameras are reliable, give a good picture, and are lightweight—a blessing when you are sightseeing. On the other hand, if you are more seriously interested in photography and want to get special effects, buy a single-lens reflex.

However, to help you decide, here is a rundown of the various types of camera on the market:

110 pocket. These are inexpensive—about $15 to $80 list—and strictly for the amateur. They are convenient to carry in a pocket or purse and are popular with people who like to have a snapshot camera wherever they go. A typical model has a 25mm f/8 lens (considered "slow" because it has little light-gathering power and needs a flash indoors and in the shade), a fixed-focus lens (5 feet to infinity) and a fixed exposure control. It takes drop-in film cartridges, so you don't have to thread the film. The flash, which is built in to the camera, recycles in ten seconds with fresh batteries and produces about 100 flashes per battery set. The flash can be used from 5 to 15 feet from the subject with fast film. The appeal of these cameras is mainly price. Disadvantages include the slow speed, the inability to take close-ups and the fact that the cameras can't produce high-quality enlargements much bigger than the usual snapshot size.

Disc. These cameras, whose list prices range from $15 to $150, produce small images and, because of the tiny negatives, the quality of the pictures isn't marvelous. As with the 110 cameras, images can't be enlarged to large dimensions and still retain quality. One popular model has autofocus and a 12.5 mm f/2.8 lens (considered "fast") with a built-in close-up lens that focuses from 13 inches to infinity. The built-in flash fires automatically if the exposure reading is below a certain level. The flash can be fired 1,200 times per set of two 3-volt batteries within a range of from 13 inches to 18 feet. The advantage of this type of camera is that its compactness (it is rectangular and flat) makes it easy to carry. Drop-in loading, automatic film advance, built-in flash and automatic exposure control also make it very simple to use.

Subminiature. For snapshooters—or spies! This kind of camera costs from $200 to $600 at list price, and it is a mechanical marvel, but it produces a very small image that doesn't enlarge well. One of the few available models has a 15mm f/5.6 fixed-aperture, fixed-focus lens with focus range of from 1 meter to infinity and electronically governed shutter with speeds of from 8 seconds to 1/500. A cube-flash adapter can be added. The camera is tiny, and it's possible to shoot a roll of film without being observed—if you know how to do it.

35mm compact. There's a wide price range for this type of camera—from $30 to $1000. All of them accept 35mm cartridges, so you can shoot black-and-white film, color negative film for prints or color slide film. The cameras have eye-level viewing, and the more expensive ones have range finders (to set the focusing distance) and accept interchangeable lenses. A few expensive models feature automatic focusing as well as total exposure automation. The picture quality is excellent. Included in this category are "point and shoot" cameras in the $30 to $300 list price range, which have built-in flash units. With a camera of the latter variety, you can take pictures indoors or outdoors under any lighting conditions. The costlier models have a few interchangeable lenses, which greatly expand picture-taking possibilities.

35mm single-lens reflex. At a list price of $200–$600, this is the most popular type of camera above snapshot level. It's for anybody and everybody, from someone who is just getting interested in photography to the professional who goes on worldwide assignments (and probably takes several SLR cameras, along with a battery of lenses). Many of the models are highly automated. Most of them use the aperture-priority system, in which the user selects a lens aperture and the camera determines the shutter speed for proper exposure. A few cameras use the shutter-priority system, in which the speed is set by the photographer and the f/stop is determined by the automated exposure system (useful for the person who wants to take photographs of such things as sports events, with a lot of movement). A third type of automation is the programmed variety, in which the user sets the film speed (ISO index number) and the camera makes the necessary aperture and speed adjustments. A number of manufacturers offer complete camera "systems," which include not only the camera but also a wide variety of lenses and accessories. Among them are: motor drive, flash units, diopter correction lenses (for eyeglass wearers), remote control units, and interchangeable focusing screens.

Medium format. The list price of these cameras is from $150 to $3000. Compared with 35mm single-lens reflex cameras, they are heavier and bulkier. The negative size is 120 rollfilm, and the most popular formats are 4, 5 by 6, 6 by 6, and 6 by 7 centimeters. The camera operates more slowly than a 35mm, but it is used by serious amateurs and many professionals. Its advantage is obvious: it provides, in a hand-held camera, a negative big enough to make big enlargements, and it can be used in a studio instead of a larger camera. These cameras are available in single-lens reflex and twin-lens reflex models.

Large format. List prices go from about $150 to $3000. This type of camera, ranging in size from 4-by-5 to 8-by-10 inches, is strictly for the advanced amateur or the professional. It must be mounted on a tripod and it accepts cut film, which must be loaded in film holders. The entire outfit is bulky, heavy and expensive. Furthermore, the film is costly when compared with 35mm or 120 film. A typical 4-by-5-inch view camera has a rising and falling front, lateral shift, revolving back (for vertical and horizontal images), accessory rollfilm back, and a variety of accessories that increase its capabilities.

Self-processing. List prices are \$25–\$300. You use this type of camera for "pictures in a minute." The prints aren't cheap, but you get them while you wait. The advantage is speed; the disadvantage is that copies are comparatively expensive. Models are available with fixed-focus or focusing lenses, exposure automation, automatic print ejection by motor drive and built-in electronic flash. This is basically a camera for amateurs, but a lot of professionals use it too, to determine proper exposure.

Photography Buyers Guide, compiled by the editors of *Popular Photography* magazine, lists and briefly describes most of the photographic equipment on the market (and gives prices). The survey includes cameras, lenses, film, darkroom equipment, video cameras and recorders. Products aren't rated or evaluated in any way, but there are buying suggestions. *Photography Buyers Guide* is available on newsstands from October to mid-May or by mail from **PHOTOGRAPHY BUYERS GUIDE,** ***P.O. Box 603, Holmes, PA 19043.***

PHOTOGRAPHIC AND DARKROOM EQUIPMENT SUPPLIERS

When asking for prices and buying photographic equipment, remember that there are variables and add-ons. Be sure you know exactly what you need and what you are actually getting. The New York Better Business Bureau suggests that you ask whether what you are buying is ready to use, whether it needs additional equipment (such as a lens adapter) and whether all components of the equipment are made by the same manufacturer.

Bi-Rite Photo and Electronics, ***15 East 30th Street, New York, NY 10016.***
Telephone: questions, 212-685-2130; orders, 800-223-1970.
Write or telephone with name and model number for prices.
MC, V.
Sells cameras, film, calculators, telephones, video equipment, watches.
Minimum order \$60.
Returns: money back if merchandise returned within 15 days.
Established 1981.

Bi-Rite was recommended to me by Eric Zuesse, author of *Bargain Finder,* a book on New York discount stores. He told me that Bi-Rite had the lowest prices. I checked, and they did seem to beat the other stores in this book by one or two dollars on photographic equipment.

Although Bi-Rite sells electronic equipment, I think its strength is photographic. When on three occasions I have asked about Walkman-type units, the store has not had what I wanted.

Garden Camera, ***145 West 30th Street, New York, NY 10001. Telephone: questions, 212-868-1420; orders, 800-223-5830.***
96-page catalogue, $3, or call or write for specific prices.
AE, MC, V.
Sells photographic, audio, video equipment; computers; telephones and answering machines; typewriters; radar detectors.
Returns: money back if merchandise returned within ten days in condition received.
Established 1969.

Garden Camera has a good reputation for satisfactory service. On one occasion when I asked for a price quote, the salesperson told me that they won't quote on things that are not currently in stock. Considering that being sold something and then finding you have to wait for it is a major annoyance, I consider that a praiseworthy policy. If you can get a good price at Garden, I think this is the place to buy.

Olden Camera and Lens Company, ***1265 Broadway at 31st Street, New York, NY 10001. Telephone: information, 212-725-1234; orders only: computers, 800-221-6312; photographic equipment, 800-223-1444; video equipment 800-221-3160.***
Send self-addressed, stamped envelope or telephone 9 A.M. to 6 P.M. for specific prices.
AE, DC, MC, V.
Sells photographic and darkroom equipment and supplies, office equipment.
Minimum order $7.95.
Returns: money back if merchandise returned within ten days, credit after that.
Established 1937.

This well-known New York store provides several services for locals. It arranges computer, photographic and video courses, and it has a spring sail sale, when the staff takes customers out on a sailboat and allows them to try Leica cameras and buy them at "used" prices if they want. No wonder Olden boasts of many celebrity customers.

The store doesn't sell many instant cameras, but it has a large "high-end" inventory of photographic and darkroom equipment, with plenty of single-lens reflex cameras. I bought a popular Pentax by telephone here at a good price, and it was quickly mailed to my daughter in college. My only complaint (and probably it was my fault) was that when I was comparing prices, the salespeople didn't mention that the price they gave me did not include the case. An Olden spokesman told me that the store does sell parallel imports but informs customers if that is what they are buying.

Olden also sells IBM and IBM-compatible computers, as well as major lines of video equipment.

Prestige Photo and Electronics, ***373 Fifth Avenue, 2nd floor, New York, NY 10016. Telephone: questions, 212-683-6715; orders, 800-223-2626.***

In the U.S. and Canada write for specific prices.
MC, V.
Sells photographic equipment and some televisions, radios and personal stereos.
Returns: money back if goods defective, otherwise credit, but must be returned within 15 days.
Established 1976.

Prestige, on a Fifth Avenue second floor with a sign saying "Come Up and Save," clearly sells mainly by mail and telephone. The tiny store, up a dark flight of stairs, is packed with huge cartons—there's almost nothing on display, and offices all around are filled with men shouting into telephones. Besides photographic equipment, Prestige sells supplies such as paper and out-of-date film for 99 cents a roll (when I was there).

Sunshine Cameras, ***2606 North Kings Highway, Myrtle Beach, SC 29577. Telephone 800-845-0693; in South Carolina, 803-626-9961.***
Write or telephone 12 noon to 6 P.M. Monday through Friday for specific prices.
AE, DC, MC, V.
Sells cameras, video and audio equipment.
Returns: money back if merchandise returned within seven days in brand-new condition, with all the factory packing and blank warranty card.
Established 1979.

Sunshine sells cameras (*every* camera, says the owner) and accessories but no darkroom supplies. I have been comparing prices, and one or two here have been even lower than New York discount prices (in fact, when I told a New York storekeeper, he told me that he didn't believe Sunshine would actually sell at that price). Other prices have been higher than those in New York.

The owner says he has a very large stock of video machines and 20 people answering telephones. He also says he never sells parallel imports.

Wall Street Camera Exchange, ***82 Wall Street, New York, NY 10005-3699. Telephone 800-221-4090; in New York State, 212-344-0011.***
Catalogue, $4.95 ($5.95 in Canada).
MC, V.
Sells photographic equipment for professionals and amateurs; electronics (including scanners, security systems, radar detectors); office equipment (typewriters, calculators, copiers).
Minimum order $25.
Returns: no refunds, credit or exchange if returned within seven days.
Established 1952.

Wall Street claims to have invented the idea of taking used equipment in partial exchange for new. You write in and describe your equipment, and the Wall Street people will give you the price range within which their actual offer will fall. Once they receive the equipment, they make a final offer.

On their parallel imports, they offer their own guarantee (they have a repair shop), or you can buy an extended guarantee that is effective nationwide.

FOCUS and 47 ST. PHOTO (Appliances and Electronics section) also have large stocks of photographic equipment and supplies.

Accessories

Spiratone, ***135-06 Northern Boulevard, Flushing, NY 11354. Telephone: questions and in New York State, 212-886-2000; orders, 800-221-9695.***
44-page catalogue, $1 in the U.S. and Canada.
AE, CB, DC, MC, V.
Sells photographic and video accessories.
Returns: none.
Established 1941.

This widely respected firm was recommended to me by two professional photographers. Spiratone manufactures accessories of good quality that sell for substantially less than better-known brands. Buy things such as filters, viewers and extension tubes here. The lenses are also of good quality and can be adapted for use on almost any camera.

Paper

Light Impressions Corporation, ***439 Monroe Avenue, P.O. Box 940, Rochester, NY 14603. Telephone: questions, 716-271-8960; orders, 800-828-6216.***
64-page catalogue in February, $2 in the U.S. and Canada.
AE, MC, V.
Sells Kodak photographic papers at 15% discount, supplies for framing; has custom mat-cutting service. Main stock consists of acid-free products for safe storage, preservation and display of paper, photographs and negatives, but these are not sold at a discount.
Returns: money back with prior permission.
Established 1969.

Light Impressions has a marvelous collection of supplies for preserving and showing photographs, including albums, file boxes and framing gear—all top-quality and full-price. Also top-quality (fresh from Kodak) but sold at a 15% discount is the complete range of Kodak papers, including the hard-to-find Elite Fine Art paper, large paper for murals and postcard paper, ready-cut and printed to make postcards.

GARDEN CAMERA (described above) sells the more common papers at about 30% off, but there is a rather high minimum order.

BUYING SECONDHAND

Buying used equipment makes sense for people who are not interested in the latest features but want high-quality stuff at lower prices. Prices for used equipment should be about 25 to 30% below prices for comparable new equipment.

According to Ken Hansen (see below), secondhand Leicas are likely to be particularly good buys, as there are quite a few available. (Often people buy Leicas and then find that buying the whole system is going to be prohibitively expensive, so they switch to other brands.)

Cameras are one of the trickier things to buy secondhand, so buy from a reputable source and *always* get a guarantee (repairs are expensive). If you buy from a private individual, the price will probably be below a dealer's price, but in that case insist on shooting a roll of film before you pay in full, and make sure you can get your money back if you are not satisfied. Don't buy a camera that shows signs of rough handling or heavy use.

Ken Hansen Photographic Co., ***920 Broadway, 2nd floor, New York, NY 10010. Telephone 212-777-5901.***
Write with details of what you want.
MC, V.
Sells cameras and equipment for studio photography and professional photographers by Canon, Contax, Hasselblad, Leica, Linhof, Nikon, Sinar.
Returns: full refund if equipment returned within ten days; guarantees for 90 days to three years, depending on equipment.
Established 1976.

Ken Hansen has an excellent reputation and mainly sells top-of-the-line equipment to professionals and very dedicated amateurs (he has no darkroom equipment or autofocus, pocket or compact cameras). He also sells used cameras and other supplies for about 30% off the price of new. He says that his used equipment is tested with sophisticated machinery, looks brand-new and has 90-day to one-year guarantees. In addition to the cameras, he sells all types of lenses, and he points out that a new Leica 800mm lens costs $1600, whereas a used one costs a mere $600.

It is almost impossible to get through to Ken Hansen by telephone. Write and tell him what you are looking for, and someone will call you back. The store also rents equipment and does repairs.

CAMERA REPAIRS

New York's best camera repair shop (for professional-quality equipment only) is **MARTY FORSCHER,** ***37 West 47th Street, New York, NY 10036, telephone 212-382-0550.*** He's famous among professionals for fast, honest service. Out-of-town customers send cameras in by UPS with a letter describing the problem and saying whether they want a repair estimate first or just the repair (there's a charge of about $12 for an estimate).

PUBLICATIONS

BOOKS

In recent years, book buyers have found themselves in an increasingly difficult situation. The number of good bookstores has decreased, the independent stores often replaced by branches of the big chains, which increasingly concentrate on a small selection of fast-moving titles. The lovely used-book stores that used to dot the downtowns of even the smallest cities have been removed by urban renewal, and prices on new books have risen steadily with the tide of the chain invasion. For many people, the only way to buy a book is by mail, not simply to save money but to get the fullest selection possible. If your bookstore charges you to order a book it doesn't stock, or if you find that there are several books you need in no particular rush, try the companies selling current titles by mail.

Discount

Blackie's Books, ***39 Lowther Avenue, Toronto, Ontario M5R 1C5, Canada. Telephone 416-960-5238 (24-hour service).***
Sells any American, Canadian or British trade book in print at a 20% discount; business, medical, professional books at list price.
MC, V.
Returns: none.
Established 1981.

Roberta Bucovetsky started her mail-order book-finding service when her daughter complained that she couldn't find the books she wanted in local bookstores. Roberta will trace any book *in print* published in Canada, the United States or Britain. She supplies all trade books (i.e., those that are not textbooks or technical books) at a 20% discount.

New World Books, ***2 Cains Road, Suffern, NY 10901. Telephone 914-354-2600.***

Free page with ordering information.
Sells general trade, university press, technical and text books.
Returns: depends on the circumstances, but don't return anything without getting permission first.
Established 1961.

As long as you don't mind waiting, you can get general hardback and the more expensive paperback books in print from New World at a 30% discount, any university press book in print at a 15% discount and most medical or technical (but not legal) books in print at a 10% discount. Whenever I'm not in a hurry, I order from New World and I have been absolutely satisfied with its service. The most popular current books come from a "jobber"; other books have to be ordered from the publisher, which takes longer. Everything I have ordered has taken from three to six weeks to arrive.

Remainders

As we all know, remainders are not necessarily unwanted and unworthy. On the contrary, they may be books that publishers were overly optimistic about. Many is the popular book printed in moderate or even huge numbers that is remaindered, while books with more modest printings are not.

People seem to agree that these are the best catalogues of publishers' overstock:

Barnes and Noble, ***126 Fifth Avenue, New York, NY 10011.***
18 free catalogues a year.
AE, DC, MC, V.
Sells remaindered books and own reprints, records and videocassettes.
Returns: 30-day money-back offer.
Established 1873.

In recent years, this has become the country's leading dealer in remainders, most of them sold by mail. Some 8.5 million people are on its lists, so you probably receive one of its catalogues already. Steady customers can receive monthly installments. The remainders are a catholic choice, from last year's best-sellers to imports and reprints (a 12-volume scholarly reprint of Hakluyt's *Voyages,* for example, reduced from $275 to a mere $99.50). Barnes and Noble is increasing the number of new paperbacks it sells, but these are sold at full price. However, many softcovers are also included among the remainders, and there is a growing selection of records and videocassettes of foreign and classic films at reduced prices.

Daedalus Books, ***2260 25th Place NE, Washington, DC 20018. Telephone 202-526-0558.***
Catalogue, free in the U.S. and Canada, published in January, May, September.
AE, MC, V.

Sells trade and university press remainders, mainly in literature, visual and performing arts, philosophy and history.
Returns: money back.
Established 1980.

"Lasting value" is what Robin Moody and Helaine Harris look for when choosing Daedalus books, and, as they say, their prices are 50 to 90% off. The selection is a particularly literary one; the company advertises primarily in the *New York Review of Books,* and the books are appropriate for that audience. I'm always impressed by the number of handsome books available and the originality of the choice. As often as not, the remaindered hardcovers are cheaper than the paperbacks of the same titles that have been issued since. Daedalus was recommended by Allen Pasternack.

Edward R. Hamilton, ***Falls Village, CT 06031-0358.***
Free price list.

I have never managed to get Mr. Hamilton to send back one of my forms or to answer my notes. But he (or someone) is there, and I buy from him all the time. Large, newspaper-style catalogues listing lots and lots of mainly middle-brow books arrive regularly, and prices are tempting (many books cost $4 and $9), so I almost always end up buying several. The books are unconditionally guaranteed. Earlier this year I bought a cookbook, decided I didn't like any of the recipes and returned it after several weeks. I got a refund check promptly.

The Scholar's Bookshelf, ***51 Everett Drive, P.O. Box 179, Princeton Junction, NJ 08550. Telephone 609-799-7233.***
Free catalogue.
MC, V.
Sells scholarly books in art, music, literary criticism, history, philosophy and religion.
Minimum order $10.
Returns: none.
Established 1974.

In recent years, scholarly books have become more and more expensive, and at the same time university presses have taken on an increasing number of areas that used to be the hands-off domain of commercial publishers, such as art books, poetry and literary translation. It's therefore particularly useful for those interested in the more serious products of publishing to write for the catalogues of The Scholar's Bookshelf, an enterprise that specializes in university press remainders. Its enormous seasonal catalogue is filled with fascinating titles and though you may not be interested in the more monographic ones, there are a great many that are sure to tempt you.

Strand Bookstore, ***828 Broadway, New York, NY 10003. Telephone 212-473-1452.***

Catalogues, free in the U.S. and Canada.
AE, MC, V.
Sells new books and remainders.
Returns: money back or credit, depending on situation.
Established 1944.

Strand is New York's largest used-book store, advertising what it calls 8 miles of books on its many shelves. The store reminds one of the vast emporia that used to fill lower Fourth Avenue in New York, and many of its offerings survive from the twenties and thirties. But the store is best known for its new books sold at half price, reviewers' copies that have been passed on, usually in mint condition. The store's frequent catalogues are aimed at out-of-towners and list, alphabetically, a choice of the store's vast holdings. Newest titles are not listed, but if you want to gamble, you can always write to see if Strand has a copy of whatever you want. The major catalogue offerings are remaindered stock and some rare titles. A recent catalogue, for instance, listed Willy Grohmann's famous book on the painter Kandinsky for $350. But you are as likely to find a book for $1.95. The catalogues are very much like the store itself, reflecting a huge stock of art books as well as an enormous range in every conceivable field. They are quite unlike the other remainder catalogues, which concentrate on books published within the previous two or three years.

Books from Britain

When the pound is low, it makes sense to look at British catalogues for books, both recent and classic. The main advantage of buying from England is that the better bookstores issue marvelous catalogues. Seasonal lists will keep you posted on everything that appears in any scholarly field of interest as well as give general readers' information. The disadvantages are, of course, having to wait for the book and the fact that many British hardcovers are still physically inferior to their American counterparts. But prices can be substantially lower, even on trade paperbacks, and the choice is very wide indeed. If you have any specialized interests, try the two major university bookstores, Heffer and Blackwell's. If you simply want a current title or can't wait for the American edition of your favorite English author, Hatchards in London is likely to stock it.

W. Heffer and Sons, ***20 Trinity Street, Cambridge, CB2 3NG, England. Telephone 223-358351.***
Free specialized price lists.
MC, V.
Sells books in all subject areas, records and cassettes.
Returns: damaged or imperfect books replaced.
Established 1876.

Blackwell's, ***Broad Street, Oxford, OX1 3BQ, England. Telephone 865-244944.***

Free specialized price lists.
MC, V.
Sells new and secondhand books, music, records and tapes, publications from all parts of the world, including hard-to-find European, Indian, scarce and out-of-print books.
Returns: "only accepted on imperfect or incorrectly supplied goods."
Established 1879.

Hatchards, ***187 Piccadilly, London, W1V 9DA, England. Telephone 1-439-9921.***
Free catalogue, free list of large-print books.
AE, MC V.
Sells general interest books, but no technical or text books.
Returns: judged on each case.
Established 1797.

I have been buying British books from Hatchards for years. I pay with a credit card and find the whole thing very easy. The other day I ordered a book for my mother that her local English bookshop claimed didn't exist. Hatchards quickly sent me a postcard telling me they had dispatched the book. Hatchards also "offers to obtain" books from all over the world and searches for secondhand books. It sells large-print books and has a rebinding service.

Children's Books

Heffer's Children's Bookshop, ***30 Trinity Street, Cambridge, CB2 3NG, England. Telephone 223-358351.***
Free 84-page catalogue.
MC, V.
Sells children's books, records, cassettes.
Returns: imperfect and damaged books will be replaced.
Established 1876.

Whatever the exchange rate, it is always worth buying children's paperbacks from England. Whereas American publishers seem to put only the most popular books into paper, in England there are all sorts of classic and more interesting children's books selling for under or around $5 in paper.

Heffer's publishes a free catalogue with no illustrations but one-line descriptions of well over 1,000 books. Also listed are over 50 cassettes with English actors and actresses reading well-known books, from *Charlie and the Chocolate Factory* to *Alice in Wonderland;* these cost about $7 each as I write.

Heffer's has customers all over the world and makes things easy. You can pay with an ordinary personal check into its account in New York or Toronto (it has accounts in ten other countries too).

Libraries

If you are dissatisfied with your local library, suffering from recent cuts in funding, don't be driven to desperate measures such as buying hardback books.

Join one of New York's famous private libraries and save money. Both libraries use the same system for out-of-town members: members get monthly lists of new acquisitions and send in lists of book requests and say how often they want to receive the books (two a week, one a month or whatever). Books are mailed out by the library (postage costs and a small handling fee for each parcel are deducted from a mailing deposit that the member has supplied). Members return the books in the same mailing envelope, using return labels supplied by the library, and pay the same amount of postage the library paid.

These two have roughly the same holdings. Some members use them as they did the old rental libraries—it's clear that biographies, mysteries and current best-sellers are most in demand.

Mercantile Library Association, ***17 East 47th Street, New York, NY 10017. Telephone 212-755-6710.***
Membership fee: $45 per year.
Established 1820.

The Mercantile Library does not, not, not have a business collection. It is a general membership lending library that happened to be founded by merchants. There is a 200,000-volume collection, and a monthly newsletter lists new acquisitions. Out-of-town members send a list of books they want and at least $10 for a postage fund, out of which is deducted a $1.50 postage and handling fee for each parcel. The library is proud of the fact that if three people reserve a book, it buys a second copy so that waiting time is cut down. If three people ask for a book the library doesn't have, the book is bought, no matter whether the library approves of the book or not.

New York Society Library, ***53 East 79th Street, New York, NY 10021. Telephone 212-288-6900.***
Out-of-town membership fee: $80 per year.
Established 1754.

The best-known of the New York private libraries has a collection of 175,000 books and adds over 300 titles each month. The New York Society Library is housed in a handsome old building that is very much like a private club and has comfortable reading and reference rooms. But you can have a mail membership if you like, which entitles you to read the latest additions to the library as well as use its collection. Out-of-town members get a list of new acquisitions with their first order each month. They give a $15 deposit, from which is deducted postage and a 75-cent handling fee for each package.

MAGAZINES

As far as I can see, the services for students and educators have better general rates than those of magazines' introductory offers to the public, and, at least in my case (see below), American Educational Services didn't, when it came down to it, seem to be desperately interested in the exact details of my connection with academia, nor, as far as I know, did it check to see that my daughter actually is currently pursuing her studies at Oberlin, Ohio, as I claim she is.

I am not sure whether most people realize that any magazine subscription can be cancelled at any time for any reason and payment for the remaining issues must be returned to you. When publications make magnanimous-sounding offers about your being able to cancel your subscription at any time and get a refund for remaining issues, they are merely mentioning your legal right.

American Educational Services, ***419 Lentz Court, Lansing, MI 48917. Telephone 517-371-4618.***
Free list of discounted magazines.
MC, V.
Sells over 200 magazines at a discount to college students and educators (teachers, principals and administrators).
Returns: money back on undelivered issues.
Established 1974.

I had just resubscribed to the *New Yorker* when I heard about this firm and saw that it was offering the magazine for $20 a year instead of $32. So I quickly cancelled my own subscription and, through American Educational Services, gave myself a gift of the *New Yorker* in the name of my daughter who is in college. Nobody seemed to mind that it was I who signed the check (maybe they can guess that her money is really mine anyway).

Publishers Clearing House, ***382 Channel Drive, Port Washington, NY 11050.***

Publishers Clearing House offers popular and special-interest magazines at varying discounts. Two months after I had subscribed to *Consumer Guide,* I saw it on this list for $8.95 (I had paid $11.97). Some of the discounts are insultingly small; for instance, on the sheet I looked at you would save a laughable 68 cents on 14 issues of *Family Handyman.* Others are better and you can get up to 50% off.

RECORDS AND CASSETTES

As the head of a record company said to me, the way to save on tapes—obviously—is to make your own by recording from friends' records or tapes or from the radio, and it's the method most people use. But there is at least one person in the world who thinks it's immoral—my friend Clement Meadmore, who says, "I'm grateful to the musicians who play the fairly unpopular kind of jazz I like and I don't want to deprive them of their royalties."

The way to save on records is to buy "cutouts"—records that have been discontinued from a record company's regular stock—or "overruns"—records that were issued in too great quantities, so the manufacturer decided to sell off a certain number at lower prices, even though sometimes the record remains generally available at regular prices. The records are brand-new and in exactly the same condition as records that are sold at full price.

Note that some record companies mark cutouts by drilling a hole in the outer edges of the records, removing their plastic covers or slicing off a bit of the jackets.

If a mail-order company is out of a record or cassette you have ordered, it will most likely issue a credit slip. If you don't want one, be sure to ask when ordering for your money back on out-of-stock records.

Andre Perrault International, ***Box 5629, Virginia Beach, VA 23455. Telephone 800-833-2400; in Virginia, 800-572-2224.***
Free classical music catalogue and jazz catalogue.
MC, V.
Sells records, cassettes and compact discs.
Returns: defective goods replaced.
Established 1962.

This widely praised importer of European classical music tapes and records, apart from a few specials in each catalogue, has rather ordinary prices on LPs and cassettes. However, a competitor at New Angel recommended Perrault to me on the grounds that Perrault gives the best prices on compact discs. As

I write, there are so few manufacturers of CDs, and the CD field is in such a state of flux, that most discounters offer no special prices on CDs. I don't know whether it will last, but at the moment Perrault stands out as a great source of compact discs.

Berkshire Record Outlet, ***428 Pittsfield-Lenox Road, Lenox, MA 01240. Telephone: questions, 413-637-2415; orders, 800-992-1200.***
Price list in February, June, October; free in the U.S. and Canada.
MC, V.
Sells classical records and cassettes, closeouts and overruns.
Returns: money back if merchandise unopened with receipt; otherwise "an egregiously defective disc will be replaced for another copy of the same title."
Established 1974.

Berkshire has an enormous list of classical cutouts and overruns. This mainly mail-order firm belongs to Joseph Eckstein, who worked at Sam Goody's New York record store until he decided to combine his love of music with a move to the country. Now he goes to Europe three times a year to pick and choose among cutouts and overruns. He rejects half the records and cassettes he is offered and ends up with an impressive range of records and cassettes that are either not available in the United States or list here for several times his price. As I write, prices start at $2; most are about $4 or $5.

Chesterfield Music Shop, ***226 Washington Street, Mount Vernon, NY 10553. Telephone 914-667-6200.***
Catalogue, free in the U.S. and Canada.
AE, DC, MC, V.
Sells records and cassettes, mainly classical.
Refunds: exchange on defective or incorrect merchandise returned after one playing within a month, $1 charge.
Established 1946.

Chesterfield supplies catalogues of its regular stock, most of which is sold at a small discount (and most records in the Schwann catalogue can be provided at 20% off list price). The store also produces sale catalogues with special buys and cutouts and says that discounts can go as high as 70% on these records.

International Tape and Record Club, ***315 West 36th Street, New York, NY 10018. Telephone 212-594-1690.***
Free catalogue ($2 in Canada) published in January, April, July, October.
Sells records and cassettes, including smaller labels and imports.
Minimum order $20.
Returns: defective merchandise exchanged.
Established 1963.

International produces regular catalogues of classical and pop LPs and cassettes, and each issue has pages of cassettes and records at low prices: pop, rock, country and western, soul and blues. The firm boasts of giving a 15 to

20% discount off the list price of any record in the Schwann catalogue. It was recommended by Allen Pasternack.

Musical Heritage Society, ***1710 Highway 35, Ocean, NJ 07712. Telephone 201-531-7003, 201-531-7004 or 201-531-7005.***
Catalogue in January, $2 (sometimes out of print at end of year).
MC, V.
Sells classical records, cassettes and compact discs; beginning to sell jazz.
Returns: money back, credit or exchange if returned within 60 days.
Established 1962.

This popular mail-order distributor has been heartily recommended to me by several record buyers. Musical Heritage Society makes recordings in the United States from European and American master tapes and sells them for prices that are below those of other recordings of the same music. It is sometimes said that the quality of the records is not as high as that of higher-priced European records, but most people agree that Musical Heritage Society records are value for money.

You can get the catalogue of about 3,000 records and buy from that, or you can join the Society. It is a "negative option" club—members receive information every three weeks and automatically get certain tapes and records unless they send in a card refusing them. Tapes and records cost $2 or $3 less to club members. Warning: Heritage compact discs are sold at the market rates.

New Angel, ***308 Vine Street NW, Washington, DC 20012. Telephone 800-446-7964.***
Free price list.
MC, V.
Sells imported classical, rock and jazz records and some domestic cutouts.
Returns: defective records replaced; credit given for unopened, unplayed records returned within 30 days.
Blue Angel established in 1980, bought and renamed by new owners in 1985.

The Blue Angel used to sell boxed sets of classical and rock recordings from Europe—with some amazing bargains among them. The new owners still sell the boxed sets but have added single LPs too. They continue to import superior European pressings, and sell them at prices they say are a dollar or two lower per record than inferior U.S. versions of the same music. They also sell some cutouts and overruns from U.S. firms. Their best-seller is a complete set of the 14 original Beatle albums with the original covers, pressed in Germany and selling, as I write, for $119.95.

Rainbow Music Service, ***200 Farnham Road, South Windsor, CT 06074. Telephone 203-644-4855.***
Price list, $2.
MC, V.
Sells budget and current records, compact discs, cassettes.

Returns: unconditional replacement or credit.
Established 1978.

Owner Tony Concatelli stocks out-of-print rock, folk, blues, picture discs (album cover pressed directly into record) and unofficial live releases, as well as many budget reissues. He says that customers are especially pleased to find records by out-of-print performers who have recently become popular and whose records are very hard to find (Harry Nilsson, Babies, Guess Who, Black Oak Arkansas and Bachman-Turner Overdrive, for instance). He also has a free search service for records and music-related books, magazines and posters. Tony Concatelli started the service after one of the established services charged him $50 to search for an old Alan Price record. After a year, he asked for his money back, and six months after that he got it back. The Rainbow search service is cleverly organized. A monthly list is sent out to scouts around the country, who are actually Rainbow customers who spend their free time browsing around record stores anyway and are pleased to earn extra money.

You can also order any in-print record, cassette or compact disc through Rainbow at a discount. As I write, most records and cassettes cost $8.98 and are available here for $6.98. Most compact discs have a list price of $15.98 and cost $13.98 here. Rainbow was suggested to me by reader Allen Pasternack.

Record Hunter, ***507 Fifth Avenue, New York, NY 10017. Telephone 212-697-8970.***
Price list, free worldwide, or write for specific prices.
AE, DC, MC, V.
Sells classical, popular, jazz, spoken and children's records and cassettes.
Returns: merchandise exchanged if still sealed or if defective.
Established 1945.

This old and well-known New York store with a comprehensive stock offers a small discount on everything it stocks. Not to be missed are the special one-week sales featuring rock-bottom prices. The special sales are announced in the Arts and Leisure section of the Sunday *New York Times* and in quarterly special-sales catalogues. The Record Hunter also has weekly "label" sales, when all records by a certain manufacturer such as CBS, Polygram or RCA are reduced. Jay Hunter tells me that he has customers who telephone every Monday to find out what the sale of the week is.

As for requests, when I wrote and asked what Alfred Deller records are stocked, it took me about three weeks to get an answer (perhaps because it was near Christmas). The answer was minimal but perfectly satisfactory, consisting of the listing from the Schwann catalogue with the Record Hunter price.

Rose Records, ***214 South Wabash Avenue, Chicago, IL 60604. Telephone 312-987-9044.***
Free 16-page price list.
MC, V.

Sells records, cassettes and compact discs.
Returns: exchange or money back on defective recordings.
Established 1935.

A 50-year-old family business, Rose is the biggest and best-known record store in Chicago. It stocks more records than are listed in the Schwann catalogue, but its catalogue lists just a sprinkling of them. The catalogue list is small but does give very good prices on cutouts of classical, country, sound track and children's music, as well as jazz. It also gives a 20% discount on most records and cassettes in the Schwann catalogue.

Roundup Records, ***P.O. Box 154/CC, Cambridge, MA 02140.***
Catalogue, $2.
MC, V.
Sells records and cassettes on independent labels.
Returns: credit given for sealed LPs; only defective unsealed records can be returned.
Established 1976.

No pop, not much classical, but this firm does have a splendid selection of folk, jazz, reggae and country and western music and anything else from over 350 independent companies. All records are sold at about 25% off list prices, and shipping costs are low. Roundup Records has been widely and well reviewed. It was also recommended by a customer, Allen Pasternack, who says that the stock of the smaller, hard-to-find labels is impressively complete and that the prices are the lowest he has seen for smaller-label records.

Wayside Music, ***P.O. Box 6517, Wheaton, MD 20906-0517.***
Price list free in the U.S. and Canada.
Sells avant-garde and contemporary music on small foreign and domestic labels.
Returns: defective records exchanged.
Established 1980.

Wayside Music sells, by mail only, "farther out" music: modern jazz; electronic, progressive and experimental music—the kind of stuff that college radio stations play, as owner Steve says. At the beginning of the year a green list of imports goes out to customers, then every three months a white list of domestic and imported cutouts and overstock is mailed with prices that are mainly from $1.50 to $6. When I spoke to Steve, he told me that he'd just been selling a double album, "Talking Heads" by Talking Heads, for $6.50, and several Tangerine Dream records for $4 each. Wayside was recommended for its good prices by reader Allen Pasternack.

W. Heffer and Sons, ***20 Trinity Street, Cambridge, CB2 3NG, England*** *(see under Books) has a free "Classical Music Records and Cassettes" catalogue.* **Blackwell's Music Shop,** ***38 Hollywell Street, Oxford, OX1 3SW, England*** *(also under Books) has free music catalogues.*

SPORTS

BACKPACKING AND CLIMBING

Burt Greenspan of Bold Ventures says that money-saving strategies in buying backpacking and climbing equipment are important. Buy equipment that is as simple as possible, that does not need to go back to the manufacturer for repairs but can be fixed in the field. Buy low tech rather than high tech—simple strong tents that can be put up quickly, for instance. He also says to buy as little as possible and buy things that you can use for several purposes; for instance, wear your clothes in your sleeping bag and get a lighter bag so that you both save money and have less to carry.

Seasonal Sales

Preseason sales in camping and climbing equipment take place after Easter, and postseason sales are in September and October. Recently buyers of sporting equipment have been in luck—interest in climbing and backpacking has topped out, so competition among outfitters has been fierce to get rid of previously consigned goods. In some parts of the country there have been warehouse sales offering 60 to 75% off.

Recreational Equipment (REI), ***P.O. Box C88125, Seattle, WA 98188. Telephone 800-426-4840.***

This co-op (which has a $5 lifetime membership fee) has regular prices but also famous sales for which people line up for hours. There are highly recommended catalogue sales in January for everyone and sales in late February for members only. At other times there are telephone sales when, if you call in, they'll tell you what is reduced.

Mail and Telephone Sources

Bold Ventures Ltd, ***455 Linden Street, Winnetka, IL 60093. Telephone 312-441-9073.***
Price list, March/April (none available in February), $1 in the U.S. and Canada.
Sells hardware and software for rock climbing and mountaineering; tents, packs, sleeping bags and clothing for outdoor activities. Brands handled: Eureka tents; Camp Trails, Karrimor packs; Climb High, Forrest, Salewa, SCM hardware; Simmond tools.
Returns: credit if merchandise returned within 30 days.
Established 1979.

Three climbers have a very small business of making climbing harnesses and selling them, plus selling well-known brands of backpacking and climbing equipment by mail. In the early days, their price list gave their discount prices, but some manufacturers objected, so they now give list prices and offer "quantity" discounts—10% off if you spend over $100, 15% off for over $150 and 20% off for over $200. As one of the partners points out, the moment you buy more than one of the larger items, you are over $200.

One of the partners, Burton L. Greenspan, a known "equipment freak," loves talking about equipment and will advise customers who write or call. This sounds like a place to get first-rate advice from someone who is continually testing equipment and believes in the importance of getting the right tool for the job.

Campmor, ***810 Route 17 North, P.O. Box 999, Paramus, NJ 07653-0999. Telephone 800-526-4784; in New Jersey, 201-445-5000.***
Free catalogue.
MC, V.
Sells backpacking, bicycling, camping clothing and supplies.
Returns: money back on anything returned in perfect condition within six months.
Established 1977.

This popular store was recommended to me by custom tent maker Jack Stephenson (he's unbiased—it doesn't sell his stuff). This is what Jack says: "Best place for value for money. Years of experience show in a good practical selection of equipment for everything from backpacking to roadside camping. Brand name goods, such as Eureka tents, for 20 to 30% below prices at other sources." Campmor vice president Frank Kosco is more modest; he says that, although discounts are sometimes 15 to 20% off list price, other times they are only 5 to 10% off. Anyway, people seem to agree that this is the best place for reputable brands such as Camp Trails, Cannondale, Eureka, Lifa, Slumberjack and Woolrich at discount prices.

Gander Mountain, ***Box 248, Highway W, Wilmot, WI 53192. Telephone: questions, 414-862-2331; orders, 800-558-9410.***

132-page color catalogue, free in the U.S. and Canada.
MC, V.
Sells camping, hunting and fishing gear.
Returns: unconditional guarantee.
Established 1960.

A color catalogue displays clothes and "outdoor sportsman supplies." There are many well-known brand names such as Barbour, Duofold and Woolrich. Although the choice isn't anywhere near as great as that at the more known catalogue houses, prices are better. Some prices I checked: Oxford cloth shirts for men and women cost 20% less than similar shirts at L. L. Bean's. Melton 10-ounce-per-yard cotton chamois shirts cost 30% less than Eddie Bauer's, and 8-ounce-to-the-yard plaid flannel shirts cost 40% less than Eddie Bauer's 7-ounce-to-the-yard flannel shirts. Gander was recommended to me by three different readers.

Good Stuff from Tom's Place, ***1 Owens Gorge Road, General Delivery Tom's Place, CA 93514. Telephone 619-935-4875.***
Free information.
Sells sleeping bags.
Returns: money back if bag returned in new condition.
Established 1983.

John Fischer of the Palisade School of Mountaineering in California recommends this bag (he has used it) as good value for money. As I write, the bag costs just under $200, which is roughly 25% less than bags of similar quality. Most bags use 550 fill power down, whereas this bag has white Hungarian down of 650 fill power, which means a warmer bag for the weight (it weighs 2 pounds, 12 ounces). The bag also has tuck (concealed) stitching on the baffle, because the most common reason for return of bags is snagged baffle stitching. The bag has no side blocks, so you can shift the down to where you need it (underneath in warmer weather). Another feature is that the draw cord is inside instead of outside, so you get down up to your neck instead of a couple of inches of fabric as with other bags.

As you might guess by the design of the bags, Guntram Jord, who runs this small business, is a climber himself. His main business is making superior down comforters that are sold by Whole Earth Access (*described in the General section*) under the name of Phoenix.

Mark Pack Works, ***1803 East Shore Highway, Berkeley, CA 94710. Telephone 415-540-7225.***
Free mail-order sheets.
MC, V.
Sells day packs and rucksacks; a full range of soft luggage; duffel, gear and sports bags.

Returns: defects in workmanship and materials repaired free.
Established 1977.

This firm was recommended to me for sturdy and attractively designed rucksacks and soft luggage. Although prices aren't rock-bottom, they are about 5 to 15% lower than prices for goods of equivalent quality. The fabric is all cordura nylon, and seams are all double-stitched and taped.

Mountain High Ltd, ***824 West Graf, Ridgecrest, CA 93555. Telephone 619-446-5643.***
Free price list.
Sells mountaineering equipment, cookware, a few sleeping bags by Caribou and Camp 7, a few internal-frame packs, and freeze-dried food by Mountain House.
Minimum order $25.
Returns: money back if the item is unused and returned within 15 days.
Established 1981.

A husband and wife run this firm as a hobby and hope to make it a full-time business in a few years. At the moment they have a very small warehouse but try to keep a little of everything in stock. If they do have what you want in stock, they mail it out the next day; if they don't it usually doesn't take long to get.

Overhead is low and prices are well below those at most other firms. When I compared prices, an MSR stove cost 25% less than at Eastern Mountain Sports, and a Sigg cookset from Switzerland cost 25% less than at EMS. The Wild Things "Freney" pack cost 8% less than at Mountain Tools (below).

If you want to order by telephone, evening or midafternoon are the best times, as the owners are often out.

Mountain Tools, ***P.O. Box 22788, Carmel, CA 93922. Telephone 408-625-6222.***
Free catalogue, free tent list.
MC, V.
Sells hardware and soft goods for rock, snow and ice climbers and expeditionary mountaineers.
Returns: money back if merchandise returned within 30 days in new condition.
Established 1980.

John Fischer of the Palisade School of Mountaineering recommends this mail-order firm. He says that it has a very good reputation and is growing fast. He also says that it has low overhead and so offers reasonable prices on the brand name American- and European-made climbing equipment it carries.

Larry Arthur, one of the owners, doesn't claim to give discounts but does say that prices are lower for equivalent quality. He also says that the staff consists of skilled climbers who have firsthand experience with the products. They have in-depth knowledge of the latest techniques and applications for the goods they sell, so they can give advice to the beginner or expert.

Finally, if you are in need of a friend (and who isn't?), try them. Larry Arthur says, "We encourage people to contact us and in the process many become friends."

Stow-A-Way Industries, ***P.O. Box 957, East Greenwich, RI 02818. Telephone 401-885-6899.***
General catalogue for campers and the storage food market, leaflet for sailors.
MC, V.
Sells dehydrated food—house brand and nationally known manufacturers such as Alpine Aire, Dri-Lite, Mountain House, Richmoor, Smokey Canon, Yurika.
Returns: money back on unopened packages.
Established 1963.

Stow-A-Way mixes and packages dehydrated food that it says is much less expensive than the nationally known brands. Dehydrated food is more compact than freeze-dried and less expensive. The problem is that while fruits and vegetables aren't bad, meats are definitely not as tasty as freeze-dried.

Stow-A-Way has a handy service for hikers: by arrangement, it will mail foods to post offices along the trail.

Other Sources

Jack Stephenson, manufacturer of superb tents and sleeping bags, says that local discount and surplus stores are worth combing for bargains. About 90% of what is sold is junk, but occasionally you might find something like a beautifully made sleeping bag, or a ski parka with synthetic fill and 1.9 ripstock cover for under $20. He also says, don't forget Sears Roebuck. The so-called good-quality stuff isn't so good, but the two superior qualities—"better" and "best"—generally *are* OK.

BICYCLING

In each January issue, ***Bicycling*** magazine publishes a buyer's guide "to help you find the best bike for your money." According to technical editor Jim Redkay, the magazine tests only bicycles at a level where "a significant difference in comfort and performance" shows. Below that level are "heavy, clunky 'kid's' bicycles." List prices start at just under $300 as I write, and Jim Redkay says that you can sometimes find lower prices on these bikes after the season, from August to December. If you can't find an issue of *Bicycling* locally, you can buy from this address. Check the current price. **BICYCLING,** ***33 East Minor Street, Emmaus, PA 18049. Telephone 215-967-5171.***

Seasonal Sales

New bicycles are rarely sold below list price. But out of season, November through February (especially January and February), you can sometimes find discounts of about 10% off regular prices at bicycle shops. Mail-order firms also reduce prices during the off season.

Mail and Telephone Sources

Bicycling magazine investigated mail-order companies for its January 1986 issue and found (surprise, surprise) that if you know exactly what you want and are willing to buy it sight unseen, ordering by mail can save you time and money. *Bicycling* found the following factors in the mail-order stores' favor: convenience, better selection and the fact that prices are about a third off retail prices. Against mail-order stores: more mix-ups, less service (you have to choose and install without help from the store) and shipping costs.

Because you are on your own, only people who have the skill to assemble their own bike and the know-how to adjust it for a correct fit should buy a whole bike by mail. But accessories are different; first-rate products can easily be ordered through a catalogue or by telephone, and prices are about 25% lower than at the average walk-in store. With some prices the difference can be as little as 15%, but with others it can be as much as 50%. Reader Charles Flynn tells me that he had to buy a chain locally, and he was charged $33 for a certain chain selling for $16 by mail. He also says that prices in the mail-order advertisements in *Bicycling* are so low that many bicycle shops now refuse to carry the magazine.

Bickerton Rowlinson, ***9, Little Mundells, Welwyn Garden City, Hertfordshire, AL7 1EW, England. Telephone 707-320223, 707-320224, 707-320225 or 707-320226.***
Leaflet and prices, $2.
Sells the Bickerton portable bicycle.
Returns: money back.
Established 1982.

The reputable Bickerton portable bicycle (weight: 22 pounds) was originally designed for commuters. The idea was to ride the bike to the train, fold it up, put it on the luggage rack and then, at the other end, unfold it and ride to work. In fact, the bike is used for longer distances, and there is now a single-speed model for town and three- and five-speed models for hilly areas. The bike got a good review in *The Next Whole Earth Catalog,* in which an owner says it solves the problem of theft—take it indoors with you—and portability—you can store it in its own bag and take it on public transport, in a car or on a plane. The Bickerton was designed by a man who was responsible for design and development for Rolls-Royce and de Havilland. This firm belongs to him and a friend, and it manufactures and sells the bikes. Prices range from about $280 to $330 plus airfreight charges to the United States of about $70.

Bike Nashbar, ***411 Simon Road, Youngstown, OH 44512. Telephone: questions, 216-782-2244; orders, 800-345-BIKE.***
56-page catalogue, $2 for next four issues.
MC, V.
Sells bicycles and equipment, including parts, tools, clothes and exercise equipment. Brands handled: Colnago, Woodrup, Guerciotti, Campagnolo, Shimano, Sun Tour, Cannondale, Specialized, Eclipse, Rhode Gear, Cycle Pro, Dia Compe, Zeus, Vetta, Avocet, Cinelli, KKT, Sakae, Sugino, Blackburn, Wolber, Michelin, Vittoria, Zefal, Sedis, Spenco, Sergal, Brancale, Bell.
Returns: 100% satisfaction guaranteed.
Established 1974.

Bike Nashbar, a mail-order giant, produced a frugal black-and-white catalogue—but now has burst into color. When *Consumers' Checkbook,* the Washington-based consumer magazine, compared prices of accessories such as helmets, locks, pumps and racks, they were all very close to 25% (some a smidgen more, some a smidgen less) below local bike shop prices.

Performance Bike Shop, ***P.O. Box 2741, Chapel Hill, NC 27514. Telephone 800-334-5471; in North Carolina, 800-544-4583.***
Free color catalogue.
MC, V.
Sells bicycle frames and components; specialized tires; bicycling clothes by Cannondale and Sergal; shoes by Diadora and Detto; accessories; tools by Campagnolo and Park.
Returns: unconditional money-back guarantee.
Established 1981.

One of the biggest and best of the mail-order discount firms. Performance sends out 3 million color catalogues a year, and it is one of the few firms that allow you to ask service questions on the toll-free number. Furthermore, the staff makes a point of being willing to inform and advise. If the telephone answerer can't tell you what you need to know, he or she is supposed to pass you on to a technical person.

Performance also sells a completed regular (touring) and a completed racing bicycle made to its own specifications in Japan. By cutting out all middlemen and having a policy of large volume and lower profit on these, the Performance people told me that they sell the bicycles at roughly 20 to 30% below the price of similar bicycles sold in shops. The bikes cost about $25 to ship anywhere in the country. When I telephoned in January, the bikes were on special sale at just under $400, and they are put on sale at various times of the year. When I asked one of the technical people how a person who isn't a cycling buff could compare prices on this bike, he said that, if you dare, you could take the Performance catalogue page with the specs into a shop to compare. Otherwise you could take note of the important specs and ask the shop what it could show you that met them.

Buying Secondhand

A good way to save money on ready-made bikes from well-known manufacturers is to buy secondhand. Used bikes in average condition go for about 50% of the new price, and in excellent condition for about 75%. You can try the usual ways of finding secondhand goods locally (bulletin boards and newspaper advertisements), and sometimes bike shops allow customers to post notices. But the best way to find a used bike is through a cycling club. There are always enthusiasts among club members who are longing to sell their current bikes to trade up, and buy more expensive models. Such bikes are likely to be in good condition. Bicycle shops usually can help you find the nearest cycling club, or else write to: **BICYCLE USA,** ***6707 Whitestone Road, Suite 209, Baltimore, MD 21207, telephone 301-944-3399.*** Send a stamped, self-addressed envelope and 25 cents to this national organization for a list of clubs in your state.

Sales

Emily K, ***539 State Street, Santa Barbara, CA 93101. Telephone 805-966-5748.***
Brochure, $1.

Superb bicycling clothes are all reduced by 20 to 50% each January and September. Telephone for sale prices; they are not given in the brochure.

See the Travel section for lists of people who are willing to give touring cyclists a free bed for the night.

BOATING

The information in this section is largely from ***Practical Sailor,*** a very helpful twice-monthly for anyone interested in value for money. It specializes in comparing and assessing sailboats and sailboat gear, as well as giving advice on buying and using boats and equipment. Advice is based on evaluations performed by the editorial staff and user reports from readers. The publication carries no advertising. Contact: **PRACTICAL SAILOR,** ***Subscription department, Box 971, Farmingdale, NY 11737. Telephone 800-227-5782.***

Mail and Telephone Sources

Prices are generally very high at local ship chandlers. Chandlers have the problems of high waterside rents and turnover that, except in a few populous areas, is not huge. Several specialist mail-order firms have a larger stock and much lower prices than most chandlers, and discounts range from 10 to 40% off list price. In a reader survey, *Practical Sailor* found fewer complaints than it expected against discounters (both walk-in and mail-order). *Practical Sailor* also decided that consumers' fears over buying from discounters by mail are unfounded, at least in the case of reputable firms.

Most reader complaints about mail order involved delays in delivery. With one or two exceptions, most firms take between two weeks and two months to deliver. To minimize timing problems, order by telephone with a credit card and make one or two big orders a year, planning ahead of time for anything you know you'll need.

Two types of products that are tricky to buy from discounters are electronics and sails. Whether or not it's worth buying electronic equipment at a discount depends on what the equipment is and what your skills are. Some electronics need checking and calibrating before installation, and some customers need advice when installing complicated equipment. If you think you might need help with new electronic equipment, buy from a full-service boat yard or dealer.

Sails are another case in point. Ater investigating the subject, *Practical Sailor* found that with sails you get what you pay for. Discount sails are an intelligent choice for day sailing and people who don't care about performance, but not for those who care about speed or who sail in heavy weather or offshore.

Boat Owners Association of the United States, ***880 South Pickett Street, Alexandria, VA 22304. Telephone 703-823-9550.***
304-page catalogue, free with membership in Boat Owners Association.
MC, V.
Sells boat equipment.
Returns: money back if merchandise returned unused in original carton within 30 days.
Established 1966.

Boat Owners Association of the U.S. has a well-organized and easy-to-use catalogue with a limited selection of goods in high demand. Prices are 30 to 35% off list prices, and service is the best among the mail-order discount firms. This is a very good source for weekend sailors and power boat owners, as the stock is mainly geared to their needs.

Boat Owners is a membership organization (with a fee of $17 per year, as I write); it is probably not worth joining for the shopping alone, but there are many other benefits. Ask for details.

Defender Industries, ***P.O. Box 820, 255 Main Street, New Rochelle, NY 10801-0820. Telephone 914-632-3001.***
196-page catalogue, $1.50 in the U.S. and $2.50 in Canada, published in February.
Sells marine supplies.
Minimum order $10.

Returns: money back minus refund charge if goods returned within 30 days.
Established 1938.

An excellent stock of serious boating gear from fiberglass supplies to life rafts, a good selection of hardware and electronics and a complete inventory of resins and cloths for boat building and repair are available. Defender doesn't advertise, doesn't accept credit cards, doesn't have a toll-free number and publishes a cheap catalogue. So prices are really low—about 30 to 35% off list price (and the firm will meet any advertised price).

E & B Marine, ***980 Gladys Court, P.O. Box 747, Edison, NJ 08818. Telephone 201-287-3900.***
130-page catalogue, free in the U.S. and Canada.
AE, CB, DC, MC, V.
Sells brand name marine accessories for power boats and sailboats, pumps, boating apparel, electronics, navigation aids, skiing equipment, tools, hardware, safety equipment, cleaners and more.
Minimum order $10.
Returns: requests must be made within ten days, returned goods must be in the manufacturer's original carton.
Established 1956.

E & B has a good inventory, complete in hardware and accessories and especially strong in cleaning supplies, galley wear and on-board amenities. Prices are generally 25 to 30% off list, but the interesting bargains are the "loss leaders"—popular things such as fire extinguishers, boat shoes and so on—featured in the advertisements and in the catalogues.

Goldberg's Marine, ***202 Market Street, Philadelphia, PA 19106. Telephone: questions and in Pennsylvania, 215-829-2200; orders, 800-BOATING. BOATING.***
Free catalogue in January, March, June, October (in Canada, $2 in U.S. currency).
AE, MC, V.
Sells pleasure boating equipment for power, sail and fishing boats. Manufacturers handled: Attwood, Boat Life, Chelsea, Danforth, Fenwick, Guest, Ray Jefferson, Penn Reels, Ritchie, Sitex, Seth Thomas, Uniden.
Minimum order $25.
Returns: credit on damaged merchandise returned within 30 days.
Established 1946.

One of the oldest, largest and best-known of the discounters, Goldberg's has a complete selection of everything from hardware to clothing. There are seasonal "specials" but, apart from those, prices aren't the lowest. Discounts vary from 15 to 25% off list. There are plentiful stocks of most things sold, so there is less chance here of delays because of the store having to reorder.

M & E Marine Supply, ***Box 601, Camden, NJ 08101. Telephone: questions, 609-858-1010; orders, 609-858-0400.***
340-page catalogue, $2 in the U.S., $5 in Canada. Free sale flyers.
MC, V.
Sells boating equipment.
Returns: money back within 30 days if receipt is enclosed.
Established 1946.

M & E has one of the most complete inventories of equipment and gear, especially strong in diving, fishing and waterskiing equipment. Prices are 15 to 20% off list.

Sails USA, ***P.O. Box 1868, 137 Preble, Portland, ME 04104. Telephone 800-341-0126; in Maine, 207-772-4335.***
Free information sheets.
MC, V.
Sells made-to-order sails, sail covers, storm sails and jib bags.
Returns: lifetime warranty on material, cut and workmanship.
Established 1975.

Sails USA has excellent off-season discounts during its sales each year from the end of October through December. In addition, any sails bought here can be traded in for 20% of the purchase price, and there is a repair service.

However, please see the introduction to this section for what *Practical Sailor* advises regarding discount sails.

Skipper Marine Electronics, ***3170 Commercial Avenue, Northbrook, IL 60062. Telephone 800-621-2378.***
Catalogues, free in the U.S. and Canada, published in January.
MC, V.
Sells marine electronics for boaters, sailors and fishermen. Goods from over 50 manufacturers stocked, including Furuno, Si-Tex, Raytheon, Datamarine, Icom, Standard, Uniden.
Returns: depend on the circumstances.
Established 1970.

Skipper has a complete selection of high-quality electronics and, in fact, claims to be the largest marine electronics dealer in the world. Skipper also has a superb reputation, and it provides same-day shipping on most orders. Unlike most discount stores, it services whatever needs it before delivering it (radios, for instance, are pretuned and ready to install and use). There are three full-time technicians who can help customers having difficulty operating equipment by "walking them through" correct procedures over the telephone. Products are also repaired here. Prices are 25 to 30% off list.

British Sources

British yacht equipment has an excellent reputation, and prices are dramatically lower in Britain than in the United States. It is safest to buy things that will not need repairs or servicing, such as winches, sextants, foul-weather gear and safety gear. It is riskier to buy expensive, sophisticated equipment that will not have an American guarantee if bought abroad, but some people do take the chance (see the Yachtmail list below).

English catalogues consist of just listings without details. You'll need to do research and decide what you want through U.S. sources.

Cruisermart, ***Shoreline (Yachtmen) 36/37 Eastern Esplanade, Southend-on-Sea, Essex, England. Telephone 702-68574, 702-615678 or 702-64346.***
160-page catalogue, $3 (bills, postal order or International Reply Coupons).
Sells yacht equipment.
Returns: money back or credit, depending on situation.
Established 1964.

This is one of the better-done English catalogues. Choice is limited, but there are many worthwhile buys. Prices are particularly good on Lewmar winches and Henderson pumps.

Thomas Foulkes, ***Sansom Road, Leytonstone, London, E11 3HB, England. Telephone 1-539-5084.***
Free price list in January and April, $1 airmail.
AE, DC, MC, V.
Sells a complete range of boat equipment.
Returns: money back if merchandise unsuitable and returned unused.
Established 1953.

Foulkes has the biggest selection in London and offers many things that are hard to find. Prices aren't the absolute lowest, but the firm is experienced in export and is pleasant to deal with.

Topgear, ***38 Blenheim Close, Pysons Road, Broadstairs, Kent, CT10 2YD, England. Telephone: questions, 843-602343; orders, 843-588732.***
16-page catalogue, free in the U.S. and Canada.
AE, MC, V.
Sells yacht fittings, accessories and equipment.
Returns: money back.
Established 1979.

Topgear has a small but fully illustrated and easy-to-read catalogue. It has a limited selection but the lowest prices on Henri-Lloyd foul-weather gear and Avon dinghies and life rafts.

Yachtmail, ***Admiral's Court, The Quay, Leamington, Hampshire, England. Telephone 590-72784.***
30-page price list, $2 (refundable).
MC, V.
Sells equipment for large yachts: navigational and electrical instruments, supplies and fittings for above and below deck, clothing, safety equipment, tenders and life rafts, books and chandlery.
Returns: unconditional money back guarantee.
Established 1966.

The price list is just a list of products with code numbers, but export prices (minus taxes) are given, as are shipping costs to the United States. Service is satisfactory. Prices are very good. I compared some last year and found that the Autohelm 3000 autopilot, for instance, cost about $479 (including *everything*—airmail, insurance, duty) from Yachtmail and about $700 in the United States. Avon inflatable boats cost, including shipping, 30% less than in a U.S. store.

Owner Tom Crumby, at my request, looked at his sales figures for the last six months and found that the following were most popular with American customers (in order of preference): autopilots (Autohelm, Seafarer Mini Seacourse, Aries Vane Gear), life rafts and inflatable boats (Avon), satellite navigators (Walker), echo sounders (Seafarer and Space Age), sextants (Zeiss, made in East Germany—not on sale in the United States and much less expensive than the sextants available here, according to Tom Crumby), stoves and heaters (Taylor Paraffin), winches (Lewmar), logs and other electronic equipment (Seafarer, Stowe, Walker) and anchors and anchor windlasses (Simpson-Lawrence).

Used Boats

When *Practical Sailor* is asked, "What new boat shall I buy?", the editors reply, "Why not a *used* boat?" The advantage of buying a used boat is not only that it is cheaper to buy but also that its value doesn't depreciate. A boat usually continues to be worth what it is worth in its third year, unless styling, performance or construction methods make the boat obsolete. Another advantage is that if you buy from a reputable dealer, the boat will be a known quantity.

The disadvantage of buying a used boat is that it is much harder to do—you have to search, research and haggle. Moreover, as with many used products, there is no warranty.

If you do decide to buy a used boat, don't buy one with structural defects. Even if the price is low enough to allow for repairs, the actual cost of many repairs can't be known until the full extent of damage is discovered, so estimates can be misleading. On the other hand, certain expenses, such as rerigging, are predictable and can be accurately allowed for.

FISHING

Buying Fishing Tackle Advantageously

By Angus Cameron

Saving money in the purchase of fishing tackle is often complicated by angling mystique. An aura surrounds fly tackle, a subtly pervasive atmosphere that seems to dictate that only the products of certain manufacturers or handcraftsmen will suffice; to buy other than these declasses the angler who descends to such practices. Because of this elitist aura that fogs over the tackle choice, one has to know his mentor very well indeed. Although expert advice from old, experienced anglers is indispensable, it is important that the beginner seek such advice from several sources in order to escape what one angler I know calls the "Hardy trauma," an affliction that makes you feel that unless your fly reels are Hardy's imported from Alnwick, England, you might as well give up even considering fly fishing. The truth of it is that several much less expensive fly reels, such as the various Pflueger Medalist reels, are just as effective and may outlast their overseas rivals.

The best way to save money in buying fishing tackle is to make sure you are not forced to buy the same item of tackle twice. It is tempting (to beginners) to buy the $30 item instead of the $60 item, but in some cases the cheaper version simply will not perform the task you are asking it to. To buy a cheap fly rod and then find you cannot cast with it is penny wise and pound foolish.

Buy as your first rod the best one your purse permits. That does not mean that only a $600 split fly rod will suffice. On the contrary, a $175 graphite rod may serve you better (and certainly enable you to cast farther), weigh less and be less tiring to cast with than the more expensive bamboo rod. Or, though heavier than graphite, a fiberglass rod can be quite adequate, too, at a considerably lower price than graphite.

Note: If you *do* covet a fine split bamboo fly rod, remember that prices in Britain are much lower than they are here, even with duty. F. S. Sharpe in Scotland, for example, makes a split bamboo rod (that is also impregnated) of the same quality that you find here in the United States but at much lower prices.

Seasonal Sales

Around the middle two weeks of March, many full-price tackle stores have preseason sales. In order to get customers in and buying, a limited number of products are sold at reduced prices. The best sale prices are usually to be found at the postseason closeout sales around October and before Thanksgiving, when stores get rid of excess inventory.

Mail and Telephone Sources

Generally speaking, catalogue houses offer the lowest prices, and, happily, once the angler gets on one catalogue list, his or her name is soon on a dozen others. Being on several fishing tackle catalogue lists permits the bargain-seeking angler to do comparative shopping. Beginners may need some advice from an expert friend in order to understand specifications at first, but they'll soon learn to differentiate between an open-bale spinning reel and a spin-casting reel.

For starters, make sure you get the catalogues of the following mail-order houses. Also check with friends to discover mail-order houses in your own area. Small local houses often offer prices lower than those at the better-known companies. Above all, don't pay the gouge prices charged by certain mail-order houses whose imprimatur has become trendy among the affluent.

Dan Bailey's Fly Shop, ***P.O. Box 1019, Livingston, MT 59047. Telephone 406-222-1673.***
Free color catalogue.
AE, MC, V.
Sells everything for fly fishing.
Returns: satisfaction guaranteed.
Established 1938.

This famous store has 35 people making hand-tied flies for customers in the United States, Canada and 30 other countries. It outfits for fly fishing only and stocks equipment for serious fly fishers, such as insect-collecting kits, stream thermometers and books. Prices are not the lowest—they are in the medium range—but there is a mail-order sale in the fall during which selected goods are reduced.

Cabela's, ***812 13th Street, Sidney, NE 69160. Telephone: questions, 308-254-5505; orders, 800-237-4444.***
Free spring fishing catalogue.
MC, V.
Sells fishing equipment and sports clothes.
Returns: unconditional refund.
Established 1961.

Cabela's is well known for good quality and low prices, and it has been recommended by two anglers and a backpacker. Several catalogues of outdoor clothing and equipment are published each year, but only the spring catalogue has a substantial stock of fishing equipment. Nationally known brands and

Cabela's own are carried, and there are occasional flyers announcing the sale of discontinued stock at even lower than usual prices.

Donegal, ***677 Route 208, Monroe, NY 10950. Telephone 800-356-3005; in New York State, 914-782-4600.***
Free catalogue.
AE, MC, V.
Sells fishing rods, flies, outdoor clothes, shirts. Major brands for fly fishing such as Scientific Angler and Hardy. Clothes by Barbour and Willis and Geiger.
Returns: satisfaction guaranteed.
Established 1976.

This friendly store has recently moved to a 150-year-old stone dairy barn with a wood-burning stove and sun deck. Owner Ted Simroe says that New Yorkers like to come up for the day, have lunch nearby and spend hours reading the books, browsing around the fishing gear, asking questions and talking to other customers.

The specialty is the highest-quality fishing clothes and supplies. Much is imported from Europe, but Ted Simroe says that, as Donegal buys direct from manufacturers and not from wholesalers, prices are lower than those charged for goods of equivalent quality elsewhere. You can especially save on the tackle and clothing made expressly for Donegal. Their "very, very" fine ragwool sweater costs $23.50, as I write, whereas the equivalent nationally known brand costs $45. Customers who buy a lot here get on the "preferred customer" list and are offered special small finds at lower prices.

If you want advice on what to buy, Ted Simroe says that his people will spend several hours with you in person and can also give their basic recommendations and evaluation of new equipment on the market by telephone and mail.

Fishin' Tackle Place, ***114 Fairwood Avenue, Charlotte, NC 28203. Telephone: questions, 704-332-3320; orders, 800-982-0436.***
Catalogue in February, $2.
MC, V.
Sells fishing tackle accessories, flies, rods, reels, vests.
Brands: Berkley, Daiwa, Fenwick, Garcia, Normark, Penn, Scientific Angler, Shimano.
Returns: money back if merchandise returned for any reason.
Established 1982.

Tom Barnhardt, who runs this mail-order discount firm, says that prices on smaller items such as bait are about level with prices at retail stores, but that prices on more expensive products such as rods and reels can be as much as 30% off going prices at most stores. Special sales of closeout items are held from December to February.

Kaufman's Streamborn, ***P.O. 23032, Portland, OR 97224. Telephone 503-639-6400.***
Free catalogue at the end of January.
AE, MC, V.
Outfits anglers for fly fishing and fly tying. Stocks Orvis and Scientific Angler rods, Hardy and Ross reels.
Returns: satisfaction guaranteed, but please return goods with apparent damage within ten days.
Established 1970.

Kaufman's has everything for fly fishing in several price ranges, including heavy equipment for steelheading and salmon fishing. Jerry Swanson of Kaufman's says that the best way to get value for money when buying is to make sure that your initial purchase is the right one. All the people at Kaufman's are anglers who know and use the equipment, and they will give specific advice. You can probably even speak to someone who has been fishing wherever you are planning to go (Alaska, for instance). Telephone, says Jerry; a $5 or $10 call may save you a couple of hundred dollars.

Pennsylvania Outdoor Warehouse, ***1508 Memorial Avenue, Williamsport, PA 17701. Telephone 800-441-7685; in Pennsylvania, 800-282-8731.***
Free fly fishing catalogue and archery catalogue.
Sells full selection of fly fishing and archery equipment.
Returns: satisfaction guaranteed.
Store established 1934, mail-order business established 1981.

Pennsylvania Outdoor Warehouse started as a local discount firm and then went into mail order, advertising the lowest prices in the nation. Although it no longer makes that claim, vice president John Matter says that its prices, on almost everything but "pro shop" equipment, are about 20 to 25% below those of most walk-in stores—lower than Orvis, Bauer, Bean and even lower than K Mart. He says they have the local K Mart "screaming for mercy."

Do It Yourself

Many fishermen tie their own flies and make their own lures. The primary reason is almost never to save money—they do it as an interesting hobby. Nevertheless, the flies do cost less than half price if you tie your own, and some fly tiers become so adept at it that they take it up professionally as a sideline. Most catalogues list fly-tying tools and materials as well as components for other kinds of lures. A salmon fisherman friend of ours once figured that he can tie salmon flies costing from $2.50 to $3.50 each at retail for less than 50 cents each. He also ties his own nylon tapered leaders for a small fraction of the retail cost of prepared leaders.

Rods

Many anglers go one better and not only tie their own flies but also make their own rods from rod blanks and other rod-making components (guides, ferrules, tip-tops and so on) supplied by houses like Dan Bailey's, Cabela's, Donegal, Kaufman's and other mail-order outfits. Substantial savings can be made, and it doesn't take an expert to make rods either. Blanks and components come with detailed instructions.

Buying Secondhand

If you want expensive bamboo rods, think of buying secondhand ones—they are usually considerably less expensive than new ones. Len Codella, of Thomas and Thomas, says that there is little danger of being swindled when buying used rods and reels by mail or telephone (charlatans aren't common; you can always get your money back). The main danger is of being disappointed. Make sure you buy from professionals who know how to evaluate and describe equipment accurately.

Thomas and Thomas Rod Makers, ***P.O. Box 32, 22 Third Street, Turners Falls, MA 01376. Telephone 413-863-9727.***
Free listing of used tackle.
Sells used rods and reels.
Returns: money back on "classic rods" if returned within three days, no returns on reels and "handyman specials."
Established 1969.

These makers of very fine custom bamboo rods (President Reagan gave one to the Australian prime minister) also have a flourishing business in high-quality used rods (mostly bamboo). There are two sections of the list. The first is of "classic" rods, which are "immediately fishable." These generally sell for 25 to 35% below the new price. But, as prices depend on supply and demand, rods from popular custom makers that have a one- or two-year waiting list sell for full price. With those rods, the perk is instant gratification. The other section is of "handyman's specials," which are run-of-the-mill rods no longer being produced. These are less expensive (many cost $60 or $70) and need work. After fixing, revarnishing and so on, some people use them to fish with, others use them as decorations.

GOLF

Seasonal Sales

The best time to buy clubs is after the Fourth of July, when pro shops and golf stores start reducing prices to clear merchandise for the end of the season. Sometimes if certain items are not selling well, their prices will be reduced even before the Fourth.

Mail and Telephone Sources

Nevada Bob's Golf and Tennis, ***3333 East Flamingo Road, Las Vegas, NV 89121. Telephone 800-634-6202; in Nevada and for advice, 702-415-3333.***
Free price list.
AE, MC, V.
Sells golf and tennis equipment and clothes. Golf equipment by Dunlap, Prima, Wilson and others.
Returns: money back on unused items, but there is a 10% restocking charge on some.
Established 1974.

This chain of 123 golf and tennis stores sells by mail all top pro-line equipment for golf and tennis at lower prices than in its walk-in stores. It also has golf books and videotapes. If you are in need of advice on such questions as which equipment will improve your handicap or your game, telephone the 702 area code number and ask to speak to a pro.

Professional Golf and Tennis Suppliers, ***7825 Hollywood Boulevard, Pembroke Pines, FL 33024. Telephone: 305-981-7283.***
Price list, free in the U.S. and Canada.
AE, DC, MC, V.
Sells golf, tennis, racquetball and running equipment and clothing.
Returns: satisfaction guaranteed, but there is a 15% restocking charge for a refund or credit instead of an exchange.
Established 1979.

Professional Golf and Tennis Suppliers sells the usual golf equipment and gives information over its toll-free line. If you want help, ask for the PGA-certified golf professional or owner Jeff Flitt. Professional also makes custom-fitted golf clubs in its own workshop. Ask for the customer data sheet, on which you give information to have clubs made to your own specifications.

Telepro, ***17622 Armstrong Avenue, Irvine, CA 92714. Telephone 800-854-3687; in California, 714-250-9142.***
Free brochure, or telephone for prices and advice.
MC, V.
Sells golf clubs and equipment by Browning, Dunlop, Hogan, Lynx, MacGregor, Ping, Powerbilt, Shamrock, Spalding, Tigershark, Stan Thompson and Wilson.
Returns: if goods returned unused within 30 days, they may be exchanged with a deduction for shipping; if customer wants money back, there is a shipping charge and 10% restocking fee.
Established 1939.

When I telephoned Telepro to ask about golf clubs for a beginner, I spoke to one of the two telephone answerers, Suzy. Suzy was extremely helpful, explained why the MacGregor and Hogan clubs I had suggested would be difficult for a beginner, gave me plenty of information and advice and offered to send me material to help choose. She suggested I try clubs out at a pro shop and look at the ads in golf magazines for information.

Do It Yourself

Golf club repairs are relatively simple if you are at all handy, and the savings are tempting. If you change your own grips, you can save about 60% of the price that a golf or pro shop would charge. If you do your own refinishing, you can save about 80% of the cost and perhaps do a better job.

Assemble your own irons and you can get a complete set for roughly $100. Finish your own clubs and save about 40% of the list price of similar clubs.

Custom Golf Clubs, ***10206 North Interregional, Austin, TX 78753. Telephone 512-837-4810.***
Free golf repair catalogue and golf accessories catalogue.
MC, V.
Sells golf club components, custom-made clubs, complete inventory of golf accessories, used balls.
Minimum order $10.
Returns: money back if merchandise returned unused.
Established 1969.

Ken Brugh of Custom Golf Clubs says that a set of irons you assemble yourself from components costs around $100, about half what the same irons cost made up and sold by the store and about a quarter of what pro lines cost. Custom has a free one-page sheet of instructions on replacing grips, a book for beginners called ***Golf Club Design and Repair*** (price: $5.95) and, to give more help, a toll-free telephone number that you can call to speak to a trained staff member who will answer repair and assembly questions. It has 72,000 accounts of hobbyists and professionals around the world who make or repair clubs.

This firm also sells used golf balls (graded A, B, and C) at half price or less according to grade. It also has X-outs, balls that have been rejected by manufacturers and that many people use for practicing.

Golf Day Products, ***3015 Commercial Avenue, Northbrook, IL 60062. Telephone: questions, 312-498-1400; orders, 800-433-GOLF.***
Catalogue, 50 cents ($3 in Canada).
AE, MC, V.
Sells supplies to make and repair golf clubs and putters.
Minimum order $20.
Returns: money back if goods returned within 45 days.
Established 1970.

Golf Day sells wooden clubs with ready-sanded shafted heads (in persimmon, laminated maple or stainless steel). You wind the whipping around the neck, stain, fill, spray finish and add grips. The price of these clubs will be roughly 40% less than the list price of brand name clubs, yet they will have the same kind of grips and true temper shafts.

The catalogue also sells materials for repairs: changing grips and broken shafts and refinishing. None of these are hard to do (instructions are in the catalogue), yet you can save as much as 60 or 80% of the cost of having some of those repairs done professionally. The store owner, John Harvey, sells his own book, ***Golfer's Repair and Maintenance Handbook,*** for $6.95, and he will answer further questions by mail (not telephone).

This is also the place for finished specialty clubs and balls plus golfing accessories, but these are all sold at full price.

Sales are in June, July and August; some prices are reduced by about 15%.

SKIING

Seasonal Sales

The way to save on new ski equipment and clothes is to buy at the sales. Each season's unsold equipment goes on sale in March (and sometimes in February) and then again between August and October. As ski gear is so seasonal, everything except for the most specialized stuff is put on sale. (In March it's to make room for summer goods, and in August and September it's to make room for the new season's models.) Reductions are typically between 25 and 40%, but can be as much as 70%, so are well worth planning for.

Buying Secondhand

Good, usable ski equipment can be bought at ridiculously low prices at the "swap meets" (one-day sales) that ski clubs hold—most often in the fall, around November. Members about to buy the latest equipment bring in their old gear to get rid of it, so you'll find skiable stuff almost given away: $100 boots for $7, cross-country poles for $2 to $3, bindings for $3 to $5. Sometimes local shops contribute brand-new equipment that hasn't sold.

Ski clubs will tell you when they have sales. Get the names of local clubs from people where you ski or ask for the addresses of clubs from **THE UNITED STATES SKI ASSOCIATION** ***(Att. Nordic, freestyle or recreation), 1750 East Boulder Street, Colorado Springs, CO 80908, telephone 303-578-4600.*** Send a self-addressed, stamped envelope if you write.

In addition, some shops, glad to see skiers throw out old equipment and buy new, don't see the sales as competition and will tell you about clubs and sales.

Do It Yourself

If you are adept with needle and thread and are willing to put in the time, you can make top-quality ski clothes for about 40 to 50% off what the classier brands such as Head, Roffee and White Stag cost. The firms listed below use and sell the same types of materials that the better manufacturers use: durable fabrics with a high thread count that won't ravel or snag, as well as hollow-core insulating materials, such as Thinsulate, that are warmer than the cheaper polyester used in less-expensive ski wear.

Daisy Kingdom, ***217 Northwest Davis, Portland, OR 97209. Telephone 503-222-9033.***
30-page sale catalogue, $1 in the U.S. and Canada.
MC, V.
Sells kits to make ski clothes for men, women and children.
Returns: credit.
Established 1970.

This firm sells complete kits for ski clothes. They are sold for about 15% off during a sale in the spring.

Donner Designs Company, ***P.O. Box 7217, Reno, NV 89510. Telephone 702-826-1288.***
Catalogue, $1 in the U.S. and Canada. Fabric swatches, $2.
MC, V.
Sells patterns, fabrics, notions and insulation for outerwear.
Returns: money back if goods returned as received within six weeks.
Established 1972.

Donner specializes in master patterns that each customer can adapt to his or her own size, so this is an excellent source for the hard-to-fit. Shapes are what owner Honor Jones calls "designer/functional"—rather fashionable—and there are fabrics in many colors. Furthermore, besides Gore-Tex, Du Pont insulation, and imported stretch fabric, there are specialty goods such as stirrup fabric, Polar fleece, Lycra, buckle pads and boot hooks. In fact, almost anything you are likely to need for making outerwear is stocked. If you don't see it in the catalogue, ask for it.

Sale: there is a corn snow sale every March through April 15, when overstock is reduced by 20%.

Green Pepper, ***941 Olive Street, Eugene, OR 97401. Telephone 503-345-6665.***
16-page catalogue, $1. Fabric swatches, $2.50.
MC, V.
Sells patterns to make sportswear, fabrics for sportswear such as cotton chamois, Thinsulate, Gore-Tex and Polar fleece.

Returns: money back if goods returned in original condition within 60 days. Established 1973.

Green Pepper is the place for you if you want a relatively straightforward sewing project. Owner Arlene Haslip says that her instructions have been praised by Renee Schulz, who tested kits from most manufacturers for her book *Sew for Snow* and decided that Green Pepper's patterns are suitable for novice sewers. (They do, however, take time, attention and patience.) One man who hadn't sewn before astonished the Green Pepper staff by starting with the hardest pattern of all, the zip-apart ski suit, and thereafter sewed ski clothes for his entire family. Green Pepper styles are classic, but colors and fabrics change with the fashions.

ANNE PAREE (see main listing under Perfumes) sells Vuarnet, Porsche Carrera, Ted Lapidus and Yves Saint Laurent sunglasses at about 30 to 45% off American list prices. For instance, when the best-selling Porsche Carrera black folding sunglasses cost $119 in the United States, they cost only $74.15 plus $5 surface postage from Anne Paree. And Vuarnet sunglasses cost between $30 and $54 from Anne Paree when they were $49 and up in the United States.

47 ST. PHOTO (see main listing under Appliances and Electronics) sells Ray-Ban and a few Porsche Carrera sunglasses at a smaller discount. The black folding Porsche Carrera, for instance, cost $99 at 47 St. when they were $74.15 at Anne Paree and $119 generally.

TENNIS

Each year ***Tennis*** magazine reports on lab and court testing of about six tennis rackets in the March, May or June, September and November issues. In the December issue there is a list of every racket available, with key characteristics noted. *Tennis* is sold by subscription, on newsstands and by mail from: ***Circulation Department, Tennis Magazine, 5520 Park Avenue, Trumbull CT 06611.*** Single issues cost $3.50 each (which must be paid in advance).

Seasonal Sales

If you need to try your racket before buying, you may find after-season sales (January/February and July/August) at pro and other full-price shops, although these are more common for clothes than for equipment. There are sometimes manufacturers' sales on equipment at odd times through the year. During after-season sales, clothes are often sold at about 20% off, or even more.

Mail and Telephone Sources

If you already know what you want, and don't need to try your equipment before buying, get it from one of the firms below. As the owner of a full-price tennis equipment store said to me, prices at the discount mail-order firms are "ridiculously cheap—walk-in stores just can't compete."

Lombard's, ***1861 Northeast 163rd Street, North Miami Beach, FL 33162. Telephone 305-944-1166.***
Price list, $1.
MC, V.
Sells tennis rackets for adults and children; tennis clothes and accessories, including Bard stringing machines; Lobster and New Prince ball machines; squash rackets, Vitamaster exercise machines, running shoes.
Returns: unconditional money-back guarantee.
Established 1944.

Bernie Lombard says that there is nothing special about Lombard's, except that it is the oldest in the business and tries to give the lowest prices and best service. What is best service? Speedy delivery, fewer mix-ups, guarantees on merchandise and nothing listed that is not in stock. Mr. Lombard says that he has no exclusives but does occasionally stock better brands of tennis clothes, such as Ellesse and Fila, at a discount.

Professional Golf and Tennis Suppliers, ***7825 Hollywood Boulevard, Pembroke Pines, FL 33024. Telephone 305-981-7283.***
Free price list.
AE, DC, MC, V.
Sells golf and tennis equipment and clothing; raquetball and running equipment. Tennis rackets by Prince, Kennex, Reebok, Le Coq Sportif and others.
Returns: 100% satisfaction guaranteed, but there is a 15% restocking fee on goods returned for money back or credit (no restocking charge on exchanges).
Established 1979.

This is another walk-in and mail-order store that sells most popular brands of tennis equipment. Owner Jeff Flitt says that the phone number isn't just an order number—the telephone answerers know the inventory. Most of them play tennis and can advise on such questions as stringing, size and how new models play.

Samuels Tennisport, ***7796 Montgomery Road, Cincinnati, OH 45236. Telephone 800-543-1153; in Ohio, 800-543-1152.***
Free price list, or telephone for prices.
MC, V.
Sells tennis rackets, clothes and accessories (but clothes are not listed on the price list).
Returns: money back if goods returned unused within 30 days.
Established 1981.

This small new firm prides itself on its service. All the telephone operators are good players and have used the equipment, says the manager, Steve

Glimcher. Orders are not taken for goods that are not in stock, and so everything arrives within the week.

Major brands of equipment, clothes, shoes and accessories are sold, including top-of-the-line clothes by Fila, Ellesse and Tacchini. But these last cost list price unless you are lucky and find a few leftovers on sale at the end of the season. When I telephoned, for example, Ellesse warm-ups were on sale because they hadn't sold as well as expected.

Sportline of Hilton Head, ***3720 Alliance Drive, Greensboro, NC 27407. Telephone 800-438-6021; customer service, 919-292-5781.***
Catalogue planned, $1, or telephone for prices.
Sells tennis clothes, equipment and accessories; racquetball clothes and accessories; basketball shoes; running shoes; some swimming apparel; Vuarnet sunglasses.
Returns: one-year guarantee on "Sportline" clothes; with equipment, depends on manufacturer's guarantee.
Established 1983.

Co-owner Sheila Mays says that she normally carries all the major brands of tennis rackets in every grip size and weight and that she can ship them out within 48 hours. After Christmas, when supplies are lower because she is waiting for spring deliveries, she will always tell a customer whether what he or she orders is in stock or not.

Charlie and Sheila Mays visit the clothing factories and try to do selective shopping—picking clothes that are really good value to sell by mail. Mrs. Mays says that she and her husband will stock well-known brands that they are not so impressed with in the shop, where shoppers can judge for themselves, but by mail they try to stick to tougher clothes that will hold up well in the wash.

Buying Secondhand

Another way of saving on rackets is to find a store or a pro shop that sells used ones. Prices on used rackets vary according to how much use and abuse the racket has taken and whether the model is obsolete, but you can get some really good deals this way.

Do It Yourself

Tennis String International, ***Box 1151, Berkley, MI 48072. Telephone 800-245-0208.***
Free price list.
MC, V.
Sells tennis racket grips and strings.
Minimum order $30.
Returns: defective synthetic strings exchanged, no guarantee on natural gut.
Established 1977.

You can change your own and your friends' and family's tennis racket grips and save half the cost. You have to do several, because there is a $30 minimum at this firm and the nationally known grips cost only $2.25 to $7. Tennis String International sells the leading brands (Fairways and Gamma Gut are the most popular).

If you want to start a hobby or small business of restringing, you first have to buy a restringing machine (there are used ones around) but after that can save about 80% of the cost by doing your own. TSI salespeople will answer customers' how-to questions on their toll-free line and will refer you to the **United States Racket Stringers Association** if you mean business.

TELEPHONE SERVICE

Webcor 758 two-line multifunction telephone. When the list price was $119, the price at 47 St. Photo was $29.95.

TELEPHONE SERVICE

LONG-DISTANCE CARRIERS

Now that the telephone system has been deregulated, there are a lot of muddled people around. Most of us agree with Russell Baker's indignant cry in the *New York Times,* "I'm tired of being urged to spend precious time thinking about things like 'telecommunications.' I am especially tired of being urged to think about telephones." Anyone who feels the same way, yet has an uncomfortable feeling that he or she is paying too much for long-distance telephone calls, will be pleased to hear about the two services described below. For a reasonable fee, they will do the thinking for you in a personalized comparison of long-distance companies. You may be able to save quite a bit of money—possibly 15 to 19% of your bill if you are now using AT&T and live in a major metropolitan area with several companies to choose from. You'll save less if there are only two or three long-distance carriers servicing your area.

Whether you compare rates for yourself or get one of the organizations described below to do the work, remember these points:

You are not necessarily monogamously wedded to your primary carrier. Even if you change carriers, you can still use AT&T, or any other carrier, whenever you want, simply by dialing an access code. And for about $5 (as I write) you can change again or go back to Ma.

You may find smaller or regional companies (in the yellow pages under Telephone Companies) in your own area that may not reach the whole country but may serve the places you call and have lower prices than the major companies that service much of the country.

Most people tend to make long-distance calls to a few specified numbers (of friends and family) at certain regular times. It is therefore important to take your own calling patterns into account when comparing rates.

Groups That Will Compare Rates for You

Consumers' Checkbook is a program of the nonprofit Center for the Study of Services, which "helps consumers get the most for their money when they buy services." If you want to find out which long-distance telephone service would save you most money, but don't want to do the calculations yourself, you can pay *Consumers' Checkbook* to do them for you. Send in a list of long-distance calls from up to three "reasonably typical" phone bills, and the *Checkbook* people will send you a page listing what the same calls would have cost you with the other major long-distance companies servicing your area. They will also send a chart comparing billing and service features of the companies.

Charges for this comparison service are on a rising scale, depending on the size of your long-distance telephone bill (as I write, prices go from $10 to $75 for home telephones—more for businesses). *Consumers' Checkbook* finds that 15 to 19% is the average saving of people in major metropolitan areas who switch from AT&T to another carrier. The address to write to is: **CHECKBOOK'S COMPUTERIZED LONG-DISTANCE COMPARISON,** ***806 15th Street NW, Suite 925, Washington, DC 20005. Telephone 202-347-9612.***

Consumers' Checkbook also publishes a thorough booklet, ***The Complete Guide to Lower Phone Costs,*** for people who are willing to do quite a bit of work themselves. The booklet contains detailed ratings of the major long-distance companies in terms of cost and quality of service. In spite of the ratings, you still have to work out which one will save *you* most money, because that depends on your own habits—where you call at what time of day, and so on. The booklet also contains advice on how to save on installation and repairs, how to cut the cost of local services and much more. *The Complete Guide to Lower Phone Costs* ($6.95 postpaid) is available from **LOWER PHONE COSTS,** ***806 15th Street NW, Suite 925, Washington, DC 20005.***

For a mere dollar, the nonprofit **Telecommunications Research and Action Center** sells an excellent and very helpful chart that compares rates and features of the main national long-distance carriers, "TRAC Residential Long-Distance Comparison Chart." The rates are updated every six weeks.

TRAC will also compare the cost of any 30 calls you send in (from your bill or made up by you) with each of the major carriers. This costs $35 as I write, and the address is **TRAC,** ***P.O. Box 12038, Washington, DC 20005. Telephone 202-462-2520.***

Doing the Work Yourself

If you decide to calculate for yourself which would be the cheapest long-distance company, you can start with this list of major equal-access long-distance companies. Or better still (as this list will date), call the companies listed in your yellow pages under Telephone Companies.

If equal-access service is available where you live, your local telephone company will give you a list of participating companies. You may also find in the yellow pages smaller or regional companies that are not participating in equal access (you will therefore have to dial a code to use their service). These companies may not reach the whole country, but they may serve the places you call and have lower prices.

If equal access has not reached your area, you can use an alternative long-distance company by dialing a code number and using either a tone dial phone or a tone generator device.

Not surprisingly, I suppose, I have found these companies much better at answering questions by telephone than by mail.

Questions to ask:

What are your rates for five-minute calls made during the day? Evening and/or night/weekend rates for the following calls? (Assemble a list of the long-distance calls you commonly make.)

What areas may be called? Can I call within my state and to other states too? Are there areas that are more expensive to call?

Are there restrictions on time of day?

Is there a minimum monthly charge for the service?

How do you bill? After the first minute, is additional time billed in whole minutes or in smaller increments?

Are there volume discounts? (With most services "the more you talk, the less you pay," as a man at Sprint put it.)

Is there a "travel" service (so that family members can use the carrier when away from home)?

Major Long-Distance Carriers

ALLNET, ***South Wacker Drive, Chicago, IL 60606. Telephone 800-982-8888.***

AT&T COMMUNICATIONS, ***1 Empire Plaza, Providence, RI 02903. Telephone 800-222-0300.***

ITT US TRANSMISSION SYSTEMS, ***P.O. Box 732, Bowling Green Station, New York, NY 10004. Telephone 800-526-3000.***

MCI, ***MCI Building 17th and M Streets NW, Washington, DC 20036. Telephone 800-624-2222.***

RCI CORP, ***333 Metro Park, Rochester, NY 14623. Telephone 800-458-7000.***

U.S. "SPRINT," ***30150 Telegraph Road, Suite 400, Birmingham, MI 48010. Telephone 800-521-4949.***

WESTERN UNION LONG-DISTANCE SERVICE, ***1 Lake Street, Upper Saddle River, NJ 07458. Telephone 800-527-5184.***

BUYING YOUR OWN TELEPHONE

It is most certainly cheaper to own your telephone than to pay a monthly rental fee for it to AT&T. Depending on the price, it could take as little as a few months to pay off the cost of the telephone. The cost of rented telephones includes free replacement or repair if needed, but at some inconvenience to the customer, since AT&T requires that the customer bring or mail the telephone to a repair location for the free repair.

An advantage of owning your own telephone is that you can choose one that performs tricks, such as redialing a busy number, automatic dialing of numbers you call often and timing of long-distance calls. You can get a telephone with a "mute" button so that you can talk to someone in the room without the person on the other end hearing. Then there are hands-free speaker telephones and cordless telephones.

Leading manufacturers of telephones include ATC, GTE, ITT and Telcor. When Consumers Union tested telephones (see the June 1984 and May 1986 issues of *Consumer Reports*), two highly rated telephones came from ITT and AT&T. In the 1984 article, CU suggested that people who don't want to spend a lot of time shopping around could play it safe and buy from companies that did well in their tests.

If you do buy your own telephone, you must notify your local telephone company and give the telephone's ringer equivalence number and F.C.C. registration number (as explained in the instructions packed with the telephone). You must also notify AT&T and *return the old telephone to AT&T so that the company stops levying the monthly rental charge.* If you give a telephone back to AT&T and don't replace it, you should notify your local telephone company so that the company stops levying the rental charge for the outlet.

Repairs

If you buy a telephone from AT&T and it breaks, you take it to an AT&T telephone center or send it to an AT&T repair center (and pay for the repair after the expiration of the guarantee). If you buy a telephone from any other manufacturer, you may have to either send it back to the manufacturer for repairs or take it to a local repair shop. Ask before you buy.

If there are breakdowns in the lines, these are still the responsibility of your local telephone company, which installed and owns them.

SAVING ON WIRING

If you are handy enough to run wire around doors and perhaps through walls, you might want to take on some of your own new wiring. If you buy jacks and wire at stores that sell telephones, you can install new telephones, move old ones and add extensions for considerably less than your local telephone company charges. Electrical current in the telephone system is minimal, and the live parts of some of the new jacks are designed to be unreachable anyway. First, however, be sure to ask your local telephone company for its requirement on how you can legally hook into its wire system.

You may also save by replacing the local telephone company's in-place wiring if you have the company's permission in advance. But this is for fanatics only, as savings are small. I agree with Russell Baker, who says, "Being bilked for 'wire investment' is a small price to pay for not having to learn the difference between SNI and DPA." (You'll find out about them if you do your own wiring.)

If you rent your wiring, you are charged a very small monthly rental/maintenance charge (92 cents in New York as I write) plus possibly a monthly "wire investment charge" ($1.29 as I write) if the wiring was installed before April 3, 1982. And the telephone company repairs indoor wiring for free. You may want to check with your local telephone company about buying their in-place wire and assuming the responsibility for its repair.

U.S. General Supply Corporation, ***100 Commercial Street, Plainview, NY 11803.***
(Main listing under Tools in the Hobby section)
196-page catalogue, $2.

Sells jacks and wires for telephone installation and several adapters, including one that will convert a dial telephone to Touch Tone for use with the long-distance services.

TOYS

Steiff plush teddy bears. When the U.S. price of model 0203/41 was $85, the price at Kinderparadeis Hamburg in Germany was $59, including postage.

TOYS

Great buys in popular toys by American manufacturers can be found at a discount at chains such as Toys "Я" Us and at a couple of mail-order sources. These are good places to stock up, especially for Christmas and birthdays. Toys are also likely to go on sale after Christmas, in January and February, and some stores put summer toys on sale in August.

If you want toys that are different—traditional toys made of natural materials and good-looking enough to decorate a child's room, the only way to beat the outrageous prices is to buy from Germany or to make them yourself.

MAIL AND TELEPHONE SOURCES

Best Products, ***P.O. Box 26303, Richmond, VA 23260. Telephone 800-221-BEST.***
(Main listing in General section)
438-page color catalogue, $1.
MC, V.

This general catalogue has baby furniture and supplies and popular toys by manufacturers such as Coleco, Fisher-Price, Mattel and Playskool, all discounted (and shown photographed in full color). I checked two Fisher-Price toys, and they were selling for about 27% under what full-price stores charge. I also checked Monopoly, which was 50% off, and Trivial Pursuit, which was 30% off what a New York toy store was charging. This is a great place to buy mainstream American toys.

Orchard Toy and Stationery Co, ***185 Orchard Street, New York, NY 10002. Telephone 212-777-5133.***
Send stamped, self-addressed envelope or telephone any day between 10 A.M. and 4 P.M. for specific prices.
MC, V.

Sells toys by Fisher-Price, Hasbro, Ideal, Kenner, Mattel, Parker Brothers, Selchow and Righter, "plus all name companies"; electronic games; stationery; sporting goods.
Returns: merchandise exchanged if returned within 30 days.
Established 1948.

Orchard has a big stock of toys by well-known manufacturers and especially "odds and ends," as they call them, for party favors. The problem is that discounts (when I checked, Fisher-Price roller skates were 25% off, Monopoly was 20% off, and Trivial Pursuit was 15% off) will largely be eaten up by shipping costs. However, if you need lightweight party favors, or a large batch of toys, Orchard may save you money.

German Stores

Kinderparadeis Hamburg, ***Neuerwall 7, 2000 Hamburg 36, Germany. Telephone 40-343931.***
256-page main catalogue in October, two $1 bills, $7 in bills airmail. Kathe Kruse and Steiff catalogues free on request, two $1 bills airmail.
Returns: none.
Established 1982.

Spielzeug-Rasch, ***Gerhart Hauptmann Platz 1, 2000 Hamburg 1, Germany. Telephone 40-337922.***
256-page catalogue, three $1 bills.
Sells toys.
Minimum order DM 50.
Returns: credit.
Established 1896.

Well-known German toys such as Fishertechnik and Baufix construction sets, Marklin and Fleishmann H.O. model railways, Faller and Kibri lineside buildings, Kathe Kruse dolls and Steiff plush animals cost half or less in Germany of what they cost bought in the United States. As I write, for instance, a 14-inch mohair teddy bear by Steiff costs $78 in the United States, yet only $33 in Germany. One of the most expensive Steiff animals, the 14-inch Leo the Lion, costs $125 in the United States and only $57 in Germany. As Margaret Diekmann of Kinderparadeis points out, Kathe Kruse dolls and Steiff animals are "the most interesting objects to collect" because of the difference in price and low cost of mailing. But you should also be able (as I have) to save about 25% of the cost of heavier German toys, even after paying postage and duty.

Spielzeug-Rasch says that it has over 1,000 foreign customers and can answer letters in English, French and Spanish.

FISHER-PRICE PARTS

Don't throw away broken Fisher-Price toys—you can get replacement parts direct from the manufacturer. Ask for "Bits and Pieces," the replacement parts price list. There is also a complete catalogue of Fisher-Price toys, and the manufacturer will sell direct to anyone who can't find a certain toy locally. However, prices are higher than in the stores because of mailing costs. Contact: **FISHER-PRICE DIVISION OF QUAKER OATS COMPANY,** ***Consumer Affairs Department, East Aurora, NY 14052-1880. Telephone 716-687-3000.***

MAKE IT YOURSELF

These firms sell kits for the inexperienced and supplies for the competent. By making toys instead of buying them, you can save money (lots if you buy patterns and use your own materials) and also get toys that are far more interesting than the ready-made toys generally available.

Children are also usually particularly pleased with toys made especially for them. Toys we made for, and with, our daughters are the only toys they still hang on to now that they have grown up.

Cherry Tree Toys, ***P.O. Box 369, Belmont, OH 43718. Telephone 614-484-4363.***
Catalogue, $1 in the U.S. and Canada.
Sells kits, patterns and parts to make wooden toys.
Returns: money back if goods returned within ten days.
Established 1975.

Cherry Tree has the best-designed wooden toy kits and patterns I have seen—the animals are irresistible and the trucks and trains are handsome. If you are a complete beginner, you can buy cut kits that you just have to sand, glue and finish; prices for these are about 30% off those of the same toys ready-made. If you are an accomplished woodworker (and own coping saw, crosscut saw, chisel and drill), you can buy patterns, use your own wood and save much more money.

Most toys are push-and-pull toys for younger children, but there are also pull carts and a rocking horse, and owner Michael Murphy is planning wheelbarrows and wagons. Turned parts, such as wheels, are available in natural or colored wood, and toy makers' paints, finishes and tools are also sold.

Greenleaf, ***R.D. 3 Box 100 (Dept. 51), Cooperstown, NY 13326. Telephone 607-547-5136.***
Color catalogue, $3 in the U.S. and Canada.
MC, V.
Sells dollhouse kits and parts.
Returns: none; defective parts replaced.
Established 1947.

Greenleaf manufactures machine-made, die cut kits to make magnificent dollhouses of all shapes and sizes (the largest is 4 feet high). The mainly Victorian houses are shown beautifully painted in the catalogue, although in reality you must buy your own paints and do your own painting. All the houses are put together with glue, and some are fairly easy. Others are only for dedicated hobbyists, as they have fancy latticework, gingerbread trim and shingles to be put on one by one. As I write, prices go from $20 to $187. Parts such as floor tiles, shingles and electricity sets are also available. If you send Greenleaf $3, it will send a portfolio of all its models and the name of your nearest distributor.

Judi's Dolls, ***P.O. Box 607, Dept 1C, Port Orchard, WA 98366. Telephone 206-876-3954.***
20-page color brochure, $1.50 in the U.S. and Canada.
Sells patterns and supplies to make fabric dolls.
Returns: money back on unused merchandise if returned within 30 days.
Established 1978.

The first Cabbage Patch dolls were soft sculptures, made from stretchy fabric with faces molded out of the material. Now soft sculpture dolls have become a craze. Judi Ward designs traditionally cute, mostly baby dolls with large round eyes that can be made from her needle sculpture patterns. Velour is sold in skin tones, which Judi says is nicer than the more common single-knit or muslin fabric. Long-hair fur and a few other essentials are also available—you supply your own materials for stuffing and clothes. Faces can be embroidered or painted.

Pattern Plus, ***21 CC Mountain View Avenue, New Milford, CT 06776. Telephone 203-354-1894.***
16-page catalogue, $1.50 in the U.S. and Canada.
Sells patterns and kits to make cloth dolls and teddy bears.
Returns: money back if returned within 30 days.
Established 1976.

Kits and patterns to make the most lovable tousled-haired, long-legged cloth dolls, dressed in wonderful flouncy clothes, including an Afro-American pair. Kits include body fabric, face transfers, fake fur for hair and doll stockings. You provide your own fabrics, stuffing, thread and so on, which is why the kits are so inexpensive. The kits are suitable for the average sewer without special skills, but you must know how to use a sewing machine. And you do your own cutting from patterns or diagrams. You can also buy patterns, face transfers and other supplies, such as doll stockings and doll stands, separately.

Real Good Toys, ***P.O. Box 706, Montpelier, VT 05602. Telephone 802-479-2217.***
Catalogue, $2.50 in the U.S. and wherever in Canada UPS delivers.
MC, V.
Sells dollhouse kits.
Returns: none, but defective parts or kits are replaced.
Established 1972.

Superior all-wood dollhouse kits are made by this Vermont firm. Kits include general stores, mere shells, small space-saving houses for children and rambling

Victorian mansions for collectors. Everything is precision cut by hand and the plywood is of cabinet quality, so these kits are not the cheapest—as I write, the children's houses cost about $75 each. To assemble the houses, you need glue, hammer and nails.

If you send $2.50, Real Good will send you illustrated information on its products and will either put you in touch with a distributor in your area or, if there isn't one, sell to you by mail.

Son Rise Soft Crafts, ***P.O. Box 5091 CC, Salem, OR 97304. Telephone 503-362-0027.***
12-page color brochure, $1 in the U.S. and Canada.
Sells craft patterns for puppets, stuffed animals and wall hangings; supplies such as fake fur, fabric, glue.
Returns: money back if returned within ten days.
Established 1981.

A small collection of distinguished furry puppets and stuffed animals can be made from Son Rise patterns or kits: wonderful green-eyed Persian cats and long-haired Scottish terriers will probably tempt adults and older children, while lion cubs, plump teddy bears and pandas look just right for younger children. They are much nicer than most ready-made animal toys.

TRAVEL

Villa sleeping seven near a private stretch of pink sand beach in the Bahamas, recently offered for holiday swap through I.H.E.S./ Intervac. The owners were interested in an exchange anywhere at any time.

Vacation house sleeping seven on water with lake access and boat dock in Tahoe Keys, California. Recently offered for holiday swap through I.H.E.S./Intervac. The owners were interested in an exchange anywhere at any time.

TRAVEL

AIR TRAVEL

Travel Agents

You don't pay agents a thing—they get commissions from the airlines and other carriers. The travel business changes so much, and ticket pricing is so complicated, that a knowledgeable and willing agent can be invaluable in helping you find the lowest fare. An agent can also be helpful in knowing which charter companies are the most reliable. Furthermore, good agents can do things you can't do, such as pay for return trips from abroad in foreign currency to take advantage of the strong dollar. Another agent's trick is to book flights to less expensive destinations. My agent, for instance, booked a New Yorker a first-class round-trip to Dublin. The passenger actually wanted to go to London, so he took only carry-on luggage and got off in London. Buying the Dublin ticket, plus paying for the return ticket in Irish pounds instead of dollars, saved the passenger $1000 for the first-class tickets.

Ethnic Travel Agents

Some cities have "ethnic" travel agents that specialize in bulk fares and charters to one or two countries only. If you can find an ethnic agent (in an ethnic neighborhood, by word of mouth or perhaps through a newspaper advertisement) for the country you are visiting, you'll most likely get very low fares.

Do It Yourself

However, there is a problem. Many agents are paid on commission only, and some are not enthusiastic about working extra hard to find the lowest rates. Most agents will compare prices and find the cheapest way for you if you prod them a bit. But if your agent refuses or is reluctant to do research on budget travel, arm yourself with *JAX FAX*, the industry guide to international charter and low-price travel, and do some investigating yourself.

Domestically, Jesse Lemisch, a commuting history prof at the State University of New York at Buffalo, says that there is *always* a cheaper flight. Agents and airline employees can't keep tabs on the multitude of price levels, so you have to get hold of a copy of ***The Official Airlines Guide*** (available at travel agencies, airline offices and some libraries). Find out the names of *all* the airlines that fly your route; then call and interrogate each one. Ask whether there are special discounts if you book ahead of time and whether there are cheaper night flights. **OFFICIAL AIRLINES GUIDES,** ***2000 Clearwater Drive, Oak Brook, IL 60521. Telephone 312-654-6000; circulation, 800-323-3537.***

Bulk Fares

Airlines know ahead of time that on many flights they will have unsold tickets. Rather than take a total loss on those seats, the airlines quietly sell the seats at lower prices to wholesalers, who resell them at prices that are lower than any of the posted prices. These tickets, usually for less popular flights—midweek, for instance—cost about the same as charter tickets and have the advantage of being on regularly scheduled airline flights. Ticket wholesalers advertise these bulk fare tickets in newspaper travel sections (if an advertisement includes words such as "special conditions apply," this is an indication of bulk fares). Travel agents can also get hold of them and sell them to you. Bulk fare tickets are listed in *JAX FAX* (see below), which most travel agents subscribe to, and some of the firms under Discount Tickets (below) sell them.

Two Sources

Japan Budget Travel, ***10 East 39th Street, Room 402, New York, NY 10016. Telephone 212-686-2929.***
Sells tickets to Japan and other parts of the Orient.
Returns: usually none.
Established 1982.

This is an "ethnic" travel agency with mostly Japanese customers that specializes in lower-priced tickets, mainly to Japan and other parts of the Orient. Tickets are for regularly scheduled flights, often on Northwest Orient Airlines. The agency was recommended by a friend who has used it.

Sunbeam Travel, ***telephone, except California and New York, 800-AIR-ONLY. Offices: 30 North Michigan Avenue, Suite 1015, Chicago, IL 60602, telephone 312-263-7664. 1654 Wilshire Blvd, 2nd floor, Los Angeles, CA 90017, telephone in California 800-AIR-TKTS. 274 Madison Avenue, Suite 904, New York, NY 10016, telephone 212-725-8835. 1 Gloucester Street, Suite 103, Toronto, Ontario M4Y 1L8, Canada, telephone 416-922-7559. (Main office is in London.)***
Sells international airplane tickets.
Returns: "it depends."
Established 1978.

Sunbeam Travel sells tickets for international charter and scheduled flights. It deals mainly with Europe, Africa, the Middle East and the Far East. When I called in March (off season) to check prices to Rome and London, Sunbeam had the lowest prices I found anywhere. When I called for a Christmas return to Madrid, it had the lowest fares outside of charters. Off season Sunbeam was offering midweek departures on scheduled KLM flights at roughly half the regular prices and 25% off the APEX (Advance Purchase Excursion Fare). During the Christmas season it was offering merely 10% below APEX on midweek KLM flights.

The KLM flights involved changing planes in Amsterdam and therefore several extra hours of traveling. To some people the stopover is an added plus; a friend of mine just announced excitedly that she had this wonderful low-priced ticket to London that would allow her six hours of looking around Amsterdam on the way.

Charter Flights

Tickets on charter flights to Europe cost substantially less than tickets on scheduled flights run by the major airlines. There are not so many charter flights off season, but during the high season, when scheduled prices go up, there are plenty of charters at 20 to 30% below the APEX on the major airlines.

Charters are run by independent operators who hire planes, run regular (often weekly) flights and take care of selling the tickets themselves. As far as safety goes, the companies operating the planes have to maintain Federal Aviation Administration standards. But in return for the lower prices there certainly are disadvantages. The seating is more crowded, service is worse, departure times are likely to be late at night and, as the charter companies have last landing rights, the planes are more likely to be delayed. Another problem is that if at the last moment you find you can not make a flight, you lose your money, and if you change your flight, you are charged for the change. There are also minor inconveniences such as sometimes not knowing until a few days before your trip what time the plane is scheduled to leave or what airport you'll use. If all of that sounds horribly daunting, remember that there are differences *between* charter companies and that, although all of them are subject to these problems, the cheapest charters tend to be the most chaotic. Remember, too, that there are millions of repeat charter customers. My family sometimes travels by charter and we've all suffered delays, but never disastrous ones. My advice is: always, always take a very long and *very entertaining* book.

Try to pay for charter flights with a credit card. The Federal Fair Credit Billing Act allows you to complain about credit charges within 60 days of being billed. If a charter company goes out of business before you take your trip, you can complain that the bill is in error and the card company may give you a refund (this seems to be an iffy area). It is most sensible to book your charter through a travel agent who knows which companies are the most reliable. But if you have to do your own research, the directory that travel agents use, ***JAX FAX,*** is inexpensive ($12 a year) and lists charter flights from major airports around the country. Contact: **JAX FAX TRAVEL MARKETING MAGAZINE,** ***280 Tokeneke Road, Darien, CT 06820. Telephone 203-655-8746.***

If you want to check the record of a charter company, you can contact one of these offices: **CONSUMER AND COMMUNITY AFFAIRS, U.S. DEPARTMENT OF TRANSPORTATION,** ***400 7th Street SW, Washington, DC 20590, telephone 202-755-2220.*** It will give you the number of complaints registered against a company. **CONSUMER AFFAIRS OFFICE, AMERICAN SOCIETY OF TRAVEL AGENTS,** ***4400 McArthur Boulevard NW, Washington, DC 20007, telephone 202-965-7520.*** This office will give you a company's complaint record and will also try to help if you have a complaint against a charter company—for instance, if you are having trouble getting a refund.

Charter Companies

Council Charter, ***205 East 42nd Street, New York, NY 10017. Telephone 800-223-7402 or 212-661-0311.***

Free brochure.
Sells tickets for charter flights to 14 major European cities.
Returns: you may cancel up to the day of travel with a $50 penalty.
Established 1947.

This wholly owned subsidiary of the Council on International Educational Exchange is the oldest charter operator in the country. A student friend of mine, who is a happy customer, tells me that it has the reputation of being more expensive but more reliable than other charter companies.

Flights leave year round from New York, and there are reduced-fare connections on scheduled airlines from about 12 U.S. cities. Booking arrangements are extremely flexible—you can book round-trip or one-way, fly into one city and return from another and leave and return whenever you want—there are no time limitations. Furthermore, there is an unusual (for a charter company) sweetener—you can cancel your ticket up to the day of travel with only a $50 penalty.

Travac Tours and Charters, ***telephone 800-872-8800. 6151 West Century Boulevard, Los Angeles, CA 90045, telephone in California 213-760-9692. 166 Geary Street, San Francisco, CA 94108, telephone in California, 405-392-4610. 989 Sixth Avenue, New York, NY 10018, telephone in New York State, 212-563-3306.***

Free brochure.
Sells charter tickets to eight countries, but mostly to England, France, Italy and Switzerland.
Returns: you may cancel your flight up to 14 days before the trip with a $50 penalty; after that no refunds unless the ticket is sold.

Another charter company with a better reputation, Travac was started by two people who had worked with Council Charter (above). A spokeswoman tells me that the company uses only carriers backed by major scheduled airlines, such as Balair, the charter division of Swissair, or Transamerican, which is backed by a large and solid corporation.

There are flights from and to the East and West coasts. You can buy one-way tickets (at an additional charge), fly into one city and out of another and stay as long as you like within the same price season. There are representatives in Europe, so you can change your return flight once you are there.

Standby

Lately I've taken to traveling standby, which is not as nerve-wracking as it sounds unless you are traveling at the most popular times (midweek is best, Fridays and Sundays worst). Few airlines offer standby tickets in the winter, but it's my favorite way to travel in the summer. The cost of flying standby on the major airlines is roughly the same as taking a charter or one of the budget airlines such as People Express. Icelandair has extra-low-cost standby tickets from several U.S. cities to Luxembourg (4½ hours by train from Paris). To get Icelandair's toll-free number, call information 800-555-1212.

To fly standby in a worry-free way, you must, of course, be under no pressure to leave on a specific day. You can call up the airline ahead of time, and until the very day, to get a rough estimate of ticket availability. Then, on the day you want to go, you can buy your ticket at the airport or at the airline offices in town, going early to line up if you think it is necessary. If you *are* under time pressure, you might be able to travel "dirty," as a woman I met in a standby line last August explained. If there is a budget airline flying your route, such as People Express, you book on that as a backup.

Courier Services

One way of getting half-price airfare is to act as a messenger for a courier service. My daughters and their friends have all been couriers to London and back when they couldn't get on the budget airlines Virgin Atlantic and People Express, and when they couldn't find a suitable charter.

Courier services that specialize in the speedy delivery of documents send the documents via regular airlines (if they don't have their own planes). Smaller companies find it economical to hire free-lance messengers, whose payment is a half-price ticket or, occasionally, a free one. As a courier, your job is to accompany a crate of documents, checked in as your baggage allowance.

If you want to be a courier, find a firm that has a regular courier service to wherever you want to go. Telephone and ask whether the service can use you around such and such a date, or when its next available job is. If you can't be flexible about your dates, you should call about two months in advance.

If you get a job, you'll probably have to go to the courier service's office to sign an agreement and perhaps pay for your ticket ahead of time. On the day of your trip, you most likely meet the firm's representative at the airport, where he or she checks in the crates of documents and gives you a small package of papers to take with you. At the other end, you meet another representative, who will wait with you while the documents are unloaded (and seen through customs if the job is international). At this point you can wait around for up to two hours. If you have paid for the ticket, you'll now get your refund.

Here are a few courier services that use free-lancers, just to give you an idea of how they work. They'll probably be booked up because of being listed here. For more listings, work your way through the Air Courier Companies listed in the yellow pages.

Air Systems, ***29-20 37th Avenue, Long Island City, NY 11101. Telephone 718-268-7437.***
This company has flights to Miami ($50 as I write), San Juan, Amsterdam and London ($125 as I write) from New York. Call on the first of the month before the month in which you want to travel. The first time you work for Air Systems you must go to the office to pay for your ticket; after that you can mail in the payment. You can take one piece of check-in and one piece of carry-on luggage of your own.

Now Voyages, ***263A West 19th Street, Suite 406, New York, NY 10011. Telephone 212-620-5987.***
Now Voyages is not a courier service itself but makes a business of representing several services. Would-be couriers must pay a registration fee ($35 a year as I write). Round-trip tickets are available out of Los Angeles, New York and San Francisco to many European cities (Amsterdam, Brussels, Frankfurt, London, Milan, Paris and so on) for half price, or even less. Only carry-on luggage is allowed.

Securicor Air Couriers, ***1010 West Hillcrest Boulevard, Inglewood, Los Angeles, CA 90301. Telephone 213-973-4866.***
Has one-way tickets only (no returns) from Los Angeles to London. It uses the whole baggage allowance, so you can take only carry-on luggage. Telephone for a reservation, and then pay your fare in person at the office or by mail.

Telerade, ***Main Office: 47-45 Vernon Boulevard, Long Island City, NY 11101, telephone 718-937-1920. Chicago, 312-750-0500. Los Angeles, 213-649-4800 (call 9 A.M. to 2 P.M. for information).***
This firm has flights between New York and Los Angeles and New York and London. Couriers pay full price for the ticket in advance and then get up to half the money back at the destination if going one way or on the return if doing a round-trip. Couriers can take one piece of check-in luggage on international flights and one piece of carry-on on domestic flights.

Discount Tickets

If you can be flexible about where you go, these brokers are an excellent source. They sell leftover unsold tickets on cruises, flights and package tours at hefty discounts. The tour and cruise operators are pleased to fill places that would have been empty, you feel smug about your bargain and only the people who paid full price are annoyed.

Discount Travel International, ***205 The Ives Building, Narberth, PA 19072. Telephone 800-824-4000.***
Telephone 24 hours a day, seven days a week, for latest offers.
MC, V.
Sells airplane tickets, cruise trips, vacation packages, hotel rooms at a discount.
Membership fee.
Returns: none.
Established 1982.

This firm deals in discounted unsold tickets on charter flights and tours, as well as hotel and car rental discounts. You do have to pay a $45 membership fee but can telephone the 800 number before joining to get information. Members are given a toll-free number to call for up-to-date listings and reservations.

Moment's Notice, ***40 East 49th Street, New York, NY 10017. Telephone 212-486-0503.***
Telephone during business hours for prices.
MC, V.
Sells discounted tickets on both charter and noncharter flights. There is an annual membership fee.
Returns: money back only if trip is cancelled.
Established in 1983 as a subsidiary of a company established in 1952.

Each morning Moment's Notice calls charter companies and cruise ship companies to see what unsold tickets they have, and it then sells those tickets at prices that are discounted by up to 50%. Perhaps its most spectacular saving was for an around-the-world cruise on the world's most famous ship (I'm not allowed to mention the name, as customers who paid full fare will get hopping mad). Through Moment's Notice a couple paid $60,000 instead of $80,000 for the cruise, thus saving the sum of $20,000. Other good savings include a tour of China for $1500 that cost the unfortunates who paid full price $3000 (and in that case the booking wasn't even last-minute; the lower-priced tickets were sold ahead of time because the organizers wanted to be sure of fulfilling the necessary charter minimum). Less spectacular but still very good: I called up anonymously to ask about plane fare to Rome. There was no discount tour, just a Pan Am charter over on a specific date and a return whenever I wanted. It cost $499 round-trip. The same trip on a regular Pan Am flight would have cost $699 with the APEX (Advance Purchase Excursion Fare) book-ahead system and $899 full fare.

By far the best way of dealing with Moment's Notice is to call, give the representatives your holiday dates and ask them what they have. If you call with a very specific destination in mind, you are much less likely to find something.

Moment's Notice handles trips to most nondomestic destinations and says that the Caribbean "has the best availability of bargains of any destination." There is a $45 annual fee.

Spur of the Moment Cruises, ***10780 Jefferson Boulevard, Culver City, CA 90230. Telephone: recorded travel information, 213-838-9329; inquiries, 213-839-2418.***
Telephone for prices.
AE, MC, V (small additional charge added to credit card payments).
Sells discounted cruise bookings.
Returns: none.
Established 1982.

Spur of the Moment has cut-price bookings for cruises (more than anyone else, it claims). It has the very appealing policy of no membership fee, and you can even book through your own travel agent if you want.

Stand Buys, ***311 West Superior, #404, Chicago, IL 60610. Telephone 800-255-0200; in Illinois, 800-826-4398.***
Telephone for information and free brochure.
AE, MC, V.
Sells discounted tickets for cruises, package tours including hotels and air-only tickets. Annual membership fee.
Returns: 30-day guarantee on membership; no returns on travel.
Established 1979.

Stand Buys sells leftover tickets for charter trips that have not been filled—some include the hotel and others don't. On one day that I called, offers included a trip from Detroit to Acapulco for $449 (the regular charter price had been $699) and a seven-night New York–to–Aruba package for $609 (regular charter price: $749). Another time I called about a ticket to Mexico City; Stand Buys had a seven-day round-trip for $159 at a time when the regular fare was $307.

The problem with Stand Buys is that you have to plunk down an annual membership fee per household before you find out what's available. (However, you can cancel your membership and get your money back within the first 90 days if you have not taken a trip.) Once you join, you are given a toll-free number you can call at any time to hear the offers (usually about 35 a day for the following few days to six weeks). Trips leave from Detroit, Chicago, and

New York and go to the Caribbean all year round and to Europe in the spring and summer only.

Worldwide Discount Travel Club, ***1674 Meridian Avenue, Miami Beach, FL 33139. Telephone 305-534-2082.***
Free brochure and sample current offerings.
Members receive monthly lists of offers and a toll-free number for ordering.
AE, DC, MC accepted for the $45 annual membership fee.
Sells discounted short-notice travel tickets.
Returns: membership is not refundable.
Established 1982.

Owner Ted Hankoff says that 60% of his offerings are cruises; the other 40% are tours and airline tickets. He says his customers are mainly retired people who are free to pick up and go when a trip appeals to them. Monthly lists of tickets with three-day to three-month warnings are distributed to members. Tickets tend to be for whatever is popular in the current season. In the winter it's warm places: Saint Martin, Aruba, Jamaica, Barbados, Antigua, Hawaii, Acapulco. From the spring on it's mainly Europe.

There is an annual membership fee, which is not refundable. "We don't make wild promises," says Mr. Hankoff. "We expect people to be serious."

Coupon Brokers

The Coupon Broker, ***David Kenny, 1780 South Bellaire Street, Suite 125, Denver, CO 80222. Telephone 800-247-2891 or 303-759-1953.***
Telephone 8 A.M. to 5 P.M. for prices.
AE, MC, V.
Sells discounts on airfares to the Caribbean, Hawaii, Mexico, the Orient and the South Pacific.
Returns: none, and once a ticket is issued the name can not be changed.
Established 1979.

David Kenny sells coupons bought from "frequent flyers" who have been awarded the coupons by airlines but aren't going to use them. There are about 15 different coupons, some for use within the United States, others for the Caribbean, Europe, Mexico, the Middle East, the Orient and the South Pacific.

The coupons are for a specified dollar amount, so you don't save on short or medium-length trips, but you can on long trips (within the United States, for instance, from the East Coast to Hawaii). Mr. Kenny says that the best savings by far are on first-class tickets; savings on those range from 50% to occasionally 70%.

Besides the coupons, this firm offers discounts on certain airlines, although these vary according to the season. I called a couple of times on behalf of traveling friends and found that The Coupon Broker could give me 20% off a Mexicana Airlines ticket to Mexico City (which I hadn't been able to find anywhere else). Another time it offered 25% off the TWA APEX and economy fares to the Continent and good airfares to London from the West Coast.

When to Travel

If you can avoid traveling during the high season, you'll find that the price of plane tickets to certain destinations goes down by anywhere from 15% to as much as 50% (one travel agent told me that tickets to Greece are even more than half off during the off season). Here is a rundown of seasons, including off seasons, when prices are at their lowest. Between low and high seasons are "shoulder" seasons, when prices are somewhat lower.

Caribbean. High: Christmas through Easter. Low: May, September, October (hotels are half price too).

Europe, Middle East. High: summer. Low: winter—November 1 to March 31, but dates vary slightly according to the country.

Pacific (Australia, New Zealand, Tahiti). High: winter. Low: summer.

South America. High: winter. Low: summer.

As is the price of most things, ticket prices are based on supply and demand, and go up around holiday seasons on popular routes. Avoid traveling, if you can, around the presidents' birthdays, Easter, Christmas, college intersessions and school holidays. Prices on some routes go up by as much as 50% then. If you *do* book on crowded holiday flights, you can sometimes earn free tickets for future use by agreeing to be bumped off seriously overbooked planes and waiting for the next flight. I have known people, such as my younger daughter, who repeat the whole performance on the next flight to earn another free ticket.

If you are willing to fly *during* the holiday, while other people are making merry, you may find good discounts. For instance, in 1985 some special "turkey fares" were as much as 80% off if you booked ahead and flew between Thursday and Saturday midnight on Thanksgiving weekend.

DRIVING

The trip across country is an American institution. Going west is part of the national folklore and driving is the way to do it. If you've got no car, you can still take an all-American holiday at very low cost by driving a car for a drive-away company. Such firms, many of which have offices all over the country, specialize in delivering cars for people who are moving and would rather take a plane than drive. Dependable (below) says that many of its customers are retiring, which is why routes to sunny places are the most popular.

To drive a car you must be over 19, or, in the case of some firms, over 21; you must have a valid American or international driver's license and present up to three references and/or one or two pieces of identification such as a credit card or a passport. The car is free, of course, but you must put down a deposit of $25 to $100, depending on where you are going. The deposit is refunded when you get there. One free tankful of gas is provided, and you can take passengers to share expenses. There are time limits—three days from New York to Florida, for instance, and six days coast to coast. If you want to take a more leisurely trip, you can take a car to a midpoint and then take another one to your destination.

The important question is, of course, whether you can find a car going where you want, when you want. Popular destinations—the sunny ones such as California and Florida—are usually easy. But if you want to go somewhere out of the way, try calling various companies before you need to go to get some idea of car availability.

To find drive-away companies near you, look in the yellow pages under Automobile Transporters and Drive-away Companies.

Auto Caravan, ***2400 East Devon, Des Plaines, IL 60018, telephone 312-699-7300. 6310 West 89th Street, Los Angeles, CA 90045, telephone 213-624-6644. 110 West 40th Street, Room 403, New York, NY 10018, telephone 212-354-7777.***
Requirements vary depending on the office. Drivers must be over 21, have three references and a driver's license that has been valid for at least six months. In New York, passengers accompanying the driver must come in to the office to be fingerprinted. Cars are late models, none over seven years old. California and Florida are the most common destinations from New York. Waiting time to find a car going where you want to go varies.

Auto Driveaway, ***310 South Michigan, Chicago, IL 60604, telephone 312-939-3600. 4800 Melrose Avenue, Los Angeles, CA 90029, telephone 213-666-6100. 313 Fifth Avenue, New York, NY 10022, telephone 212-696-1414. Has 28 other offices around the country.***
Drivers must be at least 21, have two pieces of identification and come in to the office to fill out papers. Denver, California and Florida are the most popular destinations.

Dependable Car Travel Service, ***8730 Wilshire Boulevard, Beverly Hills, CA 90211, telephone 213-659-2922. 162 Sunny Isle Boulevard, North Miami Beach, FL 33160, telephone 305-945-4104. 1501 Broadway, New York, NY 10036, telephone 212-840-6262.***
American drivers must be at least 19 and have three references; foreign visitors just need a passport. Dependable says it is "very cautious" about whom it uses; the quality of the references is important. Arizona, California, Florida and Texas are popular destinations.

General American Shippers, ***4635 North Broadway, Chicago, IL 60640, telephone 312-728-0108. 6016 Woodman Avenue, Van Nuys, CA 91401, telephone 818-988-9000. 450 Seventh Avenue, Room 1804, New York, NY 10123, telephone 212-594-2690. Has 97 other offices throughout the country.***

Drivers must be 21 or over and provide two pieces of identification and one reference. The company says that drivers should call two or three days ahead and that you'll rarely have to wait more than ten days, as cars are always being delivered to obscure parts of the country.

WHERE TO STAY

Wherever you go, in the United States or abroad, there are places to stay that are much cheaper than hotels and, some people think, much nicer.

Bed and Breakfast

If you are friendly, staying in a bed and breakfast is a marvelous way to save money. Not only do you pay much less, but you also have a host and/or hostess to talk to as you start and end your day. I have several friends who refuse to go to "lonely," "alienating" and "completely forgettable" hotels, but rather always go to B&Bs where, they claim, each visit is an adventure.

I went to Washington, D.C., last spring, and the cheapest hotel I could find, even after asking various friends for advice, cost $78 for a double. I called two B&B reservation services and, giving them only four days' notice, quickly found a double for $42 in exactly the central district I wanted.

B&B is not a hotel; you don't have the privacy or the amenities. You have to tell your host roughly when you are arriving, perhaps make telephone calls in public and clean up the bathroom after you use it. On the other hand, you do have the pleasures of snooping around someone else's home. My Washington hostess was a painter: her bathroom was decorated with shells, lace and paintings; her guest room was crammed with books (Sylvia Plath, Lewis Mumford and so on) and even had a black-and-white TV. She made us a good breakfast of juice, strong, better-than-hotel coffee, scrambled eggs and muffins and talked to us while we ate it. "Never again," said my husband, who isn't very friendly and was dying to read the paper with his breakfast (he could see the *Washington Post* lying temptingly on a chair). I, on the other hand, would be happy to switch to B&Bs. I think they particularly make sense in cities like New York, where the less expensive hotels tend to be deeply depressing and sometimes (according to friends of mine who have suffered them) sinister too.

BED AND BREAKFAST, THE NATIONAL NETWORK, ***P.O. Box 4616, Springfield, MA 01101.***

If you send a self-addressed, stamped envelope, this organization will send you a list of about 28 member B&B agencies around the country. Although prices are not rock-bottom, the B&B homes are all inspected and known to the agencies. I booked my Washington stay through an affiliate.

When you want to book lodgings, you simply call or write to whichever agency serves the area you are visiting, give your dates and tell them where exactly you want to stay. The agency will tell you what's available. There is no charge to you for the referral.

I have a friend, a publisher's wife, who lets out rooms in her smartly furnished Victorian house through the New York affiliate **URBAN VENTURES,** ***P.O. Box 426, New York, NY 10024, telephone 212-594-5650.*** She says the people who come to stay are much nicer than people who go to hotels; often they are schoolteachers and retired people. (Our Washington hostess said that B&B guests are well educated, well mannered and parsimonious.)

I talked to Urban Ventures, which says it can provide just about whatever kind of lodging you want in New York. As I write, its very cheapest single is $23 a night in a "cheerful second-story walk-up" (old building); one of the most expensive is a room overlooking a garden with a king-sized bed and a private bathroom in a "beautiful, beautiful" townhouse in the posh East 80s—$100 a night for two. There are even apartments with no host. The cheapest hostless lodging is a studio apartment that costs $68 a night for two.

American Historic Homes Bed and Breakfast, ***P.O. Box 388, San Juan Capistrano, CA 92693. Telephone 714-496-7050.***
This organization will book you into any of 2,000 (often uninspected) "historic" homes. Historic means old in this case, and the agency calls 1920s houses old if they are in California. This agency handles both private homes, for which $40 is a rough average price, and also inns, which cost about the same as hotels.

BED AND BREAKFAST USA ***by Betty Rundback and Nancy Kramer. $9 plus $1 for fourth-class mail ($2 for first-class mail) from Tourist House Associates, R.D. 2, Box 355A, Greentown, PA 18426. Telephone 717-857-0856.***
This book is most useful for its listing of bed-and-breakfast reservation services in cities and popular tourist areas around the country. When I wanted to book a room in Washington, D.C., for instance, I found three reservation services listed, and two actual B&Bs. Neither of the two B&Bs worked out, but I quickly found a room through one of the reservation services. Besides the booking services, actual B&Bs are listed in every state and in Canada, but not in huge quantities. The book is updated annually.

Campus Lodgings

There are universities and colleges all over the place trying to make money by renting out those empty dorms during the vacations. Some friends of mine (he's a publisher, she's a bookseller) took their four children and their four children's friends to stay on the campus of the University of Sussex in Brighton, England. They were delighted: huge spaces, swimming pools, tennis courts and cafeterias just right for a large, noisy and impecunious family.

Accommodations on most campuses usually include singles, doubles (with communal bathrooms) and apartments with kitchens at prices between $10 and $20 per person per night in the United States. Some places reserve their accommodations for academics or academics and students, but many will take anybody.

I wrote to several British universities in May 1985 and found all sorts of tempting dwellings. In London, among other possibilities, I could have had bed and full English breakfast in the centrally located London School of Economics halls of residence. Price was from $9 to $15, depending on whether it was Easter, summer or around Christmas. (Optional extra dinners cost $3.70, but most people would probably pay $3.70 or more *not* to have to eat them.) In the summer I could have stayed at Chelsea College's King's Road residence for $15 a night, or $98 a week, but there I would have had only a continental breakfast. At the University of Edinburgh I could have had single accommodations in the center "overlooking Princes Street Gardens and commanding unforgettable views. . . ." Or I could have rented a four-bed apartment surrounded by gardens and golf courses outside the town. In Bath I could have had a house sleeping four at the family holiday center outside of town for $162.80 per week (the charge for additional people was $23 each per week). In Bath squash courts, table tennis, playing fields and swimming pool may be available if they are not being repaired over the summer. And there are lots of stately homes and pretty villages to visit in the area. These are the British campuses I wrote to:

Accommodations Office, University of Bath, Claverton Down, Bath, BA2 7AY, England. Telephone 225-61244 Ext. 622.

Business Manager, Institute of Developmental Studies at the University of Sussex, Brighton, BN1 9RE, England. Telephone 273-606261.

Conference Administrator, Chelsea College, 552 King's Road, London, SW10 OUA, England. Telephone 1-351-2488.

Administrative Officer, Conferences and Functions, London School of Economics, Houghton Street, London, WC2A 2AE, England. Telephone 1-405-7686.

Holiday Operations Manager, University of Edinburgh, Pollock Halls, Holyrood Park Road, Edinburgh, EH16 5AY, Scotland. Telephone 31-667-1971.

There are, of course, many similar setups in the United States and around the world. It shouldn't be too hard to do your own research by writing to colleges wherever you want to go. As with most things, *you'll have a better choice if you book early.* When I wrote in May, popular dates—July and early August—were already booked up at smaller halls.

If you don't want to do your own research, get this excellent booklet, which lists basic details of vacation accommodations in 44 American states and 27 other countries. Many are in or near popular tourist spots.

TRAVEL ACCOMMODATIONS GUIDE, ***$9.95 postpaid from Campus Travel Service, 1303 East Balboa Boulevard, Newport Beach, CA 92661. Telephone 714-675-9891.***

Guest-room Swapping

If you are adventurous and gregarious, here is the payoff: there are organizations you can join through which you offer hospitality to the other members and in return get almost free accommodations in private homes when you travel.

Inter Lodgings Co-Op, ***P.O. Box 7044, Tacoma, WA 98407-0044. Telephone 206-756-0343.***
Free information sheet.
Club membership fee: $45 per year.
Arranges guest-room swapping.
Returns: partial return of membership fee within 30 days.
Established 1980.

This club was started by a schoolteacher, Bob Ehrenheim, who hopes to make it his full-time occupation when he retires. He has 300 members in 45 of the American states, plus some in Canada, Australia, Germany and Switzerland. Members agree to open their guest room to other members for at least three months of the year, and in return they can stay with other members whenever they like and for as long as the other members will have them. Upon joining, you get a directory that lists information about all the other members, their homes, their interests and so on, and then you make arrangements with them individually. You don't have to bother about counting nights, as once you are a member you can use the club as often as you like, even if no one comes to stay with you. And you can look people up in your directory to find out about them before they come to stay.

There is a fee of $4 per person per night when you stay with members, which goes to pay for laundry, electricity and so on. No meals are provided, although members can make their own arrangements.

When he started the club, Bob Ehrenheim thought it would be for blue-collar workers, but in fact all the members are rather adventurous professionals—doctors, lawyers, schoolteachers and so on (one member has a house with pool in Hawaii). No one complains of too many visits. In fact, friendly members say they don't get enough visitors.

Touring Cyclists' Hospitality Directory, ***13623 Sylvan Street, Van Nuys, CA 91401.***
Send self-addressed, stamped envelope for information.

John Mosley publishes a directory of names and addresses of cyclists who agree to give other cyclists touring the country a free place to stay for the night and a shower. The directory is free, although donations are most welcome. The only way of getting a copy is by agreeing to be listed—except for cyclists from other countries, whom John gives complimentary copies to, as Americans enjoy meeting them so much.

There are members of all ages, from college kids who give their parents' address because they are living at home, to retired people. Members live everywhere from the wilds of Alaska to downtown New York. And although hosts aren't required to provide anything but a place to stay and a shower, this is a rich country, as John says, and most people end up feeding their guests. If you live on a very popular route, you may possibly get up to five visits a year, but most people listed get none or one, and a major complaint from cyclists who are longing to hear other cyclists' touring stories is that they aren't visited enough.

The people listed below publish equivalent directories for their own countries. Americans can get the directories without agreeing to be hosts.

Michael Burlace, Bicycle Australia, ***P.O. Box K499, Haymarket, New South Wales 2000, Australia. Telephone 2-264-2521.***
The directory costs $10. (You must *pay with Australian dollars; otherwise they lose in the exchange. Get Australian money from DeakInternational (see index).*
Bicycle Australia also sells cycling guides to Australia and New Zealand. Write and ask for its information package. They say that mail takes two weeks each way, so expect to wait five weeks. If you can't wait, you can telephone, but remember that the poor Australians are upside down, so check with the telephone system before calling.

Leigh Howlett, ***Rock Rose, Well Lane, St. Margaret's-At-Cliffe, Near Dover, Kent, CT15 6AA, England.***
A free list of 140 hosts is published in March. Donations are welcome. (Please give a donation, preferably in $1 bills; remember that bank charges take about $4 of any personal check you send.)

Corrie Buschman, ***Nassaustraat 19, 3583XB Utrecht, Netherlands.***
A list of 168 hosts in Holland is available for $1, payable in International Reply Coupons, which are available at the post office.
Corrie Buschman writes, "We'll be glad to receive American cyclists! They are welcome!"

Bruce O'Halloran, ***40 Amy Street, Ellerslie, Auckland, South New Zealand. Telephone 9-591961.***
To get the New Zealand list, you must agree to be a host.
Send a brief description of yourself with your address, telephone number, a self-addressed envelope and six International Reply Coupons.

US Servas, ***11 John Street, New York, NY 10038. Telephone 212-267-0252.***
For information on membership in an exchange program, send a long (number 10) self-addressed, stamped envelope.
Established 1948.

Servas (which means "service" in Esperanto) was started in Denmark by an American conscientious objector and others just after World War II. The organization's aim is to help build world peace through understanding. Servas is hoping to achieve this by encouraging people from different countries to get to know each other individually. It makes possible home stays with families, individuals and groups in about 90 countries besides the United States. It's a nonprofit group and is on the United Nations roster as a nongovernmental organization.

Membership is open to anyone who shares the aims. To join, you must be 18 or over (unless you are traveling with your family). When you apply, you will be sent the name of an interviewer, who will explain the aims of the organization to you. There is a charge of $30 a year for travelers and $10 a year for hosts (you can join as one or the other or both). If you join as a traveler, you are lent the lists of hosts for any country you are thinking of visiting. The host list includes all sorts of information such as the interests, occupations and languages of the hosts and the number of visitors they have rooms for. Using the host list, you make your own contacts. A spokeswoman for Servas told me that people of all religions and no religion belong, and that middle-class and more highly educated people seem to be attracted to the group, although that was not the intention of the organizers.

When traveling, you are expected to stay a maximum of two nights with each member, unless you are invited to stay longer. When a host, you are expected to spend time with your guests. No money changes hands between hosts and guests.

Visiting Friends, ***P.O. Box 231, Lake Jackson, TX 77566. Telephone 409-297-7367.***
Free leaflet.
Monthly news sheet describes new locations.
Membership fee: $15 for life. A fee is also charged for each trip arranged.
Arranges guest-room exchanges.
Established 1981.

Laura LaGess has a small group of about 150 members in 41 states who exchange guest rooms. Members stay with each other for one to six nights, mostly when crossing the country. Many members are genealogists tracing their family history, and they like visiting county seats where they can visit the courthouse—Boston is the most popular stopping place. Mrs. LaGess keeps the list of members herself and then tries to match hosts and guests to make sure they are compatible. She wouldn't suggest that her more conservative, sedate and proper members stay with her chain smokers with a casual lifestyle, for instance. Hosts are obliged only to offer a guest room, but all of them seem to want to give breakfast as well and some like to drive guests around and show them whatever is to be seen. Mrs. LaGess says that her members are interesting, friendly and active people, mostly in their fifties and sixties, and, although most members are married, it is a nice safe way for single women to travel. Members are welcome to bring a friend, but not pets or children.

Membership costs $15 for a lifetime, and then each visit that Mrs. LaGess arranges costs $20 for the first member stayed with on one trip, no matter how many nights (up to six) you stay, and $15 for subsequent members stayed with on the same trip.

Home Swapping

I love staying in other people's homes when they are not there. All my married life I have been rudely asking my friends whether I can move my family in while they are away on vacation. Besides being cheap, a home is infinitely more comfortable than a hotel room. There is space to sit around, books and magazines to read, perhaps toys, bikes and cribs for the children and often the offer of a car. It is nice not to *have* to have breakfast, lunch and supper in a restaurant; nice to be able to join in local life a bit by shopping for food and very nice to have enough space to enjoy relaxing at home, instead of feeling you must pound the streets all day because the alternative is lying on your bed in a hotel room.

If you don't have friends you can descend upon, there are agencies and directories through which you can arrange an exchange with strangers. The agency and directory people say that swappers mistreating each other's homes is not a problem—it almost never happens. The real problems are: (1) Maybe nobody wants your lovely home because it is in the wrong place. In this case you stand a better chance with a directory, because there are more listings. But anyway, don't give up hope; people sometimes want to visit family or friends, or see new parts of the country, in nontourist areas. (2) The people with whom you've arranged a swap may dump you when they get a better offer. To avoid this, try an agency.

Note: the more flexible you are about where and when you'll go, the more likely you are to find an exchange.

Agencies

Although swapping your home through an agency is much more expensive than swapping through a directory, it is less trouble, and there is no danger of being left stranded if the person or family you were planning to exchange with lets you down at the last moment.

Four Star Living, ***964 Third Avenue, 39th floor, New York, NY 10022. Telephone 212-772-8333.***
Telephone or write for brochure.
Arranges home exchanges.
Established 1974.

Four Star arranges for exchanges worldwide but only in places where *everyone* wants to go, says director Heidi Otto. If you don't live in California, Colorado, Florida, Utah (for the skiing) or an equally desirable place (New York counts!), don't bother to apply. You send photographs of the inside of your home, and your home must be "lent" to someone else first so that you can earn credits. Ms. Otto says that many people use second homes to build up credits. After that you can use your credits to stay where you choose (exchanges are not direct exchanges). The whole thing sounds rather grand and is expensive (in the United States, Four Star advertises only in *Town and Country*)—there is a deductible registration fee, and then the agency charges $1,000 and up for swaps arranged. Ms. Otto says that it is still less expensive than staying in a hotel. And she is probably right if there are several of you, especially if you remember that you won't have to eat out the whole time.

Global Home Exchange Service, ***P.O. Box 2015, South Burlington, VT 05401. Telephone 802-985-3825.***
Write for flyer and application form.
Arranges home exchanges.
Established 1980.

This service is run by an American schoolteacher, Tim Khan, who started by arranging exchanges for students. He has the largest number of homes in France and Great Britain, but also some in Belgium, Germany, Holland and Switzerland. Most of his American exchangers are on the East Coast and in Florida. He matches swappers and organizes an exchange of house photographs and details. After that, the homes are inspected to make sure they haven't been abused, aren't "on a railroad track" and so on. There is a lifetime registration fee of $25 for people who want to swap within the United States and $30 for people who want to swap with Europeans. Then, when a deal is arranged, there is a flat fee of $175 for swaps within the United States and $220 for U.S.-foreign swaps. Owner Tim Khan says that last year he arranged swaps for 40% of those who applied. Three to four weeks is the typical length of stay.

Home Exchange International, ***185 Park Row, P.O. Box 878, New York, NY 10038-0272, telephone 212-349-5340. 22458 Ventura Blvd., Suite E, Woodland Hills, CA 91364, telephone 818-992-8990.***
Write or telephone for brochure.
Arranges home exchanges.
Established 1979.

People east of the Mississippi contact the New York office; those west of it call California. This organization arranges swaps between Americans and people in England, France, Italy and Mexico and has a few people in the Bahamas,

Bermuda and Puerto Rico. It says that anyone with a nice apartment in Manhattan can get an exchange at any time, and that other in-demand American places are Arizona, California, Colorado (for skiing), Florida, Hawaii and cities (and their suburbs) such as Boston and Washington. But sometimes people from other countries want to go to less obvious places. When I spoke to director Linda McCall, she said she had just arranged a swap between Albany, New York, and Biarritz, and currently has someone near Marseilles who wants to go to Michigan. During the summer, most swaps are between families, who like being in the suburbs rather than the center of a city. At other times of the year, it is mostly academics and business people who want center-city swaps.

There is a lifetime registration fee of $40. You submit photographs and a description of your home and it is graded (if you can stand it!) "quality," "superior" or "luxury." Then, each time you want to swap, you let the organization know where and when (obviously people who give several countries and times are more likely to find something). Home Exchange will send you photographs and descriptions of one or two possibilities. Picky people often reject several offers before finding something they like. When an exchange is organized, there is a fee of $150 to $525, depending on length of swap and grade of home (top prices are for lengthy sabbatical stays, which this organization handles).

Directories

A friend of mine who advertised that she was willing to do a summer swap of her Connecticut house for a house in the south of France complained furiously to me, "Oh, those directories don't work. I didn't get a single answer." Well, supply and demand being what it is, and life being notoriously unfair, unless you live in a prime holiday spot, you have to do some work. You have to write up a description of your home and your part of the world, make it sound exciting and send a photocopy to as many likely prospects as possible. The less popular your home district, and the more popular the place you want to go, the harder finding an exchange will be. But don't despair—perhaps your state has great fishing or rapids shooting or something. The directory people say that even people living in highly undesirable places sometimes find swappers who want to visit friends or family.

People offer and find all sorts of arrangements through the directories: weekend swaps, exchanges of hospitality (that means you stay *with* the other person or people, and they then come and stay with you), rentals and swaps that include a car exchange. Anyway, the would-be swappers all sound most respectable, and their houses are mouth-watering—from the "New England farmhouse with mountain views, a 50′ pool, and a perennials garden" to the "recently restored luxury flat in an old palace in the center of Padua (car avail., close to Veneto, Vicenza, Verona)."

Holiday Exchanges, ***Box 5294, Ventura, CA 93003. Telephone 805-642-4879.***
Monthly listings of homes to swap and rent. Twelve issues (six back issues and six as published including your own listing), $25. Your listing and a copy of that issue only, $12.
Current owners bought business in 1978.

A photocopied list is published monthly, with roughly 30 listings in each issue. Half the listings are in the United States; the others are abroad, including Australia and New Zealand. This is a small operation, so I imagine your chances of finding something would be lower than with other organizations. On the other hand, the price of advertising your own home is only $12.

International Home Exchange Service–Intervac US, ***P.O. Box 3975, San Francisco, CA 94119. Telephone 415-382-0300.***
Catalogue published end of January, end of March and end of May.
Subscription fee: $45 plus $3.75 mailing charge; 20% discount for senior citizens. MC, V.
Established 1977.

This organization has teamed up with European Intervac, so it has about 4,000 listings a year, many of which are foreign (of the directories I saw, this one had the most listings outside the United States). The large, efficient-looking catalogue is studded with photographs and has two pages of advice on how to swap successfully. Most of the listings look very inviting—one Christmas swap described in the *San Francisco Chronicle* starred a Colorado governor who exchanged his state mansion with round-the-clock security for a San Francisco architect's "classy Filbert Street home—with its hot tub and sweeping view of the bay." (Apparently the governor was known locally as a tightwad, and some thought he shouldn't have used state property for an exchange.)

European readers are very interested in California, Florida and New York and want summer exchanges there. Americans are much more flexible and will travel at any time. Within the United States some people even exchange houses for weekends. When International Home Exchange asked for swapping stories, it found several people who swapped about four times a year.

Loan-a-Home, ***2 Park Lane, 6E, Mount Vernon, NY 10552. Telephone 914-664-7640.***
Free descriptive leaflet.
Directory listing long-term exchanges and rentals published in June (with September supplement) and December (with March supplement). One directory and one supplement, $25; all four issues, $35.
Returns: money back if directory is returned.
Established 1968.

Here is a photocopied list of a few 6- and 12-month exchanges but mostly rentals, mainly for academics moving around and relocating business people who need somewhere to live while they look for a more permanent home. The editor, Muriel Gould, advertises her directory in the *New York Review of Books* and university publications. Photocopied sheets list about 400 apartments a year around the world, most of them in university towns. The problem is that, unlike vacationers, academics on sabbatical are necessarily so inflexible about dates and their needs that exchanges are extremely hard to come by. Muriel Gould says that it is the rentals listed in her directory that are more often used.

Ms. Gould says that about three times since the directory started people have written to complain that they hadn't got their money's worth, and each time their money has been returned.

Vacation Exchange Club, ***12006 111th Avenue, Suite 12, Youngtown, AZ 85363. Telephone 602-972-2186.***
200-page catalogue in February, 60-page catalogue in April, both $16 (with your own listing $24.70) in the U.S. and Canada. No catalogues available from November to February.
Returns: money back.
Established 1960.

Big catalogues list swappers around the United States and the world with coded descriptions of them and their homes. There were many marvelously tempting listings in the directory I saw, most of them in the United States with quite a few in Great Britain and Italy and a smattering in 38 other countries from Australia to Zimbabwe (where one company director and his wife, with a private pool and a 1½-acre garden, were willing to exchange house and car with anyone, anywhere, anytime, or to exchange hospitality, rent out their home or give bed and breakfast). The number of overseas people who want to come to the United States varies with the strength of the dollar; now that the dollar is weakening again, more people want to come to this country. The editor, Mr. Ostroff, says that many people make swapping a way of life—he has an American family living in Mexico that has done it 60 times. Home exchanges are most popular, and then exchanges of hospitality, but you can also find rentals and guest room rentals through the guide.

Worldwide Exchange, ***P.O. Box 1563, San Leandro, CA 94577. Telephone 415-521-7890.***
Lists homes, boats, trailers to exchange, rent or buy $9.95.
MC, V.
Returns: "negotiable."
Established 1979.

This is the least expensive of the guides—it costs only $9.95 (or $19.95 if you want to be listed). It is published quarterly and has about 1,000 listings a year of houses, boats and recreational vehicles to exchange or rent, as well as bed and breakfasts. The owners are proud of the fact that the listings are written in simple English and, as no codes are used, are easy to read.

Other Places to Stay

YMCA

The Y's Way, ***356 West 34th Street, New York, NY 10001. Telephone 212-760-5856.***
Send self-addressed, stamped number 10 (long) envelope (from abroad six International Reply Coupons) for information.
Books rooms in YMCAs in the U.S. and 24 other countries; runs tours and special-interest group vacations.
Established 1978.

The Y's Way is a division of the New York Metropolitan YMCA and is the central U.S. booking office. It can book rooms for you at YMCAs in 58 cities in the United States and Canada and 24 other countries. Most of their customers are students, but they welcome older people too.

Single rooms in North America with communal bathrooms cost an average of $22 as I write. Accommodations abroad are more "hotel-like" and more expensive. Prices vary, of course, but, as I write, a room for one in Austria might cost $20; for two, $30. A single room in Denmark might cost $31; and a single room with a private bath, $52.

Ideally, The Y's Way likes about two months' warning, partly because some places get booked up, and partly to confirm reservations, find alternatives and so on.

Youth Hostels

American Youth Hostels, ***National Administrative Office, P.O. Box 37613, Washington, DC 20013-7613. Telephone 202-783-6161.***
Membership fee: $10 per year for people under 18 and over 59, $20 for everyone else.

In spite of the name, this organization is for all ages. If you join, you'll get a membership card and a booklet listing about 300 hostels in the United States. You can also buy two booklets that list international student's hostels. Volume 1 is for Europe, and Volume 2 is for the rest of the world. U.S. accommodations cost about $4 to $12, and accommodations abroad cost about $3 to $10.

Youth hostels are heartily recommended by people who are sociable (there are usually a common room and cooking facilities). They are an excellent way of meeting people and marvelous for people traveling alone, as you meet people and can get traveling advice. There is also the pleasure of the occasional unusual building in a lovely setting (one American swears that she stayed in two hostels converted from lighthouses in the United States).

But other people balk at the dormitory-style sleeping arrangements and time restrictions (you have to be out from 9 A.M. to 5 P.M. and in by 11 P.M.). My daughters, for instance, claim that in many places abroad you can find B&Bs, or even hotels, that are almost as cheap as hostels (well, about twice the price—$8 instead of $4, for instance) by looking around once you get there.

OTHER WAYS TO SAVE MONEY IN EUROPE

International Student Identity Card and Work Programs

The International Student Identity Card gets you into museums and other educational institutions at reduced rates. To get a card, you need a passport-sized photograph and proof that you are a student (such as a transcript or letter from a registrar with the school seal). You can get the card at Council on International Educational Exchange offices around the country or by mail from the **COUNCIL ON INTERNATIONAL EDUCATIONAL EXCHANGE,** ***205 East 42nd Street, New York, NY 10017, telephone 212-661-1414.*** It costs $8, takes two to three weeks to process and arrives with a booklet listing places abroad that give student discounts. It is essential for certain reductions, such as the one-third discounts on British long-distance buses. However, my younger daughter claims that the Empire State Building is the only place that insists on an International Student Identity Card; in her experience any European museum or cinema offering student rates is content with a regular student ID.

CIEE also organizes programs for students of 18 and up (or 16 and up in Germany) to work in community programs with young people in Europe. You go for three to four weeks, all board and lodging are provided free and you pay only your airfare and an "administration" fee of $100.

Eurail Passes

Europe Through the Back Door, ***120 4th Avenue, Edmonds, WA 98020. Telephone 206-771-8303.***
Free budget travel newsletter.
Sells Eurail passes plus advice, books, money belts, luggage.
Returns: money back if there is "honest dissatisfaction."
Established 1975.

Rick Steves spends four months a year in Europe, lectures on travel and writes about travel (I noticed that his latest book, *Europe 101,* was recommended in the *New York Times*). He also sells Eurail passes and is a godsend to all the bewildered math phobics who can't decide whether a pass will pay off. If you telephone him, he will tell you "in a jiffy" whether you should get a pass. He says about 20% of the people who buy passes don't need them. "How can you do that?" I asked. "Won't you lose all your customers?" "Now, that's a very short-sighted view," he chided. "Maybe if I tell enough people not to buy passes, I'll get a reputation for honesty, and wouldn't that be nice?" As Eurail passes cost the same wherever you buy them, do get yours from Rick—because he will not only tell you whether you really need it but, as an added attraction, will also answer questions you have about transportation and will send a taped "critique of your itinerary." (Note: my daughters point out that Eurail passes are convenient because you don't have to wait on line for tickets.)

MORE INFORMATION AND HELP

Guestaccom, ***Claremont House, Second Avenue, Hove, East Sussex, BN3 2DJ, England.***
Hotel listing, $1 in cash or six International Reply Coupons.

A list of inspected small hotels, inns and guest houses in Great Britain that cost under $20 per person per night. Although the hotels pay to be included, I have heard from someone I trust that the list is reliable. I stayed in one listed hotel and saw another; both were exceptional value for the price. Most places are in the country, and as I write there are none in London.

Guest Houses, Farmhouses and Inns in Europe. Each year the English Automobile Association publishes this booklet of 4,000 places to stay in Europe for under $20 per person. Alas, no descriptions are given. I found, when I tried to use this booklet for Vienna, the fact that locations aren't given was very annoying (surely when choosing a hotel you want to know where in town you'll be—outskirts or center). But for small towns or used in conjunction with street maps in big towns, this comprehensive guide should be useful.

It is available from Forsyth (below) for about $10 and from December to August in British bookshops and by mail from Hatchards (see under Books).

Forsyth Travel Library, ***9154 West 57th Street, P.O. Box 2975, Shawnee Mission, KS 66201. Telephone 913-384-3440; orders, 800-FORSYTH.***
Brochure, 25 cents in the U.S., free in Canada, published in February (no brochures available November to January).
MC, V.
Sells travel guides, books and maps.
Returns: money back for any reason within 14 days; after that "we sometimes receive merchandise returned because of a change in travel plans; we refund the merchandise but not the shipping costs."
Established 1976.

A good long list of mainstream guides (including popular series such as Baedeker, Berlitz, Fielding, Fodor, Frommer), many of which will be helpful to frugal travelers. Others such as *Ford's Freighter Travel Guide* and *Castle Hotels of Europe* won't be.

Nomadic Books, ***401 Northeast 45th Street, Seattle, WA 98105. Telephone 206-634-3453.***

Catalogue, free in the U.S. and Canada.
MC, V.
Sells budget-travel guides, books, maps and language books and tapes.
Returns: money back if books are returned in mint condition within ten days and with invoice number.
Established 1982.

Nomadic has a wonderfully useful catalogue of books for "independent budget travel," as they say, from the famous Lonely Planet guide to India through *Scottish Island Hopping* and *French Farm and Village Holiday Guide* to *Backpacking and Trekking in Peru and Bolivia* and *Work Your Way Around the World.* The books are well chosen and well described, so if you are planning an unusual trip, you are very likely to find one that is an inspiration and real help.

WATCHES

MAIL AND TELEPHONE SOURCES

You can save about 20% on most well-known watch brands if you buy through American low-price stores, and much more if you buy from abroad. If you are comparing prices, don't forget that many watches come in several versions—for instance, gold-plated or solid gold and with different straps. You may be able to compare prices using a model number (if there is a long model number divided with a dash or slash, the second half represents the type of strap). Full-price stores aren't usually willing to bother with model numbers, but the low-price stores that use catalogues to order watches will usually give you the model number and the list price as well as the discount price. In the course of my checking, I found that, unless they are having special sales, regular jewelers do seem to charge exactly the list price quoted to me by the low-price stores.

Most watch manufacturers produce brochures (see the list of manufacturers) and have New York offices that you can telephone for information.

There are manufacturers—Piaget and Rolex, for example—that restrict you to buying one or two watches by mail, although you may buy them abroad and wear them in.

Duty on watches is 10 to 12% of the price paid abroad (not the U.S. price).

The Amsterdam Airport Shopping Center, ***P.O. Box 7501, 1118 ZG Schiphol Airport, Holland. Telephone 20-517-24-97; Watch Shop, 20-17-59-36 and 20-17-69-63.*** *(Main listing in General section)*
Sells, among other things, jewelry by Cartier, President, Pisano and Mikimoto; watches by Baume & Mercier, Breitling, Cartier, Casio, Citizen, Cupillard Rieme, Edox, Eterna, Fiorucci, Longines, Omega, Roamer, Rolex, Seiko, Tudor, Tissot, Yves Saint Laurent.

Mikimoto cultured-pearl necklaces start at about $100; in New York, when I compared, they started at about $460. Watches cost about a third of New

York list prices (they only problem is that, as there is no proper catalogue, you'll have to ask for a price with a model number). For instance, the man's Rolex Datejust self-winding chronometer watch (model 16013-62523) cost $2675 plus tax at a posh jeweler's in New York and only $1786 at Schiphol when I compared.

U.S. and overseas model numbers were different on Omegas, so I couldn't compare exactly. However, New York Omega told me that Seamaster 120 Titanes with gold in the bracelet cost around $2500 in the United States, whereas at Schiphol Seamaster 120 Titanes with gold in the bracelet cost about $1000. New York Omega told me that the Omega Seamaster 120 Titanes without gold in the bracelet cost around $1300 in the United States. At Schiphol, they cost about $640 and $827 when I compared.

A. Andrews and Co., ***Mail Order Department, 38-44 D'Aguilar Street, 1/F (GPO Box 2938), Hong Kong. Telephone 5-26647.***
(Main listing in General section)

The whopping catalogue of this all-inclusive mail-order store has pages of watches, actually photographed and with model numbers, so this is a convenient place to buy watches at astounding prices. In the catalogue that I looked at, there were 108 Seikos costing mainly between $65 and $130 and smaller numbers of Citizen, Casio and Rolex. I compared prices on the Omega Constellation DD 393808643, and it cost about $200 less than the Schiphol price. The Rolex Datejust 16013-62523 cost $1526, including insurance and air parcel post to the United States. At the time, the full price in New York was $2675. Assuming you had been charged 12% duty, you still would have saved about $965 of the U.S. list price. When I wrote to ask for price quotes on specific watches, Andrews replied instantly with a well-organized letter that gave watch prices, insurance costs and air parcel post charges in Hong Kong dollars and U.S. dollars.

T. M. Chan and Co., ***P.O. Box 33881, Sheung Wan Post Office, Hong Kong. Telephone 5-496298. Office address: Flat B, Central Mansion, 14th floor, 270-276 Queen's Road C., Hong Kong.***
Free catalogue published in May.
Sells photographic equipment; Rolex and Seiko watches.
Returns: money back if goods are not in stock.
Established 1962.

This electronics firm answered my price inquiries promptly and in dollars. Prices were very similar to those of Andrews. The letter mentioned that the watches were in stock and could be mailed immediately. T. M. Chan has appeared in my other books, and I have never received a complaint about it.

47th St. Photo, ***36 East 19th Street, New York, NY 10003. Telephone 800-221-7774.***

(Main listing under Appliances and Electronics)
Sells jewelry and watches by Audemars Piguet, Cartier, Concord, Longines, Movado, Patek Philippe, Porsche, Rolex, Omega, Seiko and others.

When I compared prices, the woman's Movado Museum watch, electroplated in 14-karat gold, was selling at a Madison Avenue store for $285; at 47th St. it cost $199. However, 47th St. had no model numbers, so its model may have been an older one.

Lane Crawford, ***Lane Crawford House, Hong Kong. Telephone 5-241002.***
This well-known store with branches all over Hong Kong (it has been called the Hong Kong Harrods) replies promptly to questions about prices. Watch prices are far lower than those in the United States but about 5% higher than those at Andrews. The store gives the price in Hong Kong dollars and tells you how to convert to U.S. dollars.

Phillipus Company, ***Arcadian Shopping Center, Route 9, Ossining, NY 10562. Telephone 914-762-3300.***
Telephone for specific prices.
AE, MC, V.
Sells Concord, Longines, Movado, Rolex watches. Will special order other watches.
Returns: money back if goods returned within 14 days with receipt.
Established 1968.

Phillipus, a store that sells watches, china and glassware, stocks a few watches and will order any others upon receiving a deposit. It says that it gives roughly a 20% discount on all watches. When I asked about the Rolex Oyster Perpetual with oyster bracelet 1500-78350, Phillipus told me the list price was $1075 and its price was $800. At the same time, the Hong Kong price was about $662 and the Schiphol price, $689.

MANUFACTURERS' ADDRESSES

Manufacturers can provide accurate, up-to-date information on their products. The manufacturers listed below all sent me leaflets or brochures (without prices) when I requested them as a consumer. (When I wrote to the publicity departments as the writer of a shopping guide, almost none of them answered!)

Most manufacturers also have public relations departments that will answer questions by telephone. I have often called for more specific information than is in the brochures, and have been given all sorts of information by telephone. Maytag, for instance, helped me with price information when a repairman was quoting me outrageous prices for spare parts, Aiwa told me why my new tape recorder was squealing and two soothing people at RCA babied me through attaching my VCR to my television set and then fine-tuning the cable channels. More and more manufacturers are getting toll-free 800 numbers, so call 800-555-1212 to find out whether any manufacturer you want to telephone now has a toll-free number.

APPLIANCES

ADMIRAL, ***1701 East Woodfield Road, Schaumburg, IL 60196.***
Brochures for dehumidifiers, freezers, refrigerators and washer-dryers.

AMANA REFRIGERATION, ***Consumer Affairs, Amana, IA 52204.***
Catalogue of ovens, ranges, cooktops, refrigerators, freezers, washers, dryers, air conditioners.

BRAUN APPLIANCES, ***66 Broadway, Route 1, Lynnfield, MA 01940. Telephone 800-633-0035.***
Leaflets for handsomely designed kitchen and small personal-care appliances.

CALORIC, ***403 North Main Street, Topton, PA 19562-1499.***
Leaflets for gas and electric ranges and microwave ovens.

CARRIER, ***Consumer Relations, P.O. Box 4808, Carrier Broadway, Syracuse, NY 13221. Telephone 800-227-7437.***
Brochure of room air conditioners and full-line catalogue.

CUISINART, ***15 Valley Drive, Greenwich, CT 06836.***
Brochures for food processors and accessories, pots and pans, air surge ovens.

FARBERWARE, ***1500 Bassett Avenue, Bronx, NY 10461. Telephone 212-863-8000.***
Brochures for small electrical appliances and cookware.

FEDDERS, ***Effingham, IL 62401.***
Brochures for air conditioners.

FRIGIDAIRE, ***Consumer Services, P.O. Box 182056, Columbus, OH 43218.***
Catalogue of most appliances for washing, cooking and refrigeration, as well as trash compactors, food waste disposal units, air conditioners, dehumidifiers.

GENERAL ELECTRIC ANSWER CENTER, ***Telephone 800-626-2000.***
Brochures for major appliances such as washers, dryers, compactors, refrigerators, stoves, air conditioners; small appliances such as irons and hair dryers; television and video products.

GIBSON APPLIANCE CORPORATION, ***Telephone 800-245-0600.***
Catalogue of air conditioners, washers, dryers, refrigerators, freezers, ranges.

HAMILTON BEACH, ***95 Scoville Street, Waterbury, CT 06706.***
Catalogue of small electric kitchen appliances such as can openers, carving knives, coffee makers, mixers, food processors, toasters.

KITCHENAID, ***Consumer Affairs, 3800 Space Drive, Dayton, OH 45414. Telephone 800-422-1230.***

LITTON, ***Consumer Services, 4450 Mendenhall Road South, Memphis, TN 38101-9990.***
Leaflet for microwave ovens.

MAGIC CHEF, ***Customer Service, 740 King Edward Avenue, Cleveland, TN 37311. Telephone 615-472-3371.***
Brochures for refrigerators, freezers, washers, dryers, microwave ovens, ranges, cooktops, wall ovens, dishwashers.

MAYTAG, ***Information Center, 403 West 4th Street N, Newton, IA 50208. Telephone 515-792-7000 Ext. 8389.***
Brochures for dishwashers, gas ranges, food waste disposers, washers, dryers.

MODERN MAID, ***Advertising and Sales, 403 North Main Street, Topton, PA 19562-1499. Telephone 215-682-4211.***
Brochures for built-in ranges, cooktops and wall ovens, dishwashers, built-in toasters, waste disposers, trash compactors.

PROCTOR SILEX, ***Kitchen Collection, 71-87 East Water, Chillicothe, OH 45601. Telephone 614-773-9150.***
Brochures for Proctor Silex small appliances (irons, toasters, juicers) and Wear-Ever pots and pans.

SUNBEAM, ***Consumer Affairs, 1333 Butterfield Rd., Downers Grove, IL 60515.***
Catalogue of small household appliances such as irons, food processors, mixers, can openers; small personal appliances such as hair dryers, curlers, electric razors.

TAPPAN ADVERTISING, ***P.O. Box 606, Mansfield, OH 44901. Telephone 419-755-2011.***
Brochures for gas and electric ranges and microwave ovens.

TELEDYNE WATER PIK, ***1730 East Prospect Street, Fort Collins, CO 80525. Telephone 800-525-5302.***
Leaflets for Water Piks, electric toothbrushes, shower heads, water filters.

WARING PRODUCTS DIVISION, ***Dynamics Corporation of America, New Hartford, CT 06057.***
Brochure of small electric kitchen appliances such as blenders, can openers, ice cream makers, food dehydrators.

WEST BEND COMPANY, ***Division of Dart Industries, P.O. Box 278, R.R. 6, West Bend, WI 53095.***
Catalogue of small electric kitchen appliances such as kettles, buffet servers, woks, slow cookers, corn poppers, beverage makers, coffee makers, skillets.

WHIRLPOOL, ***Administrative Center, 2000 U.S. 33 North, Benton Harbor, MI 49022. Telephone 513-454-6803.***
Catalogue of ranges, ovens, cooktops, exhaust hoods, dishwashers, trash compactors, refrigerators, washers, dryers, air conditioners; Chambers and KitchenAid brochures.

WHITE-WESTINGHOUSE, ***Consumer Service, 300 Phillipi Road, Columbus, OH 43218. Telephone 800-245-0600.***
Brochures for refrigerators, freezers, ranges, microwave ovens, washers, dryers, air conditioners, humidifiers, dehumidifiers.

ELECTRONICS

AKAI, ***800 West Artesia Boulevard, P.O. Box 6010, Compton, CA 90224. Telephone 213-537-3880.***
Catalogue of audio components and brochures for video products.

CURTIS-MATHES CORPORATION, ***Customer Service, P.O. Box 223607, Dallas, TX 75222-0607. Telephone 214-659-1122.***
Spec sheets for televisions and VCRs.

HITACHI, ***Sales Department, 1290 Wall Street, Lyndhurst, NJ 07071. Telephone 201-935-8980.***
Brochures for radios, stereos, televisions and video equipment.

MAGNAVOX, ***Interstate 40 and Straw Plains Pike, P.O. Box 14810, Knoxville, TN 37914.***
Brochures for audio and video products.

MITSUBISHI, ***Customer Relations, 5757 Plaza Drive, P.O. Box 6007, Cypress, CA 90630-0007. Telephone 800-421-1140.***
Brochures for televisions, video equipment, compact disc players, audio components.

NAP CONSUMER ELECTRIC CORPORATION, ***Interstate 40 and Straw Plains Pike, P.O. Box 6950, Knoxville, TN 37914.***
Brochures for televisions, VCRs and stereos by Magnavox, Philco and Sylvania.

PANASONIC CORPORATION OF AMERICA, ***One Panasonic Way, Secaucus, NJ 07094.***
Brochures for Technics audio components and Panasonic VCRs, televisions, radios, tape recorders, telephones, microwave products.

QUASAR COMPANY, ***9401 West Grand Avenue, Franklin Park, IL 60131. Telephone 312-451-1200.***
Brochures for televisions, VCRs, audio systems, cassette recorders, microwave ovens.

RCA, ***Consumer Relations, P.O. Box 1976, Indianapolis, IN 46201. Telephone 317-267-6445.***

SANYO ELECTRIC, ***1200 West Artesia Boulevard, P.O. Box 5177, Compton, CA 90220.***
List of dealers around the country, who will give out brochures for Sanyo products.

SONY NATIONAL INFORMATION CENTER, ***Telephone 800-222-SONY. I've had such trouble getting through using this toll-free number that I'm including an address and regular number as well: Sony, Sony Drive, Park Ridge, NJ 07656, 201-930-1000.***
Brochures for audio, television and video products.

TOSHIBA AMERICA, ***Advertising and Public Relations Department, 82 Totowa Road, Wayne, NJ 07470. Telephone 201-628-8000.***
Brochures for televisions, VCRs, radios, tape recorders, stereo systems, telephone-answering machines, kitchen appliances and vacuum cleaners.

ZENITH, ***Public Relations Department, 1000 Milwaukee Avenue, Glenview, IL 60025.***
Brochures for televisions and VCRs.

FLATWARE AND SILVER

CHRISTOFLE SILVER, ***680 Madison Avenue, New York, NY 10022. Telephone 212-308-9390.***
Free silver plate brochure.

GORHAM, ***Att. Live the Gorham Life, 333 Adelaide Avenue, Providence, RI 02907. Telephone 401-785-9800.***
General brochure summarizing lines and brochures for flatware, holloware, sterling and silver plate.

GEORG JENSEN SILVERSMITH, ***683 Madison Avenue, New York, NY 10021. Telephone 800-223-1275 or 212-759-6457.***
Free Georg Jensen silverware and Royal Copenhagen porcelain catalogues.

KIRK-STEIFF, ***800 Wyman Park Drive, Baltimore, MD 21211. Telephone 301-338-6000.***
Brochure, $5 by mail or free from dealers in each state.

ONEIDA SAMPLE CENTER, ***Oneida, NY 13421. Telephone 315-684-6860.***
Brochure.

REED AND BARTON, ***144 West Britannia Street, Taunton, MA 02780. Telephone 617-824-6611.***
Leaflets for stainless steel, silver plate and silver flatware.

WALLACE INTERNATIONAL SILVERSMITHS, ***15 Sterling Drive, Wallingford, CT 06492. Telephone 203-269-4401.***
Leaflets for silver, silver plate and stainless steel flatware.

FURNITURE

Furniture catalogues usually cost between $3 and $10 each.

BAKER FURNITURE LIBRARY, ***Publications, 1661 Monroe Avenue, Grand Rapids, MI 49505. Telephone 616-361-7321.***
List of brochures and catalogues for sale. (Living room, bedroom, dining room and occasional furniture in several styles, as well as reproduction furniture.)

DREXEL HERITAGE FURNISHINGS, ***Drexel, NC 28619. Telephone 704-433-3151.***
Will not send a catalogue—will send a booklet on the perils of buying from unauthorized dealers—but will send a list of authorized dealers in your area so that you can go and look at the furniture for yourself.

HEKMAN FURNITURE, ***1400 Buchanan SW, Grand Rapids, MI 49507. Telephone 616-452-1411.***
Catalogue and leaflets for sale.

HENREDON FURNITURE INDUSTRIES, ***Advertising Department, P.O. Box 70, Morganton, NC 28655.***
List of furniture catalogues for sale. Living room, dining room and bedroom furniture in several styles.

HICKORY MANUFACTURING COMPANY, ***Customer Service Department, Box 998, Hickory, NC 28603. Telephone 704-322-8624.***
List of furniture catalogues for sale.

THE LANE COMPANY, ***Altavista, VA 24517-0151. Telephone 804-369-5641.***
Catalogue of bedrooms and dining room sets, cedar chests, occasional table groups, upholstered pieces, recliners. Catalogue is not free; ask for the current price.

STIFFEL, ***700 North Kingsbury Street, Chicago, IL 60610. Telephone 312-664-9200.***
Lamp catalogue for sale; check current price.

THOMASVILLE FURNITURE INDUSTRIES, ***P.O. Box 339, Thomasville, NC 27361. Telephone 800-225-0265.***
Free leaflets and list of catalogues for sale.

WHITE FURNITURE COMPANY, ***Mebane, NC 27302.***
Catalogue.

WILDWOOD LAMPS, ***P.O. Box 671, Rocky Mount, NC 27802-0671. Telephone 919-977-1577.***
List of lamp, import and screen catalogues for sale.

OUTDOOR FURNITURE

BROWN JORDAN, ***P.O. Box 1817, 1305 Progress Road, Suffolk, VA 23434. Telephone 804-934-3101.***
Outdoor furniture in several styles and materials. Catalogue is not free; check current price.

TROPITONE FURNITURE COMPANY, ***P.O. Box 3197, Sarasota, FL 33578, or 5 Marconi, Irvine, CA 92718.***
Catalogue is not free; check current price.

LUGGAGE

AMERICAN TOURISTER, ***Consumer Relations, 91 Main Street, Warren, RI 02885. Telephone 401-245-2100.***

ANDIAMO, ***Customer Service, 11520 Warner Avenue, Fountain Valley, CA 92708. Telephone 714-751-8711.***
Brochure available.

LARK LUGGAGE COMPANY, ***P.O. Box 39004, Denver, CO 80239. Telephone 303-373-6200.***
Leaflets and price list available.

WINGS LUGGAGE, ***379 Fifth Avenue, New York, NY 10016. Telephone 212-532-0566.***
Leaflets available.

PENS

PARKER PEN COMPANY, ***One Parker Place, Janesville, WI 53547. Telephone 608-755-7000.***
Pages illustrating fountain pens, ballpoints, pencils.

PHOTOGRAPHIC EQUIPMENT

CANON, ***1 Jericho Plaza, Jericho, NY 11753-1679. Telephone 516-933-6300.***
Brochure available.

HASSELBLAD, ***Product Catalogue, 10 Madison Road, Fairfield, NJ 07006. Telephone 201-227-7320.***
Brochure available.

KODAK, ***Photo Information, Eastman Kodak, Dept. 841, Building 6, 800 Lee Road, Rochester, NY 14650. Telephone 800-242-2424.***
Camera selling sheet available.

LEICA, ***Leitz Inc., 24 Link Drive, Rockleigh, NJ 07647. Telephone 201-767-1100.***
Separate brochures for their two cameras and accessories and lenses.

MINOLTA, ***Att. Consumer Relations, 101 Williams Drive, Ramsey, NJ 07446. Telephone 201-825-4000.***
Main catalogue and different brochures for different types of cameras and for lenses.

NIKON, ***Att. Consumer Relations, 623 Stewart Avenue, Garden City, NY 11530. Telephone 516-222-0200.***
Leaflets for lenses and cameras.

OLYMPUS, ***Advertising Department, Consumer Products Group, Crossways Park, Woodbury, NY 11797. Telephone 516-364-3000.***
OM systems brochure available.

PENTAX, ***Service Department, 1101 Stewart Avenue, Garden City, NY 11530. Telephone 516-222-0830.***
Literature on complete line of cameras or brochures for individual cameras available.

TELEPHONES

PANASONIC, ***One Panasonic Way, Secaucus, NJ 07094.***
Electronics brochure includes telephones and accessories.

WEBCOR ELECTRONICS, ***Att. Public Relations, 103 Charles Lindbergh Boulevard, Garden City, NY 11530. Telephone 516-794-6200.***
Catalogue of telephones.

TOOLS

BLACK AND DECKER, ***Customer Service, 710 North Park Drive, Huntvalley, MD 21030. Telephone 301-683-7100.***

MILWAUKEE ELECTRIC TOOL CORPORATION, ***13135 West Lisbon Road, Brookfield, WI 53005. Telephone 414-781-3600.***

WATCHES

AUDEMARS PIGUET, ***Att. Sales Department, 350 Fifth Avenue, Suite 7712, New York, NY 10118.***

BAUME & MERCIER, ***663 Fifth Avenue, New York, NY 10024.***
Brochure for sale; check current price.

BULOVA, ***Bulova Park, Flushing, NY 11370.***

CARTIER, ***Fifth Avenue and East 52nd Street, New York, NY 10017. Telephone 212-753-0111.***
Free brochure.

CONCORD WATCH CORP., ***650 Fifth Avenue, New York, NY 10019. Telephone 212-397-7800.***
Catalogue, $2 by mail or pick up free.

CONSUL WATCHES, ***P.O. Box 1245, Englewood Cliffs, NJ 07632. Telephone 201-568-4920.***
Leaflet available.

EBEL U.S.A. WATCHES, ***Merchandising Department, 570 Fifth Avenue, New York, NY 10036. Telephone 212-944-5757.***
Brochure available.

GIRARD-PERREGAUX, ***580 Sylvan Avenue, Englewood Cliffs, NJ 07632. Telephone 201-568-4920.***
Catalogue, $3.

INTERNATIONAL WATCH, ***580 Fifth Avenue, New York, NY 10036. Telephone 212-354-7500.***
Brochure available.

LONGINES-WITTNAUER WATCH COMPANY, ***145 Huguenot Street, New Rochelle, NY 10802. Telephone 914-576-1000.***
Brochure available.

MOVADO, ***650 Fifth Avenue, New York, NY 10019. Telephone 212-397-7800.***
Brochure, $2.

OMEGA, ***Consumer Relations Department, Omega Building, 301 East 57th Street, New York, NY 10022. Telephone 212-753-3000.***
Free catalogue.

PATEK PHILIPPE, ***10 Rockefeller Plaza, New York, NY 10020. Telephone 212-581-0870.***
Brochure, $5.

PIAGET, ***650 Fifth Avenue, New York, NY 10019.***
Brochure, $5.

ROLEX WATCH CORP., ***665 Fifth Avenue, New York, NY 10022. Telephone 212-758-7700.***
Brochure available.

SEIKO, ***640 Fifth Avenue, New York, NY 10019. Telephone 212-977-2800.***
Brochure of best-selling watches available.

UNIVERSAL GENEVE WATCHES, ***501 Madison Avenue, New York, NY 10022. Telephone 212-752-4848.***
Brochure available.

VACHERON AND CONSTANTIN, ***608 Fifth Avenue, New York, NY 10020. Telephone 212-757-3152.***
Brochure available.

PARALLEL OR DIRECT IMPORTS (A.K.A. "GRAY" MARKET)

"Gray" market goods are intended by the manufacturers to be sold outside the United States. Some manufactured goods are less expensive in other countries, especially when the dollar is strong, so some U.S. stores find it cheaper to buy foreign-made products abroad than pay the higher prices that are charged by manufacturers' authorized U.S. dealers. Cameras especially, but also electronics and cars, are imported "directly."

Direct importing is legal and has the welcome effect of making the market more competitive and lowering prices. One store owner quoted in the *Wall Street Journal* said, "It's really up to the manufacturers, if they wanted to they could solve the problem tomorrow simply by making the price here the same as it is in Europe."

However, there are possible problems for the buyer of a direct import: there will probably be no manufacturer's warranty, and instructions may be in another language.

New York stores, because they are highly price competitive, often sell directly imported goods. Since October 1985, a New York State Legislature statute that applies to retailers selling direct imports has been in effect. It states that retailers must disclose, if it's the case, that a product has no manufacturer's warranty valid in the United States. If the retailer offers a store warranty, he or she does not have to mention the lack of manufacturer's warranty. The retailer must also warn customers when the merchandise is not accompanied by instructions in English. A customer who has not been informed is entitled to a refund within 20 days. The offending store may be fined $500.

If you ever buy a product that lacks a manufacturer's warranty or instructions in English, or that has any other defect that you feel the retailer should have told you about, from a state that does not adhere to the above statute, you can complain first to the store and then to the addresses below (see the appendix on dealing with problems) that the retailer withheld "material information."

PAYING

AMERICAN READERS

Credit Cards. I prefer this way of paying, as it involves the least trouble. More details on credit cards are given in the credit card appendix.

Personal Checks. They save a trip to the bank and can be used to pay most American and foreign stores. However, personal checks can hold an order up, as most stores wait until your check has cleared (which can take up to four weeks overseas). Foreign banks will charge the recipient about $4 for converting from dollars, so if the check is for a small amount, better add $4. Never pay for a catalogue with a personal check; with such a small amount, the shop will receive less than nothing after paying bank charges.

Certified or Cashier's Checks (Bank). These can be used to speed payment but only within the United States. At your own bank, you make out a personal check, and the bank stamps it signifying a guarantee that money will be held in your account to clear the check. Once the check has been paid, it is returned to you, just as other personal checks are, so you have proof the money was paid out. My bank charges $6 for a certified check.

Money Orders (Bank). These can also be used within the United States to speed payment. At any bank, you buy a money order for the correct amount, write in the name of the store and mail it. As the money order has been paid for, the store can cash it immediately. The duplicate you receive when buying the money order is proof that you bought it, but you do not get proof that it has been cashed. My bank charges $2 for a money order.

International Money Orders or Checks (Bank). Fill out a form at the bank, and you will be given an international money order (it may be called an international check at your bank) to mail to the store. There is no delay at the other end, and your bank will work out the exact rate of exchange for you. My bank charges $4 for an international money order.

Cable Transfers (Bank). Banks claim this takes two working days. In my experience it usually takes a little longer. If you know the bank and account number of the store you are buying from, the money can be delivered directly.

Otherwise your bank chooses a bank near the store and notifies the store that the money is there. My bank charges $20 for a cable transfer.

Money Orders (Post Office). To send money within the United States, you can buy a money order at the post office for any amount between $1 and $700 and send it yourself. Charges are 75 cents for sums up to $25, and $1 for $25.01 to $700. People on rural routes can avoid a trip to the post office by having their postman buy the money orders for them.

International Money Orders (Post Office). To send money abroad, you can buy at the post office an international money order made out to the store you are dealing with. The post office mails the order in the right currency, and you get a receipt. It costs $2.

CANADIAN AND BRITISH READERS

Personal Checks. These are unpopular with and not accepted by most American firms, as they are slow to clear and the bank charges the recipient about $4 for converting to U.S. currency. Firms in other countries seem to be less fussy, although most do wait for the checks to clear (up to four weeks). Add $4 for the bank charges the recipient will have to pay.

Bank Drafts. This is the best way to pay. At any bank, buy a foreign currency bank draft for the right amount in the right currency and mail it yourself. The store can cash it immediately.

Cable Transfers. Your bank puts the money straight into the store's account (if you know the bank branch and account number) or into a nearby bank and lets the store know by cable that it is there. This method is speedy but pricey.

Post Office Money Orders. At the post office you can buy a foreign currency money order, but this is sent by the post office, so it arrives inconveniently separated from your own letter to the store.

AUSTRALIAN READERS

Bank Drafts. These can be bought at the bank in foreign currency. They are inexpensive and the best way to send money abroad. For greater speed, the bank can send a cable transfer.

CREDIT CARDS

ADVANTAGES

There is an advantage to paying for merchandise with a credit card instead of with a check or cash. The Fair Credit Billing Act rules that if you buy something within your own state or within a hundred miles of your home with a credit card that is "not delivered as agreed," you can not be charged for it. This act protects you in case of a mistake (your sofa arrives but it's the wrong color) but not in case of a dispute over quality.

To protect your rights in these cases, you must first contact the store owner. If he or she doesn't settle the matter to your liking, *write* (don't telephone) the bank that issues your card within 60 days of the "billing error."

An advantage of using MasterCard and Visa for foreign transactions is that MasterCard and Visa policy on currency conversion is to use the interbank rate. The interbank rate is the wholesale rate banks charge each other for transactions of at least $1 million. (It is the interbank rate that newspapers print—the previous day's lowest wholesale rate.) This is lower (and better for the card holder) than the rates you'll get anywhere else—banks, hotels or foreign exchange specialists. MasterCard has a new policy as of March 1, 1986: instead of the initiating (the store owner's) bank doing the conversion, MasterCard will do it and make no profit at all. With Visa it is still the store owner's bank that sets the currency exchange rate, but Visa's policy is to give card holders the interbank rate with a charge of one-quarter of one percent. If you ever think you have been overcharged on a Visa currency conversion, ask the bank that issues your card to contact the store owner's bank for an adjustment. This is also worth remembering when traveling.

CHOOSING A CARD

Bankcard Holders of America says that it is important to look at your own shopping habits when choosing a credit card. If you pay your credit card bills *in full* every month (i.e., you don't borrow money), then, of course, you are not charged interest, and the interest rate of your card is unimportant. In this case you should get your MasterCard or Visa from a bank that has no annual fee (Bankcard Holders of America has a list of these).

However, if you don't pay your credit card bill in full every month, then you should definitely look around for banks that offer cards at low interest rates. *Consumer Reports* found in a survey of 133 bank credit cards (reported in the January 1985 issue) that the interest rates banks charge differ widely. At the time of the survey, the country's ten largest banks charged from 18.8 to 20.4% interest on card holders' unpaid balances, whereas some smaller banks offered rates as low as 13 to 17%.

BANKCARD HOLDERS OF AMERICA (Consumer Action Agency), ***333 Pennsylvania Avenue SE, Washington, DC 20003. Telephone 202-543-5805.***
Free publication list.
Membership fee: $12 per year.
Established 1980.

This nonprofit organization was started by an ex-congressman who saw that, what with Reagan and company cutting back government funding, an independent organization was needed to inform consumers about credit.

BHA sells leaflets that are plenty of help if you are choosing a credit card: a short list of a few of the banks that give out credit cards without charging an annual fee costs $1.95, and a list of banks that have credit cards with a low interest rate costs $1.

BHA also sells pamphlets on subjects such as the differences between various types of credit cards; how to establish a credit history if you are a recent graduate or divorced woman; and what your rights are under the Equal Credit Opportunity Act and the Fair Credit Billing Act. BHA also has a hotline for members' questions.

FEDERAL TRADE COMMISSION, ***Public Reference Branch, Sixth Street and Pennsylvania Avenue NW, Washington, DC 20580. Telephone 202-523-3598.***

The FTC gives out several useful leaflets, similar to Bankcard Holders' but free: "Fair Credit Billing" describes your rights as a card owner and what to do in disputes over billing; "Equal Credit Opportunity" explains your rights in applying for credit and what to do if you suspect you are being discriminated against; "Women and Credit Histories" tells how to get credit if you are having difficulties because you have no credit history.

SHIPPING FROM ABROAD

MAIL

Most parcels can be delivered exactly as domestic parcels are, and this is by far the easiest method for anyone who doesn't live inside an airport. If there is any duty, it is paid to the postman along with a $2.50 duty-handling charge, which the post office calls "postage due." However, there is a limit to the size and weight of a parcel that can be shipped by mail—it must not weigh more than 22 pounds, and the length and circumference of the parcel must not add up to more than 72 inches. This means that the length of the parcel is measured in the usual way, but the width is measured with tape right around the parcel.

AIRFREIGHT

This method is used mainly for single objects that are too large to go by mail—audio equipment and such. Cargo of any size can be sent by airfreight and is charged according to weight, volume and distance (there is a minimum charge). The goods arrive at the airport nearest your address that has customs facilities, and you are notified of the arrival. You then go with identification and the bill from the store (for customs) to the airport during office hours and see the parcel through customs (storage is charged if you don't go within five working days). If you want to employ a broker to get the parcel through customs, the airline can give you a list of firms.

SEAFREIGHT

This method is for large items such as furniture, and collecting your purchases is a nuisance. Some stores will arrange delivery all the way to your door by an agency; others just arrange delivery to your nearest port. If merchandise is delivered to a port, the steamship company will tell you when it arrives. You can then call a trucking firm to see it through customs and deliver it to your door, or you can save the flat fee of about $100 and get the goods through customs yourself. If you do it yourself, you take the bill of lading and the bill for the furniture, both of which the store will have sent you, and go to the steamship company to have the bill of lading stamped; then you go to the customs house. Your crate will probably be opened, inspected and closed again, and you pay the duty. Then, with a certificate of clearance, you or your truckers can take the goods away.

AVOIDING AND DEALING WITH PROBLEMS

AVOIDING PROBLEMS

Before trying a new firm, you can check on the firm's reputation with various offices. Better Business Bureaus around the country keep records of complaints against firms within their area. Some state, county and city government consumer protection offices also keep records of complaints. The best place to get BBB and consumer protection addresses is from the U.S. Government's bursting-with-useful-information ***Consumer's Resource Handbook,*** available free from ***Handbook, Consumer Information Center, Pueblo, CO 81009.*** Produced by the U.S. Office of Consumer Affairs, the handbook has instructions on how to complain, addresses of Better Business Bureaus and government protection offices around the country and many other useful government and corporate addresses.

You can get a free directory with only BBB addresses from **THE COUNCIL OF BETTER BUSINESS BUREAUS,** ***1515 Wilson Boulevard, Arlington, VA 22209. Telephone 703-276-0100.***

DEALING WITH PROBLEMS

Most people hate complaining and returning goods and so do I, but I still think it's a good thing to keep companies on their toes, and it can be profitable too. I got $50 by complaining to White-Westinghouse that it had sent two repairmen (and charged me $50 for the second) for my clothes washer, when only one was needed. My husband got a $50 credit by complaining to United Airlines when it made him miss a connecting flight in Denver. And my friend Felicity got two free meals *and* a promise that the restaurant would send the price of the original meals to an organization to help the starving when she complained that she and her beau suffered (mild) food poisoning.

If you have a problem with a firm, first contact it (if you write to the firm, *keep a copy of your letter*). Give it a brief description of your problem and what you would like done about it (new merchandise or money back). Also send a copy (never the original) of your check, money order or credit card slip. Then contact whichever of the places listed below seems appropriate:

Better Business Bureaus will mediate between consumers and both local and mail-order firms and keep a record of complaints against firms. **THE BETTER BUSINESS BUREAU OF METROPOLITAN NEW YORK** is at ***257 Park Avenue South, New York, NY 10010, telephone 212-533-6200.*** Addresses of the other bureaus are in the U.S. Government's free *Consumer's Resource Handbook* (address above).

THE BUREAU OF CONSUMER PROTECTION, ***Federal Trade Commission, Washington, DC 20508,*** will forward your letter to the offending firm but, apart from that, does not deal with individual cases. It gathers records of, investigates and sometimes takes to court firms about which there are many complaints.

State, county and city government protection offices. There are government consumer protection offices in every state plus some counties and cities as well. They are quite often placed in the state attorney general's office, but may be in a mayor's office, governor's office or elsewhere. What the office will do varies according to the state and budget. If there are several offices in your area, find out which one helps resolve complaints. Many offices will "mediate," as it's called, i.e., contact the offending firm for you. If your local office (or, in the case of a mail-order problem, the firm's local office) *will* mediate, it is said to be a good place to get results. Some offices keep records of complaints against firms and give out information of various kinds. See below to find out how I fared at the hands of two consumer protection offices.

Mail-Order Problems Only

Your problem is the post office's responsibility, even if you ordered by telephone, *if* you ordered from a catalogue that arrived by mail. The Washington headquarters will forward your complaint to the Postal Inspector nearest the offending firm, and he or she will contact the firm. The post office claims to be good at resolving complaints because it can withhold mail from misbehaving firms. Contact: **CHIEF POSTAL INSPECTOR,** ***United States Postal Service, Washington, DC 20260.***

MAIL ORDER ACTION LINE, ***Direct Marketing Association, 6 East 43rd Street, New York, NY 10017, telephone 212-689-4977,*** will also complain for you to the offending firm. DMA keeps a list of firms with unresolved complaints against them.

Complaining to the Media

I found out about this organization because someone complained to it about *me.* (A Chicagoan turned me in for not sending a book she'd ordered. I wasn't trying to cheat her, I swear—I'd misaddressed the parcel.) Twenty-three TV and radio stations around the country are affiliated with the **Call for Action** network. Through it trained volunteers give advice to people entangled in red tape "with veterans' benefits, Social Security, utilities, Medicare." They also try to get consumer complaints resolved and are said to be quite effective (they certainly got me hopping). The hitch is that some affiliates can't handle all the complaints they get, so they have to choose the most serious or the most representative. To get a list of affiliates, write to: **CALL FOR ACTION NATIONAL OFFICE,** ***575 Lexington Avenue, New York, NY 10022. Telephone 212-355-5965.***

My Own Adventures

New York State is strong on consumer protection and has many offices. At one point I tried three.

Some offices will forward your letter of complaint to the offending firm and, if the complaint is not settled, will advise you on how to proceed. For example, I complained to the New York City Bureau of Consumer Protection about a washing machine repairman who I thought had overcharged me (the final bill was huge). My complaints were (a) that he had claimed to have replaced two parts, whereas I claimed he had just fixed the old ones, and (b) that he had charged for cleaning my filter, whereas I thought he was just doing it out of the kindness of his heart (as my previous repairman had). In New York State, repairmen are supposed to give a written estimate before starting work.

Seven weeks after writing to the Bureau of Consumer Protection, I got a form letter saying that the bureau would forward my letter to the repairman. Six weeks after that I got another form letter from the bureau saying that "the company has refused to make any refund or other adjustment" and that the bureau was unable to assist me further because "your complaint basically involves a disagreement between you and the merchant regarding what occurred." The bureau advised me to go to an attorney for advice or go to small claims court. I was actually quite contented with this advice (which I didn't follow) because when the repairman made his third visit to fix the same problem and left his third huge bill, I was away. He left the bill with my daughter, I never paid it and I think he never asked me to because of the bureau's involvement.

I also complained about the washing machine repairman to a state Office of Consumer Protection. Nineteen days later I got a personal letter from the Director of the Office of Consumer Protection near the repairman's post office box. The director advised me that if I wished to take the matter to small claims court, it should be done in New York City. "I question, however, whether you would be successful." Quite useful advice, I thought.

When I complained to the New York City Better Business Bureau about my washing machine repairman, my letter was forwarded to the repairman's district. Six days after I wrote, that BBB office sent me the BBB complaint form with a letter saying that "the BBB cannot become involved in disputes concerning prices charged for products or services. Therefore, the part of your complaint about being 'overcharged' cannot be included on the form, except as it applies to work not done." All perfectly reasonable, but I procrastinated, never filled out the form and so cannot report whether the BBB would have been effective.

CLOTHING SIZE CHARTS

Since clothing sizes vary according to the manufacturer, always add measurements.

Dresses, Knitwear, Lingerie

British	10	12	14	16	18	20	22	24	26
United States	8	10	12	14	16	18	20	22	24
Continental	38	40	42	44	46/48	50			
*Inches	32/34	34/36	36/38	38/40	40/42	42/44			
*Centimeters	81/86	86/91	91/96	96/102	102/107	107/112			

Women's Hosiery

British and United States	8	8½	9	9½	10	10½	11
Continental	0	1	2	3	4	5	6

Men's Shirts (collar sizes)

British	14	14½	15	15½	16	16½	17	17½
United States	14	14½	15	15½	15¾	16	16½	17
Continental	36	37	38	39	40	41	42	43

Men's and Women's Shoes

British	3	3½	4	4½	5	5½	6	6½	7	7½	8	8½	9	9½	10	10½
United States	4½	5	5½	6	6½	7	7½	8	8½	9	9½	10	10½	11	11½	12
Continental	36	—	37	—	38	—	39	—	40	—	41	—	42	—		

* The numbers in inches and centimeters refer to the bust and hip measurements, respectively.

METRIC CONVERSIONS

Length

1 inch	2.54	cm
1 foot	.30	m
1 yard	.91	m
1 mile	1.61	km
1 millimeter (mm)	.039	in.
1 centimeter (cm)	.39	in.
1 meter (m)	3.28	feet
1 kilometer	.62	mile

To convert kilometers to miles, divide the number of kilometers by 8 and multiply the result by 5.

Weight

1 gram	.04	ounce
1 kilogram	2.2	pounds
1 ounce	28.35	grams
1 pound	.45	kilograms
1 ton	.91	metric tons

Liquid

1 liter	1.06	quarts
1 quart	.95	liters

CUSTOMS CHARGES

DUTY IN THE UNITED STATES

Returning U.S. residents who have been away for 48 hours or more receive an exemption from duty of $400 on personal and household goods obtained abroad and brought back with them. The next $1000 worth of purchases and gifts is dutiable at a flat rate of 10%.

In addition, most articles—including alcoholic beverages, cigars, cigarettes and perfume—made in certain designated Caribbean and Central American countries are admitted duty-free under the Caribbean Recovery Act. Certain articles from developing countries may also enter the United States duty-free under the Generalized System of Preferences (GSP).

Duty is being gradually reduced in most categories. For up-to-date information on duty, ask your nearest Customs District Office or write or telephone the **OFFICE OF INFORMATION AND PUBLICATIONS, BUREAU OF CUSTOMS,** ***U.S. Treasury Department, Washington, DC 20026, telephone 202-566-8181.*** This office sends out a **"List of Duty Rates on Most Popular Overseas Purchases"** and other useful free leaflets:

"Know Before You Go" gives general information about what is and is not allowed into the country and gives telephone numbers for 43 Customs District Offices around the country.

"GSP and the Traveler" gives a long list of developing countries (including countries such as India and Mexico) whose "popular tourist items" are allowed into the United States free of duty.

"Import Requirements" explains regulations to people importing for their own personal use, as well as people thinking of going into an importing business.

"Importing a Car" explains regulations and gives advice to people thinking of bringing a foreign-made car into the United States.

"Trademark Information" lists certain foreign articles bearing "prohibited" trademarks recorded in the Treasury Department, such as certain perfumes, cameras, watches and audio equipment that must not be brought into the country with the trademark on. However, it is perfectly legal to bring in the articles with their trademarks removed. If you want to bring something in that has an import-restricted trademark, you can do one of two things: you can ask the shop you buy the article from to remove the trademark, or you can wait until it arrives and is inspected by U.S. customs officers. If they feel it is necessary, a form declaring that you agree to remove the trademark yourself will be sent for you to sign. After signing the form, you mail it back, and the merchandise will be forwarded to you in the normal way.

Here is a list of approximate U.S. Customs Charges for 1987.

LIST OF U.S. CUSTOMS CHARGES 1987

Automobiles:
Passenger—2.5%.
Bags:
Hand, leather—5.3–10%.
Beads:
Imitation precious and semiprecious stone—4.7–6.7%.
Ivory—4%.
Binoculars (prism), opera and field glasses: Free.
Books: Free.
Cameras:
Motion picture, over $50 each—3.8%.
Still, over $10 each—3.0%.
*Cases, leather—5.8%.
Lenses, mounted—6.6%.
China other than tableware:
Bone—6.6%.
Nonbone—2.1–9%.
China tableware:
Bone—8%.
Nonbone, valued not over $56 per set—26%.
Nonbone, valued over $56 per set—8%.
Cigarette lighters:
Pocket—7.2–10%.
Table—4.8%.
Clocks:
Valued over $5 but not over $10 each—30¢ + 6.4%.
Valued over $10 each—45¢ + 6.4%.
Crystal: 6%.
Dolls:
Stuffed—Free.
Other—12%.
Drawings, done by hand: Free.
Figurines, china: 9%.
By professional sculptor—3.1%.
Film:
Unexposed—3.7%.
Exposed—Free.

Fur:
Wearing apparel—5.3–7.4%.
Other—3.4–7.4%.
Furniture:
Wood chairs—3.4–5.3%.
Other than chairs—2.5%.
Bentwood—6.6%.
Gloves:
Fur—4%.
Horsehide or cowhide—15%.
Handkerchiefs, linen, hemmed: 5.5%.
Ivory, manufactured: 4.2%.
Jade:
Cut, but not set, suitable for jewelry—2.1%.
Articles of jade—21%.
Jewelry, precious metal:
Silver constituting chief value, valued not over $18 for twelve—27.5%.
Other—6.5%.
Leather:
Flat goods, wallets—4.7–8%.
Other—Free–5.3%.
Music boxes: 3.2%.
Paintings, done entirely by hand: Free.
Pearls:
Loose or temporarily strung without clasp
Natural—Free.
Cultured—2.1%.
Imitation—8%.
Permanently strung or temporarily strung with clasp attached
or separate—6.5–11%.
Perfume: 4.9%.
Postage stamps: Free.
Printed matter: Free–5.3%.
Radios, solid-state radio receivers: 6%.
Shavers, electric: 3.1%.
Shell articles: 3.4%.
Shoes, leather: 2.5–20%.
Skis and ski equipment: 3.5–5.5%.
Sound recordings: Free.
Stones, cut but not set:
Diamonds—Free.
Others—Free–2.1%.
Sweaters, wool: 7.5–25.5%.
Tape recorders: 3.9%.
Toys: 7%.
Watches:
Mechanical-type—(depending on jewels) plus
Digital-type—3.9%.
Gold case—6%.
Gold bracelet—14%.

Wearing apparel:
Embroidered or ornamented—8–35%.
Cotton and linen—3%.
Man-made fiber, knit—3¢/lb. + 19.2%–13¢/lb. + 32.5%.
Man-made fiber, not knit—3¢/lb. + 15.1%–14¢/lb. + 27.5%.
Silk, not knit—7.5%.
Wool, knit—7.5–23%.
Wool, not knit—9.5%–24¢/lb. + 21%.
Wood, carvings and articles of: 5.1%.

*Cases imported with camera are classifiable with the camera.

DUTY IN CANADA

Canada has different rates of duty, depending on the country the merchandise comes from: one for "Most Favored Nations," which includes the United States, lower rates for Britain and the Commonwealth and undeveloped countries and another rate for "general." Besides duty, most incoming goods are charged a federal sales tax of 11%.

Canada has regional customs offices in Calgary, Halifax, Hamilton, London, Montreal, Quebec, Regina, Toronto, Windsor and Winnipeg and a marvelously helpful office that will tell you by telephone or mail the exact duty for anything you are thinking of importing: **CUSTOMS AND EXCISE INFORMATION UNIT,** ***360 Coventary Road, Ottawa, Ontario K1K 2C6, Canada. Telephone 613-993-0534.***

Here is a list of approximate Canadian duty on goods imported from the United States in 1986. Sales tax is also charged unless noted.

Appliances:
Large (refrigerators, washing machines, etc.)—14.2%.
Small (can openers, irons, sewing machines, etc.)—generally 13% but can range from free for popcorn makers to 16%.
Audio equipment—11%.
Video equipment—8.9%.
Typewriters—2.6%.
Books: no duty or sales tax.
Cameras: 10%.
China:
Dinner sets—12.4%.
Figurines—11.1%.
Clothes:
Cotton—32.5%, no sales tax.
Silk—20.4%, no sales tax.
Synthetic—20.8%, no sales tax.
Wool—25%, no sales tax.
Cosmetics and perfume: 13.4%.

Flatware:
Silver—12.4%.
Stainless-steel—18.4%.
Linens (sheets, tablecloths, etc):
Over 50% cotton—22.5%.
Over 50% synthetic—25%.
Records: 15%.
Toys and games: 13%.
Shoes: 23.1%, no sales tax.
Sports equipment:
Baseball—12.4%.
Golf clubs—13%.
Fishing rods—11.1%.
Tennis rackets—12.4%.
Tents—25%.

DUTY IN BRITAIN

For up-to-date information on duty and VAT payable on goods from the United States and other countries (rates differ according to country), contact your nearest customs and excise office or the **Secretary, HM Customs and Excise, King's Beam House, Mark Lane, London EC3R 7HE.**

INDEX

AAA All Factory Vacuum Cleaner Service Center, 13
Absolute Sound, 25
Ace Leather Products, 189
air conditioners, 11–15
airplane tickets, 285–293
Air Systems, 290
Al's Luggage, 190
Allan Tom and Co. Burlington Arcade Shop "L", 50
Allnet, 275
Altenberg Piano House, 197
Aly's Hut, 64
America's Pharmacy, 135
American Association of Retired Persons (AARP), 175
American Auto Brokers, 35
American Council of Life Insurance, 178
American Dental Association, 134
American Discount Wallcoverings, 167
American Educational Services, 239
American Historic Homes Bed and Breakfast, 297
American Kennel Club, 216
American Society of Travel Agents, 288
American Veterinarian Medical Association, 220
American Youth Hostels, 307
Amica Mutual, 173
Amsterdam Airport Shopping Center, 115, 311
A. Andrews and Co., 115, 312
Animal Veterinary Products, 217
Annex Furniture Gallery, 153
Antartex Ltd., 51
Apple/Boston, 74
appliances, 11–19, 121–128, 149
  advice, 13
  large, 126–128
  repair, 13
  small, 14–16, 126–128
archery equipment, 263
architect's supplies, 138
Art-Max Fabrics, 79
art supplies, 137–139
Ascot Chang Company, 48
Sam Ash Music Stores, 192
ASPCA, 215
AT&T Communications, 275
W. Atlee Burpee Company, 111
Audio Advisor, 25
audio equipment, 11–19, 21–32
  high end, 25–32
  kits, dynaco, 28
Audio T., 29
Audio Unlimited, 26
Auto Caravan, 295
Auto Driveaway, 295
Automobile Importers Compliance Association, 40
Automobile Invoice Service, 34
automotive equipment, 121
Automotive Information Council, 33

B and M Yarn Company, 84
baby goods, 123
backpacks, 248–251
Dan Bailey's Fly Shop, 261
Bakers's Shoes of Cambridge, 65

bank drafts, 326
Bankcard Holders of America (consumer action agency), 126
Bankers National, 176
barbecues, 160
Barnes and Noble, 234
Basic Guide to Dog Training and Obedience, 220
beans, 91
Beautiful Beginnings by Spencer, 209
beauty aids, 122
Beauty Buy Book, 209
bed and breakfast, 296–297
Bed and Breakfast, The National Network, 296
Bed and Breakfast USA, 297
bedspreads, 161–165
  crochet, 162
beer-making supplies, 96
A. Benjamin, 148, 169
Berkshire Life, 177
Berkshire Record Outlet, 242
Bernie's Discount Center, 14
Best Brothers Paint and Wallpaper Outlet, 167
Best Products, 121, 139, 279
Better Business Bureau of Metropolitan New York, 186, 332
Bicycle Australia, 300
Bicycle USA, 254
bicycles, 121, 252–254
bicycling, 251–254
  advice on equipment, 253
  clothes, 253
  frames, 253
  free lodging for cyclists, 299–300
  parts, 253
  portable, 252
  secondhand, 254
  tires, 253
  tools, 253
Bicycling, 251
Bike Nashbar, 253
Bi-Rite Photo and Electronics, 227
Bimmers and Benz, 40
Bizzaro Rubber Stamps, 206
Blackie's Books, 233
Blackthorne Gardens, 102
Blackwell's, 236
Blackwell's Music Shop, 245
blankets, 161–165
  camelhair, 116
  cashmere, 116
  wool, 120
Dick Blick Company, 137
blinds, 168
  custom cut, 161
Bloomingdale's by Mail, 123
Boat Owners Association of the United States, 255
boating, 254–260
  apparel, 256–259
  electronics, 256–259
  hardware, 256–259
  life rafts, 256, 259
  navigational aids, 256–259
  safety equipment, 256
  tools, 256–259
  used, 259
Bodnant Garden Nursery, 107
Bold Ventures Ltd., 248
Bondy Export Company, 15
books, 123, 233–239
  beer, wine and soda making, 96
  car prices, 35
  children's, 237
  computer, 68
  dog training, 220
  libraries, 237, 238
  music, 194, 207
  pet, 217, 219
  remainders, 234–236
  travel, 309–310
Boston Computer Exchange Corporation, 76
The Boston Computer Society, 74, 78
bowls, 144
Boyles Furniture Sales, 154
breads, 92
Briggs and Little Woollen Mills, 85
Britex by Mail, 79
Brown and Company, 186
brushes, paint, 166
bulbs, 102, 111
Bumble and Bumble, 129
Corrie Buschman, 300
Buy Phone America, 126

Cabela's, 261
cable transfers, 325
  foreign, 326
cacti, 104
cakes, 92
calculators, 12, 15
cameras, 15, 17, 121–128, 225–231
  repairs, 231
George Campbell, 93
camping, 124, 247–251
  advice on equipment, 248
  backpacks, 248–251
  cookware, 250
  freeze-dried food, 250, 251
  sleeping bags, 248–251
  tents, 248–251
Campmor, 248
canvases, 138
Car Buying Tips, 33
Car/Puter International, 36
cars, 33–44, 126–128
  accessories, 42
  brokers, 35–37
  direct importing, 39–40
  European delivery, 39–40
  "Importing a Car" (government pamphlet), 337
  parts, 43
  price quotes, 35, 36
  rental discounts, 127
  stereos, 26
  tires, 41–44, 126
  wheels, 41–44
carpets, 127–128
Ross Carson, 217
Casselryds Gla o Porselin, 143
cassettes, 241–245
  remainders, 234
Catherine, 211
CB radios, 18
ceiling fans, 13
Center for Auto Safety, 34
Central States Co-operatives, 90
Dick Cepek, 41
ceramics, 137
cereals, 91, 92
T. M. Chan and Co., 312
W. W. Chan and Sons, 51
Charlie's Place, 52
charter airlines, 287–289
Checkbook's Computerized Long Distance Comparison, 274
checks
  cashier's, 325
  certified, 325
  personal, 325, 326
cheese-making supplies, 92, 160
Cherry Tree Toys, 281
Chesterfield Music Shop, 242
children's clothes, 60–61
Chiltern Seeds, 112
china, 119, 126, 127, 143–151, 169–171
  Arabia, 120
  Danish, 117
  hand-decorated, 211
  Irish fine bone, 117
China Products Company, 116
Louis Chock, 62
chocolates, 90, 95
cigars, 45–46
Clairol Evaluation Salon, 130
Clark Color Laboratories, 223
Clark County Coalition Health Systems Agency, 174
Classique Perfumes, 212
Cleo Ltd., 81
Clery's Department Stores, 117
cloisonné ware, 116
clothes, 47–66, 123, 124, 127, 128
  accessories, 211
  bathrobes, 163
  children's only, 60–61
  cotton, 53
  knitwear, 53–58, 117, 119
  made to measure, 48–50
  nightwear, 48
    embroidered, 162
  pants, 52
  raincoats, 52
  scarves, 211
  shirts, 52
    embroidered, 162
  shoes, 64–66
  sporting, 248–251, 262, 265, 266
  ties, 211
  underwear, 52, 61–63

Clothkits, 58
coffee, 95
  makers, electric, 161
Cohasset Colonials by Hagerty, 157
Coles Appliance and Furniture Company, 11
Comb Company, 122
comforters, 162, 163
Communications Electronics, 75
Community Audio, 26
compact discs, 241–245
Comp-U-Store International, 126
Comp-Used, 77
Computer Plus, 70
computers, 15, 18, 67–78, 122, 126, 127
  accessories, 18, 203
  books, 68
  discs, 74, 75
  furniture, wooden, 158
  paper, 74, 75
  ribbons, 74, 75
  software, 72–74
  tables, 137
  used equipment, 75–77
  user groups, 77–78
Conn Music Centers, 197
Conroy-Lapointe, 70
Consumer Reports, address, 4
Consumer Reports Auto Price Service, 34
Consumer Reports Books, 178
Consumer Thrift Club, 127
Consumers Union, 177
Cook Brothers, 139
cosmetics, 209–213
Council Charter, 288
Council on International Educational Exchange, 308
Country Life Natural Foods, 91
The Coupon Broker, 293
courier services, 289, 290
crafts
  Chinese, 164
  materials, 137–139
Lane Crawford, 313
Creativity Yarns, 85
credit cards, 325, 327–328
D. J. Cremin and Sons, 144
Cruisemart, 258
cruise tickets, 291–293
curtains, 157
  lace, 117
Custom Golf Clubs, 266
Custom Quality Studio, 224

D&A Merchandise, 62
Daedalus Books, 234
Daisy Kingdom, 268
Damart, 64
DeakInternational, telephone number, 6
Defender Industries, 255
Den Permanente, 117
dental work, 133–134
Dependable Car Travel Service, 295
Deva, 52
Dial-a-Brand, 11
A Dictionary of Finance and Investment Terms, 183
Disc World, 75
Discount Brokerage Corporation of America (DBC), 186
Discount Travel International, 291
diving equipment, 257
doilies, 164
do-it-yourself
  beer-making supplies, 96
  cars, parts, 43
  cheese-making supplies, 92
  clothes, kits to make, 58, 60
  dolls, 83
  fishing flies, 263
  furniture, 156
  golf club repairs, 266
  haircuts, 131
  pet health care, 220
  sweater patterns, designer, made to order, 87
  telephone, installing your own wire, 276
  tennis equipment, 271
  toys, 281
  wine-making supplies, 97
dolls, supplies to make, 83
Donegal, 262
Donner Designs Company, 268
draperies, made to order, 157
drugs, 134–136
Drummer's World, 196

Dublin Walen Company, 82
Durey Libbey, 94
Dutch Gardens, 104

E & B Marine, 256
East 33 St., 16
Eastcoast Software, 72
Frank Eastern Company, 203
Edgewood, 43
The Edinburgh Woollen Mill, 53
Edmunds Publication Corporation, 35
800 Software, 73
Elderly Instruments, 195
Eldridge Textile Company, 161
electronic equipment, 11–19, 121–123, 126–128
electronic keyboards, 12
Emily K, 254
energy-saving products, 123
engineer's supplies, 138
envelopes, 204
Essential Products Company, 212
Eurail passes, 308
Europe by Car, 38
Europe Through the Back Door, 308
Euro-Tire, 42
exercise
  equipment, 127, 253
  machines, 270

Fabrica Sant'Anna, 144
fabrics, 79–87, 157, 167
  camel hair, 81
  cashmere, 81
  lace, 79, 80
  linen, 82
  mohair, 80
  silk, 80–82
    for sportswear, 268
Facsimile, 27
Famous Smoke Shop, 45
Fidelity Brokerage Services, 186
figurines, 120, 145, 150, 151
  Chinese, 116
Filofax, 118
Michael C. Fina, 169
firewood, 158
Fisher Price, 281
Fishin' Tackle Place, 262
fishing, 260–264
  advice on equipment, 262, 263
  equipment, 249–251, 257
  fly, 261
  secondhand, 264
flatware, 168–171
  Danish, 117
  pewter, 148
floor polishers, 13
flours, 91
Focus Electronics, 15
food, 89–95
Marty Forscher, 231
Forsyth Travel Library, 309
Fortunoff, 169
47th St. Photo, 17, 312
Foto Electric Supply Company, 11
Thomas Foulkes, 158
Four Star Living, 302
Frank Music Company, 200
Franklin and Lennon Print Company, 165
Friends of Animals, 220
Frosig, 145
fruits, 91
  dried, 92
fuel, 159
  buying groups, 160
furniture, 11, 121, 123, 124, 126–128, 151–158
  Danish, 117
  do-it-yourself, 156
  Shaker, kit form, 157
  shipping, 152

Gander Mountain, 248
Garden Camera, 228
gardening supplies, 101–114
  tools, 111, 123
Gas Mileage Guide, 33
General American Shippers, 295
General Electric Answer Center, 14
generators, 122
Gered, 145
Giardinelli Band Instruments Co., 200
gift wrapping paper, 205

glass, 119, 120, 126, 127, 143–151, 169–171
  Danish, 117
Global Home Exchange Service, 303
Goldberg's Marine, 256
golf, 264–267
  advice on equipment, 265
  balls, used, 266
  clubs
    components, 266
    custom-fitted, 265, 266
    repairs, do-it-yourself, 266
Golf Day Products, 266
Good Stuff from Tom's Place, 249
grains, 91
gray market, 324
Great Fermentations, 97
Greater New York Trading, 149, 170
Green Pepper, 268
Greenleaf, 281
Growth Stock Outlook, 185
Guestaccom, 309

Edward R. Hamilton, 235
Handart Embroideries, 162
handbags, 211
Handbook of Vehicle Importation, 40
handkerchiefs, 164
  Irish linen, 144
Hans Hansen, 146
Ken Hansen Photographic Co., 231
R. Harkness and Company, 108
Harmony Video and Computers, 71
Harrods, 117
Hatchards, 237
Health Advocacy Services, 135
health aids, 122, 136
health equipment, 135
Heffer's Children's Bookshop, 237
W. Heffner and Sons, 236, 245
Hero Arts Rubber Stamps, 206
Hill Brothers, 65
R. Watson Hogg, 57
Holiday Exchanges, 305
holloware
  pewter, 148
  sterling, 148
Holmfirth Wools Ltd., 85
home exchange, 303–307
Home Exchange International, 303
honeys, 92
Hong Kong Tourist Association, 48
hotel discounts, 127
housewares, 121, 123
How To Use the Value Line's Investment Survey: A Subscriber's Guide, 183
Leigh Howlett, 300
The Hulbert Financial Digest, 184
hunting equipment, 249–251
The Hutton Shop, 49

The Iams Company, 217
ice cream makers, 161
Icemart Mail-Order Department, 53
Ikea Mail Order, 119
Illinois Audio, 27
inks, 138
Insider Indicator, 185
The Institute of Highway Safety, 34
insurance, 173–180
  automobile, 173–174
  health, 174–175
  homeowner, 175
  life, 175–177
Insurance Information, 177
Insurance Information Institute, 178
The Intelligent Investor, 184
Inter Lodgings Co-op, 299
International High Fi, 27
International Home Exchange, 305
International Tape and Record Club, 242
Intersonics, 29
investment, 181–188
  books, 183
  discount brokers, 186–187
  newsletters, 184
Investment Quality Trends, 185
Iron Horse Antiques, 141
ITT–US Transmission Systems, 275

J and J Dog Supplies, 218
J & R Music World, 18
J-R Tobacco Company, 46
Jaffe Brothers, 91
Peter De Jager Bulb Company, 104

Jamieson & Smith, 86
jams, 92
Japan Audio Trading, 30
Japan Budget Travel, 286
Jax Fax Travel Marketing Magazine, 288
Jen's Fashion, 49
Jerry's Artarama, 138
jewelry, 17, 117, 121, 122, 128, 150, 209
  Chinese, 164
Jingles Advanced Hair Training Center, 130
The Jompole Company, 149, 170
Peter Jones, 118
Judi's Dolls, 282
juices, 91, 92

Merit Kaplan Paint Supply, 166
Kathleen's, 54
Kaufman's Streamborn, 263
Kennel-Aire, 218
Kennel Vet, 219
Kevin and Howlin, 82
Kinderparadeis Hamburg, 280
kitchen, appliances, 11–15
kitchen, supplies, 121–125, 145, 160–161
  equipment
    bread making, 160
    cheese making, 160
    food preservation, 160
    sprouting, 160
    yogurt making, 160
knitting
  patterns, made to order, 87
  yarns, 84–87
knitwear, 53–58, 119
  Aran knitwear, 117
W. Kordes' Sohne, 108
E.C. Kraus Wine and Beer Making Supplies, 98
Edith Kressy Designs, 60
Krider Nurseries, 102

lace, 79–80
  curtains, 117
Laces of the World, 80
lacquerware, 116
lamps, 128, 137, 144, 151–156
Lands' End, 54
leather, 189–190
Leeds Luggage Shop / Kay Sherman Luggage, 190
L'eggs Products, 63
E. B. LeGrice Roses, 109
Leslie's Bootery, 65
Harris Levy, 163
libraries, lending, 237–238
life rafts, 256, 259
Light Impressions Corporation, 230
lighters, 115
lighting fixtures, 157
Limericks, 163
Limoges Unic, 145
Lindenberg Seeds, 109
linen, 116, 161–165
  bed, 123
  handkerchiefs, 144
  Irish, 117
liqueur flavors, 97
Loan-a-Home, 305
Loftin-Black Furniture, 155
Logic Soft, 71
Lombard's, 270
Lone Star Percussion, 197
Lower Phone Costs, 274
luggage, 122–123, 126–128, 189–190, 249
LVT Price Quote Hotline, 12
Lyle Cartridges, 28

magazines, 238–239
mailing supplies, 205
Mallory's, 155
Mandolin Brothers, 195
Marechal, 146
Mark Pack Works, 249
Market Logic, 185
Martin's Manhattan, 38
Mary Alice Scenic Stamps, 206
mattress pads, 163
MCI, 275
M & E Marine Supply, 257
meats, 92
Mellinger's, 113
Mercantile Library Association, 238
Mermaid Fish Supplies, 94
Mesa Garden, 104
Metropolitan Music Store, 198

Micro Information Publishing, 72
J.E. Miller Nurseries, 105
Moffat Woollens, 59
Moments' Notice, 291
money orders
  bank, 325
  foreign, 326
  international, 325, 326
  Post Office, 326
Monoghans, 55
Mountain Ark Trading Company, 96
Mountain High Ltd., 250
Mountain Tools, 250
mountaineering equipment, 248–251
Music Exchange, 201
music, sheet, 201
  out-of-print, 201
  school, 194
  string, 199
Musical Heritage Society, 243
musical instruments, 191–201
  accessories, 193, 197, 199, 200
  ethnic, 196
  repairs, 195, 196
  secondhand, 191, 192
  vintage, 194, 195
mustards, 90
Mystic Color Lab, 224

napkins, 144, 161–165
  hand-embroidered, 162
NASCO, 90
The National Association of Life Underwriters, 174
National Co-operative Business Association, 90
National Insurance Consumer Organization (NICO), 173
National Software Lending Library, 74
National Tire Dealers and Retreaders Association, 43
Nationwide Auto Brokers, 36
natural foods, 91–92
Nemet Auto International, 39
Nevada Bob's Golf and Tennis, 265
New Angel, 243
The New Contrarian Investment Strategy: The Psychology of Stock Market Success, 184
New England Cheesemaking Supply Company, 92
New World Books, 233
New York Society Library, 238
Newark Dressmaker Supply, 83
Nomadic Books, 310
Nordiska Kompaniet, 118
Now Voyages, 290
nuts, 91, 92, 94, 95
NYPIRG Fuel Buyers Group, 160

M. O'Brien, 30
office equipment, 16–19, 124, 203–207
  copiers, 204
  furniture, 137
  typewriters, 204
  wooden file cabinets, 158
Official Airlines Guide, 286
Bruce O'Halloran, 300
Padraic O'Maille, 55
Offshore Imports, 42
Olde Discount Brokers, 187
Olden Camera and Lens Company, 228
olive oil, 90
Orchard Toy and Stationery Co., 279
organs, 127
outdoor equipment, 123
Ovest Financial Services, 187

Pacific Brokerage Services, 187
paint, 138, 165–167
Palmetto Linen Company, 164
Anne Paree, 211
Park Seed Company, 103, 112
Joseph Patelson Music House, 201
Patrick's Nursery and Sun Garden Seeds, 106
Pattern Plus, 282
patterns, designer sweater, made to order, 87
PBS Livestock Drugs, 221
PC Software Interest Group, 74
Pearl Paint Company, 138, 166
pearls, Mikimoto, 115
Pennsylvania Outdoor Warehouse, 263
pens, 15, 115, 138
Percy's TV and Video, 12
Performance Bike Shop, 253

perfumes, 120, 209–213
  copies, 212
Andre Perrault International, 241
The Personal Computer Book, 68
Personal Investing, 184
Petco Animal Supplies (Animal City Division), 219
pets, 215–222
  adopting, 215
  advice, free, 217
  equipment, 217–220
  food, 216
  purebred, 215
  supplies, 217–220
  veterinarians, 220
Phillipus Company, 313
photographs, processing by mail, 223
photography, 223–231
  cameras, 128, 225–231
  equipment, 12, 15, 121, 122, 128, 224–231
  repairs, 232
  secondhand, 231
Photography Buyers Guide, 227
pianos, 127
pickup trucks, 128
picture frames, 137, 138
Pigs and Fishes, 207
pillows, 161–164
pillowcases, 161–165
  hand-embroidered, 162
N. Pintchik, 166
pipes, Peterson, 120
Pitlochry Knitwear, 59
place mats, 162
platters, 143–151
  handpainted, 144
porcelain, Chinese, 116
  boxes, 146
Post Wallcovering Distributors, 168
pottery, hand-painted, 144
power tools, 121–125, 140–141
Practical Sailor, 254
Prescription Delivery Systems, 136
Prestige Photo Electronics, 228
printmaking, 137
Professional Golf and Tennis Supplies, 265, 270
Publishers Clearing House, 239
Purchase Power, 128

Q Audio, 31
Quill Corporation, 203
Quota Phone National, 128

Rachel's Boutique, 61
racquetball
  clothes, 265
  equipment, 265
radar detectors, 12
Rainbow Music Service, 243
raincoats, 52, 56
  Aquascutum, 119
  Burberry, 119
RCI Corp, 275
Real Good Toys, 282
Record Hunter, 244
records, 241–245
  children's, 244
  out-of-print, 244
  picture disks, 244
  remainders, 234
  search service, 244
Recreational Equipment (REI), 247
Reekies of Grasmere, 55, 80
Reject China Shop, 146
Retired Persons Services, 136
Frank Richards, 193
Ridgewood Wine and Beer Supplies for the Home Brewer, 98
W.S. Robertson, 55
Robin Importers, 149, 170
Roby's Intimates, 63
rock climbing equipment, 248–251
rocking chairs, 157
Rogers and Rosenthal, 150, 170
Rose and Company, 187
Rose Furniture Company, 156
Rose Records, 244
roses, 108
Roundup Records, 245
Bickerton Rowlinson, 252
Rubberstampede, 207
rubber stamps, 206–207
F. Rubbrecht, 164
A. Rubinstein and Son, 56

Rudi's Pottery, Silver and China, 150, 171
rugs
  Foxford, 120
  Oriental, 154
  shampooers, 13

S and S Sound City, 18
Sails USA, 257
St. John's Knitting Wool, 86
sales, seasonal
  appliances, 10
  audio, 16
  art supplies, 137
  backpacking, 247
  bicycles, 254
  camping equipment, 247
  clothing, 47
  fishing equipment, 260
  flatware, 168
  gardening, 101
  linen, 161
  paint, 165
  silver, 168
  ski equipment, 267
  tennis equipment, 269
salmon, smoked, 93
Samuels Tennisport, 270
Vidal Sassoon, 130
The Scholar's Bookshelf, 235
A. B. Schou, 147
Charles Schwab and Company, 187
Nat Schwartz and Company, 150, 171
screens, Oriental, 154
Sears Roebuck and Company, 124
secondhand
  audio, 31, 32
  bicycles, 254
  computer equipment, 75
  fishing rods, 264
  musical instruments, 191
  photography equipment, 230
  ski clothes, 267
  ski equipment, 268
  tennis equipment, 271
  tools, 141
  vacuum cleaners, 13
Securicor Air Couriers, 290
security devices, household, 18
Security Mutual Life, 177
seeds, 109–111
Select Information Exchange, 184
Selfridges, 119
Sensible Sound, 25
Service Merchandise Company, 122
sewing
  doll patterns, 83
  machines, 127
  supplies, 83
Shaker Workshops, 157
Shannon Mail Order, 119
Shar, 199
shavers, 15
sheets, 161–165
  satin, 162
shipping, 329, 330
  airfreight, 329
  mail, 329
  seafreight, 329
shoes, 64–66
  running, 270
shower curtains, 163
sickroom equipment, 124
Muriel Siebert and Company, 188
silver, 148, 149–151, 168–171
Silver and Horland, 193
Sitlani Custom Tailors, 50
skiing, 267–269
  clothes, 268
  secondhand, 267
  sunglasses, 211, 269
Skipper Marine Electronics, 257
Skrudland Photo Service, 224
Skye Crotal Knitwear, 56
sleeping bags, 248–251
Snowflake Kits, 86
soda drink flavors, 97
Software Exchange, 74
Son Rise Soft Crafts, 283
SOS: Save on Shopping Directory, 3
Sotz, 113, 140
soups, 92
Soyfoods Center, 96
The Spice House, 94
Spielzeug-Rasch, 280
Spiratone, 230
sporting goods, 121, 122

Sportline of Hilton Head, 271
sports equipment, 247–272, 280
  advice, 248, 250
  clothes, 248–251, 262
Spur of the Moment Cruises, 292
squash rackets, 270
Stand Buys, 292
standby airflights, 289
stationery, 203–207, 280
R.C. Steele, 219
Stereo Cost Cutters, 28
stereo equipment, 126
Stereophile, 25
Stetchers, 120
Stock Market Logic, 184
Oy Stockmann Ab, 120
Stokes Seeds, 110
Stow-a-Way Industries, 251
Strand Bookstore, 235
student work programs, 308
Sunbeam Travel, 286
sunglasses, 15, 211
  skiing, 269
  tennis, 271
Sunshine Cameras, 229
supermarket discount coupons, 127
Sweater Market, 57
swimsuits, 271
Michael Swiss, 211

tablecloths, 144, 161–165
  hand-embroidered, 162
  lace, 164
  linen, 164
tapes, audio, 18
tea, 95
Telecommunications Research and Action Center (TRAC), 274
telephones, 12, 17, 18
  accessories, 18
  answering devices, 12, 15, 17
  cordless, 15
  repairs, 276–277
  service, 273–277
    groups that compare rates, 274
    long-distance carriers, 273–275
Telepro, 265
Telerade, 290
Teletire, 42
televisions, 11–19
  consoles, swivelling, 158
tennis, 269–272
  ball machines, 270
  clothes, 265, 270–271
  equipment, 265
  grips, 271
  stringing machines, 270
  sunglasses, 271
Tennis Magazine, 269
Tennis String International, 271
tents, 248–251
Texere Yarns, 87
Thai Silk, 80
Anne Thomas Fabrics, 82
Thomas and Thomas Rod Makers, 264
Tierney's Gift Shop, 147
tires, 41–44, 126
  bicycle, 253
tofu, making supplies, 96
tools, 121, 125, 139–142
  bicycle, 253
  boating, 256–259
  hand and power, 123, 128
  libraries, 141
  painting, 166
  secondhand, 141
  woodworking, 158
Topgear, 258
Touring Cyclists' Hospitality Directory, 299
towels, 161–165
toys, 121, 122, 124, 279–283
  dollhouse kits, 281, 282
  fabric dolls, patterns and supplies to make, 282
  German, 280
  puppets, patterns for, 283
  stuffed animals, puppets for, 283
  supplies, 283
  wood, kits, patterns and parts for making, 281
Training Your Dog: The Step-by-Step Manual, 220
Travac Tours and Charters, 288
travel, 285–310
  agents, 285, 286
    ethnic, 285

travel (cont.)
  bed and breakfast, 267, 296
  campus lodgings, 297–298
  charter flights, 287–289
  coupon brokers, 293
  courier services, 289, 290
  directories, 304–307
  discount tickets, 291–293
  Eurail passes, 308
  guest-room swapping, 299–302
  home swapping, 302
    agencies, 302–304
    long-term, 304, 306
  standby, 289
  work programs for students, 308
  YMCA, 307
  youth hostels, 307
Travel Accommodations Guide, 298
trees, 102, 105–106
  fruit, 105
  nut, 106
  seeds, 112
Le Tricoteur, 57
trousers, 52–54, 56, 58
  Daks, 119
  made to measure, 49–51
Truman College Co-op Center, 90
Tuli-Latus Perfumes, 213
tweed, 117
Twenty First Century Audio, 28
typewriters, 12, 15, 17, 127, 128, 204
Typex Business Machines, 204

umbrellas, 211
USAA Life Co., 176
United States Box Corporation, 205
U.S. Department of Agriculture
  Plant Import Office, 107
  Publications Office, U.S. Forest Service, 159
U.S. Department of Energy, Technical Information Service, 33
U.S. Department of Health and Human Services, 174
U.S. Department of Transportation
  Consumer and Community Affairs, 288
  National Highway Safety Administration, 41
U.S. General Supply Corporation, 140, 277
United States Racket Stringers Association, 272
The United States Ski Association, 267
U.S. "SPRINT," 275
The Urban Farmer, 110
Urban Ventures, 297
US Servas, 300
Utex Trading, 81
Utrecht, 138

Vacation Exchange Club, 306
Vacations, *see* Travel
vacuum cleaners, 12–16, 128
  used, 13
vans, 128
vases, 116, 144
vegetables, canned, 92
The Vermont Country Store, 13
veterinarians, 220
The Victoria and Albert Museum, Publications Department, 205
Victoria's Secret, 64
video equipment, 11–19, 21–32
  high end, 25, 29
vinegars, 90
  supplies to make, 97
Visiting Friends, 301
vitamins, 135, 136

wall coverings, 167, 168
  murals, 167
  prints, made to order, 167
wallpapers, 166, 167, 168
Wall Street Camera Exchange, 229
Wall Street's Insiders, 184
Walnut Acres, 91
Russ Walter, 67
Warren of Stafford, 81
watches, 15, 17, 18, 115, 116, 121, 126–128, 311–313
watercolors, 138
waterskiing equipment, 257
Wayside Music, 245
WCB Computers, 71
wedding veils, 164
Philip Weinkrantz Musical Supply Company, 199
West Manor Music, 194

Westaway and Westaway, 58
Western Union Long-Distance Service, 275
Whirlpool Cool Line, 14
J.C. Whitney, 44
Whittard and Company, 95
Whole Earth Access, 58, 122, 140, 160
The Whole Earth Software Catalog, 72
Wholesale Veterinary Supply, 221
Wichita Band Instruments Company, 200
Wiggle Worm Haven, 114
Wilco Trading Co., 164
Windsor Gift Shop, 151, 171
Wine and the People, 98
wine, supplies for making, 97
woks, 161
J. Wolsk and Company, 95
Woodcraft Supply Corporation, 157
woodwork, supplies for, 137
World of Music, 194
Worldwide Discount Travel Club, 293
Worldwide Exchange, 306

Yachtmail, 259
yarn, 81, 84–87
  Aran wool, 117
Yield House, 158
YMCA, 307
Young Idea, 61
youth hostels, 307

Zabar's, 90, 95, 160